Praise for *The Perpetual Prisoner Machine*

Dyer supplements meticulous research with argumentative anger and
verve to make a strong case that what has been called the "prison-
industrial complex" is preying on largely minority and
underclass segments of our society."
Publishers Weekly

Dyer's insights into the workings of the
"perpetual prisoner machine" make this book
essential reading for anyone who is trying to make sense of
society and the state of American democracy."
Southland Prison News

[A] good assault on destructive social policy."
San Diego Union-Tribune

Dyer's assertion that America is profiting from prison-building is
ultimately accurate: Our streets are safe, the social order is
stable, and law-abiding citizens are secure.
Richmond Times-Dispatch

[P]rovides an ideal place to begin looking at the issue of why most
states spend more money building prisons than schools.
Kirkus Reviews

The Perpetual Prisoner Machine is a bold and deep-probing analysis of
our criminal justice system. It raises serious questions about
crime and punishment which reflect not just on our prisons,
but on our profit-driven society.
Howard Zinn

This is one of the most important books about the state of
this nation that has come along in years. The fact that we have
become the new Soviet Union, the new South Africa, when it comes to
incarcerating our own citizens is perhaps our most shameful
accomplishment of the past decade. The brilliance of Joel Dyer's
book is that he just doesn't state that sad and compelling fact,
he gives us the why behind it—how politicians, lawyers, and
corporations have profited by frightening the public into believing
that we must lock up as many people as possible.
Michael Moore, Filmmaker,
"Roger & Me" and "The Big One"

The Perpetual Prisoner Machine

The Perpetual Prisoner Machine

How America Profits from Crime

by Joel Dyer

Westview
PRESS

A Member of the Perseus Books Group

Copyright © 2000 by Westview Press, A Member of the Perseus Books Group

Published in 2000 in the United States of America by Westview Press, 5500 Central Avenue, Boulder, Colorado 80301-2877, and in the United Kingdom by Westview Press, 12 Hid's Copse Road,
Cumnor Hill, Oxford OX2 9JJ

Find us on the World Wide Web at www.westviewpress.com

Library of Congress Cataloging-in-Publication Data
Dyer, Joel.
   The perpetual prisoner machine : how America profits from crime / Joel Dyer.
      p.   cm.
   Includes bibliographical references and index.
   ISBN 0-8133-3507-8 (hc).—0-8133-3870-0 (pb)
      1. Criminal justice, Administration of—Economic aspects—United States.
2. Crime—Economic aspects—United States.   3. Fear of crime—United States.
4. Imprisonment—United States.   5. Corrections out—United States.   I. Title.
HV9950.D94 1999
364.973—dc21   99-045576
                                                                         CIP

Design by Heather Hutchison

The paper used in this publication meets the requirements of the American National Standard for
Permanence of Paper for Printed Library Materials Z39.48-1984.

10   9   8   7   6   5   4   3   2   1

For Sam,
in the hope that your generation
will be wiser than mine

Contents

Acknowledgments   ix

Introduction   1

1   A New Commodity   9

2   The Crime Gap   27

3   Violence for Profit   53

4   Manufacturing Fear   83

5   The Politics of Public Opinion   115

6   The Weapons of War   153

7   Collateral Damage   177

8   Same Old Logic, Same Old Problems   199

9   The Hidden Costs of Private Prisons   223

10 Sidestepping the Restraints of Democracy   239

11 Pulling the Plug   265

Notes   283
Index   309

Acknowledgments

Once again, I must thank all the folks at Westview for making this book both possible and better than it would have been without their input. In particular, I appreciate the efforts of my editor Rob Williams, whose suggestions proved invaluable, as did his help in keeping this project on course and as near to on schedule as encouragement could produce. I am likewise thankful for the efforts of Laura Parsons, with whom I had the privilege of working along the way, and for those of Michele Wynn, who continues to save me from myself. And finally, on the Westview front, I would like to thank Marcus Boggs for his continued support for my writing projects, which I truly believe stems more from their potential to impact the debate than their ability to make a buck. Such support is, indeed, a rarity in this day and age, and I can give no higher compliment to anyone in charge of a publishing house.

As is always the case, it is those living under my roof who have been most inconvenienced by the writing of this book. Thank you, Ellen and Sam, for your love, patience, and support. I know it wasn't easy. Although he doesn't live in my house or, unfortunately, even in my region of the country, I am extremely grateful to my brother Paul for his encouragement as well as for his many valuable insights regarding this project, without which this book would have been less than it is.

There are many other people and organizations that have directly or indirectly contributed to the completion of this book. Unfortunately, space will not allow me to properly dispense the accolades each deserves. Even so, I must acknowledge a few. I owe a great debt to Daniel Burton-Rose, who furnished me with the invaluable research materials without which this book would not exist. Also, I could not have written this book or any other without the efforts of Susan Lindley and Ron Jong. For his quarter of a century of good company, helpful insights, and unparalleled road trips, a very special thanks to Dave Hutton. And finally, thanks to those organizations whose work in the areas of prisons, politics, and media has added immeasurably to this project: The Center for Responsive Politics, Fairness and Accuracy in Reporting, The Sentencing Project, and The National Criminal Justice Commission, to name a few.

This book exists through grace for which I am most thankful.

Joel Dyer

The Perpetual Prisoner Machine

Introduction

Trying to figure out what went wrong with the U.S. criminal-justice system at the end of the twentieth century is no simple task. It reminds me of when I was a kid sitting in my grandfather's barbershop in Purcell, Oklahoma. You looked in the mirror in front of you and saw your reflection in the one behind, and it created an infinite number of images forever diminishing in size—each image's existence dependent upon the one that came before. The harder you strained to see the beginning, the further away you realized it was. And so it is with the problems confronting America's justice system.

To understand all the misguided efforts that have shaped modern penology, you would literally have to trace the shrinking images back to the ancient kingdoms of Egypt and Babylonia, for it is there that we find the roots of the modern prison system and the beginnings of its demise. That being the case, I have narrowed the focus of this book to an examination of only the most recent backward step in the evolution of the criminal-justice system—a significant leap that, though less than three decades old, has had a more profound impact on American justice than anything that came before.

The United States now incarcerates between 1.8 and 2 million of its citizens in its prisons and jails on any given day, and over 5 million people are currently under the supervision of America's criminal-justice system. That's more prisoners than in any other country in the world, an estimated 500,000 more than Communist China and just a few more than Russia, which offers the United States its only real competition when it comes to imprisonment.[1] But perhaps the most telling comparison of penal systems can be found in the statistics kept in the archives of our own Department of Justice. Today's 2 million prisoners represent a prison and jail system ten times larger than that which existed in the United States a mere twenty-nine years ago.[2] This unprecedented rise in the number of prisoners in the U.S. prison system reflects the largest prison expansion the world has ever known.

By way of comparison, the United States now locks up about five to seven times as many people as most other industrialized nations—nations whose crime rates are often similar to ours, but which have chosen to deal with the majority of their nonviolent offenders outside of prison walls through drug rehabilitation programs, various forms of community service, and well-supervised probation and parole.[3] These alternatives to incarceration are both more effective when it comes to reform and cost billions less per year to implement. Once again, a quick look at the Justice Department's archives tells us that U.S. authorities are well aware of these programs and their obvious advantages over our prevailing policy of prison as the first choice for dealing with nonviolent lawbreakers because at one time, prior to the current prison expansion, we used to practice them ourselves.

So why is it that only America has abandoned these alternative programs in favor of a policy of mass imprisonment? Proponents of growing the prison population point to an increase in crime as justification for this trend. But Census Bureau statistics reflect that crime rates have been relatively flat or falling for the last three decades, which would seem to indicate that another explanation for our liberal use of incarceration is needed.[4] I believe that a more likely motive for our having launched the largest prison expansion in history can be found in the corresponding "largest" increase in criminal-justice expenditures in history. Or put another way, the motive behind the unprecedented growth in the U.S. prison population is the $150 billion being expended annually on criminal justice,[5] much of which eventually winds up in the bank accounts of the shareholders of some of America's best known and most respected corporations. Although this explanation is admittedly controversial, I believe that it is fully supported by the evidence.

As the subtitle of this book suggests, the pages that follow will examine "how America profits from crime" and, I think more important, how this profiteering is impacting our culture. When I say "how America profits from crime" I do not mean "how much it profits" per se, though such facts and figures will receive some treatment. Still, if someone wants to read a detailed description of the dollars and cents being generated by the prison industry, there are certainly better sources than this text for such fiscal information.

The purpose of this book is to expose and examine a political and economic chain reaction that I believe is largely responsible for the majority of the growth in the prison and jail population during the last three decades. I have chosen to describe this chain reaction as a "prisoner machine" because as I began to research the impact caused by various techniques for profiting from crime, it became clear that each such method had become somewhat dependent upon the others for its success, not unlike the gears of a machine that must be meshed in order to turn. I have added the word "perpetual" to the book's title because the machine is self-sustaining, meaning that it has the ability to create new prisoners by way of the prisoners it has already created.

The perpetual prisoner machine is an impressive and complicated mechanism that owes its incarnation to no single power. It was during the late 1970s and early 1980s that the original three components of the machine appeared on the scene as the result of three separate and initially unrelated occurrences: the accelerating consolidation of the media industry, the rise in influence of political consultants, and the emergence of an organized prison-industrial complex that is perhaps best described as a collection of interests whose financial well-being rises and falls with the size of the prison population. As a result, the media, our elected officials, and the corporations that compose the prison industry each developed a unique method for turning crime into some form of capital—individual techniques that were, in the beginning, not particularly dependent upon one another for their success.

Subsequent changes within our political system—primarily the increasing use of public opinion polling and the rapid increase in the cost of political campaigns—have affected the various components of the machine the way the lightning bolt affected Frankenstein's monster. They caused these previously separated components to mesh and begin to function as a single mechanism that is considerably more efficient and powerful than any of its gears were on their own.

There is no adequate way to describe the function of the machine in only a few paragraphs, but just to give you a general idea of where this book is going, I offer this limited explanation. In the 1980s, when the media corporations decided to dramatically increase their use of violent, crime-oriented content as a means of increasing ratings or pickup rates and thereby enhancing their profits, it created a by-product—an exaggerated apprehension of crime throughout the general population. According to behavioral scientists, the majority of Americans now base their worldview more on the mediated messages offered by television than upon their own firsthand observations. As a result, nearly 80 percent of the public now believes crime to be one of the biggest problems confronting America, despite the fact that most of us are safer now than we were in the 1970s.[6]

Unfortunately, the arrival of this media-created anxiety over crime coincided with the rise in influence of the poll-taking political consultants. In the 1980s and 1990s, it has become the norm for these politically powerful consultants to use their public-opinion polls and their access to campaign funds to ensure that their candidate-clients' platforms on particular issues, such as crime, are not in conflict with the opinion of the majority of targeted voters. This increase in the importance of polling, coupled with the existence of the public's exaggerated concern over crime, explains in large measure why the vast majority of politicians from both parties have now fully embraced the politically expedient "hard-on-crime" position. That's to say that our war on crime is not rooted in rising crime rates but is rather the result of the rise in the public's concern over crime, which has been wrought not by the criminals in the real world but by the images of the criminals who now break into our living rooms nightly through the window of television.

Although the anxiety over crime that is driving our nation in a hard-on-crime direction is not based in reality, the criminal-justice policies being derived as a result are more tangible. Mandatory sentencing, including "three-strikes" laws and "truth in sentencing," are the weapons of the war on crime that have increased our prison population ten times over in recent years—an extraordinary increase that would not have been financially feasible without the participation of the third gear of the machine, the increasingly privatized and politically influential prison-industrial complex.

By the late 1980s, the prison expansion had begun to reach what should have been its economic limits. State after state had built countless new prisons, only to see them quickly filled by hard-on-crime sentencing measures. The majority of taxpaying voters were beginning to express their concern over ever-increasing corrections costs, as exemplified by the fact that they began to vote down many of the bond issues needed for new prison construction. Considering that most states were under court order to reduce overcrowding, this refusal by voters to allow state governments to create bond debt for prisons should have spelled the end of the war on crime—but it wasn't to be. Private corporations and politicians who were benefiting from the expansion came up with an alternative plan. If state governments couldn't get their voters to approve the general-obligation bonds historically needed to construct new prisons or they simply wanted to save their general-obligation bond capacity for more popular projects, then American Express, Allstate, Merrill Lynch, GE, Shearson Lehman, Wackenhut Corrections Corporation, Corrections Corporation of America, and others would raise the construction money the states needed by underwriting lease-revenue (a.k.a. lease-payment) bonds that don't require voter approval or by actually building the prisons themselves and then charging the states to house their inmates in the privately owned facilities.

In the end, this market intrusion into the justice system means that politicians can simply *divert* tax dollars out of existing programs such as education, child welfare, mental-health care, housing, and substance-abuse programs to repay the market and its investors for having put up the money to construct the prison facilities. If finagled properly, this diversion of funds does not require voter approval. In many ways, it's as if the prison expansion is now being funded by way of a credit card issued by the prison-industrial complex—a high-interest credit card that the taxpayers have no control over when it comes to spending but are nonetheless still being required to pay for at the end of the month.

I'm sure that private industry's rescue of the war on crime seemed like a good idea to politicians at the time. After all, it allowed them to continue to exploit the hard-on-crime platform as a means of growing their political fortunes à la Willie Horton. But in reality, the prison-industrial complex's "plan B" has turned out to be all too similar to the credit-card debt that has destroyed the finances of many a consumer. Taxpayers are paying far more for the market's prison system than they would have paid if they had been willing to pass the prison bond issues at the ballot box in the first place. Although the new prisons being built by investors and corporations have been wildly profitable for the prison-industrial complex, they have failed to provide the relief from overcrowding sought by the states because they too have been filled by hard-on-crime sentencing guidelines as quickly as they have been constructed. After thirty years and over 1,000 new prisons and jails, the system is now more overcrowded than it was when the expansion began, with most jurisdictions now operating at 15 to 30 percent over capacity.[7]

As a result of investors and corporations being willing to fund the construction of prisons that the majority of voters have shown increasing hesitance to bankroll, the budgets of corrections departments all across America have exploded. In many states, corrections expenditures have increased by more than seven times just since 1980, and they are still rocketing upward by at least 7 and up to more than 10 percent per year in many jurisdictions.[8] Picking up this ever-growing tab for prisoners is where the "perpetual" aspect of the machine kicks in.

Because much of the funding for corrections is now coming at the expense of social programs that have been shown to deter people from criminal behavior in the first place, I believe it is entirely accurate to say that the more prisoners whose incarceration we pay for through this diversion of funds, the more future prisoners we create.

Based on conversations I have had with criminologists both here and abroad, it appears that most of the civilized world finds the U.S. decision to use prisons to fight crime—a decision that flies in the face of research that strongly suggests that incarceration rates have little or no influence over crime rates—to be quite illogical. This low opinion of our justice system stems from the understanding that living in poverty is the most important factor in determining who is most likely to wind up in prison. That being the case, it is nonsensical to take money away from programs that fight poverty or help people to rise above its influence to pay for more prison cells. This poorly thought out fiscal maneuvering is playing a crucial role in one of the most significant human migrations in our nation's history—a migration that has seen hundreds of thousands of low-income citizens uprooted from their urban communities and relocated into places with names like Chino, Leavenworth, San Quentin, and Jolliette.

For the most part, America's prison population is being harvested from our growing fields of urban poverty. Since these fields are disproportionately composed of minority citizens, so too is the new prison population. By 1992, one out of every three black men in the United States between the ages of twenty and twenty-nine was under the supervision of the criminal-justice system. In some cities such as Washington, D.C., and Baltimore, 50 percent of black men between the ages of eighteen and thirty-five are now under the watchful eye of the Justice Department. Seventy percent of those being sent to prison these days are black or Hispanic, even though statistics tell us that these minorities are not committing anywhere near 70 percent of America's crimes.[9]

For example, blacks compose only 13 percent of monthly drug users, yet they are arrested five times as often as whites on drug charges, and once arrested, they are twice as likely to receive a prison sentence as their white counterparts and, on average, that sentence will be 20 percent longer than one doled out to a white offender.[10] This multiple is

the result of race-biased law-enforcement practices and court proce-
dures, and it helps to explain why in many states, blacks are filling prisons at a rate of ten to one over whites. It is estimated that if this prison
expansion continues for twenty more years in its current discriminatory
manner, we will eventually find ourselves imprisoning over 6 million minority citizens.[11]

This is the effect of the perpetual prisoner machine on American society at the end of the twentieth century. In short, the machine has
overpowered the forces that historically determined the size and composition of the prison population—namely, the crime rates, the overall
health of the economy, and the progressive ideal of reform over punishment.

Before we move on to the first chapter, I should point out that I do
not believe that our current prison expansion will continue for another
twenty years at its same rate. The truth is, it can't. Such an expansion
would eventually consume nearly every dollar of every state budget in
the union. There would be no public education, no infrastructure, no
anything except for prisons, and that simply isn't going to happen. So
the real questions become: How far will this prison madness go? How
long will the perpetual prisoner machine be allowed to run unimpeded?
How many hundreds of billions of tax dollars will it divert into the bank
accounts of the prison-industrial complex? How many millions of lives
within our low-income communities will it devastate? And who, in the
end, will turn it off?

I do not know the answers to these questions, but I can tell you this:
The machine will never be disabled by those who built it—the media,
the politicians, those who compose the prison-industrial complex, and,
most important, the shareholders of the corporations involved. They
simply have no incentive to do so. For them, crime has become a valuable commodity. And if we want to get rid of this machine, we will have
to do it ourselves. There are ways to accomplish this task, and I truly believe that it is in the best interest of the majority of Americans to pull
the plug sooner rather than later.

A New Commodity

As you drive through the streets of Youngstown, Ohio, it's not hard to
find the usual reminders that we live in a market-driven culture. Electronic bulletin boards nailed to buildings that house investment firms
flash their alternating messages of current temperature and the latest
stock quotes, a newspaper headline questioning whether Wall Street
will catch the Asian flu can be seen through the foggy plastic of a coin-
operated box, and at every turn, vibrantly colored billboards and other
signs testify to the products we cannot live without or as to the way we
should live—"Just do it."

We have become so accustomed to seeing these images that represent the capitalistic forces that shape our lives that they tend to blend
together in a meaningless information stew, this ingredient being no
more important than that one. "Drink Coke," "Invest in Microsoft,"
"Vote Republican," "Supersize your fries"—it's all the same, or so it
seems after a while. But on the outskirts of Youngstown there is one
more sign, one last symbolic message from the market that we cannot

allow to be blended into the jumble. It may look like more of the same, but nothing could be further from the truth.

The words "Yesterday's closing stock price" hang on a nondescript placard near the road that runs past the Northeast Ohio Correctional Center. And though these may be the only words on the sign, the message being conveyed is not nearly as simple as it initially appears. The stock price being quoted is for Corrections Corporation of America, the largest of the new private-prison companies that have sprung forth from America's decision to turn punishment into a booming industry. As of January 1999, the company has 67,992 beds in sixty-eight facilities in three countries, and it has more than quadrupled the value of its stock since 1993.[2] Times are good at CCA. To this the sign bears witness.

But if we're not careful, we can easily miss the deeper meaning behind this innocent-sounding piece of corporate PR. What the sign is really telling us is that anyone—anyone with money, that is—can now profit from crime. And this new development in our criminal-justice system has major implications for our culture. By placing a call to a broker, any American with a few bucks can begin to build wealth so long as the prison population continues to grow, a disturbing revelation when you consider that the same people who can now profit from the current prison expansion also have the power—by way of the voting booth—to insure that it continues. It's a sort of societal conflict of interest, but not one that has regulators concerned.

To understand the full impact of this interjecting of market forces into our justice system, we must look behind this nondescript sign in Youngstown. Like Alice's magic mirror, it can be our portal to a previously invisible world—a world where crime is good; recidivism, a business plan; prisoners, a valuable commodity. And as we will see, like Wonderland, it is a place filled with deceptive illusions.

A Sizable Motive

If, as I have stated previously, profit is the primary motivation behind the ten-fold increase in the prison population that has occurred in the last twenty-nine years, then it stands to reason that the potential for making money from this business of "justice" must be quite substantial—and it is. In fact, the business of turning crime and prisoners into profit has become one of the fastest-growing industries in the nation, an industry with hundreds of billions of dollars up for grabs each year. Corrections is now the fastest-growing category in most state budgets, and each year, more of this taxpayer money is finding its way into the bank accounts of companies in the private sector.

As of February 1999, the most recent statistics available from the federal government for criminal-justice expenditures were for fiscal year 1992. In that year, the combined tab for law enforcement, corrections, and courts at the federal, state, and local level was $94 billion, up from $61 billion in 1988. People in the Justice Department have told me that they believe that the costs for criminal justice have continued to rise at least as quickly since 1992. If this observation is accurate, then 1999 will find the United States spending somewhere in the neighborhood of $150 billion on criminal justice, and we should expect to crack the $200-billion barrier by the year 2002. In comparison, the entire U.S. defense budget for 1999 is $296 billion.[3]

In 1980, when the corrections budget was a comparatively paltry $6.8 billion, there were only a handful of private corporations that benefited financially from the prison population.[4] They did so by providing goods and services to the various Departments of Corrections (DOC) under contracts secured through the bidding process. But that was prior to the emergence of an organized prison-industrial complex whose arrival spelled the end of the days when prison industry bids were typically handled by some bureaucrat in a stuffy, windowless office, peeling open a handful of envelopes to determine who would get the striped-uniform concession.

Today's prison industry has its own trade shows, mail-order catalogs, newsletters, and conventions, and literally thousands of corporations are now eating at the justice-system trough. At a typical trade show in the 1990s, 700 to 1,000 corporate vendors can be found standing amid a maze of neon signs, looking to secure their share of the taxpayer dollars being doled out by an army of corrections and law-enforcement officials from all levels of government who have come to be wined and dined on the industry tab. A quick look at the web site of the Corrections Yellow Pages, a listing of over a thousand companies that serve the prison business, shows twenty-nine upcoming events in 1999 alone.[5] Attending one of these "justice" trade shows these days feels no different than showing up at a gathering sponsored by the computer or auto industries—meaning that they are a combination of showbiz, commerce, and party, where millions, if not billions, of dollars change hands.

Walking the block-long aisles of vendor booths illustrates quickly just how blurred the line between public and private interests has become in this new industry. It is easy to watch the laughing, drinking, back patting, glad-handing, buying, and selling that is going on and to forget that all this business and merriment has come about as a result of the imprisonment of millions of Americans. This blurring of lines raises one of those troubling chicken-or-egg questions: Did this Vegas-style atmosphere spring to life because the corrections budget has grown to $50 billion annually, or did the budget increase 700 percent in only eighteen years because of this Vegas-style atmosphere, where spending taxpayer money seems to have become just another form of revelry for public officials?[6] Answering this question is hardly an academic exercise. If the latter is even partially true, which I certainly believe it is, then how many hundreds of thousands of lives are being adversely affected because we have turned the administration of justice into a free-market experiment?

Supplying goods and services to prisoners, guards, and police has become a massive market. Some estimates have it at more than $100 billion annually.[7] But this figure actually seems low when you consider the size of the market we're talking about. Think of it in these terms: At the beginning of the current prison expansion, the size of the entire prison population was roughly equivalent to the population of Lexington, Kentucky. In 1999, the number of those incarcerated in the United States is equal to the combined populations of Albany, Anchorage, Austin, Bakersfield, Birmingham, Boise, Fort Lauderdale, Toledo, and Spokane. And this is just the prisoners.[8] Law-enforcement personnel and prison guards represent another 1.5 million potential customers for the corporations of the complex, as do private security officers, who now number over 2 million.[9]

As you can imagine, getting an exclusive contract to supply goods or services to the populations of the cities listed above would be an incredibly lucrative market, and so it is with the prison population. For example, someone has to provide the housing for all these prisoners. At the rate the system is growing, we are currently constructing enough new cells to house an inmate population equal to the size of a city such as Boulder, Colorado, every year.

Since 1990, the United States has been constructing enough prison facilities to hold an average of 92,640 new beds per year, and these beds are not cheap. As of 1998, the cost for creating a new maximum-security bed was $70,909; for medium security, it was $49,853 per bed; and for minimum security, the price was $29,311 for each bed added. In January 1998, the total cost of new prison construction and renovation ongoing at that time was estimated to be $3.88 billion, and this is just to construct the cells. This figure doesn't take into account the increased annual operational costs for these new beds, which is somewhere in the area of $1.3 billion a year for every new 92,640 beds added.[10]

It has been said that you can tell a lot about a culture by its great public works. If this is true, then America at the end of the twentieth century will be at least partially remembered as the society of imprisonment. The days of building public works like Grand Central Station, Hoover Dam, and the Golden Gate Bridge have given way to two decades dominated by building structures surrounded by razor wire. Building prisons has become so commonplace that this business of making cells now has its own newsletter, the *Construction Report*, to keep vendors up to date on new projects. Perusing a copy of this industry flyer leaves the reader with little doubt as to the quantity of funds being poured into this growing sector within the business of imprisonment. In any given issue, the newsletter reports on the simultaneous construction of dozens of new facilities: an 800-bed addition to the detention center in Jefferson County, Colorado; a 500-bed complex in Redgranite, Wisconsin; a 350-bed juvenile facility in Pendleton, Indiana; a 3,100-bed jail in Harris County, Texas; 300 new beds in Ontario County, New York; a 300-bed jail in Hopkins County, Kentucky; a 400-bed increase to Iowa's Fort Dodge Correctional Facility, and on and on. In 1996 alone, construction began on twenty-seven federal prisons and ninety-six state facilities.[11]

The incredible amount of money being poured into prisons has lured some of the biggest construction firms in the world into the business, among them Turner Construction, Brown and Root, and CRSS; well-known architectural firms such as DLR Group, KMD Architects, and DMJM; and a variety of Wall Street financiers. Underwriting prison construction by selling tax-exempt bonds is now estimated to be a $2.3 billion annual industry in itself.[12] Some corporations such as Corrections Corporation of America and Wackenhut have gone so far as to establish publicly traded real-estate investment trusts (REITs) that focus exclusively on building and owning prisons. Yet as lucrative as prison construction and ownership are, they represent only a small part of the profits being derived from crime and prisoners.

In the 1990s, the variety of corporations making money from prisons is truly dizzying, ranging from Dial Soap to Famous Amos cookies, from AT&T to health-care providers to companies that manufacture everything from prefab cells, leather restraints, cooking utensils, food, leg bracelets for home monitoring, security systems, razor wire, computer programs, knife-proof vests, laundry detergent, and so on. To give you an idea of what a small exclusive contract on a captive audience of prisoners can be worth, consider that in 1995 Dial Soap sold $100,000 worth of its product to the New York City jail system alone—one jail system.[13] When contracts for entire states are up for grabs, the stakes get considerably higher. When VitaPro Foods of Montreal, Canada, contracted to supply inmates in the state of Texas with its soy-based meat substitute, the contract was worth $34 million a year.[14] And the profits from soap and soy pale in comparison to more lucrative contracts such as those for phone service inside the prison walls.

Based on the number of booths at recent trade shows, there are approximately eighteen telephone companies competing for a share of the prisoner market. But unlike the free world, in prisons such competition doesn't result in lower prices. The prison telephone market now generates more than $1 billion a year by charging exorbitant rates—rates often five times higher than those you or I pay—to the families of inmates who are billed for their incarcerated loved one's collect calls. One pay phone in a prison can generate as much as $15,000 per year. That's approximately five times more than the average revenues generated by a pay phone in the general population.[15]

The profits are so enormous that prisons, public and private, do not choose their inmates' phone service provider based on which company offers the lowest price, but just the opposite. The prisons often choose the company willing to give the prison administration the largest share of the profits, and quite often the company promising to kick back the most money to prison management is the corporation charging the most to the prisoner's families. This is the kind of market abuse that results from a captive population that cannot take its business elsewhere.

Health care is another industry that does quite well with a captive clientele. Contracting to care for prisoners has become a billion-dollar industry.[16] Despite the hefty price tag, health care in our prisons is absolutely dismal. I know of inmates who have dropped dead of heart attacks after having complained of chest pains for weeks but never having been granted access to a doctor. Prisoners with severe mental problems are often locked in solitary confinement because it's cheaper than providing medication and making sure that it is taken regularly. HIV patients don't have access to the expensive drug cocktails that have greatly increased the life expectancy of AIDS patients on the outside. Such poor care is largely the result of having established a completely backward reward system for the companies that bid for inmate health care, which is to say that the less health care these corporations actually provide to prisoners, the more money they get to keep for themselves.

In addition to the typical services one thinks of when it comes to the prison population, an assortment of strange new industries has been born from the trade in prisoners—quite literally, the trade in prisoners. Prisoner brokers now place inmates in for-profit facilities for Departments of Corrections across the nation. These brokers charge taxpayers $2.00 to $5.50 per day per inmate placed. For instance, when the State of Colorado wanted to find beds for 500 of its inmates in 1995, it called Dominion Management of Edmond, Oklahoma. The company found an old mail warehouse equipped with bars in Texarkana, Texas, that could hold the prisoners, albeit twenty-six to a single cell with only one bathroom. For this placing of phone calls, the Colorado Department of Corrections agreed to pay Dominion $365,000 a year for as long as the inmates were in the Texas facility. Perhaps more than any other single element within the prison industry, this brokering of human beings makes clear that we have truly turned our prison population into chattel at the end of the twentieth century.[17]

I did some experimenting on my own in this sector of the prison trade in 1995. In less than five hours, I placed calls to nearly every state Department of Corrections in the United States. I found out which states had prisoners they needed to place and which states had or knew of empty beds to put them in. It was fast and it was simple. It is difficult to understand why government officials are willing to pay millions of dollars a year to prisoner brokers for a service that they could easily perform for themselves in a few hours on the phone, but such disregard for the taxpayer's interest is commonplace in today's prison industry. It reminds me of the $600 wrenches and $1,200 toilet seats that have become so commonplace in the defense industry.

Another method for profiting from the prisoner trade is that of prisoner transportation. A number of private companies, some of which are owned by the private-prison corporations, are now moving prisoners back and forth across the nation for a per-head fee. The increasing use

of out-of-state private prisons during the last decade has greatly escalated the numbers of prisoners being transported across state lines.

For instance, Texas is housing somewhere in the neighborhood of
5,000 inmates from fourteen different states. That's a lot of transportation. Although most forms of interstate commerce are highly regulated,
shipments of inmates are not. Moving cattle or chickens across state
lines is considerably more regulated than this shipping of the human
commodity, and it's not nearly as profitable. Due to lax regulation and
oversight, prisoners are often bounced from one holding facility to another while the transport companies seek to maximize their profits by
making as few trips as possible. As a result, it can take weeks for an inmate to be moved from one prison to the next. Being placed in the care
of the poorly trained private guards who work for these companies for
such long periods of time helps to explain why the incidence of prisoners being abused during transport is on the rise. In recent years, a number of female prisoners have reported that they have been raped while
being moved cross-country by all-male staffs of transportation companies. As of March 1999, there were at least three lawsuits alleging rapes
by employees of prisoner transport companies pending in Colorado
alone.[18]

Many rural communities—which are enduring falling crop, livestock,
and oil prices, not to mention the transfer of traditionally rural jobs to
Third World labor markets—have become major players in the new
prison industry. In an effort to lure badly needed jobs to their communities, many a rural county has turned to prisons as a "recession-proof"
economic resource. Such counties now actively compete for the privilege of having prisons—public or private, or both—sited in their region.
Before Cameron, Missouri, was chosen as the location for the Western
Missouri Correctional Center, which opened in 1989, it had to beat out
thirty other rural communities that were trying to land the same complex. Why so much competition for a prison? Journalist David Lamb put
it this way: "They don't pollute, they don't go out of business, they don't
get downsized."[19] And they can bring millions of dollars into the economy.

For example, when rural northern New York lost its dairy and mining
industries, civic leaders turned to prisons as an economic cure. Towns
like Dannemora, which now houses the Clinton Correctional Facility,
have become totally dependent on the prison business for their survival.
Clinton's 1,198 jobs pour $2 million in payroll into the local economy

every week, and Clinton is only a drop in the bucket for a region swimming in prison dollars. Northern New York has gone from having two prisons in the 1970s to eighteen today, and these new prisons have accounted for a $1.5-billion construction boom and have created an annual windfall of approximately $425 million a year in salaries and operating expenses for the area.[20]

With so much money and so many jobs at stake, it should come as no surprise that many of these rural communities now hire their own lobbyists and throw campaign funds at politicians in an effort to ensure that the war on crime doesn't end anytime soon. And this is a questionable practice that they have in common with other sectors of the prison-industrial complex, including juvenile-justice providers and private-prison corporations.

An investors' report issued by Equitable Securities Research in 1997 summed up what is happening in the business of juvenile justice under the headline "At-Risk Youth: A Growth Industry." By 1998, there were between 10,000 and 15,000 private juvenile-justice service providers in the United States. These companies provide everything from educational programs to management of juvenile detention centers to running wilderness camps for at-risk youth. Dealing with juvenile offenders at the local, state, and federal level has become a $3-billion a year market, but this figure is small compared to the $50 billion being spent annually for programs serving at-risk youth.[21]

Although it still has a considerably smaller market than its juvenile-justice cousin, running private prisons for adult inmates is the fastest-growing segment of the prison-industrial complex. At last count there were twenty-six private-prison corporations, but as with most industries these days, that number is shrinking quickly as consolidation has become the name of the game in the incarceration business. For-profit prison companies now operate approximately 150 facilities in twenty-eight states.[22] These private prisons house approximately 116,000 inmates from over thirty state jurisdictions as well as federal prisoners and those in the custody of the Immigration and Naturalization Service. The number of inmates in private facilities is predicted to reach 200,000 by the turn of the century and 360,000 within the next six years. In 1996, private facilities were proliferating at four times the rate of state prisons.[23]

The largest of these prison companies is Corrections Corporation of America, which was founded in 1983 and now constitutes the sixth-largest prison system in the nation, trailing only the federal system and the state systems of Texas, California, Florida, and New York. The largest shareholder in CCA is Sodexho, a multinational corporation with headquarters in Paris, France. And it's not just the shareholders in this prison company that are international. CCA also operates for-profit facilities in Great Britain and Australia. In 1998, CCA's revenues were estimated to be $695.6 million.[24]

The second-largest private-prison company is Wackenhut, a corporation that also specializes in private security. Wackenhut has annual revenues of over $1 billion derived from its prison and security ventures. Together, CCA and Wackenhut are well on their way to establishing a near monopoly in the private-prison industry. They now control 76.4 percent of the global private-prison market. In all, today's private-prison industry constitutes a $1.5- to $2-billion-per-year business. Market analysts believe that the revenues derived from private incarceration will surpass $5 billion within a decade or may do so even sooner if corporations are allowed to purchase entire state prison systems at a time, as CCA is attempting to do in the state of Tennessee.[25]

And corporations aren't the only ones benefiting from the war on crime. Public-sector employees in law enforcement and corrections have also seen their stock rise as a direct result of the war on crime in the form of increased salaries, growing numbers, and new equipment and facilities. Prison guards in California, for instance, have seen their incomes nearly double as that state's prison population has quadrupled in size. Law-enforcement budgets across the nation have also rocketed upward in the last fifteen years as state and federal governments divert more and more money into fighting crime. As of May 1999, Democrat Bill Clinton's "liberal" administration was boasting that it had increased the number of police on the streets of America by 100,000.[26] Like other entities within the criminal-justice system that benefit from the war, law-enforcement and prison-guard unions have become major suppliers of campaign funds to politicians willing to support new hard-on-crime measures that will further enlarge their numbers, the justice system, and their members' paychecks.

Prison labor is another area where both the public and private sector are cashing in on America's 2 million prisoners. Unicorp, the government entity that produces products with prison labor, now has annual sales of over $500 million a year.[27] By 1998, there were over 2,500 prison and jail industries in operation in the United States, a figure that reflects a nearly 500-percent increase in such industries in the last decade.[28] Prison industries include everything from sewing to accounting to telemarketing to the manufacture of false teeth, parts for Boeing aircraft, and the logos for Lexus automobiles. As these last examples illustrate, it's not just obscure companies that use prisoners to cut their labor costs. Large well-known corporations such as Microsoft, Spalding, IBM, Compaq, Texas Instruments, AT&T, Victoria's Secret, Eddie Bauer, Chevron, and TWA, just to name a few, are all using prisoners directly or through subcontractors as a portion of their workforce.[29]

The 1,310 industries in operation in the U.S. prison system accounted for total sales of $1.63 billion in 1998. There is no cumulative figure available for the estimated 1,200 industries operating in our jails, but it would be safe to estimate that the combined sales for jail and prison industries is in excess of $2 billion annually and could be as high as $3 billion.[30] With many states, as well as the federal government, currently considering legislation similar to the recently passed Oregon law requiring all inmates to work, it is estimated that prison labor could be generating more than $8 billion in annual sales within the next few years.[31]

Of the billions being made off this captive labor force, prisoners are generally paid between $.20 and $1.20 per hour—less at private prisons and a little more in some federal- and state-run facilities. Imagine how appealing inmate labor looks to corporations, considering that these industries are generating an average of $14.54 profit per inmate-hour worked.[32] In a foreshadowing of things to come, at least one company has already closed its data-processing operation in Mexico's *maquiladora* district in favor of a labor force from San Quentin State Prison. Other companies have laid off their entire workforces, immediately replacing them with cheap prisoner labor.[33]

In 1998, moviegoers who attended a screening of the documentary film *The Big One* saw filmmaker and activist Michael Moore trying to convince executives at Nike to stop using sweatshops in Indonesia to make their shoes in favor of laborers from Moore's hometown of Flint, Michigan. At the same time that Moore was pitching Flint workers to Nike, Oregon state representative Kevin Mannix was busy telling the shoe magnate that his state could offer the company "competitive prison labor."[34] But Mannix wasn't talking about labor costs competitive with Flint. He was describing labor costs more competitive with Indonesia, where 74 cents a day is the norm. If I was unemployed in Flint, I wouldn't be counting on a paycheck from Nike anytime soon.[35]

Moviegoers also play a role in yet another area of crime profiteering. As financially rewarding as the prison population has become for those corporations within the prison-industrial complex, perhaps the biggest winners when it comes to making money from some aspect of crime are the media corporations. Putting an exact figure on the media's crime profits is simply impossible. We know that the news business makes a lot of money by increasing its ratings and pickup rates with sensationalized news coverage of violent crime. We know that sex- and violence-filled media offerings have become the second-largest U.S. export in dollar amount.[36] We know that in the 1990s, the majority of all television programs—61 percent—contain violence, much of it related to crime.[37] We know that advertisers spent $1.4 trillion in the 1980s and are currently spending approximately $150 billion a year to plug their products in between the scenes or stories of violence.[38] And finally, we know that together, the nine media companies that now control the majority of the world's content put $110 billion in profits in the bank in 1997.[39] So even though no one can say for sure exactly how much money the media corporations are generating as a direct result of their escalating dissemination of information based on violent crime, I think we can safely assume that it is a multibillion-dollar annual venture.

No Need for Conspiracy

These are only a few of the methods being used to turn crime into profit these days. There are many more. But before anyone gets the idea that I am trying to imply that the growth in the prison population is the result of some massive corporate conspiracy designed to turn Americans into chattel, let me assure you that this is not the case.

In truth, such a grand scheme to enlarge the prison population would be far easier to combat than the real and seemingly innocent forces behind the prison system's growth. After all, if companies were making a concerted effort to work together to take away the freedom of certain individuals for economic gain, one would need only expose such a devious strategy to the public to ensure its demise. So even though there is a "prisoners-as-chattel" scenario unfolding, the explanation for why it is occurring is much more complicated than simply ascribing it to a sinister plot. To understand the real cause of the justice system's demise, we must examine one of the basic tenets upon which our nation was founded: the free market.

For example, I believe that two of the main culprits behind the current growth in the prison population are the increasing use of corporate-owned prisons and the willingness of investors to fund prison construction in the public and private sector. While being touted as a way to save money on prisons, this market intervention into the justice system has given rise to a myriad of conflicting interests that are actually feeding the current expansion and its corresponding expense. In other words, there is no conspiracy afoot designed to further the growth of the prison population. The corporations now involved in the dispensing of justice simply operate in a manner that they perceive to be in the best interest of their shareholders and the prison population grows naturally as a result of this pursuit.

In the 1980s and 1990s, the perception of what is in the shareholder's best interest—regardless of a corporation's function—has become distressingly singular: to maximize the return on investment at all costs. Anyone who has run a company in the last two decades will tell you that any business plan designed to maximize shareholder profits must include strategies that will guarantee the company is able to maintain a certain level of growth over the long haul. Such an emphasis on growth and profit may be acceptable in the computer, furniture, or automobile industries. However, this is a wholly destructive force when applied to such fundamental elements of a democracy as a free press or the administration of justice—elements that, due to the inescapable conflicts of interest born of the principle of shareholder primacy, were never intended by the framers to be placed under the absolute control of market forces. This is particularly true of a market focused on consolidation rather than competition, as is the situation today.

Nevertheless, these conflicts now exist and are a part of the economic and political chain reaction that is causing the prison population to expand far beyond its historical limits. For this reason, I believe that when it comes down to determining who is responsible for the growth in the prison population, those who own stock in the corporations that compose the prison-industrial complex and media must bear as much of the blame as the CEOs of the companies themselves, who, after all, are only doing their bidding. So if you want to implicate someone for what is happening to justice in America at the end of the twentieth century, depending on your economic status, you may have to start with the face in the mirror.

A Criminal Portfolio

December 16, 1998, was no ordinary day at my house. It was my long-awaited payday, the culmination of months of hard . . . well, actually I hadn't done anything to earn the dough, so let's just say months of waiting. What's important here is that there was money in my mailbox, a check from my recently retained stockbroker. As I held the blue-green piece of paper in my hand—ever mindful not to bend, fold, or mutilate—I couldn't help but ponder the process that had produced this windfall, the first from my recently created crime portfolio.

In an effort to "write what you know," as they say, I lost my long-cherished virginity to Wall Street in 1998. Initially, my goal was to buy one share of stock in every company that makes at least a portion of its profits via some aspect of crime, but there were a couple of obstacles to such a venture. First, as mentioned earlier, the sheer volume of companies that now profit from crime is staggering. Buying just one share in each corporation would have required tens of thousands of dollars—which brings me to obstacle number two. I write nonfiction for a living, which made overcoming obstacle number one an impossibility.

In the end, I settled for a small, representative portfolio composed of one share each in nine companies that profit from crime in one or more of the ways described previously. I chose to buy Disney, General Electric, Corrections Corporation of America, American Express, Wackenhut, AT&T, Proctor and Gamble, Microsoft, and TWA. I would have liked to have purchased one of the high-interest, tax-exempt bonds being sold to fund the construction of new prisons, but most of these bonds require a $5,000 minimum investment, which puts them financially out of reach for two-thirds of all Americans, including myself.

In economic terms, my first crime-portfolio check wasn't large, $29.72 to be exact, but in human terms, it seemed immeasurable. I couldn't get past the idea that I had made money to a certain extent as a result of someone else's life in some other community taking a tragic turn for the worse. For me, holding this check was like holding a tiny flask of perfume, but rather than enjoying the aroma, only being able to imagine the bloody, butchered carcass of the whale from whence it came.

In the micro perspective, my new money represented nothing more than business as usual in the investment world; buying publicly traded stocks, holding them for a while, then selling them at a profit or collecting dividend checks. But in the big picture, my little blue-green check represented something far more significant. It was proof that when it comes to justice, America has replaced our long-held ideals with something less, a *mechanism* for turning crime into profit.

Eventually I tossed the check from my broker on top of my coffee table, where it remained, uncashed, for several weeks. By coincidence, my crime dividend turned out to be strategically located between my couch and the television. As a result of its constant visibility in relation to the screen, the blue-green paper seemed to take on certain powers. It was as if it served as a filter or translator for the information that was pouring into my living room by way of the tube.

The evening news seemed different to me now. It was as if I had a personal stake in what I was seeing. Night after night, I watched people being arrested, handcuffed, and led away to jail or forced into the backseats of police cars. As these images of crime passed over my check, I was constantly reminded that every such scene meant that my next payday would likely be even bigger. Then I realized: It wasn't just that I felt like I had a vested interest in what I was seeing, I did have a vested interest. The pain of those on the TV screen had become my gain. In the truest sense, I owned shares in each person I saw entering the criminal-justice system. Crime, provided it stayed out of my neighborhood, had become a positive thing for me in economic terms. And I was hardly alone.

Millions of American investors have likewise tapped into this world of profit that grows every time some poor soul shoplifts food or a drug addict steals to make the pain go away. Some Wall Street analysts now watch the crime figures reported by the FBI and the Justice Department in the same way they monitor the unemployment rate or quarterly earnings reports. These crime-rate figures have become the leading indicators for the dozens of private-prison stocks and REITs devoted to prison projects, and they also serve as a crystal ball for the stocks of the many other corporations that now constitute the prison-industrial complex.

With thousands of publicly traded companies now cashing in on crime, virtually all the people who own stock or invest in any of the more than 2,000 mutual funds now in operation—an estimated 69 million people, or 44 percent of all U.S. households[40]—are deriving at least a small portion of their profits from crime. Perhaps *USA Today* said it best in a June 1996 article under the headline "Everybody's Doin' the

Jailhouse Stock."[41] It seems the old adage "Crime doesn't pay" has been rendered obsolete for millions of us.

I am not trying to imply that investors are somehow evil. The truth is, most people are ignorant about this issue. They either don't realize that they have become a cog in the perpetual-prisoner machine or they have not considered the ramifications of having become one. Case in point: The California teachers' union has been an outspoken critic of hard-on-crime policies such as that state's harsh three-strikes law, yet the teachers' pension fund invests in private-prison companies that owe much of their success to hard-on-crime sentencing measures such as the three-strikes law. It's a safe bet to assume that most California teachers have no idea where their pension money is being invested, and the same can be said of millions of other investors who, more often than not these days, have turned over their portfolio responsibilities to any number of fund management gurus.

Even when investors take an active role in building their own portfolios, trying to screen out companies that have become a part of the prison-industrial complex is a sizable challenge because corporations have worked hard to keep such activities out of the limelight. I suspect that even the majority of stockbrokers have no idea that they are helping their clients to participate in crime profiteering when they get them into some of America's best known blue-chip stocks. Consider my experience when I attempted to overtly build a portfolio revolving around the companies that profit from crime and prisoners.

When I went in search of a broker, I found that the vast majority of them either hesitated or just outright refused to assist me in my venture. I had to walk into four different brokerage firms, repeating my spiel about purchasing stock in companies that exploit crime and practice "the new slavery," before I was able to buy a single share.

At first, I was told by brokers that they weren't aware of any such companies, and I suspect that they were telling me the truth. After I tossed out a dozen or so company names with detailed explanations of how each profited from crime, they were still hesitant to help me build my admittedly distasteful portfolio. I found this quite remarkable, considering that the corporations I mentioned were companies that these same people bought and sold every day.

One broker at Smith Barney told me that I was "disgusting." I would have been more delighted by this response had I not noticed that her righteous outburst trailed her inquiry as to just how much money I intended to invest. Eventually, I found a really nice fellow willing to take my business, provided I wouldn't use his name in my book or tell anyone about our business dealings. Having little alternative, and not being particularly proud of my new title of shareholder anyway, I agreed. My broker (this is my clever disguise for his identity) told me that he was afraid that if his other clients found out that he had helped me build "this type" of portfolio, he might "lose their business." Remember this point. We'll talk more about it in the last part of the book.

Obviously I could have avoided all the hassle by using a different description for my portfolio—or none at all, for that matter. I knew that using words like "slavery" (which, by the way, I am not completely convinced is an appropriate term to describe the modern prison trade) wasn't going to go over very well. I could have just borrowed some of the imaginative terms that the prison trade uses to describe itself. For instance, I could have told the brokers that I wanted to invest in "the future of corrections" or in "companies dedicated to meeting the needs of tomorrow." Such polite euphemisms, coupled with my request to purchase a piece of well-respected companies like Disney, CCA, Microsoft, GE, and the others, would have been well received. Yet such an approach wouldn't have demonstrated that when people are confronted with the facts surrounding crime profiteering—even stockbrokers who embody the ideals of the free market—they tend to disapprove of the concept.

Since millions of American investors are currently deriving at least a portion of their income from crime, we can assume that the "facts" surrounding their profit's origin are not being discussed to any significant degree. In fact, just the opposite is happening. What little information there is regarding crime profiteering that is being disseminated to investors is quite misleading, conveying a message designed to convince those who own a stake in America's prisons that their profits are the result of a rational, beneficial, and even necessary market development.

After all, what could be wrong with making money by supporting corporations whose actions are intended to make our society safer from the criminals who have all but taken over our streets? The answer here would of course be "Nothing." And who would argue that if it takes the participation of corporate America and its investors to build enough prisons to hold enough criminals to lower the crime rates, that such market intervention isn't a good thing? Obviously, the answer here is "No one." However, these answers ring true only if criminals are taking over our streets and the market's participation in the justice system is making us safer and lowering crime rates—but these things aren't happening. These notions are based on persuasive, though inaccurate, hard-on-crime rhetoric—rhetoric that has its roots in numerous criminal-justice myths that have been widely disseminated throughout the general population but which are in direct conflict with much of the hard data relating to crime in the United States.

2

The Crime Gap

Prior to the current prison expansion, growth in the prison population tended to reflect growth in either the crime rates or the general population. In other words, the current prison expansion in our past could be assumed to have resulted from a tenfold increase in the crime rates or in the general population, or in some combination thereof. But can these historical influences over the size of the prison population explain the growth that has occurred in our prisons during the last three decades? Hardly.

According to the National Crime Victimization Survey (NCVS), the Census Bureau's mechanism for measuring crime, our nation's overall crime rate between 1973 and 1982 was relatively flat, a little up in this category one year, a little down the next. An examination of the years between 1983 and 1999 shows that the rate of people being victimized by crime was actually declining.[1] Clearly these are not statistics that would warrant a 1,000-percent increase in incarceration rates—unless, of course, these flat and declining crime rates could somehow be attributed to the growth in the prison population, but most experts do not believe that this is the case. As for the impact of America's overall population growth on the prison population, it is estimated that less than 8 percent of the total increase in the number of men and women behind bars can be attributed to this factor.[2]

Since the forces that historically determined the size of the prison population cannot account for what has happened in our prison system of late, we must look elsewhere to find the explanation for this growth. I believe that to understand the true causes of today's prison expansion, it is necessary to compare the trends in the crime rates during the last few decades with trends in the nation's perception of crime for the same period. To chart the latter, we must look back at public opinion polls conducted during the last few decades.

With few exceptions, polls conducted in the 1950s, 1960s, and 1970s reflected that crime was not a priority issue among the public. During these decades, pollsters found that Americans were mainly preoccupied with war (the Cold War or the Vietnam War, or both); the economy, particularly inflation; and civil rights issues. But things began to change approximately twenty years ago. In the last two decades of the twentieth century, war would still occupy the American conscience, but it would be a different kind of war.[3]

Since the early 1980s, when ultraconservative president Ronald Reagan declared the current "war on crime" by telling a television audience that to win this new war against criminals would require the same level of commitment it took to win World War II, crime has been at or near the top of the public's stated concerns in nearly every poll. Americans have truly become convinced that they are living in a war zone. By 1992, an incredible 41 percent of Americans believed that they were "unsafe" when walking in their own neighborhoods after dark, which is a much higher level of crime fear than in any other industrialized nation, even though a number of these other nations have similar, if not higher, crime rates than our own.

Even more disturbing, this crime anxiety appeared at a time when statistics tell us that the vast majority of people—with the exception of those living in pockets of urban poverty—were actually safer than they had been during the 1970s.[4] Recent polls indicate that the level of "crime anxiety" among Americans has continued to grow in the 1990s. One poll found that an incredible 79 percent of the U.S. population now believes that crime is one of the biggest problems facing our nation.[5] It seems clear that something more than the real incidence of crime is influencing the way that we see the world around us.

In a healthy society, if you were to superimpose a graph showing the public's level of concern about crime from year to year over a graph depicting annual trends in the crime rates, you would expect to see two lines that moved in close relation to one another. Such movement in tandem would be an indication that a population's apprehension regarding crime was tied to the occurrence of crime, or, put another way, that people's fear of crime was based on the realistic odds that they might be victimized by crime.

In direct contrast to this healthy model, if we were to overlay a graph of the crime rates in the United States since 1980 with a graph of the public's concern regarding crime for the same period, we would find two lines moving in divergent directions—concern rising as crime is actually falling—thus creating an ever-widening breach as the two measures move toward the end of the century. I believe that the mindset reflected by this growing chasm is what accounts for the other set of ever-diverging lines that appear when we compare crime rates to incarceration rates. Allen Beck, chief of corrections statistics for the Bureau of Justice Statistics, has compared these latter two measures in recent years and has noted that the trend line representing the number of inmates has soured by more than 60 percent in the 1990s, while the line for the crime rate has been declining by double-digit percentages during the same period.[6]

I believe that the same forces that have helped to create the chasm between our impression of crime and the real danger afforded by crime and the resultant diverging trends in crime rates and incarceration rates are controlled by the entities that have the most to gain by fighting a war on crime and increasing the prison population, namely, law-enforcement agencies, politicians, and members of the prison-industrial complex. This is not the first time in our history that those with a financial or political stake in fighting a war have worked to sever the public's impression of events from reality.

On January 17, 1961, President Dwight Eisenhower used his farewell speech to warn Americans that the military-industrial complex had gained a dangerous level of influence over our political system and its defense policies. In Eisenhower's words, "In the councils of government, we must guard against the acquisition of unwarranted influence, whether sought or unsought, by the military-industrial complex. The potential for the disastrous rise of misplaced power exists and will persist. . . . We should take nothing for granted."[7]

In particular, Eisenhower was concerned over the fact that the defense industry was using its influence on Capitol Hill to put forward the perception that there was a severe "missile gap" between the United States and the Soviet Union, the idea being that Soviet military capabilities were far superior to our own and that we needed to spend much more money on defense in order to restore the balance of power and thereby keep America safe. In response to the fear created by "missile-gap" propaganda, the public enthusiastically supported the government's massive increases in defense spending at the beginning of the Cold War.

Eisenhower used his last words as president to issue his warning because he understood that there was, in fact, no "missile gap." The former general was privy to information that clearly exposed this gap as a ploy by the defense industry and the politicians it financially supported to justify diverting more tax dollars into the corporations and government agencies that comprised the military-industrial complex.

I believe that Eisenhower's warning is as applicable today as it was in 1961. The only difference between then and now is that the "missile gap" of the military-industrial complex has given way to the "crime gap" of the prison-industrial complex—the idea this time around being that there is a war going on in our streets between criminals and the rest of us and that the criminals are way ahead. In the 1980s and 1990s, elected officials being financially supported by the prison-industrial complex have repeatedly told us that we must spend more, more, more of our tax dollars on law enforcement and prisons if we want to close the gap and once again restore order and safety to America.

Unfortunately, this latest ploy seems to have worked as well as the "missile-gap" propaganda did. Not since the Cold War increases in defense spending has any sector of government experienced such dramatic increases in expenditure as those in the criminal justice arena. During the last twenty years, corrections spending has actually escalated three times as fast as defense expenditures.[8] We are now pouring hundreds of billions of dollars into the bank accounts of the prison-industrial complex and its shareholders, even though an examination of the crime rates certainly seems to indicate that such spending behavior is simply not warranted. It appears that the complex has successfully managed to unbind criminal justice expenditures from the realities of crime, attaching them instead to the more easily manipulated public impression of crime.

That being the case, I will use the rest of this chapter to examine four criminal-justice "myths" that have been and continue to be widely disseminated by individuals in law enforcement and government as propaganda designed to spark public support for our current hard-on-crime policies. These myths are partially responsible for the public's ongoing belief in the existence of the "crime gap," and they help to explain the current popular support for the concept of a war on crime.

Myth 1: Violent Crime Is on the Rise

The most widely reported source regarding crime is the Uniform Crime Report (UCR). This report is tabulated by the Federal Bureau of Investigation and is based upon arrest reports provided by over 17,000 separate police departments from across the nation. Most media corporations use the UCR nearly exclusively to report on crime because it is convenient to do so. The report breaks down its information on a state-by-state basis. As a result, the UCR has become the most-often-reported measure of crime in America.

But is the UCR an accurate gauge for crime? Most criminologists say "No." According to the National Criminal Justice Commission (NCJC), a thirty-four-member organization comprised of criminal justice experts, scholars, and professors formed in 1994 for the purpose of evaluating the state of the criminal-justice system, "Most criminologists consider UCR figures inaccurate because they tend to exaggerate fluctuations in crime—a fact that is at least partly responsible for the public misperception that crime is rising."[9]

The first reason for this "exaggeration" cited by NCJC research is that the techniques used by the police for reporting crimes have been greatly improved by computer technology. For example, in 1973, there were 861,000 aggravated assaults reported to police departments in the United States, but because of the archaic techniques used for keeping track of such information, the police recorded and passed on to the FBI only 421,000 of those assaults. By 1988, things had changed radically on the technology front. With the help of computers, police were able to record and pass on to the FBI 910,000 of the 940,000 assaults reported that year.[10]

The numbers make it clear that assaults really didn't go up much between 1973 and 1988, yet the number of assaults recorded by police more than doubled. This same scenario took place with regard to other types of crimes as well, including robbery and rape. As a result of nothing more than better record keeping, the statistics contained in the UCR inaccurately reflected that the crime rates had virtually doubled during this fifteen-year period.

Better record keeping is only one of the reasons the UCR tends to exaggerate crime rates. The method used by police departments for tabulating their statistics is also flawed. Police departments count those arrested for committing crime rather than the number of crimes committed. In other words, if three people were to assault someone or if four juveniles were to rob a house, the police would register three assaults and four robberies with the FBI instead of one of each. In addition, because the UCR is based on arrest information and evidence of crimes, changes in the laws or the addition of new laws will show up as increases in crime rather than as adjustments to the statutes. Similarly, adding more police, which naturally results in more arrests, also tends to be reflected as an increase in crime rather than simply as an increase in policing.

Largely as a consequence of these numerical peculiarities, the FBI's UCR showed that crime had pretty much exploded between 1973 and 1988, when in reality it had been statistically flat or falling, and this imaginary "explosion" became the political justification for declaring the current war on crime, resulting in radical changes to the sentencing guidelines and subsequently causing the massive growth in the prison population. If you're wondering why law-enforcement agencies would allow such a misconception regarding crime to influence public policy, ask yourself this question: Did law enforcement during this time period have a vested interest in conveying the perception that crime was escalating rapidly? The answer is: absolutely.

During the 1980s and early 1990s, and in some places still, many law-enforcement budgets were greatly affected by the crime rates in a given area; that is to say that during this time frame, rising crime rates often related to increasing budgets and salaries. For example, the 1994 Federal Crime Control Act allocated its funds based solely on crime rates. Determining funding in this manner means that the higher the number of crimes reported by law enforcement in a particular jurisdiction, the more money it receives. With such incentives, it makes sense that the UCR report would show that crime was always going up during this period. Experts believe that the practice of basing financial allocations on crime rates created an important incentive for police departments and the FBI to exaggerate their crime figures upward. "The more dangerous the streets are perceived to be by the public," says Steven Chermak of Indiana University at Bloomington's Department of Criminal Justice, "the easier it is for source organizations to justify additional spending and budgetary and personnel increases."[11] But the times have changed, and so have law enforcement's incentives with regard to the crime rates.

What Goes Up

After fighting the war on crime for more than a decade while reports on crime rates simultaneously continued to reflect increases in lawbreaking, the public started to question the massive expenditures for the war in light of the lack of success being reflected in the UCR. As a result, the pressure to inflate numbers that existed from the late 1970s to the early 1990s reversed itself into a pressure to skew them downward, thus demonstrating that we were winning the war. Since 1993, the UCR has reported substantial decreases in the crime rates, and these decreases have been widely hailed as proof by politicians, corrections personnel, and law-enforcement agencies of success in the battle against crime and therefore as justification for continuing the current prison expansion and further increasing law-enforcement budgets.

This convenient logic was described by Steven Donziger of the NCJC in *Atlantic Monthly*. "If crime is going up," said Donziger, "then we need to build more prisons; and if crime is going down, it's because we built more prisons—and building even more prisons will therefore drive crime down even lower."[12] Such thinking is like determining criminal-justice policy with a flip of a coin that has a prison on both sides. But in 1998, proof that law enforcement's crime figures were being fudged downward began to surface.

Gil Kerlikowske, former police commissioner of Buffalo, New York, told the *New York Times* that the new pressure on law enforcement to prove that it is winning the war on crime through lower crime figures "creates a new area for police corruption and ethics."[13] Kerlikowske went on to point out that the promotions and pay raises that were once linked to escalating crime rates have, in the 1990s, become increasingly tied to statistics showing that crime has been reduced. As a result of the new need to demonstrate that crime-war expenditures are justified, one police department after another has been caught fabricating lower crime rates.

In Boca Raton, Florida, the police chief gave his blessing to a captain on the force who systematically downgraded property crimes such as burglaries. Instead of listing these robberies as such, they were recorded as vandalism or trespassing. This bogus reporting method allowed the city to report a fictitious 11 percent drop in its felony rate for 1997.[14]

Unfortunately, Boca Raton was not an isolated event. In 1998, crime figures from New York, Atlanta, and Philadelphia were all found to have been underreported. Considering the size of these cities, these instances of underreporting by themselves could account for a fair-sized percentage of the decrease in crime reflected by the UCR between 1993 and 1998. For instance, Philadelphia skewed its crime rate downward so severely that it was forced to completely withdraw its figures from the FBI's UCR report for the years 1996, 1997, and at least the first half of 1998. Since the City of Brotherly Love accounts for 2 percent of all the nation's homicides, its withdrawal from the report could reflect an inaccurate 2 percent decrease in America's murder rate.[15]

The FBI, which also has a vested interest in showing that we are winning the war on crime—the bureau needs to justify the addition of nearly a thousand new agents and significant budget increases since 1990—claims that it will attempt to adjust for the absence of Philadelphia's crimes and the other cities' bogus reports. But as is always the case with law enforcement's UCR figures, we will just have to hope that they do so, even though such accuracy would likely work to law enforcement's financial detriment.

Because of the incentives for law enforcement to exaggerate the crime numbers either up or down depending on its needs, many experts are now warning that the media and politicians should not rely upon the UCR when it comes to informing the public or determining criminal-justice policies. Unfortunately, it appears that this warning has not been heeded. Politicians continue to escalate the war on crime, now claiming that we are finally winning, and the majority of media outlets continue to regurgitate UCR figures without the slightest hint to the public of their potential inaccuracy.

The Other Crime Rate

What is most perplexing here is that we do not have to be so dependent upon the biased information provided by law-enforcement agencies to determine the threat posed by criminal activity. As I mentioned earlier, there is another report available regarding the rates of crime, one that is widely accepted within the criminology community as more accurate. The National Crime Victimization Survey is conducted by the Census Bureau and is based upon a massive nationwide telephone survey using scientific polling techniques to determine who was victimized by what crimes. The survey's information is compiled in a fashion similar to the Nielson television surveys.

Because of the manner in which the NCVS is compiled, crimes that are never reported to police can still be measured. A person whose stereo was stolen, whose property was vandalized, or who was assaulted or even raped, yet did not, as is often the case, contact police, will still have that crime counted by the Census Bureau. For this reason, as well as because the Census Bureau, unlike law enforcement, has no vested financial interest in fluctuations in the crime rate, most criminologists view the NCVS as a more realistic measure of crime. Determining which measure of the crime rates is more accurate is becoming increasingly important due to the UCR's influence over crime policy and the fact that the UCR and the NCVS have reported significantly differing levels of crime during the past twenty years.

Although it's true that law enforcement has a financial motive for tinkering with the crime rates, I still believe that the main reason for the discrepancies between these two measures is in their design and in the interpretation of their data. For instance, if you create new laws, you create more crime. If you put 100,000 additional police officers on the streets, they will find more crime. If you weaken the rights of citizens in such a way as to allow more random searches without probable cause, you will uncover more transgressions of the law. If you allow racial profiling, you will arrest more minority criminals. All of these things have come about in the last twenty years. As a result, the number of people being arrested for crimes, particularly drug-related crimes, increased dramatically in the 1980s.

According to the UCR, the incidence of crime must have gone up because reported crimes and arrests went up, but this simply isn't true. The UCR doesn't take into account all the other variables that have caused more people to be arrested and more accurate reports to be filed. The fact that such variables have no effect on the NCVS, which measures victims and not criminals, explains why criminologists prefer it as a method for measuring crime. Think of it like this: Let's say that there is a particular stretch of highway where the speed limit used to be seventy miles an hour but now it is fifty-five miles an hour. Using UCR methods, law enforcement could claim that people are driving faster than ever before on this stretch of road because more speeding tickets are being issued than ever before. But a closer examination would reveal that the vast majority of the tickets have been written to people driving sixty-five miles an hour and that the number of tickets doubled because there are now twice as many officers patrolling the highway. In truth, the speed of drivers on the road has decreased from the days when the speed limit was seventy. The increase in tickets did not come from an increase in speed but rather from other variables, just as the increase in crime reflected in the UCR in the 1980s and early 1990s did not have to come from an actual increase in crimes.

If, in fact, the NCVS's statistics on crime are more accurate than the UCR's, then one could certainly argue, as many experts have, that the hundreds of billions in taxpayer dollars being expended on the war on crime and its resulting increase in incarceration are largely unwarranted. But once again, those with a vested financial stake in fighting this war point to economic research that would seem to justify continuing the current policy of using prisons to fight crime.

Myth 2: Prisons Save Us Money

A 1987 study conducted by the Justice Department's National Institute of Justice reported that the billions of dollars we are spending on the prison expansion are, in fact, a bargain. The NIJ study claimed that although it only costs around $25,000 a year to keep a criminal in prison, such incarceration saves America $430,000 per inmate because of the losses that would result from the inmate's additional crimes if that criminal were not locked up.[16] Saves "$430,000 per inmate"? The NIJ's figure makes it sound as if every drug addict and petty thief in the joint must be living in a mansion and driving a Lexus when they're not behind bars. So exactly how did the Justice Department arrive at these intriguing figures?

First of all, the report assumes that any criminal not in prison would commit no less than 187 additional crimes a year. According to Franklin Zimring, director of the Earl Warren Legal Justice Institute at the University of California and an outspoken critic of the NIJ's economic justification for mass incarceration, the Department of Justice incorrectly used a simple mean average in its formula. In other words, a shoplifter who might commit hundreds of crimes a year is averaged in with a bank robber who might commit one to two crimes a year, and both are shown to be capable of committing an estimated 187 additional crimes each. Zimring says that using the median, or midpoint, would be a more accurate measure of potential crimes. By his estimate, a more realistic figure is something like fifteen potential additional crimes per criminal per year, a figure 92 percent smaller than the Justice Department's estimate.[17]

And what about the rates of reoffense? The NIJ study calculates that *all* criminals not in prison would be constantly committing new crimes at a rate of one every 45.6 hours, 365 days out of the year. But several modern studies on recidivism have shown that only 22 to 34 percent of convicted felons reoffend within the first three years after their release. These same studies also found that drug offenders, who now constitute the majority of all prisoners, are actually the least likely group to recidivate. And those in prison for marijuana violations—one-sixth of all federal prisoners—have been found to pose little threat for ever reoffending.[18]

When we view the NIJ figures in light of these recidivism studies and in conjunction with Zimring's observations, it would appear that the prison cost analysis by the Justice Department is exaggerating the additional potential crimes of those behind bars by many times over. And the inaccuracy of this report does not end here.

The NIJ also played fast and loose with its estimate of the average cost of each of the imaginary 187 crimes. It suggested that each crime would cost society a whopping $2,300. But the only way to arrive at this figure is to insert the total cost of U.S. law enforcement into the formula. To get to $2,300 per crime, you have to figure in the combined cost of all the cops in America at all times of the day or night, regardless of whether they are directing traffic, guarding a public building, rescuing a drowning victim, or just doing paperwork, as well as the total cost of law-enforcement administration.[19]

Another reason that this report has met with such skepticism in the criminology community is the fact that it claims that prisons save us money, yet it doesn't compare the $25,000 per year, per inmate cost of incarceration to prison alternatives such as drug-treatment programs and supervised probation, which cost around $3,500 per person per year, or even intensive probation, at $6,500 per person per year.[20] To truly claim that America's prison expansion is saving the public money, the Justice Department would need to compare the U.S. "prison" solution to the alternative approach being taken by the other industrialized nations or even to our own policies as recently as thirty years ago. Such a comparison would clearly reveal that the United States has embarked on the most costly path to fighting crime available, not the most economic. Herb Hoelter, a director of a criminal-justice consulting firm, was not surprised by the Justice Department's declaration that prisons are a cost-effective way to fight crime. Regarding the 1987 study, Hoelter told *Financial World,* "The people at the NIJ have been cooking the books for years."[21]

Incredibly, the information in this report continues to find its way into the minds of the American public through the media. In December 1998, I picked up my local newspaper, the *Daily Times-Call,* only to find an editorial written by the paper's staff citing the figures from this report and encouraging readers to tell their elected officials to spend more money on the war on crime so that they can save more money in the long run. It seems to me that this kind of "spend to save" logic would be more appropriate in an episode of *I Love Lucy,* where the dingbat redhead could regularly be expected to get laughs as she spent $500 she didn't have just so she could save $50 at a 10-percent-off sale.

So just how much is America saving through mass incarceration? At the beginning of this push toward "saving" money through imprisonment, we were spending about $3 billion a year on corrections. By 1992, this figure had climbed to $31.4 billion, and in 1999, it is estimated (the actual figures will not be available from the Justice Department for another six years) that the cost of corrections will have escalated to approximately $50 billion.[22] Allowing for inflation, our current "spend-to-save" policy is costing us at least eight times more than the justice policies that were in place prior to the war on crime with its plethora of mandatory sentences. And what have we gotten in return for all this increased spending? The crime rates are nearly the same today as they were three decades ago. I would venture to say that only government could look at these facts and figures and interpret our current course of action as somehow being cost-effective. Can you imagine a corporate CEO trying to convince shareholders that increasing expenditures eightfold for little or no benefit is a good value?

Myth 3: Prisons Decrease Crime

Despite the significant differences between the NCVS and UCR crime rates and the controversy surrounding the costs associated with our current policy of increased incarceration, virtually everyone, regardless of whether they have a vested financial stake in the war on crime, agrees that the crime rates are currently falling. What they don't agree on is "why" they are falling.

If your newspaper is like mine and you want to see a perfect example of the difference in opinion that now exists regarding the effect of the prison expansion on crime rates, just go back and read the articles that appear each year right after the release of the FBI's UCR. In 1998, Colorado's largest daily, the *Rocky Mountain News* of Denver, ran a couple of lengthy articles following the report's release about the continuing decline in the crime rates. These articles included interviews with a wide variety of "experts" who attributed the drop in crime to several factors. Taking the articles as a whole, the reader was left with the impression that crime rates were falling because of the increasing size of the prison population, the overall health of the economy, an increased law-enforcement presence, the decline of crack cocaine, and the demographic shift caused by the aging of the baby boomers.

However, a closer examination of which sources attributed the drop to which reasons reveals a disturbing trend. With rare exception, those who attributed the decline in crime to more cops and more prisoners had something in common. They were either politicians or people employed in law enforcement or corrections. With similar consistency, those experts who did not have a vested financial stake in the war on crime excluded the increase in law enforcement and the boom in the prison population from their explanation for why the crime rate was dropping.

"It's tough to find a correlation between higher incarceration rates and lower crime rates," said Alfred Blumstein, dean of the School of Urban and Public Affairs at Carnegie Mellon University. Blumstein's opinion that there are no hard data to support the argument that more prisoners result in lower crime rates is widely shared by those in the field of criminology. Barry Krisberg, former president of the National Council on Crime and Delinquency, concurred: "No one thinks that California today is safer than ten years ago, even though we have twice as many people locked up."[23] Similarly, in its 1995 report, the NCJC stated:

> One would think that the extraordinary expansion of the criminal justice system would have made at least a small dent in the crime rate. [But] the increase in the prison population did not reduce crime, nor did it make

Americans feel safer. In fact, some criminologists have argued that the overuse of the penal system for so many small-time offenders has actually created more crime than it has prevented.[24]

Even some within corrections have admitted that hard data to support increasing the prison population as a means of fighting crime are hard to come by. During the 1980s, Colorado's prison expansion accounted for a 300-percent increase in the state's prison population and a 500-percent rise in CDOC costs to taxpayers. Despite the state's decision to increase the inmate population as a means to fight crime, Scott Hromas, director of planning and analysis for the CDOC, publicly acknowledged, "I don't know of any research that would show that longer sentences have had any effect on the crime rate at all." He was right, of course, because no such research exists.[25]

But such reality-based insight has had little bearing on the decision-making at the CDOC, as evidenced by the fact that Colorado has done nothing but escalate its prison expansion in the 1990s, even though crime rates in Colorado and across the nation have been falling for at least the past seven years. It is now estimated that by 1999, Colorado's prison budget for annual operations will surpass half a billion dollars for the first time and the prison population will have once again doubled in size since Hromas's admission that the expansion was likely having no impact on the crime rates.[26]

Obviously, not everyone outside of those with a vested interest in enlarging the prison population agrees with this opinion that imprisonment does not affect crime rates. James Wilson, a respected political scientist, is among those who have voiced their belief that the drop in crime in the 1990s is the direct result of increasing the number of prisoners.[27] Yet despite such assertions by prison proponents, most of those adhering to the pro-prison position admit that data to date that support their claims are less than conclusive. Although supporters of enlarging the prison system as a means to fight crime find the evidence put forward by prison critics to be equally inconclusive, there is a large body of statistical data that suggest that adding prisons has had little effect on crime rates.

In the 1980s, when the current prison expansion really began to pick up speed, those who supported incarceration as a means to fight crime put forward a logical-sounding argument. They claimed that most crimes are committed by a small percentage of career criminals. Therefore, they concluded, if we were to double the size of the prison population and double the lengths of sentences, we would see a substantial drop in crime, something along the lines of, say, 15 to 18 percent for robbery.[28] I must admit that on one level this argument seems to make more sense than the one put forward by the academics, who tell us that there is no correlation between incarceration rates and crime rates. But the evidence is in, and it certainly seems to support the "no-correlation" position.

We did, in fact, double the lengths of many sentences as well as the size of the prison population during the 1980s. Then, just for good measure, we doubled the number of prisoners again in the 1990s. Based on the claims by those who support using incarceration as a means of fighting crime, we should have experienced at least a 30-percent decline in the crime rates as a result of this massive increase in the prison population, but we didn't. The prison experiment has failed to produce the significant decline in the crime rates that were promised when the buildup began.

Another piece of evidence that supports the "no-correlation" position can be found by examining the crime rates of our northern neighbor during the last decade. Paralleling what has happened in the United States, Canada's violent-crime rate began declining in 1991. In fact, Canada's homicide rate fell by an impressive 9 percent in 1997, bringing it to its lowest level since 1969. What makes Canada's situation so interesting is that its rate of incarceration barely increased at all in the 1990s, while ours went up dramatically. Considering that both nations experienced similar and simultaneous drops in violent crime while varying wildly on their incarceration practices, it would appear that something other than increasing the prison population was likely behind the decline in violent crime experienced by both countries.

It is possible to make countless domestic comparisons as well that show the lack of connection between imprisonment rates and crime rates. For instance, North and South Dakota have similar populations, cultures, and crime rates, even though South Dakota imprisons three of its citizens for every one person locked up in North Dakota.[29] Between 1980 and 1986, the U.S. prison population increased by 65 percent, but during this same time period, violent crime *decreased* 16 percent. Yet between 1986 and 1991, while the nation's prison population was enlarging by 51 percent, violent crime *increased* 15 percent.[30] During at least fifteen of the nineteen years that California increased its prison population between 1974 and 1995, its crime rate went up, not down.[31]

Oklahoma has a population of 3.5 million and incarcerates approximately 21,000 of its citizens. Minnesota has a population of 4.5 million and only imprisons around 5,000 of its citizens. Yet Minnesota has a lower crime rate than Oklahoma, as well as a much lower recidivism rate for those who are released from its prisons.[32] According to Justice Department figures, several of the states with the highest incarceration rates have higher violent-crime rates than other states with even larger populations and lower incarceration rates. The bottom line is that having more prisoners does not translate into having less crime. Similar statistical analysis on the number of law-enforcement officers versus population reveals a similar finding: Having more cops does not necessarily translate into having less crime. It is not uncommon for a smaller city with a larger police force to still have more crime than a more heavily populated city with fewer officers.

The Reason for Crime's Decline

Assuming that those who attribute the falling crime rate to factors other than more prisons and law enforcement are correct, then what forces are responsible for the current reduction in crime? Most experts attribute the drop in crime to a combination of factors that include the overall health of the U.S. economy, which has been on the upswing for seven straight years. For the first time in decades, the economy has created jobs for urban youths who had previously turned to the drug trade for their income.

The belief that it is jobs and not prisons that are pressuring crime downward is supported by the demographics of our prison population, which shows that two out of three inmates were unemployed or earning less than $5,000 per year at the time of their arrest.[33] This being the case, it stands to reason that if jobs have been provided for some of those at the lower end of the economy, even lousy minimum wage jobs as most of them are, then crime would drop as a consequence. History also supports this economic theory, as evidenced by the fact that other periods marked by a robust economy such as the 1950s likewise experienced decreasing crime without an increase in law enforcement or prison population.

Experts also point to the decline of the crack cocaine subculture as having had a major impact on the crime rates in recent years. A 1998 study by Bruce Johnson and Andrew Golub, scholars at the National

Development and Research Institutes in New York City, found that a decline in crack use accounts for a good portion of the decline in crime. Johnson and Golub report that "the primary reason" for the decline in crack use among juveniles is not the war on drugs but rather "the negative role models in their lives. They [juveniles] clearly do not want to emulate their parents, older siblings, close relatives or other associates in their neighborhoods who were enmeshed with crack."[34] Alan Fox, dean of the College of Criminal Justice at Northeastern University, also believes that the decline of crack has been a major factor in falling crime rates. Fox observed that "[h]omicide and robbery were the two crimes most impacted by crack markets, with the biggest increases, and now as crack markets have declined, homicide and robbery have led the way down."[35]

Another important factor exerting downward pressure on the crime rates is the maturing of the baby-boomer generation. The vast majority of all crimes are committed by people when they are in their teens and twenties. Because baby boomers constitute such a large percentage of the population, their age has likely been having a significant impact on the crime rates for decades. The teenage years of the boomers may well have accounted for the increase in crime in the 1960s. Similarly, their maturing beyond the criminal years has likely accounted for a good portion of the decline in crime that began in 1983, as reflected by the NCVS.

When I interviewed experts for my research on this book, the vast majority of those who lacked any financial stake in the war on crime supported the position that some combination of these non-crime-war factors were responsible for the bulk of the downward movement in the crime rates since 1991. Most also shared the opinion that the size of the prison population was a relatively insignificant factor in the decline of crime or, in direct conflict with yet another myth being put forward by those who support the prison expansion, they thought it had actually hindered the falling rates.

Myth 4: Prisons Rehabilitate

Supporters of the prison expansion, primarily politicians, have long argued that sending more people to prison for longer periods will make society safer because it will either reform more criminals or at least keep lawbreakers off the streets for a certain period of time. Although this argument may sound good to those who have a very limited understanding of what goes on behind the prison walls—say, for instance, suburban voters—to those who have done research in our prisons, this argument is viewed with great skepticism because it fails to take into account the "prisonization effect."

"Prisonization" is a term used to describe the central truth of prison life—namely, that in order to survive in prison, an inmate must comply with prison-society structure above all else. Behavioral scientists refer to the unwritten rules that govern this violent prison structure as the "prisoner code," and they have found that the life-or-death pressure to live by this code is far more powerful than any other force behind prison walls, including efforts at reform.

In a prison study conducted prior to World War II—the first of many similar studies that have reached the same conclusion—sociologist Donald Clemmer confirmed the failure of rehabilitation within the prison structure. Clemmer suggested that reform was basically impossible within prisons because of what he termed "prisonization." Clemmer found that people placed in prisons almost immediately took on the customs and culture of the penitentiary out of necessity. He believed that in order to survive in prison, an inmate had to adopt the "prisoner code" and become affiliated with an existing group within the facility. Unfortunately, once prisoners are assimilated in this way, the sociologist found that they are completely immune to all reform efforts, and worse, many will actually begin to exhibit additional criminal behaviors. Clemmer's research led him to the conclusion that the "prisonization effect" explains why prisons tend to function more as "crime schools" that increase the likelihood of future criminal behavior rather than as a deterrent to crime or as a means to reform.[36]

Perhaps the best way to understand this concept of prisonization, aside from spending time behind bars, is to try and imagine yourself being thrown into prison. What would the experience be like? Would it be similar to joining a country club? After all, that's what politicians these days tell us prison life is like. Or would it be like the prisons in those low-budget flicks in the faded boxes at the back of the video store? You know, the ones set in a women's prison where horny, chesty, heavy-on-the-hairspray bimbos wearing tank tops spend ninety minutes trying to seduce the guards. Let me assure you that the term "country club" paints no more accurate a portrait of prison life than the sexy vision of incarceration provided by Hollywood. Both of these versions of life behind bars are fiction designed to appeal to an audience for the benefit of the one spinning the story.

So what would it really be like if you woke up tomorrow and found yourself behind bars, where you didn't know another soul? It could well be like this:

> I was laying in my bed when seven or eight inmates came to my bed, pulled the blankets off me, put it on the floor and told me to pull my pants down and lay face down on the blanket. I said, "No," and was punched in the face by one of the inmates. The inmate that punched me stated if I did not get on the floor the other inmates would gang up on me.
>
> I got on the floor and my pants and shorts were pulled off. Two inmates spread and held my legs apart while two more inmates held my hands in front of me. While I was being buggered from behind another inmate would make me suck his penis. This continued until all the inmates had attacked me and I heard one of them say it was 1:30 A.M. so let's go to bed. They put me on the bed, covered me with the blanket and one of them patted me on the behind saying, "Good boy, we will see you again tomorrow night."[37]

Or how about this initiation into a life behind bars?

> I was in the cell at 1801 Vine when four Negro boys started bothering me for not having underwear on. Then when we got on the Sheriff's van and started moving they told everyone that I didn't have on underwear . . . they started moving close to me. One of them touched me and I told them to please stop. All of a sudden a coat was thrown over my face and when I tried to pull it off I was viciously punched in the face for around ten minutes. I fell to the floor and they kicked me all over my body including my head and my privates. They ripped my pants from me while five or six of them held me down and took turns fucking me. My insides feel sore and my body hurts, my head hurts, and I feel sick in the stomach. Each time they stopped I tried to call for help but they put their hands over my mouth. . . . While they held me they burned my leg with a cigarette. They threatened my life and said they'd get me if I told what happened. . . . I can just about breathe because my nose and jaw seem to be broken in many different places.[38]

The idea of being sexually assaulted conjures up a repugnant vision for most of us, and I suspect that the reality of these assaults is considerably worse and more psychologically damaging than we can possibly imagine. The two descriptions of sexual assault above came from a 1968 report issued by the Philadelphia District Attorney's Office, which had ordered an investigation to determine the frequency and type of sexual assaults taking place in the local jails. The investigation found that sexual assaults were endemic in the Philadelphia prison system. In only a twenty-four-month period, the report documented 2,000 such assaults on 1,500 victims by 3,500 aggressors. The report concluded that "virtually every slightly built young man committed to jail by the courts—many of them merely to await trial—is sexually approached within hours of his admission to prison. Many young men are overwhelmed and repeatedly 'raped' by gangs of inmate aggressors."[39]

I used the information generated from this thirty-year-old report because, incredibly, it is one of the only sources in existence for information concerning the frequency of sexual assaults on prisoners. Such attacks are apparently as widespread in the prison system today as ever. I say "apparently" because it's impossible to quote Justice Department statistics for such attacks because no state or federal agency bothers to collect data on sexual assaults behind bars. Such abuse is clearly not a priority for the justice system. One report published in recent years came from Human Rights Watch in 1996. That report, like the 1968 investigation, found that "sexual abuse is endemic to prisons across the nation."[40] In his 1996 book *Violence,* respected researcher and physician James Gilligan reported that approximately eighteen rapes per minute occur in prisons. That's 168,000 sexual assaults behind bars every week, or nearly 9 million per year.[41]

In 1997, five women who had been held in Corrections Corporation of America's private prison at Florence, Arizona, filed a lawsuit claiming that the institution's guards regularly raped the women inmates. The company was eventually forced to place a large number of its guards on administrative leave. One source told a reporter for *CounterPunch* magazine that approximately fifty guards were involved in either the assaults or the subsequent cover-up.[42]

Sadly, sexual assaults are just one of the dangers waiting to twist the minds of those unfortunate enough to be sentenced into our prisons. Race wars behind bars, extortion, rival-gang conflicts, guard abuse, random violence, and the demand for absolute loyalty to an inmate's fellow prisoners—loyalty that often requires committing additional crimes behind the walls—are all factors in the prisonization effect.

"I felt like almost wanting to take my own life," said inmate Tony Fountain, testifying before a U.S. magistrate in 1996 concerning a particularly cruel torture device used by Alabama prison guards. Inmates refer to the device as "the hitching post."

"I defecated in my clothes," continued Fountain. "I felt like a child. I felt helpless and humiliated. I wanted to strike back at those in authority who had put me there. Defecating on myself and being forced to stay that way for hours. . . . I have nightmares about the situation." Fountain was one of twelve inmates who filed suit in an effort to do away with the hitching post.[43]

The guards refer to the hitching post as a "restraining bar" and acknowledge that these bars exist at many prisons. Prison officials claim that the bars are an effective method for dealing with inmates who refuse to perform the work they are assigned. Prison officials told the court that they shackled Fountain to the bar not because he refused to work but because he failed to keep up with the other inmates. As a result of his poor work performance, the six-foot one-inch Fountain was chained to the four-foot bar for an entire day.

The bar's low height forced the inmate to stand hunched over throughout the experience. Not only that, but Fountain had been wearing a coat in the early morning when it was cool. He was forced to leave the coat on all day, despite the fact that the temperature climbed to over 90 degrees. In addition, Fountain also told the magistrate that he was given no water, food, or toilet breaks throughout his ordeal. Fountain acknowledged that he hadn't kept up with the others, but he explained that it wasn't for a lack of effort. You see, Fountain has a congenital back problem that has left his left leg partially paralyzed.

These are just a few examples of the activities that prevail inside the concrete-and-steel facilities that our elected officials like to refer to as "country-club" prisons. I can assure you that these stories are not the sensationalized rare exception to prison life; rather, they are representative of the physical and mental tortures that shape nearly all those unfortunate enough to find themselves thrown into our system, where such violence and abuse are the stuff of everyday life. Prison is a place where survival quickly becomes the only thing that matters. As you can imagine, it is nearly impossible for an inmate to make rehabilitation a priority under such stressful conditions.

In an interview that appeared in the December 1998 issue of *Vanity Fair*, Christopher Stone, the head of New York's Vera Institute of Justice, described prisons as "factories for crime" where the strong rule the weak. He noted that even though most inmates will only spend about two years behind bars, it is two years that will shape their future actions forever. Such was apparently the case with Tom William (Bill) King.

On February 25, 1999, Judge Joe Bob Golden sentenced Bill King to death for his part in the racially motivated murder of forty-nine-year-old James Byrd Jr., a black man who lived in King's hometown of Jasper, Texas. Byrd had been hitchhiking near his home in June 1998 when Bill King and allegedly two other men stopped and offered him a ride. The three men then drove Byrd to the outskirts of town, where they wrapped him in a logging chain that they then hooked to the bumper of their pickup truck. The men then proceeded to drag Byrd down an asphalt road until his arm, shoulder, and head were severed from his body. Why? Because Byrd was black is the easy answer, but prisonization may be the more accurate explanation.

Ronald King, Bill's father, says his son was not always a murdering racist. In fact, the older King claims that Bill was an average kid until he had a minor run-in with the law that sent him into the Texas prison system for two years. According to his father, Bill King went into prison as a normal young man who had messed up once, but he came out from behind bars a different person, an angry and dangerous man who hated blacks and other minorities. Bill King's attorney, C. Haden "Sonny" Cribbs Jr., echoed the older King's view, telling jurors, "What happened [in prison]? I don't know. What I do know is that he wasn't a racist when he went in. He was when he came out."[44] While in prison, Bill King tattooed his feelings of racial hate up and down both arms, a symbol that he had joined a white supremacist prison gang.

In speaking about King's initial prison experience, Brian Levin, former associate professor of criminal justice and director of the Center on Hate and Extremism at Richard Stockton College, told *NBC Nightly News* in 1999 that Bill King's racist murder of James Byrd Jr. was exactly the kind of thing that should be expected when "you dump a young kid in prison where racist gangs are a way of life." Levin went on to say that "prison is a crash course in hate." Just as the tattoos on Bill King's arms were a permanent fixture, apparently so too was the transformation that had taken place in his mind in just two short years behind bars. All indications are that in an effort to survive the horrors of day-to-day life in his earlier prison experience, the slightly built five-foot seven-inch King fell prey to the effects of prisonization.

Unfortunately, Bill King's experience is not unique. In order to be safe within the prison culture, inmates have little choice but to seek out the protection of a prison gang such as the Aryan Brotherhood, a violent anti-Semitic, antiblack organization. In prison, inmates have no family or friends to protect them; only the gang can prevent them from being regularly raped and beaten. Thus, for most inmates the gang becomes their family, their support, their protection, and most of all, their teacher. In America, thousands of men and women who have been thrown into the prison environment for minor nonviolent offenses such as drug use have been forced to choose between being a victim of rape, beatings, extortion, and murder or becoming a rapist, batterer, extortionist, or murderer. Many have chosen the latter because their instinct to survive made it a rational choice.

Today's prisons are not a blueprint for rehabilitation. Although not everyone returning from prison will commit a vicious murder in the manner of Bill King, many of those released will exhibit some behavior resulting from their prisonization scars such as alcohol and drug abuse, wife and child battery, rape, or an overall escalation in their willingness to use violence as a first resort. Such behavior learned behind bars greatly increases the odds that those sentenced into our prisons will someday return to a cell as recidivists.

"The internal prison culture is a far more powerful influence than any attempts at rehabilitation," wrote Thomas Mathiesen, professor of sociology of law at the University of Oslo in Norway. Like Clemmer, Mathiesen believes that the [prison] culture makes the prisoner more or less immune to attempts by the prison system to urge readjustment. "In more popular terms," Mathiesen has said, "the prison in a cultural sense first of all functions as a 'crime school.'"[45]

In practical terms, prisonization really means that sending nonviolent criminals to prison, as opposed to placing them in outside-the-prison programs such as drug rehabilitation or putting them under well-supervised probation, actually increases the odds that these inmates will reoffend upon their release as a result of being forced into a prison setting where reform is all but impossible and learning a willingness to break the law is often a means to survival. Considering that the vast majority of those being sent to prison in the 1990s have been convicted of nonviolent crimes, mostly drug offenses, and that 17 percent of the entire prison population is now composed of individuals who had no previous criminal record prior to the arrest that resulted in their imprisonment, one can't help but question the wisdom of such sentencing.[46]

The fact that prisons serve as crime schools likely explains why enlarging the system has not had a significant effect on the crime rates, except perhaps to keep them higher than they would have been otherwise.

Sentences Have Changed, not Crime

We have embarked on a great social experiment. No other society in human history has ever imprisoned so many of its own citizens for the purpose of crime control.

—Marc Mauer, Atlantic Monthly, *December 1998*[47]

So, of the massive increase in the prison and jail population during the last three decades, what percentage should we attribute to an increase in crime? The answer is: little to none. Even the right-leaning CATO Institute attributes the increase in the numbers of those being incarcerated to other factors. It estimates that 7.7 percent of the increase is attributable to population growth, and 5.3 percent has resulted from the massive increases in law-enforcement spending. As for the bulk of the new prisoners, the institute's research found that nearly 70 percent of the overall growth in the prison system is attributable to incarcerating people who—previous to the sentencing changes resulting from the "war on crime," particularly changes to the drug laws—would have been punished with community service, fines, probation, or a very short stay in jail or would not have been punished at all.[48]

Despite rhetoric to the contrary being put forward by politicians and those in law enforcement and corrections, it is not changes in criminal behavior that have caused the prison population to swell but rather changes in the laws and the sentencing guidelines. I believe that, for the most part, Americans have encouraged their elected officials to make these changes because they are operating under a societal fear stirred into existence by "crime-gap" propaganda.

In 1993, I read a newspaper article that has always stood out as a first-rate illustration of the media's role in feeding this idea that crime is escalating out of control and that we must spend more of our tax dollars to fight it or suffer terrible consequences. The reason this article is such a good example is that it contains both of the elements of the crime-gap propaganda—information to make us fear crime and the promise of safety in return for increased prison spending.

The twelve-inch story began with the following sensational claims: "[C]rime is exploding," paroled prisoners are constantly committing violent crimes that victimize "you, your friends, and your neighbors," and the state prisons are being filled faster than they can be built, which means that more violent convicts must be released prematurely to free up space.[49]

"Well done," I remember thinking to myself as I read this piece for the first time. In less than three column inches, the reporter had managed to convince a few hundred thousand readers that they were living in a war zone of crime where even walking the street should be seen as an act of courage or foolishness. The article's lead was truly compelling; unfortunately, it was also completely inaccurate.

At the time the article ran, the crime rate in Colorado was down 5 percent from the previous year and was hovering at a level virtually identical to what it had been twenty years earlier. In reality, the "crime explosion" referred to in the story was nothing more than a media bomb threat. But the misinformation being conveyed didn't stop there. According to statistics at the time, readers—unless living in a low-income minority neighborhood where crime rates were significant—were not being victimized by anyone, including recent parolees. That's because the vast majority of violent-crime victims in Colorado in 1993, just as today, were young, impoverished blacks and Hispanics, not the suburban-dwelling white folk who made up the vast majority of the paper's readership—not to mention the fact that only a small percentage of violent crimes, 2 to 4 percent, are attributable to parolees. The only accurate claim in the article's sensationalized opening barrage was the one about filling prisons as fast as they could be built. That part was quite true.

Now that the article had gotten their attention by terrifying readers with crime inaccuracies, it was time for the money pitch. The last half of the piece was used to explain how the Colorado Department of Corrections needed to spend hundreds of millions of dollars to build four new prisons in order to once again make us safe. I suspect that most readers breathed a sigh of relief as they read how the new prisons that they would soon be paying for were going to make it more difficult for inmates to get paroled and consequently make it harder for them to commit the atrocious crimes alluded to in the article. But such a feeling of relief wasn't warranted. It was all an illusion. Neither the fear instilled by the article's lead nor the subsequent comfort brought by the news of new prisons had any basis in reality. Colorado citizens were not in danger, at least no more in danger than at previous times during the last thirty years, and the new prisons would have no effect on the crime rates.

The myths we have discussed here are certainly effective at wrongly convincing the electorate that crime is more pervasive and violent than it truly is and that we should therefore spend more money on prisons and law enforcement to keep America safe. But I believe there is an even more significant reason that most Americans now believe that crime is one of the biggest problems, if not *the* biggest problem, facing our nation—namely, that the media increasingly use sensationalized violent content to increase audience share, and thus profits, in both news and entertainment programming.

3

Violence for Profit

The crime myths being put forward by politicians and those employed within the prison-industrial complex are only partially responsible for America's belief in the existence of the fictional "crime gap." Research tells us that the vast majority of us—95 percent—shape our impression of crime and criminal justice primarily from the mass media, of which television is easily the most influential.[1] In other words, whatever it is that we believe about crime, right or wrong, we likely have the owners of media to thank. So what exactly is television's message when it comes to crime?

Considering that the majority of all television programming contains scenes of violence and that television news programs now report considerably more violent crimes than ever before, I believe that we can safely conclude that television is telling us that crime is more pervasive and violent in character today than it has ever been.[2] When we couple this television message about crime with the crime myths previously discussed, it only makes sense that the majority of Americans would develop a certain degree of anxiety regarding the crime issue.

Understanding that media corporations have greatly escalated their use of violent content during the last two decades is important because it helps to explain how the public's impression of crime has managed to free itself from the bounds of the actual occurrence of crime. This is to say that the public's belief in the "crime gap" is being inspired more by the quantity of our exposure to the images of crime in the media than by anything else.

Thanks to modern communications technology, which now makes it possible to access literally hundreds of different television stations at any given time, we now hear about or "witness" on our TV sets far more crimes than we did in the past, even though there have been other periods when crime was as bad or even worse in some categories than it is today. For instance, "street crime," a category on which the media in the 1990s often focus their attention, was actually worse in the 1930s and at different times during the nineteenth century than it has been in the last three decades. Such crimes were even more prevalent in the 1970s than they are in the 1990s, even though the public seldom heard the term "street crime" twenty-five years ago.[3]

I believe that the public's growing anxiety over crime can be largely attributed to the fact that most people are unaware that the role of the news media in our democracy has changed substantially in recent years. The concept of a free press that serves the public interest has been replaced with a profit-driven news industry that chooses a fair amount of its "news" content based upon that content's perceived ability to increase viewership and thereby ad revenues. Because most Americans still believe that the press is operating in its former incarnation, it is only natural that people would assume that if more time is being allotted to reporting sensational violent crimes, then there must be more such crimes being committed.

Based upon the chasm that now exists between what we believe about crime as a society and the facts regarding crime, it appears that America has entered into a new and dangerous age where communications technology has become more powerful than reality itself when it comes to shaping our attitudes and beliefs. It seems that the growing number of psychologists and sociologists are correct in warning us that for the first time in our history, we are forming our worldview based more upon the mediated messages from our television sets than upon what we observe with our own eyes. The negative implications of this shaping of our worldview from television are more enormous for our justice system than perhaps for any other single element of our society. I say this because, as a rule, it is the messages and images of sex and violence that are being exaggerated by media far more than any other subject matter. Is our bombardment with sex having a negative impact? Probably, but that's another book. It is our being inundated with images of violence, much of them pertaining to crime, that is working to reshape American criminal justice.

The August 1995 issue of *American Demographics* reported:

Crime has become a hot issue for a number of reasons, beginning with the media. The public's concern with crime rises and falls in lockstep with media reporting about the issue. High profile crimes create sensational news coverage. And the greater the news coverage, the larger the proportion of Americans who cite crime as the most important problem facing the country.[4]

Even those within the media industry acknowledge the power of TV news over public opinion. According to a 1994 analysis in the *Public Perspective* by Jeffrey D. Alderman, director of polling for NBC News, "[P]ublic concern with crime follows news coverage of crimes with an exactness that proves the importance of the media in shaping public opinion."[5]

On the network news front, a 1995 study conducted by the Center for Media and Public Affairs (CMPA) found that the coverage of crime on all three network news programs increased dramatically between 1991 and 1993. In fact, it basically tripled from 571 crime stories to 1,632.[6] Even more disturbing, the same study found that between March 1992 and February 1993, there had been a sixfold increase in the number of people who believed that crime was the nation's biggest problem.

In addition, two separate studies conducted in 1998 examined local news content, only to discover a similar pattern. The research found that violence now constitutes 43 percent of local news content. Violent content now takes up more time on the evening news than educational, political, and social reporting combined.[7] What makes the findings of these television studies so important to our discussion of the "crime gap" is the realization that this increasing coverage of violent crime came during a time span when real crimes were on the decline.

The exaggeration of violence and crime by the news media these days has become so rampant that veteran newsman Robert MacNeil now refers to the nightly news as "body-bag journalism at 11." While receiving the 1999 Fred Friendly Award for journalistic excellence, MacNeil told the audience that PBS's *NewsHour* is "the one newscast that hasn't dumbed itself down or sold out to viewers who have become catnipped on a diet of sensation and crime."[8]

A study of Colorado newspapers revealed that the print media also distort the reader's perception of crime by exaggerating the coverage of sensational violent crimes while underreporting on nonviolent criminal activities. This study noted that the amount of crime coverage was consistently high, regardless of whether the crime rate was falling.[9] A similar study by the *New Orleans Times-Picayune* found that articles regarding murder and robbery constituted 45 percent of all crime coverage, even though these categories represented only 12 percent of actual crimes.[10]

The old adage "If it bleeds, it leads" has always been true in the news business, but never to its current exaggerated level. And it's not just news programming that is escalating its use of violent content. On the entertainment side of things, the escalation in violent content is even more pronounced.

A 1995 study by the Center for Media and Public Affairs found that between 1993 and 1995, the total number of violent scenes in entertainment programming increased by a mind-blowing 74 percent. Programming that included violence involving gun play more than tripled in this three-year period, rising by 334 percent.[11]

This study also showed that life-threatening violence—defined as assaults with deadly weapons and brutal beatings—more than doubled. Even the violence found in TV commercials increased by 30 percent. In 1995, there were 948 scenes of violence in commercials on one average day of television. That's almost equal to the *total* number of violent scenes found during a whole year in overall television programming just three years earlier.

Since 1995, things have gotten worse still. A study financed by the cable industry and released in 1998 found that 61 percent of all programs contain violence. Violence in programs screened by the networks increased from 53 percent in 1995 to 67 percent in 1997. The most violent programming is on pay-TV cable, where the study found that 92 percent of the shows contain violence. The number of TV shows with antiviolent themes fell from 4 percent to 3 percent.[12]

As a result of such dramatic increases in violent content across the board in television programming, a study by the American Psychological Association found that the average American child is exposed to over 8,000 murders and 100,000 other assorted acts of violence before ever entering junior high school.[13] A similar study by the American Medical Association reported that the typical American child spends an average of twenty-seven hours every week in front of the TV set. Because of this heavy viewing practice by kids, the study found that by the time these same children turn eighteen years old, they will have watched over 40,000 murders and 200,000 other assorted acts of violence.[14] The American Pediatric Association reported that by the time of high-school graduation, they will have spent more time in front of the TV than performing any other activity, with the exception of sleep.[15]

These last figures make perfect sense when considered in light of the findings of the 1993 to 1995 study conducted by the CMPA, which researched and analyzed the violent content contained in just one average day of television programming for each of the three years. In 1995, the study found that there were 1,738 scenes of violence on the day studied.[16] That's an average of ten violent scenes per hour on every single channel, twenty-four hours a day. Astonishingly, the 1,738 violent scenes documented by the study didn't include the violence found in commercials or the "real" violence found in nonfiction programming such as the local and national news, *Hardcopy, Inside Edition, Cops, American Detective,* or the dozens of other sensationalized pseudo-news programs and video composites that are now being piped into our homes. If it had, the number of violent scenes would have risen substantially. A 1994 study by CMPA that looked at all programming found 2,605 acts of violence on one random day of television programming.[17]

Since the experts tell us that our impression of the world is being shaped more by media content than reality, it stands to reason that it's a good idea to discuss who is doing the shaping and why. Like Dorothy in the *Wizard of Oz*, I believe our impression of the world around us will change significantly when we pull back the curtain and expose the controllers of the image and their motives.

Market-Driven News

What is the most powerful force in America today?
Answer: Public opinion.
What makes public opinion?
Answer: The main force is the press.
Can you trust the press?
Answer: The baseball scores are always correct (except for the typographical error now and then). The stock market tables are

correct (within the same limitation). But when it comes to news which will affect you, your daily life, your job, your relation to other peoples, your thinking on economic and social problems, and, more important today, your going to war and risking your life for a great ideal, then you cannot trust about 98 percent (or perhaps 99 ½ percent) of the big newspaper and big magazine press in America.

But why can't you trust the press?

Answer: Because it has become big business. The big city press and the big magazines have become commercialized, or big business organizations, run with no other motive than profit for owner or stockholder (although hypocritically still maintaining the old American tradition of guiding and enlightening the people).

— *George Seldes, journalist,* **The George Seldes Reader**[18]

In addressing the new market pressures on the newsroom, Walter Cronkite has said:

Nearly every important publishing and broadcasting company today is caught up in the plague of the nineties that has swept the business world—the stockholder demand to increase profits. . . . Adequate profits are clearly necessary for survival, but stockholders in too many cases demand superprofits. Compliant managements play the game that stock value is the only criterion of success. In the news business, that isn't good enough. The lack of a sense of public service begins today with the ownership of too many newspapers and broadcasting companies—that is, the stockholders. Stewardship of our free press is a public service and a heavy responsibility. It should not be treated the same as the manufacture of bobby pins, or of automobiles.[19]

It shouldn't be, but it is. As more and more newsrooms have become controlled by fewer and fewer shareholder-driven corporations, the conflict of interest between shareholders and the public, which journalists are supposed to serve, has increased in intensity. American corporate law makes it clear that management's first priority is to the shareholder. This concept of shareholder primacy means that CEOs at media corporations are literally required to consider their company's stock price as more important than its content, a fact that does not bode well for the news business.

A free press is essential to a democracy. In fact, one cannot exist without the other. Although it's true that those who have historically owned the content we call "news" have, for the most part, always demanded that their companies show a profit, it was with the understanding that performing the indispensable role of public watchdog was an expensive proposition and, therefore, only a certain range of profit could be realistically expected. But this is no longer the case. As pointed out by Cronkite, superprofits are now the requirement.

Those who own shares in today's newsrooms demand that their fiscal performance be equal to any other business. If buying stock in a company that manufacturers sprinkler systems can generate a 17-percent return on investment next year, then the newsroom must do equally well or run the risk of losing its investors to more lucrative market opportunities.

Unfortunately, producing proper news content cannot be entirely budgeted in advance. It's one of the drawbacks to viewing news as a business, or at least it should be. In a healthy news environment, it is the importance of the stories themselves that ultimately dictates expenditures. Costs for news content can vary wildly, depending on the circumstances surrounding a particular story. For example, a report that exposes government corruption may take weeks or months and cost tens of thousands of dollars to produce, and then, when the report is aired or printed—provided it doesn't expose a steamy sex scandal à la Clinton-Lewinsky—it may pull only a small audience share. In other words, it will likely lose money or at least prove less profitable than more sensationalized news.

The fact that such "important" journalism is expensive and does not draw particularly high ratings explains its rapidly diminishing role in modern, profit-driven news organizations. In today's newsrooms, it's likely that the only reason that some expensive stories are still being produced is that they allow news departments to maintain some level of credibility with the public. In the 1990s, the difference between *Hardcopy, Inside Edition,* and the networks' nightly news programs is not which sensationalized crime stories get reported and continually updated, because all cover this "O. J." genre with equal intensity. The difference is that the networks still throw in enough "important" news to separate themselves from their tabloid cousins while still generating much of their profit from the same sensationalized violent content.

A news report about a particularly gruesome murder in Tennessee has no relevance to news consumers in California except for its morbid entertainment value. Yet such gory regional stories are composing a larger percentage of national news content every day because they take only a few hours to throw together, cost next to nothing to produce, and can draw a big audience. On any given day of the year, there is far more news available to report than there is time and space allotted to do so. In the past, deciding which stories would be presented to the public was determined by which information was deemed most important to the public's right to know. Today, thanks to shareholder primacy, costs, and a story's potential to increase ratings, which together really mean generating profits from advertising, are increasingly the determining factors in the news-selection process.

Let's face it, GE, Disney, and Viacom didn't buy networks because they were inspired by the importance of a free press. They bought them because they offered a number of advantages, among them advertising revenues, the ability to plug their own products cheaply, the ability to better control negative stories about their more questionable business practices, and because owning a network newscast creates special access to those politicians who control the various industries owned by the parent company—and such access, just as in the case of access purchased with campaign funds, can be worth billions in today's global economy.

In describing the political influence that comes with owning the news, Lawrence Grossman, former head of NBC News, says, "For media conglomerates, news is mostly a useful corporate adornment. In the global pursuit of new business, new contracts, new franchises, new licenses and new government concessions, news divisions give their parent companies special access to top public officials and influential decision-makers."[20]

Likewise, shareholders in these corporations are less concerned with journalism's higher calling than they are with the bottom line. They don't care if newsrooms report a Watergate, a celebrity fluff piece, or a sensational crime story as long as the most profitable "news" gets its space. That being the case, which type of content do you suppose a non-journalist CEO, who can draw a seven-figure salary only so long as the shareholders are pleased with their commitment to the bottom line, is going to demand from the news division?

If you're not sure of the answer, just turn on your TV or think back to some of the more heavily covered national stories in recent years: the murder of JonBenet Ramsey, the death of Princess Diana, John Wayne

Bobbitt's severed penis, the Columbine school shootings, the love-gone-wrong saga of Joey Buttafuoco and Amy Fisher, the murder of Nicole Brown Simpson and the subsequent trial of O. J., the murder trial of British au pair Louise Woodward, the parental murders of the Menendez brothers, and so on and so forth.

Did these stories merit coverage as national news? In some instances, they did. But none of them deserved anywhere near the amount of coverage that they received and, incredibly, in some cases are still receiving. In 1999, years after an incident that should never have been reported beyond a local newspaper, all of America is still receiving periodic news updates about the trials and tribulations of John Wayne Bobbitt and his surgically reattached sex organ. The story of Lorena Bobbitt, John's knife-wielding ex-wife, was aired in the time slot opposite the Super Bowl in January 1999, admittedly in an attempt to draw women viewers who were angry about their husband's football-watching habits. In February 1999, I sat down with my newspaper, only to find yet another update on the six-year-old Fisher-Buttafuoco saga. Additional updates of this same meaningless story ran in my newspaper in April and May 1999 as well. Such dependence on the sensational may be good for ratings and reader pickup, but it's bad for journalism and the public it once served.

For decades, media owners knew that their television news programming was going to lose money. It was the one area of the TV business that was still looked upon as a public service—the price a company had to pay for free access to the airways. But no more. At the end of the twentieth century, as far as the media conglomerates and their shareholders are concerned, *Murphy Brown*'s newsroom is no different than that of Dan Rather, Peter Jennings, or Tom Brokaw. All are expected to pay their own way and produce hefty profits.

To make this requirement of the market a reality, budgets have been drastically slashed in network newsrooms, making responsible journalism difficult to impossible. According to media critic Jim Naureckas, "[U]nder Cap Cities, ABC—like the other two networks which had also changed hands in the 80s—was under heavy pressure to cut costs and make its news operation profitable. By 1987, about 300 news staffers had lost their jobs, one-fifth of all news employees."[21]

In writing for the *Nation*, author and media critic Mark Crispin Miller of Johns Hopkins University stated that this radical cost cutting in news departments that is now being dictated by the networks' parent companies "portends the death of broadcast journalism."[22] In the end Miller may be correct, but for now, newsrooms must produce the same amount of content with fewer people and greatly reduced budgets. Enter the need for sensational violent-crime content.

With the trimmed-down staffs at most newspapers and television stations, reporters in the 1990s are often expected to turn out several stories a day—stories that, while quick to produce, will still draw an audience. In order to accomplish this daunting task, journalists, out of necessity, tend to produce sensational coverage that can be completed by placing only a few phone calls, and more often than not, such stories are those concerning crime and violence, where the facts can be easily gathered from a single source—law-enforcement agencies.

TV reporters have the dual hardship of diminishing resources and very small time slots. The slots are shrinking because the time allotted to advertising is going up. A 1998 study found that a number of thirty-minute news programs studied now give more time to commercials than to the news itself.[23] It's hard to describe a complicated issue like campaign finance reform in two minutes or less, but it's easy to say that an "unidentified man shot a liquor-store clerk at the corner of Fifth and Harvey after taking $62 out of the cash register."

In writing about television violence for the *Atlantic Monthly*, Scott Stossel noted that "[s]cary and crime-ridden though the world is these days . . . prime-time television presents a world in which crime rates are a hundred times worse."[24] He's right, and the media's presentation of such an exaggerated vision of crime is taking its toll on all of us. The market's demand for sensational, cheap-to-produce violent content means that the news no longer reflects an accurate picture of our world but rather an accurate picture of a world designed to please shareholders.

The end result of determining which stories get aired based on their potential to draw an audience rather than on their importance has turned the news business into something substantially less important. Consider the decision made by network executives in 1999 when it came time for the president of the United States to offer his defense in his impeachment trial. The Associated Press reported that despite its historical importance, the networks had decided not to provide live coverage of the president's defense because it would have cost the corporations owning the networks millions in advertising revenues had they interrupted regular programming.[25] It would seem that Garrison Keillor is on to something in his remarks about the news these days: "It is as bloody as Shakespeare but without the intelligence and poetry. . . . If you watch television news you know less about the world than if you drank gin out of a bottle."[26]

Choosing the Message

According to news director Bob Suren:

> If the product is unappealing, just as in any other business, news organizations have to adapt by reorganizing, realigning, or terminating operations. Newspapers have to sell newspapers, sell ad space. They are not public utilities. They are businesses. We are in a business and I believe that you do what you have to do, legally, ethically, to get folks to watch your show. . . . We are owned by people who want to make money: they really don't care if I lead with a murder or not; they just want to know if anyone was watching.[27]

In her book *Making Local News*, Phyllis Kaniss described the importance of "doing what you have to" to draw an audience. "The difference in a rating point can mean hundreds of thousands of dollars to a station. . . . Crime is an important topic news organizations use . . . because it bolsters readership and circulation."[28] In their 1967 study titled *Crime and Publicity*, A. Friendly and R. L. Goldfarb likewise noted crime coverage's importance to increasing a media corporation's audience and revenues: "In a competitive situation where there are bound to be occasional and continual battles for readers and revenue, the usual weaponry is the reporting of crime."[29] And it's not just any crimes; sensational violent crimes are the ones that have been found to increase ratings and revenues the most.

Numerous studies have documented that violent-crime coverage increases the number of viewers and readers for a TV station or newspaper. Such studies and polls have been conducted not only by academics interested in media content but also by the news corporations themselves, which use the information to shape their future content to further increase profits.[30] As a result of emphasizing crime stories that will draw the largest audience, violent crimes now compose between 40 and 50 percent of all crime coverage by news organizations, even though crimes where someone is injured make up less than 3 percent of all crimes committed, and the rarest crime of all, murder, accounts for 60 percent of this coverage.[31]

In the 1991 book *Good Murders and Bad Murders*, author W. Wilson described the use of murder as a means to profit by the media. "The information market for murder thrives, and the media respond to that market as would any entrepreneur." Such sensational crimes contain "the intensity of drama, the centerpiece of a true crime story, the remote tragedy of a terrorist attack, and the sardonic humor of a grade B movie."[32]

More often than not, when a particularly gruesome murder occurs, it quickly becomes a lead story for news organizations, both local and national. Professor Steven Chermak of the Department of Criminal Justice at Indiana University at Bloomington has described such stories as "super primary" because "[n]ews organizations are willing to commit a larger number of financial and personnel resources to [these] stories because of their ability to attract more consumers."[33] So can one type of murder actually generate more profit than another for the media? Definitely.

Consider the tragic 1999 school shooting at Columbine High School in Littleton, Colorado, where thirteen students died at the hands of two fellow classmates armed with homemade bombs, rifles, and a semiautomatic pistol, who later committed suicide themselves. First of all, let me say that this tragedy did deserve to be the lead story on the national news for at least one day and possibly several more. But as is increasingly the norm in the 1990s, the Columbine story was milked for every dollar it could generate by the media for no less than eight full weeks following the incident. The *Today Show* did a live broadcast from the scene of the crime. Barbara Walters of *20/20* immediately jumped into the fray. In fact, every morning show and news magazine devoted major time to Columbine, as did the pseudo-news programs like *Hardcopy*, the network news, and the cable news programs.

As a result of the unprecedented saturation coverage allotted the Columbine tragedy, viewers all across the nation were exposed to every emotional nuance the case had to offer. We watched the murders unfold live on cable news programs and the networks for nearly a full day. We then saw the most sensational scenes repeated again and again over the next few weeks in segments interspersed with tearful interviews with grieving students, parents, teachers, and community leaders. Then came the days of expert opinion—interviews with a wide array of professionals from law enforcement to child psychology. Cameras looked on as celebrities such as the duchess of York and survivors of the Oklahoma City bombing made their way to the makeshift memorial of flowers and memorabilia located in the park next to the school. Television cameras took us inside the bedrooms of the young victims, where we saw their favorite stuffed toys and their sports trophies. Grieving parents told us about their lost child's favorite foods and hobbies—about bright futures that would never be realized. And finally, we attended every single tear-filled funeral via television.

In all, the Columbine tragedy generated hundreds upon hundreds of hours of media coverage. So why were we exposed to so much emotional footage of this event? I find the answer to this question most disturbing. The answer is: because the Columbine tragedy is the kind of story that can generate tens of millions of dollars in advertising revenues. Ratings for cable stations and other news programming skyrocketed during the sensationalized Columbine barrage, and as Kaniss pointed out, a single rating point can be worth hundreds of thousands of dollars to a station, and we're talking about much more than one point here.

In the saturation coverage during the week following the shooting, audience ratings for Fox News Channel were up an incredible 59 percent in total households over the previous week. CNN had a 41 percent ratings gain during the same period, with a 52 percent gain in prime time. MSNBC increased its ratings by 46 to 56 percent depending on the time of day, and CNBC improved its ratings by 34 percent during prime time. Although cable programs had the biggest ratings increases, the networks also experienced incredible gains. NBC's *Nightly News* increased its total audience share by 11 percent with coverage of the tragedy. ABC's *World News Tonight* was up 3 percent, and even lowly CBS showed an increased audience share on the nightly news. In short, Columbine was big business for the corporations that own the airways.[34]

Chermak's research into what types of crimes can generate the most profit sheds some light on why the media tend to exploit tragedies such as Columbine. Chermak reported that news organizations' "super primary" stories tend to be murders in which the victims or killers are very young, very old, or very rich, have a level of celebrity status, live in an area where crime is very infrequent, or hold positions of authority in the community such as a schoolteacher, cop, or religious leader. Rare types of violence such as murder with multiple victims, a serial killer, or the presence of an unusually morbid element such as cannibalism, decapitation, or a long period of torture before the murder are also an audience draw.

The bottom line is that sensational murders that are out of the norm draw far more viewers/readers than the "usual" murder of a transient, a dope dealer, or a typical working stiff. Such nondescript murders are generally relegated to the back pages of a newspaper or the tail end of a local TV newscast, and they certainly don't make it into the national news.

Analyze the news content that comes into your home on any given day and you will easily be able to spot this marketing-of-mayhem pattern: JonBenet (young and in a low-crime area with millionaire parents), Jeffrey Dahmer (cannibal), Nicole Brown Simpson (married to a celebrity, nearly decapitated), and the Columbine tragedy (young killers from wealthy families, multiple young victims in a low-crime area). These are the stories that lead the national newscast, while equally murdered John Doe, who drove a truck for a living, gets a few seconds at the end of the local news or no mention at all. This practice of exaggerating the coverage of the exceptional violent crime makes it seem to the viewer/reader that most crimes are such. In journalism in the 1990s, abnormal is the norm, and this fact helps to explain our society's exaggerated apprehension over crime.

Not only do news organizations choose to cover a disproportionate number of sensational violent crimes as a means of making money, but they cover them in a context-free manner in order to amplify their drama and save time and expense. Unfortunately, this nearly meaningless style of reporting enhances the amount of anxiety experienced by those who are continually exposed to it. We hear and see the gory details of violent crimes, but we are rarely informed about motives, demographics, or root causes for them—information that would help to alleviate the fear that we, too, may become the next victim of a similar incident.

Only 2 percent of the time are the root causes for a crime mentioned in media coverage. Motives for a crime are not discussed in four-fifths of crime stories. Police effectiveness is only reported in 4 percent of crime stories, and court effectiveness is evaluated in approximately 3 percent.[35] In the end, we are left with the terrifying impression that such horrible crimes can happen to anyone, anywhere—including to us in our own neighborhoods.

Of course it's true that these violent crimes can happen anywhere, just as it's true that any of us can win the lottery. But at least with the lottery, most of us realize that our chances of getting rich are next to nothing because the law requires the state to frequently remind us that our odds of winning big are several million to one. Making such context clear in crime reporting would serve a similar role. It would be a constant reminder that violent crimes are relatively rare phenomena that occur mostly in isolated and impoverished urban areas, and in most instances, the perpetrator and the victim knew one another. In other words, such context would convey the message that although we could be victimized by a violent crime, the odds are extremely long.

For the very reason that this is the truth of most violent crimes, it is, therefore, only the tiny percentage of violent crimes that don't fit these parameters that get all of the media attention. Sensational news coverage may be situationally correct, but overall, it conveys a false impression of crime's true frequency and character.

In his book *Victims in the News: Crime and the American News Media*, Chermak summed up the media's increasing reliance on crime. In his words:

> It is important to accept that these organizations are private businesses producing news to make a profit for their owners. . . . Crime delivered through any medium capitalizes on the public's fascination with gore and pathos. . . . Crime stories provide real life drama and entertainment that can stir a host of emotions for different audience members.[36]

The decision by media corporations to disseminate a disproportionate amount of violent content because it will draw large audiences and thereby please advertisers has become a powerful constraint on the information flow, as was predicted by Supreme Court Justice William Brennan in 1964 when he said:

> Clearly, the threat of censorship is no longer limited to state control. Private economic forces have ushered in another kind of censorship, one generally beyond the reach of the First Amendment. Like its government counterpart, censorship by advertisers denies the public access to knowledge that is crucial for making informed political and economic choices.[37]

The control, or censorship, as Brennan put it, that advertisers exert over content has escalated dramatically in the 1980s and 1990s. A 1992 report issued by the Center for the Study of Commercialism titled *Dictating Content* documented more than sixty instances where advertisers censored news stories.[38] The report contained examples such as a TV station in Minneapolis canning a story about corrupt car dealerships by their consumer reporter after the dealerships threatened to pull their advertising from the station.

In their book *Marketing Madness*, Michael F. Jacobson and Laurie Ann Mazur also cited several examples of advertiser censorship in recent years, including the case of critic Joseph McBride, who wrote a negative review of Paramount Pictures' *Patriot Games* in *Daily Variety*. As a result, Paramount pulled its advertising from the magazine. In response, *Daily Variety*'s editor, Peter Bart, issued a public apology to the movie company and promised Paramount that McBride would no longer be allowed to review the company's movies. One can assume that this was *Daily Variety*'s way of saying, "Come back and we promise to write only good things about your products."[39]

Mademoiselle magazine hired reporter Sheila Kaplan to do a story about women lobbyists, including a section that dealt with tobacco giant Philip Morris. Prior to publication, the magazine allowed Philip Morris, one of its advertisers, to preview the article. The tobacco company then demanded that the section about Philip Morris had to be removed from Kaplan's piece. Not only did the publication follow the orders from the advertiser, but it threatened to never run another story by Kaplan if she went public about the censorship and the subsequent kowtowing by the magazine.[40]

In September 1993, automaker Mercedes-Benz took a preemptive approach to censorship. The company sent a letter to more than two dozen magazines, instructing them to cancel all of Mercedes-Benz's advertising in any issue that ran a story that was of a negative nature regarding their product, any German products, or anything at all that might be construed to be negative about Germany. It's no wonder that the automaker found receptive ears at the publications. After all, Mercedes-Benz spent an average of $14.5 million a year on magazine advertising. Over half the publications contacted by the company signed agreements promising to comply with the automaker's orders to censor stories.[41]

These are just a few examples of how advertising is used as a means to control content. In 1992, Marquette University contacted 150 editors at newspapers and asked them about editorial interference by those who buy ads. Almost without exception, those surveyed claimed that such interference did, in fact, occur. A disturbing 90 percent of the editors told the researchers that their advertisers had tried to impact their paper's editorial content.[42] Thirty-seven percent—I suspect that this number would be higher if journalists were not so concerned with saving face—claimed that the advertisers had been successful in their meddling. The biggest effort made by the advertisers was in the area of trying to kill stories. Seventy percent of the editors had experienced pressure to do so. Other studies have found similar results. A study of business editors showed that a majority, 55 percent, had allowed advertisers to influence their editorial decisions.[43]

And it's not just trivial stories that are being altered by those who control the purse strings. In an article for the *Nation*, Mark Crispin Miller reflected on two serious breaches of the public trust. As Miller put it:

> With the [media] mergers came some hints of how the new proprietors would henceforth use their journalists: Disney's ABC News apologizing to Philip Morris—a major advertiser, through Kraft Foods—for having told the truth, on a broadcast of *Day One*, about P.M.'s manipulation of nicotine levels in its cigarettes; and CBS's in-house council ordering the old newshounds at *60 Minutes* to bury an explosive interview with whistle-blower Jeffrey Wigand about the addictive practices of Brown & Williamson.[44]

As disturbing as this type of straightforward censorship on the part of advertisers is, I do not believe that it is the most destructive form of content control impacting the public's right to know. As I mentioned previously, there is only so much time and space allotted for dispensing the news; therefore, when powerful advertisers seeking to reach a larger audience influence news executives to improve ratings, which translates into airing more sensational violent stories, they do so at the expense of "real" news. As a result of this "space" censorship, media consumers are not only left with the false impression that crime is worsening, but they are also being denied access to important information that *should* be influencing the way they view the world around them. But as I said, those who own the news these days have separated themselves from the concept that journalism's first responsibility is to the public. Consider this clarification of role made by the CEO of the network-owning Westinghouse in an interview in *Advertising Age* magazine: "We are here to serve advertisers. That is our raison d'être."[45]

This is how newsrooms in shareholder-driven media organizations choose their content in the 1990s, and it's the same principle for entertainment programming as well. Media genres such as music, the Internet, radio, and movies also contribute to our impression that crime is escalating. The music industry has been under fire in recent years for its violent lyrics, which have been linked to increasing acts of violence and suicides among teenagers. Talk radio often exploits gruesome crimes as a topic to draw listeners. One Denver talk show has been discussing the JonBenet Ramsey murder almost daily for two years. And the Internet and video games have become a veritable smorgasbord of violent content.

It should come as no surprise that the same strategy of using violence to increase revenues in television and newspapers is being implemented across all media genres. After all, consolidation in the media industry has resulted in the same handful of corporations that own the television stations and the newspapers also controlling these other sectors of the media as well, and if violence can make money in one tributary of the information flow, it can obviously be profitable in the entire media watershed.

The Spread of Sameness

In the 1980s, Ronald Reagan's faith in the free market tended to express itself in an exuberance for ignoring the antitrust laws. Reagan did for the media industry then what he did for virtually all industries: He deregulated it to some degree. Reagan made it possible for the networks to own nearly twice as many television stations as they had previously been allowed to by law.

I'm not just picking on conservatives here. What Reagan started, Bill Clinton has perfected. Under Clinton, America has had more corporate mergers than ever before in its history. There were a record-breaking 1,471 mergers in 1996, and 1998 mergers are expected to shatter that mark with the meshing of $1.61 trillion worth of corporations.[46] Democrat Clinton has also proven to be just as enthusiastic about media mergers as Reagan. Not only did he sign the monopoly-friendly 1996 Telecommunications Act, but it was on Clinton's watch that Disney took over ABC in what billionaire Warren Buffett, ABC's major shareholder, has described as the merging of the number-one content provider with the number-one distributor in the industry.[47] In other words, ABC-

Disney was exactly the type of corporate marriage that the antitrust laws were designed to stop.

Just in case anyone is still in denial with regard to the demise of the antitrust laws, the 1998 announcement of the merger between oil giants Exxon and Mobil should snap you back to reality. Not only will this merger create the largest corporation in the world, but ironically, it reunites two of the companies created when the antitrust laws forced the breakup of Rockefeller's Standard Oil monopoly a century ago. We have truly come full circle.

As a consequence of consolidation in the media industry, the number of daily newspapers in the United States by 1993 had plummeted to 1,700. Of those remaining papers, 98 percent had local monopolies over their market, and only fifteen corporations controlled the vast majority of those papers.[48] Other sectors of the media have followed the same consolidation plan. Time, Inc. now controls 40 percent of the magazine industry; Cap Cities-Disney, GE, Time Warner, and Viacom (provided its pending purchase of CBS goes through) now own the vast majority of the television airwaves in this country; and even the hallowed book industry has become owned and controlled by fewer than a dozen companies.[49]

In 1982, when Ben Bagdikian wrote his startling book *The Media Monopoly*, only fifty corporations controlled over half of the entire media business in the United States. By 1986, when he completed his first revision of the book, Bagdikian found that only twenty-six corporations controlled over half of the media empire. In 1993, when he completed his book's next update, Bagdikian reported that the number of corporations controlling the majority of the media in the United States was down to twenty.[50] So what has happened since then? As of 1998, there are only nine corporations that now control the majority of media content on the entire planet.[51]

The world's flow of information is now dominated by Time Warner (1997 sales $24 billion), Disney ($22 billion), Bertelsmann ($15 billion), Viacom ($13 billion), News Corporation ($11 billion), TCI ($7 billion), General Electric ($5 billion), Sony ($9 billion), and Seagram ($7 billion). In addition to these nine, there is a somewhat less powerful second tier of global media corporations composed of approximately three dozen companies, including Westinghouse, Comstat, Gannett, and New York Times Company, that split the remaining global market.[52]

The idea of only nine corporations controlling the majority of the world's mediated messages is disturbing enough, but it becomes even more so when you realize that these companies cooperate with each other more than they compete. The vast majority of these monopolies are actually in business with each other by way of joint ventures. In the truest sense, they have become a global media *keiretsu* (a total-production cooperative monopoly network). According to respected journalism professor Robert McChesney, "Each of the nine first-tier media giants, for example, has joint ventures with, on average, two-thirds of the other eight first-tier media giants. And the second tier is every bit as aggressive about making joint ventures."[53] This shrinking media ownership is having a profound impact on content.

In the late 1980s, a journalist friend of mine in Portland, Oregon, had a Russian guest staying in his home. One night, while the two were watching the evening news, my friend noticed that the Russian was flipping back and forth between the networks with a perplexed look on his face. Puzzled by the behavior, my friend asked him what was wrong. The man responded with a question of his own, "Who controls your news?" A little more dialogue revealed the true nature of the inquiry.

As he flipped from channel to channel, the man from Russia was astonished to find that each station was offering nearly identical coverage of the exact same events. He couldn't understand how this uniformed information flow could exist in our country because he was under the impression that the United States had a free press. He went on to explain that in Russia, all the stations also carried the exact same news, but it was because the government controlled the programming. When he saw the carbon-copy newscasts of ABC, NBC, and CBS, it was therefore only natural that he would assume that one entity was in control of America's networks as well.

I have to say, I think that the background of our Russian friend allowed him to zero in on a problem that goes unnoticed by many Americans. The government isn't pulling the strings of the nightly news, but it does appear that someone or something is making the flow of information not only incredibly uniform but also incredibly violent. The fact that so few now own so much of all news content translates into a very few people, literally a handful of people, making the decisions over "what is news" for the majority of the entire industry. And since the power of shareholder primacy guarantees that each of these executives is committed to the identical goal of producing the content that will generate the maximum profit for his or her company, it follows that news content would become relatively uniform, with an emphasis on cheap-to-produce violence that draws a large audience.

"The concentration of media power by a few giant megacorporations also contributes to 'tabloidization,'" commented movie director Oliver Stone:

> As news organizations are increasingly driven by a bottom-line mentality, the news we get becomes more and more sensational. What is the difference between *Time* and *Newsweek*? Between ABC, NBC, and CBS News? Between the *Washington Post* and the *New York Times*? For all practical purposes, none. The concentration of media power means that Americans increasingly get their information from a few sources who decide what is "news."[54]

This not-so-subtle shift from important information to profitable information in the "what-is-news" equation has led to news programming that has, for all intents and purposes, become as controlled by the shareholder's profit demands as the Russian press once was by that country's Communist regime. And because most "sensational" stories result from crime and violence, it stands to reason that the majority of what we have called news in the 1980s and 1990s has been composed of scenes of bloody carnage. And it's not just news content that has become more violent in the last twenty years. As a result of consolidation and globalization, the majority of all media content is now composed of violence as well, including nearly two-thirds of all entertainment content.[55]

McChesney's take on this was:

> A specter now haunts the world, a global commercial media system dominated by a small number of super-powerful, mostly U.S.-based transnational media corporations. It is a system that works to advance the cause of the global market and promote commercial values, while denigrating journalism and culture not conducive to the immediate bottom line or long-run corporate interests. It is a disaster for anything but the most superficial notion of democracy—a democracy where, to paraphrase John Jay's maxim, those who own the world ought to govern it.[56]

This global control of the media is a relatively new phenomenon. Until 1980, most media companies had a national emphasis, even though international trade in books, music, TV programming, and movies had been going on for several decades. According to McChesney, "Beginning in the 1980s, pressure from the IMF [International Monetary Fund], World Bank, and U.S. government to deregulate and privatize media and communication systems coincided with new satellite and digital technologies, resulting in the rise of transnational media giants."[57] As a result of the emergence of these new global supercorporations, by 1997, entertainment had become America's second-largest export in dollar value.[58] Or put another way, images of violence had become America's second-most profitable export.

Of all the programming choices available, market research has shown that violence and sex are the two most profitable forms of content on the international market because they lose the least in translation. In writing for *Atlantic Monthly*, Scott Stossel noted:

> Sex travels well. A Parisian or a Warsawian can delectate in Pamela Anderson in her bikini on *Baywatch* as well as a New Yorker can—hence *Baywatch* is the most-watched show in the world. Violence travels well. When Sylvester Stallone rains bullets on the bad guys, who duck and spew blood, a viewer in Beijing can understand what is going on as well as a viewer in Peoria. Grunting is easy to translate. That's why the *Mighty Morphin Power Rangers* is watched by 300 million children in eighty countries.[59]

Have you ever watched a sitcom produced in a foreign country like Japan and found the subtitled humor to be lacking? You're not alone. Content such as comedy is difficult to market globally because humor tends to be culturally derived and loses its appeal in translation. What's funny in one part of the world is all but meaningless someplace else. Other programming genres also lose their international appeal because they contain culture-specific or complex dialogue. When it comes to the world market, image-driven content, namely, sex and violence, are the ticket. For this reason, the multinationals that now control our media have placed a great deal of importance on creating content that is universally understood.

Dr. George Gerbner, former dean of the Annenberg School of Communications at the University of Pennsylvania, is a well-respected expert in the field of mass communications and particularly on the role of violence in the media. Gerbner has been investigating the impact of globalization on media content, and he now believes that the current mergers between production and distribution companies have not only resulted in the total control of the world market by our handful of conglomerates but have also caused the multinational monopolies to reformulate all of their content, including that aimed at the American market, in the direction of violence, much of it pertaining to crime.[60]

In Gerbner's view:

> Conglomeration brings streamlining of production, economies of scale, and emphasis on dramatic ingredients most suitable for aggressive international promotion. It means less competition, fewer alternative choices, greater emphasis on formulas that saturate more markets at a lower cost per viewer. Return on investment, attractive demographics, and low cost—rather than program quality (which may cost more)—drive commercial success. Ratings, which measure the share of the audience captured at any one time, are one side of the equation; cost is the other. Violence becomes a key ingredient of the formula.[61]

In other words, media corporations now look at the world market to determine potential profits. A nonviolent TV series that has a potential audience of 10 million in the United States and 2 million elsewhere in the world is deemed to be less desirable than a cheap-to-make action series that may reach only 3 million Americans but perhaps 50 million viewers worldwide. A perfect example of this can be found in the violent television program *Xena: Warrior Princess*, which in 1999 bumped *Baywatch* out of first place in the international market. I have yet to see *Xena* do particularly well in America's Nielson ratings, but its international appeal means that U.S. viewers will be subjected to the show nonetheless.

Most companies that produce television shows and movies barely break even on the U.S. market these days. As a result of high production costs and the fact that consolidation has left very few buyers of television programs, companies are now forced to seek their profits from the international, syndication, cable, and video markets. To guarantee the biggest return on their investments, the shareholder requirement, content producers have learned to rely on the language of "action"—the code word for violence and crime content—to break through the language and cultural barriers of international distribution.

The producer of the movie *Die Hard 2* put it this way: "Action travels well around the world, everyone understands an action movie."[62] This point was made even more clearly by Bruce Gordon, president of Paramount International TV Group, when he said, "The international demand rarely changes. . . . Action adventure series and movies continue to be the genre in demand, primarily because those products lose less in translation to other languages."[63] Stossel summed up the industry's quest for the most profitable content when he wrote: "Thus there's an overwhelming global marketing imperative in favor of the simple, the naked, and the bloody. Cheap to produce, easy to distribute—violence is the surest road to profits."[64]

New York University professor Todd Gitlin has pointed out that changes in the domestic market have also pushed the TV and movie industries toward more violent content:

> In recent years, market forces have driven screen violence to an amazing pitch. As the movies lost much of their audience—especially adults—to television, the studios learned that the way to make their killing, so to speak, was to offer on big screens what the networks would not permit on the small. This meant among other things, grisly violence. . . . We have witnessed the burgeoning of a genre unknown two decades ago: the "action movie," a euphemism for the debased choreography that budding auteurs throughout the world aspire to imitate. Aiming to recoup losses and better compete with cable, television programmers struck back: the networks lowered their censorship standards and pruned their "standards and practices" staffs; the deregulatory Federal Communications Commission clammed up; and local news fell all over itself cramming snippets of gore between commercials.[65]

Unfortunately, continually drawing an audience—whether domestic or international—with violent content demands that the violence quotient must continually be raised due to audience desensitization. What shocked people this year is all but boring the next. One need look no further than sequels to see this raising of the violence bar in action. In the first *Die Hard* movie, there were only 18 deaths, in the second, there were 264. *Robocop* killed off 32 bad guys the first time around but slaughtered 81 in his second flick. The films *The Godfather, Godfather II,* and *Godfather III* killed 12, 18, and 53, respectively.[66] It was the same trend in *Dirty Harry* movies as well. Gerbner described this more-death-more-profit pattern as "one way to get attention from a public punch-drunk on global mayhem."[67]

In 1990, Time Warner and Disney generated approximately 15 percent of their income from outside the United States. By 1997, that figure had doubled to 30 percent, and both companies project that within the next ten years, they will be deriving the majority of their profits from the international market.[68] What this means in all likelihood is that the current emphasis on violent content brought about by globalization will escalate in the future. One can only imagine the impact that such a future of violent imagery will have on an electorate already operating under the illusion that there is a "crime gap."

Don't Rock the Boat

I believe it's the role of journalists to challenge people, not to just mindlessly amuse them. . . . American journalism is disfigured by celebrity, gossip, and sensationalism. In this culture of journalistic titillation, we teach our readers and our viewers that the trivial is important.

—**Carl Bernstein,**
speaking before the Jewish Federation,
February 23, 1999[69]

As a journalist, I feel the need to try to explain why so many of my peers have gone along quietly with the transformation of the newsroom from watchdog to hawker of merchandise via violent imagery. There are a number of reasons, really. Some reporters are too young to remember that things used to be different. Some of those who have worked on both sides of the 1980s are in denial because that is easier than admitting that they have become accomplices to this crime of exploiting crime. And the rest are pretty much just trying to hang onto their jobs and do the best journalism they can under these less-than-ideal circumstances.

So what about the journalists employed by shareholder-driven media monopolies who claim that their paycheck's origin isn't influencing their work? I think journalist George Seldes summed it up best when he said, "The most stupid boast in the history of present-day journalism is that of the writer who says, 'I have never been given orders; I am free to do as I like.'"[70] Media critic Jim Naureckas has expanded on Seldes's claim by adding, "[I]t is those who are likely to do something that the boss doesn't like that get told what to do; those that naturally do what the boss wants need no such direction."[71]

In its infancy, today's "violence-for-ratings" contamination of the newsroom took a seemingly innocent form that allowed many a longtime reporter to rationalize on the decision to compromise ethics. Corporate execs wisely avoided the newsroom backlash that would have resulted had they been straightforward about demanding an increase in the amount of sensationalized violent content in their news divisions for no other reason than to increase profits. Instead of saying, "Cover this murder to increase our ratings," media owners packaged their new vision for news content in these terms: "Let's find out what our loyal viewers want to see, and then strive to meet their needs." As if *wants* and *needs* are synonymous.

These two concepts may be somewhat interchangeable in the manufacturing sector, but not in the news business, which truly is as vital a part of our democracy as the right to vote. As a result of this innocent-sounding directive, the fourth estate has been reduced to little more than an advertising delivery mechanism. Sadly, few people listened when journalists questioned this type of viewer/reader-driven decision-making within the news business. In a conversation I had with journalist Larry Bensky a few years ago, he described this new "wants versus needs" directive. "It's like having the patient tell the brain surgeon how to perform the operation. Clearly no good can come of it."

Consider the sensationalized coverage of the murder of little Jon-Benet Ramsey. Reporters from all over the country have been made to cover this story consistently for more than two years at this writing, despite the fact that very little new information has surfaced since the murder and the case has no bearing on the lives of the public outside of Boulder, Colorado. Even though it is clear that the only possible motive behind this saturation coverage of a little girl's death is to increase ratings and profits, I have found few journalists willing to admit as much on the record. Off the record is a different story.

Because I have been living in and around Boulder, Colorado, for several years, I have talked to many of the journalists who have been assigned to this murder story, and I can honestly say that nearly all of them despise being made to exploit this tragedy. But in the end, these reporters have done what they have been told to do by ownership, which is dancing to the desires of shareholders.

The exception to this off-the-record complaining was an editor for *USA Today* who had the poor taste to be candid. She described the Ramsey case as "having everything you could possibly want in a story": a young blond-headed victim, rich parents living in a beautiful mountain community, a Christmas backdrop with Santa Claus as a potential suspect. She was right. It's truly "everything you could possibly want"—if your goal is to sell more papers. This is a good example of a reporter's having shaped her view to agree with that of her publisher, in this instance, media giant Gannett. If you pull up Gannett's web site, there is a section that describes the history of the company's formation of *USA Today*. I have found no better definition of the decline of modern journalism than Gannett's own words describing the birth of this publication: "After two years of research on what readers wanted, what advertisers needed, and what technology permitted," *USA Today* was born.[72]

I am not saying that the news business was once pure as snow and is now soiled by the quest for money. I hope I won't become so nostalgic for a few more decades. As pointed out by Walter Cronkite, profit has always played a role at most news organizations. What I am saying is that in the past, when those who were committed only to the bottom line pushed, the newsroom pushed back equally hard, creating an often volatile yet fairly successful balance of power between editorial department and ownership. When today's profit-minded execs push, they tend to encounter only a small, mostly symbolic resistance.

One of the reasons for the decline of this healthy state of war between newsroom and ownership is the lack of potential employers for journalists, which has resulted from consolidation. Out of necessity, much of the journalists' commitment to the public has been redirected into a commitment to ownership. If reporters and editors in today's newsrooms want to see a future filled with paychecks, they have little choice but to become efficient at compromising their ethics and rationalizing why they have done so. Based on the sensationalized violence that often passes for news these days, it would seem that most have become adept at both.

I am not pointing a holier-than-thou finger at my colleagues. As a reporter and editor, I have experienced the pressure of the bottom line firsthand. I've been hammered on by chemical, tobacco, and restaurant corporations that advertised in publications I worked for and didn't like what I had to say about them. Such experiences can make the best of journalists desire to avoid stories that they know will make waves with ownership. And the opposite is also true. Reporters know that good coverage of a sensationalized crime will get them on the front page and earn points with management because such coverage pleases advertisers because it draws a larger audience.

Not everyone in the media business has always remained silent about the pressure exerted by advertisers and shareholders, though it might have been in their best personal interest, careerwise, to have done so. Famed journalist Edward R. Murrow spoke out decades ago about the way commercialism had trivialized news content. And on the entertainment side, Rod Serling of *Twilight Zone* fame condemned the destructive effect advertisers were having on the quality of TV dramas.[73] Shortly after his public complaints, Serling was basically blackballed from the industry. Such punishment has gone a long way toward assuring cooperation by those in the business, even those we assume would be the first to speak out critically about this type of economic pressure.

Take, for instance, Rush Limbaugh. It's fair to ask why this self-proclaimed protector of the people hasn't weighed in on the media monopoly debate. Could it be his silence is the result of the fact that he makes millions a year from his corporate keeper, media monopoly Gannett? Or how about that ever-virtuous defender of good, Pat Robertson? Oh yeah, his Family Channel—which generates millions in profit—is just a pawn in Rupert Murdoch's News Corporation empire.

Referring to Robertson's decision to become just another tentacle of the monopoly octopus, Todd Gitlin said, "Pat Robertson's willingness to sell to Rupert Murdoch, master exploiter of brainless smirkiness and sexual innuendo, shows what kind of values are in play among the movers and shakers."[74] These guys are silent because it serves their pocketbook and because the media landscape is littered with the bodies of those who *have* spoken out about consolidation or have failed to show proper editorial respect for the advertisers who back their paychecks.

One longtime newspaper reporter was terminated after he spoke out in the *Washington Journalism Review* about his employer's financially induced sensitivity to automobile advertisers.[75] Respected financial analyst Graef Crystal was fired by the *Financial World* after he wrote a column about the outrageous salaries paid to certain powerful executives. Crystal's termination came after advertisers in his publication complained to his bosses that the column represented bad press for their executives.[76] Another editor, who had previously been fired from *Philadelphia* magazine for arguing with his publisher over editorial interference from advertisers, would only speak to authors Jacobson and Mazur off the record, for fear that he would be permanently blackballed from the industry for airing dirty laundry.[77] Such exclusion from the entire industry would have been nearly impossible a few decades ago, but in today's consolidated world of media it has become a very real possibility.

This is the motive and formula for determining content, both of news and entertainment, at the end of the twentieth century. The messages being conveyed by media are those that best serve the interests of advertisers and shareholders, not the public or, for that matter, the journalist, who must comply with the wishes of ownership or run the risk of being chased from the industry. Even though this push toward violent content is altering the role of the free press as we have known it, I don't think that the demise of modern journalism is the most significant problem associated with the media's decision to greatly increase its dissemination of the images of sensational crimes. The media corporations' use of crime as a means to profit has caused an outbreak of fear that is literally spreading like a disease throughout the nation—a disease that is threatening the life of the criminal-justice system.

Manufacturing Fear

In one generation . . . America has become the first culture to have substituted secondary, mediated versions of experience for direct experience of the world. Interpretations and representations of the world were being accepted as experience, and the difference between the two was obscure to most of us.

—*Jerry Mander*, **Four Arguments for the Elimination of Television, 1978**[1]

According to Gerbner, "Whoever tells most of the stories to most of the people most of the time has effectively assumed the cultural role of parent and school."[2] If this is the case, which I believe it is, then in the 1990s it is the nine supercorporations that control the majority of the media that have primarily assumed the important societal role of storyteller. In the average American household, the television pumps its messages of violence into our minds for an average of seven hours a day.[3] As a result, TV has taken the place of our kitchen windows as our viewing point for the world.

We believe that the discrepancy between what we see in our neighborhoods with our own eyes and what we see on the screen is the result of television's ability to make us see further and more clearly into the real world. But this is not true. The television, including the news, is not showing us our world. It is not flashing its images of sex and violence for our enlightenment or even our entertainment. It is simply telling us the tales that most please those whose financial well-being is predicated upon our receiving a steady diet of sensationalized mayhem—the advertiser and the shareholder.

Make no mistake about it, advertising has become a science. Corporations now spend billions of dollars a year to hire the experts who can give them the keys to America's malleable subconscious—red cars make twice as many people buy; a pretty blond in a low-cut dress is worth an extra 10 percent; and violence, oh sweet violence, draws an audience like nothing else.

The images being pumped into our homes by way of the tube have not been left to chance, for they are far too valuable for that. They hold the secret to consumerism. They are the Holy Grail of capitalism. They are the reason that we go into debt or steal to buy things that we do not need. They provide us with the image of who we should be and then sell us all the trappings to match the picture. Nothing we see through the TV window is by accident, including its violent images.

We have been invaded by the behavioral scientists-turned-admen who have unlocked the mysteries of our minds only to sell their knowledge to the controllers of the image, who do not care if their market-driven tampering with our psyche retards our culture, our democracy, or our vision of justice. They do not care if their sensational images of violence have made us believe that we are living in the midst of a crime wave that does not exist. They do not care so long as we buy.

Mediated messages have always been a powerful influence in the world. In indigenous cultures, storytelling—a mediated message—was, and still is, the primary means of passing down the ways of a people. It's a practice that includes more than just reciting from one generation to the next an oral history of events. Storytelling also conveys the unique traits that make a people who they are. It can account for why a specific culture's behavior might be particularly influenced by the growth cycle of corn, the seeming moods of the sea, the appearance of certain creatures such as the buffalo or the eagle, the changing seasons—or violence.

As civilizations advanced, the information passed down by tribal storytellers gave way to the equally mediated messages being conveyed through the structures of school, church, and newspapers. For most of the last millennium in much of the world, it has been these powerful forces, coupled with parental input, that have determined which stories would be disseminated throughout a society. But now we find ourselves at the end of the twentieth century, and America has once again made a mammoth evolutionary leap concerning the dispensing of our culture's messages.

Thanks to the technological revolution, the role of society's storytellers that was once played by school, church, newspapers, and, to an increasing degree, even parents has been delivered into the hands of those who control the new structure of modern communications technology, particularly television. The passing of the storytelling torch is different this time around. This important responsibility has not been conveyed because this new high-tech structure is viewed as more capable of properly performing the task; rather, it has changed hands by default.

And more important, as the quote from Jerry Mander at the beginning of this chapter alludes to, for the first time ever, the interpretations and representations of the world—the stories, if you will—are being accepted as *experience* instead of as the mediated messages that they are. And the fact that this difference is obscure to most of us does not bode well for the continuation of American justice as we know it.

The arrival of television as the primary storyteller for our culture is a relatively new occurrence. Prior to 1950, less than 10 percent of American homes had a television. By 1985, the number with TV was 98 percent.[4] In the beginning, there were three channels to choose from. Now there are somewhere in the neighborhood of 500. As a result, the average American household now stares at its television set for more than seven hours a day, making it easily the single most influential dispenser of information in our homes and in our country. In the United States, more people have televisions than have indoor plumbing.[5] By the time children are six years old, they will already have spent more time in front of the TV than they will later on in their college classrooms; or put another way, they will already have learned more from television than they will learn later in university, should they be economically fortunate enough to attend.[6]

Television has literally become a centralized system that creates a shared consciousness that fulfills the societal role previously held by organized religion. The box in the corner of the den now satisfies most of our religious needs, including the needs to participate in common ritual and to share our beliefs about the meaning of life and the right way to live. Since television has become our nation's most powerful structure when it comes to communicating a common message to all strata of society, then what exactly does this mean for us in light of Mander's observation regarding our acceptance of television's mediated messages as experience? In short, it means that our society is now being guided into the future by little more than the programming desires of advertisers and shareholders, and I suspect that few would argue that this is a particularly thoughtful plan for the continuation of a healthy culture.

Before technology made it possible for us to receive our mediated messages coupled with the power of moving images, real-world experience played a dominant role in how we mentally digested our secondhand messages. In the past, we received these messages in words and then applied them to the real world we saw with our own eyes. When we received a message that conflicted with the observable reality, the message was rendered more or less impotent in its ability to affect our behavior because it was in conflict with the more powerful influence of reality. But this is no longer the case.

When television tells its stories, we do, in fact, see them happening before our eyes. In this sense, the television has literally become our window on the world. We still weigh the information we receive from television against our own experiences, but because we can witness something happening on TV—often simultaneously with the occurrence of the event (live coverage)—what we observe on the screen understandably becomes a sort of firsthand experience.

If you watched Clinton's 1998 impeachment in the House of Representatives live on C-Span, did you not experience the impeachment process? Would the experience have been significantly different if you had been sitting in the gallery next to the camera? Not really. So accepting what we see on nonfiction television programming as a firsthand experience does make some sense. Unfortunately, when we accept such imagery as experience, we are assuming that the camera cannot lie and that having a broader context would not change the relative truth of a story. These are highly flawed and dangerous assumptions.

I spent the first five years of my career as a photojournalist, and I can assure you that the images I produced were quite biased. When I covered a labor strike, for instance, my images nearly always reflected my sympathetic attitude toward the workers and my harsh opinion of management. It was not my intention to do so, but like all journalists, I'm human—no more capable of true objectivity than the next person.

During a typical labor story, I might take a close-up shot of a slaughterhouse worker's hand that was missing some fingers and run the photo

with a caption describing how the company had been cited by the Occu-
pational Safety and Health Administration (OSHA) for running its conveyer belts too fast—a practice that often results in lost digits for those
who work the line in the meat industry. Such an image obviously creates
sympathy for the workers among readers. Next, I might get a shot of
someone in management giving instructions to the sinister-looking—
they always wear those mirrored sunglasses—Wackenhut or Pinkerton
rent-a-guards whom companies hire during strikes for security purposes
as well as to perform less savory tasks such as videotaping strikers so
that the company knows who to retaliate against later. In this case, the
image conveys a cold, heartless impression of management.

So were my photos accurate? Yes, in the sense that they were not
staged and they did reflect something that was true. But they only told a
part of the story. They did not capture on film other elements that were
equally accurate. If management came out and offered food to the strikers or engaged in any other seemingly humane activities, I didn't take
that picture. In the truest sense, then, my images did not reflect reality.
This is the same problem that exists when it comes to television crime
coverage. In journalism, the sum does not necessarily equal all the
parts.

We have discussed how sensational violent crimes now make up a
disproportionately large part of the content that we see on the television
news. So are these crime stories accurate? Yes, insofar as they show real
events that have occurred in a reasonably objective manner. Then what's
the problem? The problem is, we are asking the wrong question. We
should be asking whether the overall news coverage of crime is accurate, and the answer to that question is: absolutely not.

Sensational violent crimes make up far less than 1 percent of all
crimes, yet they constitute the majority of crime coverage. We can
therefore say that the media is painting a badly distorted picture when it
comes to the overall character of crime. Likewise, if crime rates are
falling, as they have been doing for years, and the media knowingly
make the decision to radically and simultaneously increase the quantity
of crime-related content, then we can correctly describe such exaggerated coverage as conveying an inaccurate message about crime rates,
even though the rates for crime may never be mentioned specifically.

In the big picture, today's media saturation with sensational-crime
content conveys the overall false message that crime is more violent and
more pervasive now than ever before. This false message is being disseminated despite the fact that individual news images of crime are situ-

ationally accurate. This is the danger of substituting context-free mediated messages for experience. Because we correctly accept that the news coverage about particular crimes is basically true, so too do we readily accept the bigger, completely false message regarding the nature and quantity of crime.

If we continue to allow *seeing* television images of crime with our own eyes to be construed as something equivalent to *witnessing* crime with our own eyes, then there is little hope for our criminal-justice system. Eventually, our growing fear—fear generated as a result of technologically experiencing crime on a daily basis—will destroy the opportunity for justice by way of our endorsing hard-on-crime politics at the ballot box. After all, desiring to toughen the laws and increase the punishment for criminals is an understandable response for people living in a place where they witness dozens of heinous crimes every day—a place like, say, your living room, your den, or wherever you keep your television.

Aggression Versus Fear

There is a mountain of research in existence regarding the question of how violent content causes us to alter our behavior. And few subjects within this area of research have garnered more attention from the experts than the impact of television violence on our culture. There have been over 3,000 studies on this subject, and more are being conducted every year.[7]

Unfortunately, the vast majority of this research has zeroed in on the specific manner in which violence on television causes people to behave violently in the real world. I say that this is unfortunate because it means that most of what we know about violent content deals with aggressive behavior, not the creation of societal anxiety. Although fear may seem a less important by-product of violent programming than aggressive behavior to most people, I believe that it is fear that is having the more significant negative impact on our culture.

Since the vast majority of us will never commit a violent crime because we have watched too many episodes of *Power Rangers* or *Gunsmoke* or have attended one too many screenings of Clint Eastwood movies, those of us who compose the electorate tend not to be overly concerned with the question of TV content's influence on society. Sure, we know that some percentage of the population actually behaves aggressively as a result of viewing violent programming. We've heard about people who commit copycat murders after watching a movie like *Taxi Driver* or *Natural Born Killers*, but the other 99-plus percent of us aren't committing violent crimes because we watch the television or go to the movies.

I'm not trying to imply that TV's ability to cause violent behavior isn't an important subject. In fact, some experts believe that as much as 10 percent of all crimes can be attributed to television violence.[8] One ABC network study found that approximately one-fourth of all young felons locked up for a violent crime claimed that they had imitated a crime technique they had seen on television. In the month following the saturation coverage of the Columbine school shooting in April 1999, no less than a dozen schools across the country uncovered supposed plots by students to attack their classmates and teachers.[9]

What I am saying is that for many more of us, rather than causing aggressive behavior, violent content causes a fear of crime and, as a result, we should be at least as concerned with this aspect of such content. Remember the polls? Nearly 80 percent of us believe that crime is the biggest problem facing our nation even though crime rates have been dropping for years. Nearly half of us are afraid to walk in our own neighborhoods after dark, despite the fact that we are safer now than we were in the 1970s when such widespread fear did not exist. And 95 percent of us get virtually all of our information about crime from the television. It would certainly seem that there is a connection here.

The end result of having focused our violent-content research on aggression instead of on its ability to impart false, anxiety-causing impressions is that the issue of how our media-generated fear of crime is affecting our behavior has been allowed to stay largely below the radar screen of public awareness. A number of experts have repeatedly pointed out that by concentrating research efforts on aggression, critics of television programming have played into the hands of the media owners, who can dismiss their concerns as more or less inconsequential because the aggressive response appears in such a small minority of the population.

Attitudes, Beliefs, Behavior

Regardless of whether people react to violent content with aggression or fear, it is accurate to say that they have been persuaded to react in this manner. That being the case, we should take a quick look at how this process of persuasion works. One of the earliest descriptions of this awesome power can be found in Plato's *Dialogues*:

> What is there greater than the word which persuades the judges in the courts, or the senators in the council, or the citizens in the assembly, or at any other political meeting?—If you have the power of uttering this word, you will have the physician your slave, and the trainer your slave, and the money-maker of whom you talk will be found to gather treasures, not for himself, but for you who are able to speak and to persuade the multitude.[10]

In modern psychological terms, Plato's understanding was that the "message" is the key to persuasion. The philosopher was at least partially correct. I say "partially" because we now know that the "message" is just one of the factors that can cause people to change their attitudes toward someone or something. The "message" represents what today's behavioral scientists refer to as the "central" route to persuasion.

In the last fifty years, we have come to understand that there are other powerful routes to accomplishing persuasion in addition to the "central" one. These secondary paths to persuasion are known as "peripheral" routes and include such factors as who is delivering the message, what that person looks like, how often we hear the message, and whether we are promised a reward for adjusting our attitude. Advertisers take full advantage of these "peripheral" routes when they string together images that send us hidden messages such as "Buy this product and men or women will find you more attractive." To understand how both central and peripheral messages work to persuade us, we must first understand that there is a difference between attitudes and beliefs.

Psychologists define attitude as a "general and enduring positive or negative feeling about some person, object or issue."[11] Our *attitudes* are different from our *beliefs,* which result from the information we have about a certain subject. For instance, "I love ice cream" is an attitude. "Ice cream is cold" is a belief. This difference is important because it is our attitudes, not our beliefs, that ultimately determine our behavior.

Understanding the different roles of attitudes and beliefs goes a long way toward explaining why a person who is afraid of being victimized by criminals (attitude) yet believes that prisons are being overused for nonviolent offenders (belief) can be expected to vote for a political candidate who promises greater public safety by continuing to incarcerate millions of nonviolent citizens. The attitude of fearing criminals directs our voting behavior despite the obvious conflict with our beliefs regarding the use of the prison system.

In summary, "persuasion" is the process of causing someone to change *attitudes,* not *beliefs.* This change can be accomplished based upon the "message," or central route, as described by Plato, or it can be based upon any number of peripheral routes. All of these routes play an important role in the process of persuasion when it comes to the media and our attitudes regarding crime. In many ways, the elements of persuasion found in the media's presentations of crime are not that different from those found in the repetitive messages of an advertising campaign.

The Fear-of-Crime Ad

While poll results indicate that feelings about crime and punishment are more complex than is commonly understood, such complexity is only rarely translated into media coverage. Although crime frequently soars to the top of the nation's list of major problems, those who follow public opinion have concluded that it is driven more by the media treatment of crime than by changes in crime rates.

—National Criminal Justice Commission, 1995[12]

An attractive female reporter stands outside an upscale apartment complex. In the background we can see a body being loaded into an ambulance. The blood-stained sheet is pulled over the victim's head to confirm the presence of a corpse. The reporter tells us that this is the last of three victims that police found when they arrived at the apartment after receiving a call that gunshots had been fired. The reporter turns to a police spokesman who says that this is one of the worst crimes he has ever encountered. The man describes the murders as "execution style" and tells the viewers that police are looking for witnesses and that people in the area should exercise extreme caution until a suspect or suspects can be apprehended.

Next, our reporter strolls over to a woman who lives in the complex. The woman is holding her hands over her mouth and is clearly distraught. She tells the viewing audience that she can't believe what has happened. "I always thought that this was a safe place," she says. "I mean, there are a lot of kids that play around here. We have a security gate." The reporter asks her if she is going to consider moving, in light of the murders. "I don't know. Maybe," responds the neighbor, who had clearly not considered moving until the question was asked. Finally, the reporter turns to the camera and offers a closing remark in her most sincere voice: "A lot of people who call these apartments home are very upset tonight. This is the kind of tragedy that most of us assume will never happen in our own neighborhoods. But as the residents here have learned all too well, it can happen anywhere. Back to you, Bob."[13]

If you are one of the 258 million Americans, 95 percent of us, who credit television newscasts as your primary source of information regarding crime,[14] I suspect that the above example of news coverage sounds all too familiar. In fact, it probably sounds nearly identical to what you saw and heard on your local newscast last night, last week, and last month. To the average citizen, this oft-repeated style of crime coverage seems anything but extraordinary, but to behavioral scientists, such repetitive messages of violence are a reason for concern.

Before we dissect the messages being conveyed by TV news coverage of crime, let's examine the central and peripheral "messages" found in a surprisingly similar source of information, an automobile ad that has been running on TV recently. The commercial shows a driver, a very attractive woman, in a sleek black utility vehicle hopelessly stuck in a downtown traffic jam. Just as the driver is starting to despair, she reaches downward and shifts the vehicle into four-wheel drive. She swerves out of the snarled traffic by driving though a construction site full of potholes, which eventually allows her to escape the crowded, noisy cityscape. After a few moments, she reaches a beautiful, rural setting where empty roads wind their way toward a mountain range on the horizon. By the commercial's end, our model is grinning from ear to ear.

The dialogue in this commercial (the central message) simply tells us details about the vehicle and its cost. But the commercial's peripheral messages, expressed through its visual imagery, tell us a number of things. They say that if we buy this vehicle, our lives will be less hectic and that all our worries will be left behind. They tell us that attractive people, those whose opinions behavioral scientists say mean the most to us, buy this type of car. And finally, the curving mountain roads reveal that people with a sense of adventure, a quality that the experts say we all wish we had more of, prefer this particular vehicle. But does this type of "hidden-message" advertising really work to change our attitudes in the desired manner? Does it really make us want to buy that car? Of course it does.

Would companies spend an estimated $150 billion a year—an amount equal to the criminal-justice budget—on such ads if they weren't a proven commodity?[15] We may not run out and buy that car, but the underlying message that consumerism can make us happy sticks with us.

Now consider the formula for most TV-news crime coverage. First, we see the injured victim on a stretcher, a pool of blood on a sidewalk, or some other equally dramatic image that tells us that something terrible has occurred. Next, we are exposed to interviews with tearful victims, their loved ones, neighbors, or witnesses, who tell us details about the carnage that has transpired. News organizations often determine how much time a story will get during a newscast based solely upon how emotional these testimonies are, not upon a story's overall importance to the community.[16]

Eventually, we see the suspect—usually handcuffed and attempting to hide his or her face from the prying eyes of the camera—being led into a jail or put into a police car. And if it is a particularly spectacular crime, we will get to hear from the victim(s) or their loved ones on a regular basis for several months as the case makes its way through the criminal-justice system. Media corporations have found that such follow-up coverage is not only a good audience draw that requires minimal effort to produce but is extremely cost-effective as well, as often more than one story can be covered by one crew in a single locale such as the courthouse.[17] But does this type of repetitive news coverage constitute a message, and if so, what is it telling us?

When we see the pain on the faces of victims and their loved ones and hear their heart-wrenching stories, it conveys to us that being victimized by crime is physically and emotionally devastating. The impact of this part of the message is increased dramatically by such accompanying visuals as the image of splattered blood, a shattered window, or perhaps a quick camera pan of family photos from the victim's fireplace mantle. In addition to the message provided by the victim(s), loved ones, or witnesses, an attractive reporter offers the central message by telling us facts such as the address, the victim's name, the suspect's name, the nature of the crime, and the status of the case with law enforcement. Usually this description is laced with words like "tragedy," "unbelievable," "nightmare," "unnecessary," or "war zone." The reporter's physical appearance makes all of the messages, both central and peripheral, have more impact.

As for the peripheral messages in such coverage, there are plenty. Most often, the suspects we see on our TVs are black—blacks are twice as likely as any other ethnic group to be shown as criminals on TV, even though the majority of crimes are committed by nonblacks—and this of course tells us that we should be afraid of "those people."[18] When we see the suspect being led into a jail or pushed into a police car, the message is that law enforcement is swift and proficient and that we must depend upon it for our safety. A suspect who attempts to hide his or her face from the camera tells us that criminals are cowards who can not own up to what they have done. Suspects that do face the camera are considered to be callous and unrepentant for their actions.

In other words, we perceive the actions of the prisoner to be negative no matter what form they take. This is because we view criminals through the lens of a preexisting negative bias. And finally, the image of a handcuffed suspect being led to jail confirms that crime equals punishment. And we are thrilled with this concept because we have become angry at the suspect as we have seen the pain of the victims with our own eyes. In many ways, you could describe the uniformed and repetitive news coverage of violent crimes as an ad designed to sell us on the fear of crime and the need for more law enforcement—an ad that is clearly working on the majority of us.

As much as all of us would like to believe that we are above the power of television when it comes to its ability to persuade us this way or that, it just isn't true. Our being influenced by advertising or similar repetitive messages such as those regarding crime does not depend on our intelligence or even on our awareness that someone is manipulating us. It simply depends upon our exposure to the images. The fact that we do not run out and buy a new car does not mean that the message has not affected our subconscious in some way.

Methods of Persuasion

Over the last fifty years, behavioral scientists have spent a great deal of time researching the process of persuasion. Their findings have now become the science upon which the advertising industry is built. Because each of us is different, it can be expected that the success or failure of individual persuasion techniques will very greatly depending on the targeted subject's background—ethnicity, education, gender, and so on.

With that in mind, I have chosen to take a brief look at seven factors that help to explain how TV's violent content persuades us to alter our attitudes and subsequently our behavior when it comes to crime and criminals. Although few of us are likely to be heavily influenced by all seven, fewer still are completely immune to their influence. In the end, most of us are likely being influenced to varying degrees by some combination of these powerful persuaders. My descriptions of these seven persuaders rely heavily on the work of Richard E. Petty and John T. Cacioppo as published in their book, *Attitudes and Persuasion: Classic and Contemporary Approaches*.[19]

Vicarious Classical Conditioning

This particular persuader helps to explain not only why watching television violence makes us overly concerned about crime but also why we tend to accept television experiences as real-life experiences. Since the first studies examined vicarious classical conditioning in 1962, we have been aware that repeatedly being exposed to the suffering of others does affect our own attitudes and subsequently our behavior. The first study of vicarious conditioning involved an experiment where subjects were repeatedly forced to witness what they thought was a person experiencing pain from an electrical shock. Each time the fake shock was sent through the body of the model, the lights dimmed and the model flinched.[20] Eventually, those witnessing the shocks began to grimace each time the person jerked, and in the end, those witnessing the theatrics showed their discomfort at nothing more than a dimming light. In other words, they were sharing the seemingly painful experience of the model vicariously.

So what happens to television viewers who are repeatedly exposed to the very real fear and pain of those who have been victimized by violent crime? To some degree their fear, pain, and anger become our fear, pain, and anger vicariously. And this vicarious fear and pain changes our attitudes regarding crime and criminals in a manner similar to what might be expected to happen were we victimized ourselves. Because of this tendency to experience things vicariously, we can emotionally experience what we see on TV. Once again, our viewing of television becomes a sort of hybrid between mediated message and firsthand experience.

Vicarious conditioning helps to explain why a body of research, including the 1994–1995 *National Television Violence Profile*, has found that the more a person watches television, the more fearful that person becomes, and this fear results in a feeling of vulnerability that ultimately leads to anxiety.[21]

Incentives

Another powerful factor in persuasion is "incentives." For our purposes, "incentives" are defined as "promised or expected rewards." For example, the statement "We must spend more tax dollars on education" is a weak argument when it comes to persuading people to let go of their money. "We must spend more tax dollars on education in order to save our children and our way of life" is a much more persuasive argument because it offers a strong incentive in the form of saving kids, and so forth. So what is the incentive in the message of crime coverage as well as in virtually all modern political campaigns? The answer is: public safety. Whether it's the image of a handcuffed suspect being led to jail or a politician telling us that more prisons will make us safer, the crime message's incentive is always the same: "public safety." Politicians in particular use this incentive persuader come election time in the form of the hard-on-crime rhetoric.

The reason that hard-on-crime political rhetoric works so well to motivate voters is because "fear," coupled with an "incentive," is one of the most powerful persuasive forces known, according to behavioral scientists. In *Attitudes and Persuasion*, Petty and Cacioppo noted:

> In sum, fear-arousing messages are effective in inducing attitude change particularly when the following three conditions are met: (a) the message provides strong arguments for the possibility of the recipient suffering some extremely negative consequence; (b) the arguments explain that these negative consequences are very likely if the recommendations are not accepted; and (c) it provides strong assurances that adoption of the recommendations effectively eliminates these negative consequences.[22]

If you are thinking that these three points sound like the outline for virtually every candidate's crime position since the Willie Horton ads devastated the Dukakis presidential campaign in 1988, you're right. Politicians now know, through modern polling techniques, that we are afraid of crime. Consequently, their savvy handlers—the political consultants—have convinced them to use the research of behavioral scientists and advertising agencies to help them create an anticrime argument to persuade us to vote for them. They simply follow the formula described by Petty and Cacioppo's book: (1) it is no longer safe for our women and children to walk our streets; (2) if we do not stop coddling criminals and start punishing them, there will be more and more victims, and next time, it could be *your* wife, *your* daughter, or *your* elderly mother; and finally, (3) if you elect me, I will work to put an end to "country-club" prisons, and I will vote for the three-strikes law that will keep the most dangerous criminals off our streets forever.

It's right out of a psychology textbook, and it works like a charm. That's why the 1995 *Report of the National Criminal Justice Commission* noted that nearly all politicians elected to a national, state, or local office in the previous ten years had followed this hard-on-crime formula to persuade us to give them our vote.[23] Because our feelings about crime are generated from our TV sets instead of reality, this anticriminal formula for being elected even works in places where crime is virtually nonexistent.

A few years ago, the residents of a small tranquil town in rural West Virginia told pollsters that the single most pressing problem in their community was violent crime. This was quite extraordinary, considering that the town had not had a single murder in over two decades and street crime was virtually nonexistent. The only violent crimes taking place in this town were those happening in the residents' living rooms on their TV sets. But rather than pointing out the absurdity of the community's crime anxiety, a local candidate built his campaign platform around an anticrime message that went so far as to promise to completely abolish parole for all individuals convicted of a violent act, even though there were no such people in the community.[24] This hard-on-crime rhetoric not only resulted in the politician's election but also confirmed to the population that their fear of being victimized was justified. Media-generated fear, coupled with the politically promised incentive of safety, is an extraordinarily powerful one-two punch that transports men and women to the voting booth to pull the hard-on-crime lever.

The Source

There is a mountain of scientific studies that have found that the "source" of a message can be a more powerful persuader than even the message itself. Research in this area reveals that the most powerful sources are the ones that hearers of the message believe to be nonmanipulative or physically attractive, or both. In other words, if we suspect that the source is trying to change our minds, we are more likely to reject the message. Since we tend to view movies and other fictional media as entertainment and not as an attempt by anyone to persuade us toward a particular way of thinking, fictional crime messages are actually empowered. Under this same theory, journalists can also be assumed to be very powerful persuaders as well, because the public believes them to be objective, agenda-free sources for information—even though, as we have seen, this is a misconception that doesn't take into account the profit motive in selecting content.

Not only are TV news anchors perceived to be objective, they are generally hired because they are attractive physically, and this, too, adds more power to their messages of fear. Research tells us that when the source of the message is "good-looking," we tend to be more easily persuaded by the information presented. One study actually found that when we receive information from two sources, an "expert," on the one hand, and a "pretty face," on the other, we are more likely to be persuaded by the message of the attractive person, even though intellectually we know better than to do so. It is another example of a powerful peripheral route to persuasion. Our "I like attractive people" attitude overrides our belief that "experts on an issue are the best source for reliable information."

Mere Thought

"Mere thought" is a process of persuasion that can be best described as what goes on in our minds in between the crime messages. Psychologists tell us that our thought processes are controlled by "schema." According to Petty and Cacioppo, a schema is

> a preexisting bias a person has that provides a framework or structure for beliefs on a particular issue. In addition to organizing beliefs, a schema can be viewed as a subjective theory that guides a person in processing information. The schema helps the person decide what to attend to and what to ignore and tells the person how different pieces of the information should be related.[25]

Here's an example of how "mere thought" works with a schema: You really love ice cream. You meet a person, spend a little time with them, and decide that you like them. The subject of ice cream never comes up in your conversation. But because of "mere thought," psychologists tell us that there is a strong possibility that you will assume that the person you met likes ice cream. You like ice cream. You like the new person. Therefore, the new person must also like ice cream. This method of thinking provides us with another important element of thought known as "balance," which we will discuss in a moment. In essence, "mere thought" is the process of using our preexisting bias, or schema, to fill in the blanks about people or issues. Behavioral scientists believe that the end result of this process is that it leads to more extreme or exaggerated attitudes regarding the world around us. The more we think about something we like, the more we will tend to ignore its negative qualities, and therefore, we like it still more. The opposite is also true.

Since we are never presented with the root causes of crime (poverty, and so on) as a part of the crime message, we do not hear or see anything regarding criminals that might elicit any emotional response other than fear, anger, or contempt. As a result of being exposed to context-free crime messages, the majority of us have a preexisting negative schema toward criminals. Since the stories told by media and politicians convey that being victimized is painful, we can assume that as we apply "mere thought" to these messages of apprehension, we will fill in the blanks with additional anxiety-inducing information. The end result is that the level of our fear and hatred of criminals becomes more extreme than what even the exaggerated one-sided messages of the media and politicians warrant, let alone the crime rates.

Balance

As I mentioned previously, the notion of "balance" is important to our mental well-being. Behavioral scientists have developed what is known as the "balance theory," and this theory sheds still more light on our attitudes toward crime. Imagine that "balance" is the part of our thinking that is exposed to some degree when we are shown flash cards with a word on them and are requested to say the first thing that pops into our mind. For example:

Flashcard: ice cream
Response: "tastes good" or maybe "fattening"

It doesn't matter whether you think positively or negatively about ice cream. What is important is to see that your mind is organized in a manner that makes sense to you and gives order to your world. Psychologists tell us we have a strong need for this order, or "balance," as they call it, because it helps us to feel that we are in control of our surroundings. On a very basic level, it helps us to make easy sense out of complicated issues.

Research has found that when we are *out* of balance, we experience an unpleasant state of tension, hence our desire to remain *in* balance. When we are presented with information (messages) that creates imbalance, our minds naturally reformulate our attitudes to restore balance. For instance, the notion that "ice cream" "tastes good" works for you until your doctor tells you that you're going to have a stroke if you don't lose the fat. At first, there is imbalance because of the new message. Then, in an effort to restore balance, your attitude changes to "fat-free ice cream" "tastes good." You were persuaded by the doctor's message and had to adjust your thinking to maintain balance and avoid tension.

Ask your friends to blurt out a corresponding word to the prompt word "crime" or "criminal." You will find that most of us feel balanced with responses such as "punishment," "victim," "death," "prison," or some other similarly negative response. I've been playing this word game for quite a while now, and I have yet to hear the responses of "poverty" or "rehabilitation," even though one would think that these words would occasionally turn up based on our knowledge of the forces that influence people toward a life of crime.

The reason that the concepts of poverty and rehabilitation are missing in action is because most of us have subconsciously achieved a state of "balance" in our response, not to the facts about crime but to the mediated messages regarding crime. In other words, since we are confronted with the false and exaggerated crime message daily, we have subconsciously adjusted our attitudes about crime in such a manner as to avoid a tension-causing conflict with the messages that are coming in. Fearing crime and wanting to punish criminals achieves balance with our culture's mediated messages concerning crime.

Remember, it is our attitudes, not our beliefs, that ultimately determine our behavior. So even though people may believe that the justice system's first priority should be reform and not warehousing as a means of punishment, it's quite likely that their attitude has been pushed in an anticriminal direction by the oft-repeated messages of media and politicians. Experts tell us that our need for balance is capable of altering our attitudes despite our beliefs. This helps to explain why Americans are currently voting (behavior) for politicians who are dictating a form of justice (prisons should punish instead of reform) that is in direct conflict with society's stated beliefs about justice (prisons should serve as a means to reform).

Forget the Details

One of the reasons that television's violent content—both news and entertainment programming—can effectively persuade us to fear crime is because over time, we tend to remember only the message, not the specifics. A study conducted in 1949, whose findings have been confirmed many times since, found that people tend to retain the substance of a message long after they have forgotten the particulars, such as the message's source.[26] For our purposes of examining the media's violent content, this means that we remember that crime is painful, violent, and pervasive long after we have forgotten what particular crimes we saw on television last week or last month. This quirk of memory retention means that crime coverage likely has a cumulative effect when it comes to changing our attitudes toward crime and criminals. It also helps to explain why fictional violent content affects our attitudes about crime and criminals in much the same manner as nonfictional violence.

Because we forget the sources of most messages after a relatively short period of time, as far as our subconscious is concerned, mediated crime messages are all the same, regardless of whether we saw them on the news or in some forgettable late-night movie. In other words, to some degree, the fictional Hannibal Lecter—the cannibalizing criminal from the movie *The Silence of the Lambs*—becomes as much a conveyer of fear as the very real Jeffrey Dahmer. When it comes to molding our attitudes as opposed to our beliefs, fictional crime messages are quite possibly as powerful as the nonfictional variety.

One-Sided Messages

And finally, behavioral scientists have found that the most persuasive messages are those that are one-sided. We have already discussed how the vast majority of the crime messages we are exposed to certainly fit into the one-sided category, as the vast majority of what we hear and see about crime comes from only three sources—news organizations, the messages provided by entertainment content, and the hard-on-crime rhetoric of politicians. We have discussed the limited information being conveyed to viewers by television crime coverage, so let's look at the missing side, the "other side" of the news message.

Information about poverty's role as the major influence on most criminals is almost never discussed by the press, nor are the demographic realities of violent crime, such as the facts that violent crime is extremely rare, that it occurs for the most part in isolated low-income communities, and that, as a rule, the victim and the perpetrator knew each other.

As for the media's one-sided message regarding crime and punishment, the missing information that could greatly alter our behavior on this subject is found in the rarely reported economic and rehabilitative realities of incarceration. When we decide to sentence a convicted felon into our prison system, statistics tell us that we are all but guaranteeing that the individual will commit future crimes upon release as a result of the prisonization effect. Think of what this means in practical terms.

When we couple the existence of hard-on-crime sentencing laws— such as three strikes—with the power of prisonization, we are basically creating a scenario where taxpayers will eventually be picking up multi-million-dollar prison tabs for many of the people we initially sentence into prison for trivial, nonviolent offenses such as breaking marijuana laws. In 1999, one out of six federal prisoners are being incarcerated because of some marijuana offense.[27] It's a pretty simple formula: We know that somewhere in the neighborhood of 30 percent of those placed in our prison system are going to reoffend within three years of their release due in large degree to the prisonization effect.[28] And those who do reoffend three times in some jurisdictions can be sentenced to life behind bars due to the three-strikes laws. This is a recipe for economic disaster—a recipe that the media is not discussing in its context-free messages of crime.

Similarly, presenting the "other side" of crime's political arguments would also be helpful. When was the last time you heard a political speech that suggested that well-supervised parole or probation programs or drug treatment offer a criminal a better chance for successful rehabilitation than prison? Where are the politicos explaining that enlarging our prison system at the expense of social programs will, in the end, only produce more, not fewer, criminals? You haven't heard these arguments because just as two-sided news reporting works against the media's bottom line, politicians cannot speak operatively about crime without risking the outcome of their next election. In fact, in light of the media's vision of a world overwhelmed with violent crime, any politician who dared to speak about crime in accurate terms would be branded a soft-on-crime liberal by the next opponent—hardly a recipe for political success in the 1990s.

Even the crime messages being conveyed by entertainment programs are completely one-sided. The extensive 1994–1995 *National Television Violence Profile* stated, "The context in which most violence is presented on television poses a risk for viewers." This report pointed out that "[p]erpetrators [of crime] go unpunished in 73 percent of all violent scenes, and the negative consequences of violence are not often portrayed in violent programming. Only 4 percent of violent programs emphasize an anti-violence theme." The report also noted that programming rarely showed "the long-term negative consequences of violence."[29]

As a result of their findings, those conducting the study concluded:

> The majority of programs analyzed in this study contain some violence. But more important than the prevalence of violence is the contextual pattern in which most of it is shown. The risk of viewing the most common depictions of televised violence include learning to behave violently, becoming more desensitized to the harmful consequences of violence, and *becoming more fearful of being attacked*. The contextual patterns noted are found consistently across most channels, program types, and times of day. Thus, there are substantial risks of harmful effects from viewing violence throughout the television environment. (emphasis added)[30]

The Amplifier Effect

The cumulative result of constantly being bombarded with persuasive mediated messages regarding crime is what I call the "amplifier effect." For example, if you've ever watched a Senate hearing on TV violence or violence in the film industry, you have heard the industry defenders of such programming argue that they are simply *reflecting* what is happening in the world, not *causing* what is happening. But based on what we have been discussing, this is not completely true. Since we know that after a period of time we tend to remember the message yet forget the source, it stands to reason that our fear of crime is "amplified" through the entertainment industry's "reflection" of society.

Remember, crime statistics tell us that only about 3 percent of all real crimes involve physical injury to the victim, and the physical-injury category would include victims who received a minor cut or a black eye. Thus, it is obviously safe to say that far less than 1 percent of crimes could be construed to be sensational violent crimes. Yet in their attempt to mirror these sensational crimes of violence, media owners have committed the majority of their total programming to the cause. That means that for every real crime of violence that the industry claims to be mirroring, we are exposed to thousands of television violent crimes.

Fiction and nonfiction entertainment programming not only amplifies our fear by exposing us to crimes over and over again, but it amplifies our fear by only exposing us to the most gruesome examples of crimes. Consider that when the nonfiction crime show *American Detective* set out to find real crime stories with which to entertain us, it had very specific guidelines for its staff. According to one of the show's producers, employees were ordered to scour the country for the most sensational and gory examples of crime. A supervisor for the show posted on a bulletin board helpful guidelines for determining what sort of crimes qualified. The guidelines were: "Death, Stab, Shoot, Strangulation, Club, and Suicide."[31] This is hardly an accurate reflection of crime in America.

Here are a couple of other practical examples of amplifying a real crime. In 1994, Amy Fisher shot Mary Jo Buttafuoco, the wife of her older lover, Joey Buttafuoco. For no other reason than the pursuit of ratings, the media covered this event with the saturation usually reserved for an attempted assassination of a president. As if that weren't enough, all three major networks produced made-for-TV versions of the Amy Fisher story. Ratings showed that all three recreations were among the most-watched programs the week that they aired.[32] In the four years since the shooting, numerous interviews with Ms. Fisher have aired on programs where the shooting was, once again, reenacted.

In the same fashion, we were first exposed to the murder of Nicole Brown Simpson at the time the real crime occurred, again during O. J. Simpson's criminal trial, again at his civil trial, and yet again when similar plots began showing up in TV cop dramas. It has now been several years since Simpson was nearly decapitated with a knife, and even now, hardly a month goes by that this crime doesn't find its way into our homes by way of the TV screen. Even though this overkill of exposure is clearly only reflecting reality, it has likely had the same effect on our attitude toward crime as a hundred very real, very gruesome murders. Such media saturation of a crime does far more than reflect reality; it greatly amplifies the message that we should be afraid.

It would be hard to overestimate the impact of cable television when it comes to the amplifier effect. In 1998, when a deranged young man murdered his parents and later opened fire on his classmates at his high school in Springfield, Oregon, news coverage of the event was overwhelming. Network newscasts devoted one-third or roughly ten minutes of their allotted time to the story. They also interrupted other programming several times with special reports. Local newscasts did the same. A mere twenty-five years ago, this approximate one to two hours of coverage, which is substantial, would have been the extent of our exposure to this incident. But with the advent of cable, our exposure went up dramatically.

Several cable channels—Fox News, CNBC, CNN, and MSNBC—devoted as much as six hours of coverage each to the carnage that day, and both the networks and the cable stations continued to cover the violent event extensively for several days following the tragedy. The results of this massive exposure, in conjunction with similar coverage of two previous school shootings a few months earlier, are telling. Polls following the Oregon incident showed that parents had become more concerned than ever before about their children's safety while at school. Now consider how this societal impression (dangerous schools) contrasts with reality.

A study released in 1998 found that 90 percent of our public schools are safe and that violence in public schools has radically declined in recent years. But we were hardly inundated with hundreds of hours of coverage of safer schools. In fact, I only recall seeing this landmark study referred to once on an NBC newscast for approximately a minute and a half.[33]

As overhyped as the TV coverage of the Springfield shooting was, it paled in comparison to the media extravaganza that transpired following the April 1999 Columbine school shooting in Jefferson County, Colorado, where fifteen students died. Like a sequel to an action movie, the violence quotient went up dramatically in the Columbine coverage. The Columbine shooting received intense media exposure for more than two months following the tragedy. As I mentioned before, network and cable news programs, news magazines, and even the morning shows like *Today* and *Good Morning America* milked every rating point they could from the bloody shooting and its aftermath, including emotional coverage of the funerals of victims as well as the high school's graduation ceremony weeks later. If the news coverage of Springfield could make parents more afraid for their children while at school than ever before, then what would the fallout be from the unprecedented coverage of Columbine? Polls conducted a month after the shootings revealed the extent of the damage to America's psyche.

In early May 1999, a Washington-based consulting firm used focus groups from across the country in an effort to determine the mindset of voters. The groups were put together in Seattle, Oklahoma City, Denver, Los Angeles, and Baltimore and were composed of a broad cross-section of the citizenry. What the firm discovered was both disturbing and revealing. According to Celinda Lake, whose firm conducted the focus-group research, nine out of every ten participants described their view of the nation, both present and future, in negative terms, using such words as "anxious," "disappointed," "confused," and "depressed."[34]

What is perhaps most interesting about this finding is that just six months earlier, similar focus-group studies monitored by the same firm had shown that the majority of people had a positive outlook on the nation. Then why the radical reversal in opinion? Lake told reporters that the firm's research demonstrated that the negative worldview found among the focus-group participants was the result of the Columbine shooting and the air war over Yugoslavia.

Apparently, the sensationalized and saturation coverage of a gruesome crime had managed to alter people's impression of the world around them. Lake went on to tell reporters that she believes that the negative worldview sparked in large part by the Columbine tragedy will have a major impact on the political landscape for years to come, affecting issues such as pending gun-control legislation, crime bills, and even the way the 2000 presidential election unfolds.[35]

It would be hard to overestimate the media's ability to shape the public's view of the world around them, particularly when it comes to the issue of crime. In the 1990s, research has shown that many people believe that street crime is getting worse. In reality, the overall incidence of street crime has dropped. Robbery is down 17 percent during the past twenty years and forcible rape has dropped by over 30 percent, while the murder rate has remained nearly unchanged. Violent street crime in the 1990s is a full 16 percent below what it was in the 1970s. Even periods during the mid-1800s experienced waves of violence that were more severe than what we are experiencing today.[36]

It's not how much crime is taking place, it's how much crime we hear about or see on our TVs. For instance, thanks to 500 TV channels and countless nonfiction "cop" shows, we hear about more police officers being killed in the line of duty today than ever before, and as a result of "accepting mediated messages as experience," most Americans believe that more cops are being killed by criminals than ever before. Yet since 1973, the number of officers killed has dropped by more than half.[37]

In 1998, the Council for Excellence in Government conducted a study that further confirms television's ability to affect our worldview. The study looked at 2,664 television portrayals of those working in public institutions, including politicians, judges, and police. The study found that the majority of the time, television depicts these government employees as dishonest, incompetent, and mean. But more important, the council also researched how this overall negative portrayal affects the public's opinion of these officials. The study found that two-thirds of men and women between the ages of eighteen and thirty-four believe that television's negative representation of these public servants is actually accurate.[38] If television has the power to create such misconceptions regarding government employees, one can only imagine the persuasive power of television's portrayal of crime and criminals.

Misconceptions about crime exist because news organizations and entertainment programming present a false image of the overall character and quantity of crime. In response to this constant and misleading crime message, the majority of Americans today have been persuaded they are living in a much more dangerous and crime-infested world than they really are, and such an attitude is causing the nation to alter its behavior in a variety of ways.

Mean-World Syndrome

Our studies have shown that growing up from infancy with this unprecedented diet of violence has three consequences, which, in combination, I call the "mean world syndrome." What this means is that if you are grow-

ing up in a home where there is more than, say, three hours of television per day, for all practical purposes you live in a meaner world—and act accordingly—than your next-door neighbor who lives in the same world but watches less television. The programming reinforces the worst fears and apprehensions and paranoia of people.

—**George Gerbner, In Context, *1994*[39]**

In 1968, President Lyndon B. Johnson, through his National Commission on the Causes and Prevention of Violence, appointed Dr. George Gerbner of the Annenberg School of Communication at the University of Pennsylvania to analyze the content of television programming. This appointment kicked off the Cultural Indicators Project, which, in 1998, is the longest-running study of media content in the world. As a result of his thirty-plus years of research on the subject, Gerbner, often working in conjunction with other experts in the communications field, including Larry Gross, Michael Morgan, and Nancy Signorielli, has come to believe that constant exposure to the media's violent content has actually manifested itself in our society in the form of a group of disease symptoms that he has labeled "the mean world syndrome."

An overview of the sixteenth *Television Violence Profile* described the basis for and the consequences of this syndrome as follows:

The analysis of large national probability surveys indicates that long-term exposure to television tends to make an independent contribution to the feeling of living in a mean and gloomy world. The "lessons" range from aggression to desensitization and to a sense of vulnerability and dependence.

Heavy viewers are more likely than comparable groups of light viewers to overestimate one's chances of involvement in violence; to believe that one's neighborhood is unsafe; to state that fear of crime is a very serious personal problem; and to assume that crime is rising, regardless of the facts of the case. Heavier viewers in every subgroup (defined by education, age, income, gender, newspaper reading, neighborhood, etc.) express a greater sense of insecurity and mistrust than do light viewers in the same groups. . . . This unequal sense of danger, vulnerability and general unease, combined with reduced sensitivity, invites not only aggression but also exploitation and repression. That is the deeper problem of violence-laden television.[40]

There have been a wide variety of media studies that have concluded that violent content breeds fear and anxiety. The Rocky Mountain Media Watch 1997 study found that the violent content—43 percent of the total content of local news coverage—results in a fear of crime among viewers.[41] Another 1997 study, conducted by the University of Miami's communication school, found that crime coverage on the local news took up double the airtime of reports on politics, education, and health combined. According to Joe Angotti, who directed the Miami study, "I think it has a numbing effect on the public. *People withdraw from activities because of fear*" (emphasis added).[42]

The National Television Violence Profile Scientific Papers 1994–1995 stated:

> There is a general consensus in the scientific and public health fields that there are three primary harmful effects of viewing media violence: 1) Learning aggressive attitudes and behaviors; 2) Emotional desensitization toward real world violence; 3) *Increased fear of being victimized by violence, resulting in self-protective behaviors and mistrust of others.* (emphasis added)[43]

In speaking of the ability of violent content to affect television viewers, Todd Gitlin told *Wired* magazine that "the more violence they watch, the more dangerous they think the world is. They may therefore support heavy-handed, authoritarian responses to crime. . . . TV versions of violence are egregious, coarsening, and produce a social fear and anesthesia which damage our capacity to face reality."[44] I can honestly say that I have yet to find a single study of television violence that has even made an attempt to dispute violent content's ability to create an exaggerated sense of vulnerability among the public.

Since research confirms that continuous exposure to this content affects our attitudes, what exactly does this mean with regard to our behavior? Studies at the Annenberg School have found evidence of specific ways in which "the mean world syndrome" has caused many in the general population to alter their behavior. The research shows that heavy viewers of television are more likely than light viewers to have purchased new locks for their doors and guns for their personal protection and to have acquired guard dogs. They are more afraid to walk in their own neighborhoods, especially at night.[45]

Research has also found that violent content makes people more susceptible to repression by authorities. That is to say, heavy television watchers are more likely to welcome government repression in the form of a larger law-enforcement presence or diminishing protections of personal liberties if such changes are wrapped in promises of increased public safety, which will relieve the heavy viewer's anxieties. The "mean world syndrome" may actually result in a demand for repression from the government.[46]

What the research is telling us is that repeated exposure to media violence makes us more susceptible to hard-on-crime political messages, whether it's the labeling of judges as "soft on crime," declaring "wars" on crime or drugs, or calling for an increase in the use of capital punishment as a means of enhancing our security. Gerbner has concluded that this vulnerability to hard-on-crime rhetoric among those whose worldview has been shaped by media violence "has enormous political fallout." He further noted that it has become "impossible to run an election campaign without advocating more jails, harsher punishment, more executions, all the things that have never worked to reduce crime but have always worked to get votes. It's driven largely, although not exclusively, by television-cultivated insecurity."[47] This television-generated insecurity has been the focal point of a number of studies in recent years.

Dr. Grace Ferrari Levine, a professor of mass communications at Quinnipiac College, has been researching this TV content phenomenon and refers to it as "learned helplessness." In particular, Levine's studies have analyzed the impact of television news on the viewer. In 1986, she summed up her findings in an article for *Journalism Quarterly*.[48] Levine's research found that in the local newscasts she monitored, an astounding "71.4 percent of the time [of overall news programming] was given to segments where some degree of helplessness was a point of focus." This finding was similar to that of another study that had used NBC programming as a model. In the article, Levine noted that television news tends to focus on action and drama to hold the attention and interest of the audience and that it is this combination that results in an enhanced sense of helplessness on the part of the viewer.

Levine believes that this style of sensationalized news coverage raises several important questions.

Might the need for newscasts that evoke emotional response be a contributing factor in what appears to be a disproportionate emphasis on human crisis and misfortune? Might exposure to newscasts which dramatize the plight of crisis victims cultivate in viewers the sense that the environment is beyond human control? Might such a belief affect viewer expectations in regard to their own ability to effect change?[49]

Based on her research, the apparent answer to all of these questions is "yes." Levine also points out that this same trend had been confirmed by many media critics, media practitioners, and social scientists.

Martin Seligman of the Annenberg School is one of these other experts studying the effects of "learned helplessness." Seligman has reached this conclusion: "Helplessness is a disaster for organisms capable of learning that they are helpless. Three types of disruption are caused by uncontrollability in the laboratory: the motivation to respond is sapped, the ability to perceive success is undermined, and emotionality is heightened."[50]

In 1998, I asked Levine if it was accurate to say that the sensationalized structure of today's television news creates a feeling of dependence upon outside forces such as law enforcement for a viewer's safety. Although Levine did make the point that more research needs to be done on the subject, she also acknowledged that such a feeling of dependence does appear to be one drawback to the increasing amount of overdramatized news content designed specifically to lure viewers.

A Supreme Court decision in May 1999 provided further evidence that highly dramatized news coverage of crime is shaping public opinion and that the media is well aware of this fact. In a case revolving around the question of whether police departments could be sued for invasion of privacy because they had permitted members of the press to "ride along" during raids on suspect's homes, legal arguments shed light on the fact that media content manipulates viewers' impressions of law enforcement.

The legal arguments in the case were put forward by lawyers representing the police departments, but since the court's ruling threatened to eliminate one of TV's most profitable genres of programming— cheaply produced, sensationalized real-life police dramas such as Cops—no less than twenty-four news organizations filed friend-of-the-court briefs in support of the case. One argument put forward by the police and media organizations stated that allowing the media to shoot footage of actual police busts should be continued because "it promoted crime-fighting efforts."[51]

This argument raises an issue every bit as weighty as that of the right to privacy. Since when is it the news media's job to "promote crime-fighting efforts"? In the end, the court sided with privacy and against the police and media. Chief Justice Rehnquist stated, "Surely the possibility of good public relations for the police is simply not enough . . . to justify the ride-along intrusion into a home." Rehnquist also noted that journalists could accurately report on crime without going along for the ride with a camera.[52]

This case demonstrates that those who control the new dramatized and ratings-driven journalism not only realize that their content manipulates public opinion but apparently don't see anything wrong with doing so as long as it increases the size of their audience. CBS news executive Van Gordon Sauter, for example, has said that the "kind of thing we're looking for is something that evokes an emotional response. When I go back there to the fishbowl [newsroom], I tell them . . . we've got to touch people. They've got to feel a relationship with us. A lot of stories have inherent drama, but others have to be done in a way that will bring out an emotional response."[53] Sauter's last statement clearly explains the new role of journalism. It is no longer to serve the public by reporting the news but rather to create emotion through drama, which increases the audience for the advertiser.

The existence of so much research regarding the negative impact of violent content and the fact that those who control our mediated messages admit that they are intentionally dramatizing their product raises an important question: Are the media corporations aware of the damage that their sensationalized vision of crime is causing? Sadly, I believe that they are. I say this because it is clear that media owners are acutely aware of the power that media-generated fear wields within the general population.

Consider what happens every time we see a significant plunge in the stock market, for instance. We are immediately inundated with market analysts and other economic "experts" telling us that everything is "OK." News programs trot out Federal Reserve representatives to tell us that the economy is fundamentally sound and that we have nothing to fear. Following the major market correction in July 1998, we were even bombarded with fear-dispelling commercials where actors told us that they weren't worried and, more important, weren't considering selling their stocks because over the long haul, everyone always makes money in the market. Toward the end of 1998 and in early 1999, these commercials flooded the airways every time the market retreated even a few points. Such television content is clearly designed as a preemptive approach to quelling market fears.

These cliché-spouting experts, those who produce the commercials, and the media corporations who give or sell them airtime clearly realize that if a societal fear goes unchecked, it has the potential to cause damaging behavior on the part of the public—in this instance, to destroy market profits for corporations via Wall Street. For example, GE exec Jack Welch told Lawrence Grossman, his news director at the time of the 1987 stock market crash, to stop referring to the incident as "Black Monday" because he (Welch) believed that such references on television had the power to negatively impact the price of stocks such as GE's.[54]

Now contrast this oft-practiced, prop-up-the-market, media fire drill with the total silence regarding the general public's media-derived fear of crime. It would stand to reason that the deafening silence aimed toward crime fear is just as well orchestrated by those in the media business as the instant and massive effort to quash market fears. Soothing the concerns of the public when it comes to the stock market protects the media corporations' shareholders. Doing nothing to quell the nation's anxiety over crime, which results from the media's excessive use of violence to increase profits, likewise protects the shareholder—but at what cost to the rest of us?

5

The Politics of Public Opinion

The Taking Back Our Streets Act

[We promise to pass] [a]n anti-crime package including stronger truth-in-sentencing, "good faith" exclusionary rule exemptions, effective death penalty provisions, and cuts in social spending from this summer's "crime" bill to fund prison construction and additional law enforcement to keep people secure in their neighborhoods and kids safe in their schools.

—**Republican Party, Contract with America, 1994**

If I had to choose one example to illustrate the political promise of increasing public safety through hard-on-crime policies, it would be the above section of the Republican Party's Contract with America. This one paragraph represents all that is wrong with our war on crime. Based on the massive dose of persuasive misinformation being conveyed by these forty-nine words, it would have been more appropriate had the contract been dropped on Americans from fighter jets roaring overhead.

First of all, the contract is the quintessential example of designing campaign platforms based upon public opinion polls. The Republicans did a masterful job of creating a simple one-page document that speaks to virtually every issue that pollsters have determined is of great concern to the American public in a manner that appeals to the electorate's already existing opinions. Unfortunately, real facts and figures were clearly given little or no consideration when preparing this campaign tool. If the public perceived there was a problem, the contract confirmed its existence. When opinion polls suggested a fix, such as being harder on crime, the contract embraced the public's recommended solution, no matter how out of touch with reality it was.

Next, the contract illustrates how hard-on-crime rhetoric serves as propaganda—a message designed to be a powerful persuader. The title of section 2 of the contract, "The Taking Back Our Streets Act," implies that we have lost control of our streets to crime. But as we have seen, this simply isn't true. Most people are safer now than they were twenty-five years ago, and at the time the contract was written, crime was already well into its decline. The real reason for such a sensationalized heading is to reinforce the level of fear that pollsters have found in a public saturated by violent media messages.

The contract then promises that the imaginary crime wave alluded to in the title can be defeated if only we will escalate the death penalty, build more prisons, add more cops, and lengthen sentences. Once again, this sounds good to people suffering from an exaggerated sense of their vulnerability to violent crime, but in reality, the majority of criminologists believe that each of these proposed remedies has little or no impact on crime rates. That being the case, it would seem that such suggestions serve the same purpose for the prison-industrial complex in the 1990s as the imaginary "missile gap" of the late 1950s did for the military-industrial complex—they justify increased spending.

The contract even goes so far as to admit that it will fund its new prisons and other anticriminal measures by diverting money out of social programs that have been shown to be a deterrent to criminal behavior. And finally, the contract offers the all-important "incentive" through its claim that more cops, more prisons, longer sentences, and more executions will "keep people secure in their neighborhoods and kids safe in their schools." And we all live happily thereafter, I suppose.

If you still have any doubt about the purpose of the Contract with America, just compare this cliché-ridden section of the contract on crime with the previously discussed three-pronged process of persuasion described by Petty and Cacioppo in *Attitudes and Persuasion,* which as you may recall says:

> In sum, fear-arousing messages are effective in inducing attitude change particularly when the following three conditions are met: (a) the message provides strong arguments for the possibility of the recipient suffering some extremely negative consequence; (b) the arguments explain that these negative consequences are very likely if the recommendations are not accepted; and (c) it provides strong assurances that adoption of the recommendations effectively eliminates these negative consequences.

As you can see, there's a shocking similarity, and it's no coincidence.[1]

Welcome to the real war on crime—a political war of "crime-gap" propaganda designed to transform society's media-generated crime anxiety into political capital. Once again, it is not just Republicans who are playing the crime-fear game. Consider the title of Democrat Bill Clinton's latest crime legislation, announced in the White House Rose Garden on May 12, 1999—the "Twenty-First Century Law Enforcement and Public Safety Act." Not only does this title and the act to which it refers fit nearly as perfectly with the Petty and Cacioppo model of persuasion as did the crime section of the Republicans' Contract with America, but Clinton added a nice visual effect for media consumption as well. According to the press release issued for the event, Clinton announced his support for the hard-on-crime act in front of a small army of police officers, who formed a living blue backdrop by standing on risers behind the man who has become their favorite benefactor. The same man who took credit in the Rose Garden that day for having added 100,000 cops to the streets since taking office.[2] An interesting accomplishment for a "liberal Democrat."

Even though the war on crime is being enthusiastically waged by politicians of both parties, I do not think that for the most part, politicians deserve credit for launching this assault on America. It seems more than a coincidence that the beginning of the war on crime coincided with the rise in influence of paid political consultants and the subsequent increase in the use of public opinion polling as a means of shaping rhetoric and policy. I believe that it is this political evolution that is primarily responsible for meshing the cogs of the media and political components of the perpetual prisoner machine. Incredibly, this increasing use of public opinion polls has been misinterpreted by many as a positive step for our democracy.

The Source of Opinion

In late 1998, I was watching an episode of *Politically Incorrect*, a sort of celebrity-filled version of the *McLaughlin Group*. Unlike many of my peers, I believe that this show has served at least one important purpose. It has once and for all exposed the fact that the vast majority of the celebrities that America so often turns to for political guidance are, in reality, vacuous conglomerates of hair and makeup with less insight than the average third grader—but I digress. On this particular night, a discussion ensued, or rather broke out, regarding Bill Clinton's excessive use of public opinion polls to help him determine policy positions as well as what he should say, what he wears, even where he vacations.

The generally astute host of the show, Bill Maher, made an interesting observation during this segment. He implied that such dependence on the public's opinion by politicians might mean that democracy had been improved, that the people are getting more of a say in how things are being handled in Washington. Although I doubt that Maher actually believes what he said—he does not generally exhibit such confidence in the electorate's mental acuity—the crowd nonetheless erupted in wild applause. Cut to commercial.

In a different time or place, Maher's analysis of the impact of polling would certainly have had more merit than today. After all, the idea of a democracy is that government should reflect the will of the people. Unfortunately, that is not what results from government by polls in the 1990s. This line of thinking fails to take into account the source of the public's opinion, the nine or so supercorporations that now control the majority of the world's media content and their second-tier counterparts. Even in our past, when polls tended to reflect a public opinion based on the observable reality as opposed to the television, governing by the opinion of the masses was not considered a good idea.

Our country was founded upon the concept of trustee representation. That means that we elected our representatives with the understanding that only they, being paid to do so, would have the time to fully research the issues and then make their decision about what was best for their constituents based upon the facts. Governing by polls has spelled the death of trustee representation, and as a result, the facts surrounding an issue no longer carry as much weight as public opinion.

In today's political world, our elected representatives often make their important decisions, such as how to deal with crime, based upon the opinion of the masses, who admittedly base their opinions regarding crime on the distorted coverage of this issue provided by television and therefore have little or no knowledge of the facts of the issue. As a result of this chain reaction of ignorance, politicians have restructured the justice system in a manner that would be more appropriate for dealing with the quantity and type of crime in the world that we observe through our television window—an imaginary world hundreds of times more violent and crime laden than the real world.

Public opinion's influence over the modern justice system has not gone unnoticed by those who run our prisons. In 1998, in an article in the *Keeper's Voice*, a publication aimed at corrections employees, Peter Carlson, assistant director, U.S. Department of Justice, Federal Bureau of Prisons, described this new and powerful force to his peers:

> What is new and remarkable is how much weight public opinion has gained within this new freewheeling style, decisively influencing the political machinery of government. It is important to recognize in today's fast-moving, information-based society, the citizen's viewpoint has taken on new relevance for individuals in public service. We live in an age in which the public demands responsiveness from government institutions and elected leaders.[3]

This destructive practice of replacing the facts with public opinion in the legislative process did not happen by accident. It has come about as a direct result of technological advances in the campaign arena—advances pushed into prominence by the rise in importance of the political consultant—as well as through changes in the methods of funding campaigns.

The New Rulers

Consultants have been a part of America's political landscape for as long as anyone can remember. Early on, consultants tended to be lawyers assigned to a candidate by the party to handle the day-to-day managerial tasks of a campaign. Although they may have had some input into the decisionmaking process, it was quite limited compared to that of the candidates themselves or the party. But this would change to some degree in the 1930s. The following walk through the history of the political consultants relies heavily on the work of Larry Sabato of the University of Virginia's Department of Government and Foreign Affairs as published in his 1981 book, *The Rise of the Political Consultant*.[4]

In 1933, the California legislature passed a bill known as the Central Valley Project. The bill was adamantly opposed by Pacific Gas and Electric Company, which considered the legislation to be a threat to private power. In an effort to overturn the bill, PG&E threw its weight behind a citizens' initiative that would overturn the legislature's decision. Sensing that the initiative would be successful, supporters of the Central Valley Project turned to two men for help, a press agent and newsman named Clem Whitacker and a public relations wiz named Leone Smith Baxter. The two used a paltry $39,000 radio and newspaper campaign to defeat PG&E's initiative. The age of the political consultant was born, and as a premonition of the way this new age would operate, PG&E quickly hired the two men who had defeated its initiative to handle its future political affairs.

By the 1950s, political consultants were playing an increasing role in the election process. Even at this early stage in their rise to dominance, some observers could see the writing on the wall. Neil Staebler, the chairman of Michigan's Democratic Party in the 1950s, observed that "elections will increasingly become contests, not between candidates but between great advertising firms."[5] Nostradamus clearly had nothing on Staebler.

The coming of the television age increased the power of political consultants exponentially. In 1952, Dwight Eisenhower hired an ad agency to consult on his campaign. It would prove to be a shrewd move. After stumbling and bumbling his way through media coverage during the campaign, Ike's hopes for winning looked grim. But his ad agency decided to try something new. They hired the Gallup company to conduct a series of polls and used the information gathered to create themes for a series of television commercials. The ad agency believed that in a controlled environment, they could create an image of a relaxed and articulate Eisenhower to counterbalance the less-than-eloquent Ike being portrayed in news coverage. The TV spots did far more than counterbalance the news; they skyrocketed Eisenhower's popularity and thereby changed the face of electoral politics forever.

By the time Ronald Reagan ran his 1966 California gubernatorial campaign, political consultants had moved from their role of image makers into the realm of political strategists. Reagan's early attempts at campaigning were floundering. In response, his consulting firm, Spencer-Roberts, decided to make a bold move. They hired the aptly named firm Behavioral Science Corporation to research the issues that were deemed to be the most important to Californians. More significant than that, they also asked the firm to provide suggested solutions that would appeal to the electorate. Taking advantage of Reagan's training as an actor, his consultants wrote the problems and solutions on a set of index cards and had Reagan memorize the information as he would the lines in a Hollywood production. The rest is history. The modern age of political consulting—an age where the pollsters, a.k.a. consultants, decide what issues are discussed and in what fashion—had arrived.

By the end of the 1970s, the biggest and best of the political consulting firms were actually turning away potential candidate clients left and right. The consultants, who now fully believed—and to a large extent, rightfully so—that through the tools of polling and television they could determine the outcomes of elections, were now picking and choosing their clientele based largely upon a candidate's perceived malleability to their ideas. If they thought that a candidate was too set in his or her ways, unwilling to follow the script that the consultants would write based upon their own interpretations of public opinion, the firm would simply choose to work with a different candidate. After all, the firms' reputations were based upon one criterion—winning elections. Taking on a client who might adopt unpopular political positions—the "maverick" politician—was a recipe for long-term financial failure for any consultant.

With the rise in importance of the consultants, it became clear that any political wannabe who spurned the use of the media-savvy pollsters during the election process was all but doomed to defeat. More important, the opposite was also true; any candidate rejected by the established consultants had little chance of reaching office. As a result, virtually every candidate running for office since the late 1970s has done so with the aid of these new rulers of the political system and has been more or less willing to follow their instructions.

In the late 1970s, when Larry Sabato was completing the research for *The Rise of the Political Consultant*, it was not only clear that these masters of the media had become the true driving force of America's electoral process but that they had also become a powerful force in post-election policy decisions as well.

It became commonplace that after winning an election for their political client, the consultant would be retained on staff, presumably to help maintain a politico's popularity until the next round of elections. What this meant was that consultants were now advising those in office about which of their policies were popular and would translate into future votes and which might make reelection more difficult. As a result of this political evolution, public opinion began to take on an increasingly important role in policy decisions and not just in campaign rhetoric.

Stuart Spencer described his role as consultant for President Gerald Ford in 1976 in disturbingly candid terms:

> When I'm working with a client I try to get him to do things that I think are politically wise. I went to President Ford in 1976 when [Secretary of State Henry] Kissinger had trips scheduled to Africa just before the Georgia and Alabama primaries. I went to the President and I said, "Mr. President, you can't let him go to Africa before these two primaries. There are too many racial overtones in the South." But he looked me in the eye and said, "You're probably right, Stu, but I'm doing the right thing for the country." Well, I don't argue with that. I made my point, and he said no . . . I did get him to change sides on the common situs picketing bill. [The bill, strongly favored by labor, was vetoed by Ford after he'd promised to support it.] I don't even care about common situs picketing, but a lot of people on the right in the Republican party did, and it became a cause celebre.[6]

Gerald Ford is widely regarded as a man of great integrity, an old-time politician who desired doing what was right even more than being reelected. If Ford could be controlled to such an extent by his hired handlers, I shudder to think of the influence that consultants wield in this age of TV politicians like Bill Clinton and Newt Gingrich. Along these lines, Sabato has written:

> Consultants have emphasized personality and gimmickry over issues, often exploiting emotional or negative themes rather than encouraging rational discussion. They have sought candidates who fit their technologies more than the requirements of office and have given an extra boost to candidates that are more skilled at electioneering than governing. They have encouraged candidates' own worst instincts to blow with the prevailing winds of public opinion.[7]

One would assume that the consultants would try to dispute such allegations regarding their effect on the political process, but for reasons that must surely stem from vanity, they seldom do. In fact, Dick Morris,

President Clinton's consultant until he fell from grace amid a sex scandal of his own, has written two books describing his role in the Clinton administration, a role that fits perfectly with Sabato's observations.

In *Behind the Oval Office* and *The New Prince,* Morris proudly tells his readers how he developed a three-pronged approach to politics that is responsible for Clinton's rise to power. First, Morris claims that he convinced the president to use "triangulation," a process that has been described as developing a platform to include the most popular elements from both parties, thus eliminating the usual Democrat-Republican conflicts.[8] It's sort of an "all things to all people" approach.

Next, Morris turned public opinion polling on nearly every conceivable position into a daily, sometimes hourly, activity at the White House. Then, as more than one observer has noted, Morris convinced Clinton to change his stated political positions to fit the polls. And finally, Morris takes credit for developing the political tool known as the "never-ending campaign." In effect, this tool dictates that even though a candidate has been elected, he or she never quits running for office, the centerpiece of this philosophy being that governing is made subordinate to winning reelection.

What Morris has done for the Democratic president he has also done for powerful Republicans, including Jesse Helms and Trent Lott. All in all, it seems that Dick Morris is quite proud of the fact that consultants like him are now running the show in Washington. But such a reality has major implications for the rest of us.

One can only shudder when wondering what America might look like today had Dick Morris and his poll-taking peers been working their antidemocratic magic earlier this century. For instance, what would have happened during the McCarthy era? When the "hard-on-communism" senator was at the height of his popularity, only 29 percent of Americans thought he was doing the wrong thing.[9] With lopsided poll results like that, Morris and his pals would surely have pushed all of their candidate-clients onto the McCarthy bandwagon. As disturbing as this proposition sounds, I'm not sure it would have been any more terrifying than what's happening today. It seems inconceivable that even Joseph McCarthy and a bunch of poll-driven clones would have imprisoned 2 million people as a means of retaining political popularity.

The Role of the Modern Consultant

Today's political consultants have more or less taken over the tasks that once fell under the purview of the party and the candidate. They are hired to provide technical services such as direct-mail fund-raising, polling, public opinion surveys, and fund-raising from political action committees (PACs), corporations, and the donor class. They also serve as the "experts" in charge of managing the overall direction of the campaign. They orchestrate the press that turns to them nearly exclusively for their political information, a fact that accounts for the near-propaganda quality of much political reporting these days. And most significant, they play an important role in selecting which issues a candidate will concentrate on and increasingly what position the candidate will take on those issues.

Unlike Dick Morris, some consultants have actually expressed concern over their ability to control candidates. In 1979, well-known consultant Charles Guggenheim acknowledged, "We're the big experts from the outside; we are prophets from another country whose biggest problem is that they [politicians] defer to me too much. I want to get their reactions but they hold back. If I said, 'You've got to play that,' I'd be scared they'd do it unquestioningly."[10]

In the late 1970s and early 1980s, Sabato's research confirmed Guggenheim's worst fear. As Sabato said, "Consultants are having an increasingly greater voice in the setting of basic strategy and the selection of (and relative emphasis on) campaign issues."[11] I suspect that consultant Guggenheim's fear stemmed from his understanding that the enthusiastically followed instructions he was issuing to his candidate clients, though helping to ensure their election, were not based on any pertinent facts concerning the issues but rather upon what words, according to the polls, would tickle the ears of the most voters.

Since consultants like Guggenheim have expressed apprehension about their role in politics, I would suggest that the rest of us should be wholly terrified. Understanding how these "prophets" of the election process go about determining a candidate's issues is no comfort at all— polling, polling, and more polling—or as this gauging of the public's desires is described by political writer Alan Baron, "the new holy writ of American politics."[12]

Since the end of the 1970s, which marked the beginning of the modern era of polling, political consultants have primarily used five types of polling tools during the course of an election. First is the "benchmark" poll. This survey is taken in the early stages of a campaign. Its purpose is to determine the public's assessment of a candidate's strengths and weaknesses as well of those of his or her opponent. Originally, these surveys were conducted by going door to door, but as costs for such "in person" surveys have risen, most are now conducted over the phone.

Once the benchmark survey is analyzed, "follow-up" surveys are conducted. These surveys serve a couple of purposes. They help to gather more specific information about any areas of concern pointed out by the benchmark poll, or, if a candidate has adjusted the platform based upon the original benchmark poll, the follow-up survey can reflect whether the adjustment has had the desired effect on the public's opinion of the candidate.

Later in the election process, "panel" surveys are performed. These surveys involve recontacting a large percentage, usually more than half, of the people previously polled in the benchmark or follow-up surveys. This information is coupled with a new smaller survey of people not previously polled by the campaign. The purpose of the panel surveys is to determine any shifts that have occurred in public opinion during the course of the campaign—presumably to allow the candidate to shift views in accordance with public sentiment.

The next polling tool is known as the "tracking phase." This is a small, constant sampling of public opinion that goes on throughout the campaign. It usually consists of approximately 100 phone calls every night. These tracking polls are designed to question members of the public about issues that arise during the campaign. They also help the consultants gauge whether their TV commercials are proving effective. In addition, they pick up on any changes taking place in the general population's opinion about a candidate or the opponent. Although such a small sampling of opinion is relatively useless by itself, the cumulative effect of constantly acquiring such bits of information helps to map trends in public opinion.

And finally, consultants use what have come to be known as "focus groups." Small samplings of individuals are brought together in a room where they can be more or less used as human guinea pigs. Consultants often watch from behind one-way mirrors as the individuals are asked to respond to anything from campaign slogans to issue positions to individual words. These days, it is not uncommon for those who participate in focus groups to be hooked up to electronic monitors that reflect their emotional responses to every conceivable stimulus: the color of a candidate's tie, the meter of his or her voice, a candidate's believability. Pollsters have found that these electronically monitored emotional responses are a better gauge of true public opinion than the views voiced by the focus-group participants. Perhaps the best example in recent years of a politician effectively using focus groups is the case of Bill Clinton in 1998.

After Clinton finally admitted to his sexual indiscretion with Monica Lewinsky in the Oval Office, it was time for damage control. Clinton's consultants used a focus group that determined that people grew angry every time Clinton used the word "truthful," but the group reacted favorably whenever he described his sexual liaisons as being a part of his "private" life. In response to the focus-group findings, Clinton went on national TV and in a well-scripted four-minute speech, he used the word "private" no less than six times, while steering clear of any subject matter having to do with "truthfulness."[13] Support for Clinton shot up following the speech, which makes perfect sense when you consider that the speech had, for all intents and purposes, been written by the American people themselves, based upon what they wanted to hear.

Trim the Sails, Divide, and Conquer

What all of these polling tools have in common is that they are ultimately designed for two purposes. First, they allow politicians to adjust their political platform in a manner that reflects the public's opinion and will motivate a "targeted" segment of the electorate to go to the polls on election day. This is not to insinuate that all politicians are going to completely discard their personal views on an issue simply because the polls show them to be bucking public opinion—although this certainly can and does happen. In 1976, famed political consultant Robert Teeter voiced concern over the fact that many candidates are too willing to change their platform to fit the poll results. Teeter told the *National Journal,* "I've seen candidates who were far too flexible for my tastes in being willing to realign their positions."[14]

Even so, I believe that polling is often used to assist a politician in trimming the sails on issues, as opposed to outright determining them. That is to say, polling results tell politicians which parts of their platform to emphasize or exaggerate and which parts to avoid discussing publicly. In writing for the *New York Times* in 1992, Michael de Courcy Hinds described this dilemma in terms of crime. Hinds noted that both governors and other policymakers were well aware that they should be seeking alternatives to prisons because of the skyrocketing costs of incarceration. Yet after a number of interviews with elected leaders, Hinds concluded that the politicians believed that they had to ignore doing what was best for their constituents because they were uniformly afraid that supporting prison alternatives would allow them to be painted as "soft on crime" in future elections.[15] Although such political positioning increases a politician's chances of reaching and maintaining office, in the long run it means that the election process has lost its ability to inform and thereby persuade the public to alter its position on important issues such as crime when public opinion is out of touch with the facts.

The other purpose of polling is to help the consultants to assess the best way to shrink the electorate by encouraging the people composing the demographic groups that have not been targeted by television commercials and issue selection to stay home on election day. Designing a campaign to encourage low voter turnout allows politicians of both parties to avoid having to deal with issues such as crime in an operative manner. It also makes it possible for those seeking office to adopt a stance on an issue that will reward one group at the expense of another, for example, as in the hard-on-crime position, which offers a false promise of public safety to white suburbanites at the expense of low-income communities of color.

Voter apathy is disturbingly high in nearly all demographic groups, but it is the highest among the millions of Americans who live at the bottom of the economic food chain. This lack of political action by those with the most to lose is hard to understand unless you realize that apathy among the poor has long been cultivated by the powers that be. The "get out the vote" strategies of the 1960s have been replaced with technological trickery designed to "keep out the vote," when it comes to the poor.

Advancements in technology, the behavioral sciences, and polling have made it quite possible for those who oversee the election process, meaning the consultants, to greatly influence the size and composition of the electorate that will ultimately make the trip to the polls come election day. Of course, any number of things can happen beyond the consultants' control, which can result in the nontargeted electorate turning out in large numbers—a strong grassroots effort, a racial incident such as the police shooting an unarmed black motorist, or something of the sort—but as a general rule, the consultants' strategies designed to shape voter turnout work quite well.

"Pray for a low voter turnout" encouraged former Operation Rescue activist turned congressional candidate Randall Terry during his 1998 bid for political office. Terry's plan was a simple one. If most voters stayed at home on election day, his highly motivated right-wing supporters would be able to catapult him into office with less than 20 percent support among registered voters.[16] Terry was not alone in his desire to enhance voter apathy. In fact, his request for God's help in discouraging voter turnout is one of the least disturbing techniques being employed these days by political consultants and their clients in the effort to limit political participation.

And just so you don't get the idea that I'm picking on conservatives here, let me assure you that most Democrats are equally desirous of minimal voter turnouts. In the 1998 elections, Democrats and Republicans alike relied heavily on "targeted-voter" strategies developed by their consultants. The idea was that it is easier to win 16 percent of the vote in an election where only 30 percent of voters go to the polls than to try to appeal to large numbers of people with varying and often conflicting interests.

Writing for the *Progressive,* John Nichols observed correctly that "a campaign that emphasizes issues of broad popular appeal might turn off corporate contributors. That's something Democratic insiders fear since, as their party has moved further and further to the right, it has come to rely on the same Wall Street donor base as the Republicans." Nichols concluded that such action "leaves many voters with a clear sense that the political choices they make don't matter."[17] And this sense of political helplessness among the nontargeted population is exactly what the consultants are counting on.

In a conversation I had a couple of years ago with historian Howard Zinn, he made a similar point. Zinn told me that throughout our country's history, whenever the two parties have become nearly indistinguishable from one another, as is the case in the 1990s, people tend to remove themselves from the political process through apathy. It seems that the current trend toward a one-party system—a trend that has been accelerated by the rise in importance of the political consultant—has simply made a comfortable couch on election day preferable to a line at a voting booth, where a person more often than not these days gets to choose between two nearly identical candidates. In the 1990s, the choice is generally between a pro-big business, hard-on-crime, millionaire attorney claiming to be a Democrat in favor of abortion, or a pro-big business, hard-on-crime, millionaire attorney claiming to be a Republican who opposes abortion. This is too often the reality of modern politics.

If the majority of people were to actually vote, it would be nearly impossible for candidates to efficiently target wealthy demographic groups with their sound-bite-laden commercials and financial appeals. This, in many ways, would make the campaign process more difficult for politicians, and this is particularly true for Democrats, who must still maintain, though somewhat disingenuously, that they represent the concerns of poor and working-class Americans. As Nichols has pointed out, Democrats these days have become increasingly dependent upon wealthy constituents and corporations whose political desires are, more often than not, in direct conflict with those of blue-collar workers and people living in poverty.

The most important issues for families at the bottom of the economy revolve around securing jobs that pay an adequate amount to feed, clothe, house, and provide health care for their families. For our low-income communities, the issues are access to adequate services and equal educational opportunities for their children. Unfortunately, the geographic segregation of the classes that has resulted from the ongoing flight to the suburbs has made it increasingly difficult for poor America to achieve even these modest goals. Many of the businesses that once offered employment opportunities have followed the money to the outskirts of town. And when it comes to services and education, this exodus of wealth has meant that nearly every dollar spent on these necessities of life for the poor has become a dollar removed from the tax base of well-to-do suburbanites, whose taxes ultimately foot the majority of the bill for their impoverished city cousins.[18]

The flight to the burbs by those who could afford it has done much to drive a wedge between the interests of the rich and poor. In the past, when a library or a fire station was built in urban America, it would likely have benefited voters of every economic strata, at least to some degree, because all the classes lived in relative proximity to one another. But geographic segregation has put communities of varying classes at war with one another over government expenditures. Suburbanites would much rather see their tax dollars go for beautiful parks, or that increasingly popular form of class discrimination known as "open space," in their own neighborhoods than for some inner-city school that they will never lay eyes on or for fire trucks that will never spray their life-saving water on the beautifully landscaped, nearly identical homes found in suburban clusters with names like "Fawn Brook" or "Aspen Meadows."

Any campaign truly designed to speak to the needs of the lower class would have to include operative discussions of such modern political taboos as income redistribution, community-to-community diversion of tax revenues, and the racist elements and economic shortcomings of the war on crime—issues that, if put forward by Democrats, would run the risk of pushing the wealthy individuals and corporations who now pay for their TV commercials even further to the right and possibly into the waiting arms of "moderate" Republicans.

Consequently, most politicians, including modern pseudo-progressives of the Clinton ilk, have made the decision to cater their campaign platform to the desires of that portion of the electorate that political consultants tell them is most critical to victory, namely, suburbanites who are already predisposed to vote and who offer the added bonus of being able to fill campaign coffers. That being the case, the challenge for politicians is to make sure that voters from other demographic groups stay home on election day. In recent years, political consultants have devised methods that make apathy less a byproduct of disenfranchisement than a result of high-tech media manipulation.

Before the first political commercial has hit the airwaves, the political consultants and advertising executives have already experimented with polls and focus groups composed of people of every make and model. Rich and poor, black and white have all been strapped into chairs and hooked to an array of electronic gadgets designed to measure their emotional responses to all that is political. The goal of this electronic wizardry is as much designed to determine what content might encourage some demographic groups to abstain from voting as it is to determine what issues will motivate other voters.

As former Speaker of the House Newt Gingrich once observed, "When things happen that make one side's partisans unhappy, they stay home."[19] That being the case, both political parties are now spending significant time and money to search out those issues that they believe can be hyped in commercials or leaked to the press that will insure that selected "partisans" are "unhappy" and, therefore, motivated to stay home on election day. Since both sides are now courting the same well-to-do voter base, it is largely the poor who are being encouraged to stay at home so that their conflicting interests don't muddy up the political waters for either party.

By 1994, this misuse of technology, coupled with the increasing emergence of an apathy-enhancing one-party system designed to appeal to wealthy constituents, had helped to reduce voter turnout to a measly 38 percent of those registered.[20] We are often told that the "common person" no longer believes that his or her vote counts, but we are rarely informed that such political intuition is, for the most part, by design.

At the beginning of the 1980s, the period that also happens to mark the emergence of the perpetual prisoner machine, the excessive use of polling began to shift in earnest from the nearly exclusive domain of campaigns into day-to-day political life. In the 1990s, consultants such as Dick Morris and James Carville have become permanent year-round fixtures, as has excessive polling. Politicians who once used polls and consultants a few times a year now rely on them monthly, weekly, and, sometimes, as in the case of Clinton, nearly daily throughout their political careers. This shift is largely responsible for the dramatic increase in the cost of political campaigns, which have risen by five to ten times over in the last twenty-five years. The political parties and news organizations increased their spending on polling by 35 percent just between the election cycles of 1992 and 1996, a period in which approximately $500 million was paid out for political polls. Bill Clinton, who has been described as a man who "polls as often as he breathes" by Morris, spent more than $1.3 million on polling during the 1996 presidential campaign, and the Dole organization was not far behind.[21] As a result of the increasing cost for polling, television time, and consultants, being considered a top contender in a national election is now based more on a candidate's reputation for fund-raising than upon his or her political ideology.

Sadly, this is not an exaggeration. At the writing of this book, First Lady Hillary Clinton is considering a run for the Senate in the state of New York. News counts have repeatedly described her as a formidable opponent "because of her ability to raise money." The same is true of Texas governor George W. Bush and his quest for the White House in the 2000 presidential election. One political analyst after another has described Bush as the "front-runner" for no other reason than his ability to raise the most campaign funds.

The growing cost of political campaigns has greatly increased the influence of those who provide politicians with campaign funds. In addition, this need for massive amounts of money has become the central force in a process that has caused the Democratic and Republican Parties to become increasingly blended and indistinguishable, as they have adopted many of each other's platform positions, including a nearly universal acceptance of the hard-on-crime position.

Phase One: Win at All Costs

It can be argued, and many have done so, that modern campaign financing is one of the most destructive forces in America at the end of the twentieth century. That's because, in its current form, our process of funding elections has resulted in nothing short of our turning over the reins of our government to those who pick up the tab for the campaigns. Let's take a look at the political money supply, starting with the donor class—that all-powerful .0025 percent of the individuals in the United States who give money to politicians.

So who is in the donor class? What do they look like? What do they believe in? Well, first of all they are wealthy. Many are billionaires, or at least millionaires. A full one-fifth reported annual incomes of over $500,000, and four-fifths made at least $100,000. Ninety-five percent are white. Eighty percent are men. And although over 80 percent of all donors are over the age of forty-five, at least 62 percent of those are over the age of sixty.[22] Since it is these wealthy white men who have the ear of our elected officials, it is important to understand what messages they are whispering.

A 1998 study conducted by the Joyce Foundation of Chicago set out to do just that. The study found that on the whole, those who composed the donor class shared the same values. They are generally conservative on economic issues. More than one-half are in favor of tax cuts even if they have to come at the expense of public services. Most are adamantly opposed to any form of national health-care insurance. They oppose any new spending aimed at reducing the effects of poverty. They believe that the free-market system should be allowed to operate unencumbered by government, and they oppose any cuts in the defense budget. Incredibly, these are the shared values of both Democrat and Republican campaign donors, so it should come as no surprise that this list of donor opinions reads like the political platform of both parties during the last ten years.[23]

The overall largest suppliers of campaign funds are the special interests such as the prison-industrial complex, the defense industry, other such industries, and the parties themselves. The special interests include PACs, corporations, labor unions, and single-agenda ideologues who fund candidates willing to take certain positions on particular issues such as anti-abortion, pro-gay rights, or hard on crime. With some corporations giving millions of dollars a year to individual candidates, PACs, and lobbyists, it would be hard to overestimate the influence wielded by these business interests—particularly when the connections between the money supply and the all-powerful political consultants are taken into account.

In the 1990s, the role of money in politics is simple—the candidate who can get his or her hands on most of it nearly always wins. The off-year elections of 1998 were a perfect example. In the Senate, the candidate who spent the most won 93.9 percent of the time. In the House, the biggest spender prevailed in 94.9 percent of the races. So who are the biggest spenders? Incumbents. In these same elections, 90 percent of Senate incumbents and 98.3 percent of House incumbents were victorious.[24]

The top political consultants have ongoing relationships with those who provide the campaign money supply, be they the special interests or the donor class. Some consultants are actually retained by the PACs. Candidates who want access to that consultant as well as the PAC's money have to meet certain criteria. Surprisingly, for most business interests these criteria are not based so much on party affiliation or ideology as on a candidate's chance of winning the election. Herein lies the strength of incumbency.

Many corporations, PACs, and individuals in the donor class give money to Democrats or Republicans, or both, during each election cycle, demonstrating that giving is about something other than political platform. If those in the money supply are reasonably sure who is going to win a particular race, then, for the most part, that's who gets their financial backing. If they aren't sure who's going to come out on top, it isn't unusual for them to give funds to both sides.

For the most part, there is one reason for donating campaign funds. On the day after the election, everyone wants to have given money to the winner. Having done so translates into postelection access and influence. No one, except for the ideologues, has any desire to pump money into a campaign that is likely to fail. It would have no subsequent value. That is why those who compose the political money supply work so closely with the consulting firms. Such a relationship helps the entities that trade dollars for influence make sure that they are getting the majority of their money into the hands of the eventual winners, be they Democrats or Republicans.

It is this aspect of modern elective politics—where political platform has far less to do with who gets campaign funds than a politician's odds of winning the election—that has transformed America's political process into a stagnant, self-perpetuating system of incumbency rule. The consultants, who guide the flow of a significant amount of the overall campaign funds, take the position that because incumbents have all-important name recognition, they are the most likely to win an election from the onset. Because consultants consider incumbents likely to win, they advise their clients on the money side of politics to "invest" the vast majority of their funds in the incumbents. Since the incumbents now have both name recognition and more money to spend—often ten times more than their opponent—they are, in fact, all but assured of victory.[25]

This self-perpetuating formula helps to explain one of the great contradictions of modern politics, namely, why the electorate—which claims to be extremely disillusioned with Washington politicians—continues to reelect an unbelievable 96 percent of all congressional incumbents. Now consider how this consultant–money supply–incumbency process has narrowed the political spectrum on certain issues.

Because the polls taken by the consultants of both Republicans and Democrats reflect the same public opinions and because the reason for taking such polls for both parties is to allow politicians to shape their positions toward this public opinion, it has to follow that Republicans and Democrats would increasingly be putting forward nearly identical platforms in the areas where the public's opinion is the strongest. This helps to explain why the issue of crime—where the public' opinion is perhaps more unified than on any other issue, thanks to the media's exaggerated use of violent content—is the most common theme found in the campaign ads of both parties.[26]

In 1999, I asked Larry Sabato what would happen if a candidate seeking office today were to put forward a position that challenged the current hard-on-crime philosophy. In light of the fact that polls in 1999 are finding that crime and violence is still the biggest concern for the majority of Americans, Sabato responded that "they would quickly be shown the door by the PACs and the consultants." Sabato's reasoning here is simple. The poll-driven consultants and those supplying campaign funds believe that putting forward a position on an issue that goes against such strong popular opinion could well result in defeat at election time, and no one giving money wants to take a chance on wasting it on a losing campaign. Certainly, other factors can override this one issue. For instance, it's not likely that opposing the current crime policies would take money out of Ted Kennedy's campaign coffer. That's because the Massachusetts senator has such a strong base of support he would be expected to win regardless of his stance on crime.

But still, for the most part, those who pull the strings in the political world these days are dictating a "get hard or get out" message to would-be elected officials. This is one explanation for why both parties now exhibit equally conservative positions on crime and continue to push mandatory sentences, more prisons, and an increased law-enforcement presence over more effective and more cost-efficient alternatives.

Peter Carlson of the Bureau of Prisons has also noticed this bipartisan support for hard-on-crime policies. He also accurately describes its source:

> The American public is growing impatient with hearing about the horror stories of crime in our streets . . . and the number one subject in every political poll in the land is public safety. Our legislative bodies are reacting to public opinion—voices are really being heard—and elected representatives are creating our future in the prison business.[27]

It would seem that Carlson and his peers in corrections view this poll-driven prison expansion as a positive development. I suspect that this is because those who make their living from the prison population realize that their paychecks and job security are being enhanced by the new politics of public opinion.

Issues such as crime, welfare reform, defense spending, and tax cuts—issues on which opinion polls show the targeted voting public to have a strong and unified opinion—are the most susceptible to this manipulation from those who fund and run campaigns. The days of clearly defined party platforms on these issues have gone by the wayside. The main differences between today's Democrats and Republicans show up in issues like gay rights, education, and abortion, areas where pollsters find the targeted electorate to be greatly divided in its opinions. When it comes to the other issues that once defined the differences between the parties, nearly all politicians, regardless of party affiliation, have adopted a similar position, the white suburbanite's position.

For example, in the 1990s, it was a Democratic president who cut welfare spending, a move that was praised and embraced by the Republicans. And when the Republicans wanted to push global trade agreements, even though it meant selling out workers in favor of the business interests, Democrats went along. Modern Democrats like Bill Clinton have pushed for smaller government, for corporate mergers, for increasing the defense budget; they have supported making it easier for government agencies to do surveillance on citizens through wiretaps and for privatizing government functions such as social security and corrections. All of these positions were once the exclusive domain of Republicans. And then there is the issue of crime. It would be difficult to find any issue in America's history that has garnered more bipartisan support than the hard-on-crime policies of the last twenty years.

I believe that it is the pressure being exerted by those who fund campaigns and by the consultants that explains why modern Democrats have abandoned their traditional political platform to a great extent, as evidenced by the 1996 presidential campaign, when more than one political observer noted that Bill Clinton's positions on crime, immigration, law enforcement, welfare, defense, and the size of the federal government were either identical to or in some instances to the right of his Republican opponent, Bob Dole.

Such blending of party platforms makes sense considering the public's poorly thought out reward system. Ever since the hard-on-crime Willie Horton ads derailed presidential candidate Michael Dukakis in 1988 by inaccurately depicting the Democrat as supporting parole for violent offenders, the voting portion of the public has exhibited an increasing willingness to defeat any candidate who can even remotely be tagged with the "soft-on-crime" label. Consequently, as the National Criminal Justice Commission has reported, nearly every candidate at every level of elected office since 1988 has put forward a hard-on-crime position. Even individuals running for political offices that have no bearing on crime policy such as insurance commissioner or treasurer have aired anticrime TV ads as a means of tapping into the public's growing fear of crime. I believe that this simple and uniform position on crime is largely attributable to the consultants and suppliers of campaign funds, who warn their candidates that meaningful discussions of crime policy will result in their being labeled "soft on crime" and could subsequently lead to election-day defeat.

So why should politicians rock the boat on the crime issue? Clearly, in the 1980s and 1990s, they have found no incentive to do so. Under the very best of circumstances, the public's system of rewarding those who talk only in vague hard-on-crime rhetoric has forced the politician who understands the destructive nature of our current crime policies to keep quiet in order to maintain public support and thereby maintain access to the millions of dollars in funding now needed to pay for consultants, perpetual polling, and TV commercials—the three ingredients deemed necessary for political viability at the end of the twentieth century.

What I am describing is the new "natural-selection" process of American politics. For the most part, only candidates holding positions deemed proper by the money supply and the consultants are able to rise to power. Candidates who are hard on crime are seen as more viable because their crime position is in tune with the vast majority of the targeted electorate according to the polls. Such anticrime candidates are therefore the recipients of more campaign funds because they hold this popular position, and in turn, these funds make them more likely to win and stay in office. As a result of this selection process being in effect over the last two decades, the vast majority of those left in office at the end of the century are the men and woman who have always been in favor of hard-on-crime sentencing measures or those who have conveniently become hard on crime in order to stay in office. Those who might have held a position contrary to the hard-on-crime stance have been weeded out to a significant degree over the course of time.

Because of this weeding process, the public either hears the persuasive propaganda of hard-on-crime rhetoric that confirms their media-induced impression that crime is very violent and pervasive, or they hear silence from the few remaining anomalies of modern political evolution who oppose the current crime policies. This lack of debate all but ensures that the public's opinion will not change regarding crime; which means the poll results will not change; which means the recommendations of the consultants to the political money supply will not change; which means that the selection process will continue and that the prison population will likely keep growing year after year, election after election.

This general pressure being exerted by those who fund campaigns and the consultants who script campaign issues from public opinion are what I refer to as "phase one" in the development of hard-on-crime policies. At its most basic level, phase-one pressure is not specifically aimed at issues such as crime but rather at winning the election at all costs. However, because the consultants have now exaggerated the role of public opinion in the campaign and policy-creation process and because public opinion on the issue of crime has become somewhat one-dimensional in response to the media's exaggerated crime messages, the pressure to win and the pressure to be hard on crime have become nearly indistinguishable. Consequently, the majority of campaign funds—even money that is coming from sources that have absolutely no vested interest whatsoever in America's crime policies—are nonetheless having the effect of pushing politicians to be hard on crime because they push politicians to conform their political positions to what the consultants say will help them win—and in the 1990s, that's "hard on crime."

Phase Two: "Special Access"

"Phase two" of the campaign-finance system takes place postelection, or in the case of incumbents, anytime after a campaign contribution has been made. It is in this phase of the process that campaign contributors get what they paid for—access for the purpose of influencing particular policy decisions. In phase one, the pressure on the politician is exerted by public opinion polls and the necessity to do whatever it takes to win the election. In phase two, politicians are expected to repay contributors in very specific ways such as introducing or supporting legislation that will financially benefit the particular industries that have filled the campaign coffers.

Before we move on, I should point out that many politicians, most of them, in fact, readily admit that our current system for funding campaigns is broken and that they do not like it. I believe that most who voice this opinion are sincere. However, with this broken system so heavily favoring the incumbents—the only ones with the power to dismantle it—no one has been sincere enough to fix the system so far. Every year, members of both parties decry the abuses of the modern system for funding campaigns. And every year, the same politicians fail to reach agreement on how to correct the situation. It's like a scene from the movie *Groundhog Day* where Bill Murray relives the same twenty-four-hour period over and over again. Of course, following, and even during, this public display of contempt regarding campaign finance, the incumbents of both parties are busy exploiting the corrupt system to its fullest because it all but ensures their reelection.

As a sign of just how out of control things have become in our system of financing campaigns, the act of raising money is now the single most important and time consuming part of the job for our elected officials. Sadly, even politicians acknowledge that this is the situation. "I do think that the amount of time people have to put into raising money is a serious problem in the country," moaned Republican representative Vin Weber of Minnesota to the people at the Center for Responsive Politics. "There's no way you can prove the impact on the quality of Congress's work. . . . But when the members making decisions can't devote serious quality time to serious decisions, it has to [result in] a lower quality of work."[28]

This is truly an amazing and disturbing observation by someone on the inside. According to Weber, politicians are spending so much time raising money that they can't even allocate a responsible amount of time to their policy decisions. So just how much time do our elected officials spend asking consultants, lobbyists, corporations, PACs, and the rich white guys of the donor class for money? According to former Senate Majority Leader George Mitchell, a lot.

Mitchell claims that nearly every single day in his six-year tenure as the man in charge of scheduling the Senate's votes, he was asked to rearrange the chamber's schedule to accommodate fund-raising. "If I put all the requests together," said Mitchell, "the Senate would never vote. I once had my staff keep a list of such requests on one day . . . and had I honored all the requests, there could not have been a vote that day. It covered the period from 9 A.M. until midnight."[29]

It is not uncommon for a politician in the 1990s to attend several breakfast fund-raisers beginning as early as 6 A.M., a lunch or afternoon fund-raiser, and as many as six evening fund-raising events in a single day. This type of round-the-clock fund-raising is no longer limited to short spurts during the campaign season. Because a successful campaign can now require as much as $10 million, fund-raising goes on from a politician's first day in office straight through until the next election cycle.

"The worst thing about it [fund-raising]," agrees former Senator Dennis DeConcini of Arizona, "is that members have to spend so much time in the pursuit of campaign finances that I think that their ability to do really their best as legislators is jeopardized."[30] I agree with DeConcini and Weber that the ability of legislators to do good work has, indeed, been compromised, but I hardly think that the time spent on fund-raising is the "worst thing" about the process.

The worst thing is the fact that those supplying the money have done so in exchange for influence over policy decisions. And their influence over such decisions has been greatly amplified because those in Congress must now rely even more heavily on the opinions of the special interest's lobbyists because, admittedly, they don't have time to do their own independent research; they are too busy raising money from the people who are telling them how they should vote. It's enough to make you dizzy.

In an effort to enhance their ability to secure campaign funds, politicians in recent years have even begun to break one of the oldest unwritten rules of raising funds. They now specifically target the industries they oversee on their committees for campaign contributions. This practice is considered so disturbing because it clearly gives the impression that favorable legislation is being traded for dollars. Even the politicians who admit that they are selling "access" attempt to downplay or deny that such questionable pandering goes on.

Take DeConcini, for example. When he was asked if politicians like him used their committee positions to target specific donors—such as a Public Works Committee member who doles out billions in tax dollars for construction projects hitting up a corporation that constructs prisons for campaign contributions—he responded, "I never do, and I don't know anybody who does—maybe some people do—sit around and say: 'look, I'm on the banking committee, and we're doing credit unions this month. Get a list of credit unions and start calling them.' That is not how it works."[31]

Now contrast the senator's claim "That is not how it works" with this story from the Associated Press's Washington, D.C., office in October 1998:

> Craig Metz, the chief of staff to House National Security Committee chairman Floyd Spence, worked the telephone this week to reach out to key players in the defense industry his boss oversees. His mission wasn't to talk business—it was to raise money. All across Washington, lawmakers or their top aides in both parties who are in safe races are hitting the phones calling the industry friends they know best for last minute get-out-the-vote dollars.[32]

How campaign money is raised is certainly an important issue, because in the end it likely defines just how much influence has been sold. Then exactly what is it that is being bought via campaign contributions?

The answer depends on who you ask. Listening to politicians currently in office, one would assume that those who fund their campaigns get next to nothing in return for their millions in contributions.

For the most part, when the Center for Responsive Politics asked current politicians what special interests get for their campaign donations, they heard the same response over and over again: "Money doesn't buy votes, but it does buy access, and access often leads to favorable action."[33] Huh? It's as if politicians honestly find some discernible difference between selling votes and selling "access that begets favorable action." I mean, after all, what *is* favorable action? Do those we elect really believe that laundering their campaign money through a three-step process of semantics makes the end result more palatable? Or is it just that this concept of "special access" is the best excuse that anyone can come up with to explain why people giving campaign money tend to see their political desires turned into congressional action?

Taking the semantics approach, former representative Thomas Downey (D–New York) told the center, "Money doesn't buy . . . a position. But it will buy you some access to make your case." He should know. Downey is now a lobbyist and freely admits that when it comes to influencing legislation, he finds it to be advantageous to drop a grand or more to attend a fund-raising event. The former congressman says that the money allows him to get an appointment to sit down with the member of Congress. He explained, "When somebody is helping you win a campaign, you're going to at least certainly grant the request for a meeting."[34] The words that concern me here are "at least." Downey admits that donors do ask members of Congress to initiate legislation on their behalf, but he says that more often they simply want to know if a member is going to vote in a manner that will be favorable to them. I can't help but wonder if this inquiry into how a politician will vote comes with the unspoken understanding that future campaign funds may well be tied to the politician's answer. Or should I just assume that corporations, lobbyists, and PACs give millions of dollars to elected officials because they're so darned enthusiastic about democracy?

To his credit, retired senator Wyche Fowler has been a bit more candid about how "phase two" of the campaign funding system really works. The former congressman said:

> I'm sure that on many occasions—I'm not proud of it—I made the choice that I needed this big corporate client and therefore I voted for, or sponsored its provision, even though I did not think that it was in the best in-

terest of the country or the economy. It's the same rationale as in why people want to sell arms to countries that haven't got any business having these sophisticated arms. You know the argument, "If I don't sell them, well, the French will."[35]

A 1998 PBS documentary confirmed Fowler's explanation of how campaign contributions work. The documentary, hosted by Bill Moyers, showed videotapes of President Bill Clinton telling wealthy campaign donors who were attending his now infamous White House coffee fundraisers that their donations would, in fact, "buy them special access." Later in the program, in an effort to better define this "special access," Moyers interviewed Democratic Party chairman Don Fowler regarding money donated after one of these coffees by a wealthy Puerto Rican developer named Ruben Velez.

MOYERS: If Ruben Velez had been a shopkeeper from San Juan, would he have been at that coffee?
FOWLER: If he'd have been a shopkeeper, probably no.
MOYERS: People with money should not be able to buy more democracy than people without money.
FOWLER: But they do and we all know it.[36]

Then what name should we hang on this process of trading money for an extra dose of democratic prowess—a process that, as we have seen, tends to determine the political winners and losers, which issues get discussed in what fashion, and, to an alarming degree, what policies get adopted? Once again, it depends on who you talk to, but I must confess a special affinity for Jimmy Carter's take on this matter. Carter called it legalized bribery, noting in 1997 that "I don't think there is any doubt that in the incumbent administration and in the Congress decisions are heavily influenced, in many cases, by how large contributions are made."[37]

The Perpetual Prisoner Machine Lobby

When it comes to trading money for access and influence, the components of the perpetual prisoner machine operate just like those of any other special interests. Private-prison companies, media corporations, unions, communities whose economies are based on prisons, and corporations that profit from the prison population in a myriad of ways are all funneling money to politicians who are in a position to make decisions about whether their ability to profit from crime and prisoners will be enhanced or diminished. Just as the rise in the importance of the political consultants and their polls acted to mesh the gears of media and politics within the machine, so too has the influence of political contributing acted to mesh the components of the prison-industrial complex and politics and to further engage the media gear.

When it comes to throwing money at elected officials, those in the media portion of the machine spend the most per company. Seagram and Sons, Disney, Time Warner, and GE can all be found in the list of the top 100 overall campaign-fund contributors to the parties and individual candidates. For the period 1995–1996, Seagram doled out more than $2.5 million to lead the way. Disney spent $1.6 million. Time Warner contributed $1.4 million. And General Electric donated just over $1 million. Even though these are incredibly large sums, they represent only the tip of the iceberg in what media corporations paid for their access and influence.[38]

In just the six-month period between January 1 and June 30, 1997, General Electric spent $4.1 million on its overall lobbying efforts. Time Warner and Westinghouse also dropped more than $1 million each on lobbying during this short time frame.[39] And then there is that greatest of the dozen or so loopholes that politicians have built into the campaign finance laws, "soft money." Since 1978, soft money has allowed corporations to far exceed what should be their legal caps on contributing campaign funds. For the 1995–1996 reporting period, the media companies dominated the top fifty soft-money contributor's list, with Seagram at $1.9 million, Disney at $1.3 million, Rupert Murdoch's News Corporation at more than $869,700, and Time Warner at $726,250.[40]

So what exactly did these media corporations buy with their millions? Who knows? That's how the system works. You spend a few million dollars and you get to meet behind closed doors with those who write the rules for the industries from which you profit. Considering the primary role that the media plays in the perpetual prisoner machine—that of creating an exaggerated apprehension concerning crime within the general population—it isn't likely that these corporations spend much of their time lobbying for hard-on-crime legislation. That's not the aspect of crime that benefits them most, although there are exceptions to this last statement.

GE and Westinghouse do have a direct vested interest in increasing the prison population through their manufacture of products designed for law enforcement and corrections as well as through their funding of prison construction. And there are other ways that the media corporations are profiting directly from hard-on-crime policies as well. In 1997, Congress decided that though there wasn't enough money to fund the drug rehabilitation programs requested by drug czar Barry McCaffrey, it could drop $1 to $2 billion on an anti-drug advertising blitz. The vast majority of the taxpayer money being spent on anti-drug TV commercials—such as the one where an attractive model smashes up a kitchen that looks to be straight out of a Williams-Sonoma catalog—will eventually find its way into the hands of the media giants. *Advertising Age* estimates that Disney will walk away with a cool $50 million in the first year of the program alone.[41]

These examples aside, I would assume that the majority of the special access being purchased by media interests is to ensure that their monopoly control over the world media market doesn't become threatened by the enforcement of antitrust laws. And as pointed out previously by Lawrence Grossman, former head of NBC News, most of the media companies use the special access created by owning news divisions, as well as financing campaigns, to secure further revenues from international markets for the multitude of industries that their parent corporations are involved with, from media to computers to nuclear power to military weaponry.

And finally, in light of the growing public outcry over the media industry's increasing reliance on sexual and violent content, I would assume that these companies are making sure that their political beneficiaries know better than to suggest any type of censorship laws or ratings systems that could impact their ability to market such content. After all, without sex and violence it would be impossible to dominate the international market—the market that these companies are admittedly banking on for the majority of their future profits.

Other parts of the machine use their phase-two influence to push more specific anticrime agendas. Law-enforcement and prison-guard unions, private-prison corporations, those who sell goods and services to the prison system, and ideologues such as the National Rifle Association contribute money to those they believe will specifically further the hard-on-crime agenda.

In the case of the NRA, the hard-on-crime position has been interpreted as being pro guns for self-defense and also fits the conservative ideology of most of its membership, which includes a significant number of current and former police officers, prison guards, and people in rural America who tend to hold to a generally hard-on-crime position. The NRA has bankrolled numerous propaganda blitzes designed to push the hard-on-crime agenda, including the first three-strikes law that was enacted in Washington; a push to get Texas officials to spend $1 billion on new prisons; a national advertising campaign that encouraged the federal government to dedicate $21 billion to new prisons while simultaneously cutting funding for crime-prevention programs; and so on and so forth all across the nation. The NRA also pushes its hard-on-crime agenda by pouring large quantities of money into the campaign coffers of politicians, including $1.69 million in the 1995–1996 election cycle at the national level.[42]

As for the unions, law enforcement's budgets have been greatly increased as a result of hard-on-crime policies being passed on both the state and federal level, and increased budgets mean bigger salaries and new equipment for America's cops, which explains their significant financial support of hard-on-crime politicians via campaign contributions. As for the prison-guards unions, perhaps the best example of their reason to support hard-on-crime candidates can be found in California's three-strikes law.

It is hardly a coincidence that the group that has been the single biggest financial beneficiary from this law also spent the most money lobbying for its passage. In 1993, prior to the passage of three strikes, then California governor Pete Wilson had refused to support the "three strikes and you're out" citizen initiative, but there was an election on the horizon.

There were two groups in California that lobbied hard for three strikes—the NRA and the California Correctional Peace Officers Association, the union that represents the state's prison guards, parole officers, and prison counselors. Both of these groups began to pour money into Wilson's and other hard-on-crime candidates' campaign coffers. In fact, the guard's union was the governor's single largest contributor, eventually giving him over $941,000, an amount three times larger than from any other single source.[43] When it came to three strikes, the guards' union significantly outspent the teachers' union, which opposed the law, even though the guards' union was only about one-tenth the size of the teachers' union at the time. In the end, the special access purchased by the union's money paid off. Wilson flip-flopped his position and signed three strikes into law. Just in case you are wondering why a bunch of prison guards would be so enthusiastic about passing a law like three strikes, I assure you they had their reasons.

Prior to three strikes, guards made a little less than teachers, somewhere around $24,000 a year, and their union had only 4,000 members. Now that three strikes and other hard-on-crime measures backed by the union have gone into effect—the union claims that thirty-eight out of forty-four of the bills it pushed in the California legislature in the 1980s and 1990s have been enacted—guards have seen their salaries increase to approximately $55,000 per year, and their union has grown to over 24,000 strong, with nearly $10 million a year in dues coming in.[44] As one might expect, the union continues to use its ever-increasing phase-two influence to push for still more hard-on-crime measures that will further enhance its bottom line. It is a strategy that is clearly working.

In 1977, California housed 19,600 inmates. In 1998, that number had grown to 159,000. California now runs the biggest prison system in the Western world. It houses more inmates on any given day than do the countries of France, Japan, Germany, Great Britain, the Netherlands, and Singapore combined.[45] California has spent $5.2 billion on new prisons since 1977, yet it still has the most overcrowded system in the nation. It is estimated that hard-on-crime sentencing changes such as three strikes will require California to spend another $6 billion in the next ten years just to maintain its current level of overcrowding.[46]

The growth of California's prison system has not gone unnoticed by the private-prison corporations. Private-prison companies such as CCA and Wackenhut have opened Sacramento offices and are spending a great deal of time and money lobbying influential state officials in an attempt to get their share of the California prisoner market. CCA is clearly confident that its political influence will be successful, as illustrated by the fact that it is already building three prisons—one of which is costing over $100 million—even though these prisons have no contract with the state as of 1998. Not to worry, a CCA representative told the *Wall Street Journal*, "if you build it in the right place, the prisoners will come."[47] Such a financial strategy would clearly be foolish if CCA wasn't sure that with the right amount of political expenditures, the company can get what it wants.

So far, the private-prison industry seems to be spending most of its money for "special access" at the state level. This is not to say that it isn't paying attention to those at the national level who can further the financial growth of the industry. When I researched the donating habits of some of the private-prison companies and their employees, I found that the majority of their money targeted committee members who oversee different aspects of the new private-prison system. For instance, the Environment and Public Works Committee that oversees the construction of prisons, the Judicial Committee that oversees the nation's penitentiaries, and the committee that oversees interstate commerce (most private prisons house inmates from out of state and want to make sure that transporting and housing prisoners across state lines remains largely unregulated) were all targeted. Appropriately, Senator Phil Gramm, whom many consider to be the "father of modern mandatory sentencing," was also one of the biggest campaign-funding beneficiaries from the private-prison companies I researched.

But as I said, the best examples of the private-prison industry's trading dollars for "special access" can be found at the state level, where campaign funds go a little further, as shown in CCA's political network in the state of Tennessee. At one time, CCA employed seven lobbyists in Tennessee alone, and Thomas Beasily, the company's chairman emeritus and cofounder, has always had a pretty good idea where to spend his Tennessee campaign contributions. That's because Beasily is the former chairman of that state's Republican Party.[48]

In 1985, CCA made an unsuccessful attempt to take over Tennessee's entire prison system, a bold move that had support from politicians in high places, including then governor Lamar Alexander who is currently a presidential candidate for the 2000 elections. CCA offered to purchase the state of Tennessee's prison system for $250 million. The sale of prisoners would likely have gone through if not for the fact that critics of the plan were quick to point out that Lamar Alexander's wife, Honey, as well as Tennessee Speaker of the House Ned McWherter owned 1.5 percent of CCA's stock at the time. In an attempt to avoid the appearance of a conflict of interest, Honey Alexander placed her CCA stock in a blind trust, where she eventually had the kind of good fortune that Hillary Rodham Clinton had in the commodities market—that's to say that her $5,000 worth of stock turned into $100,000 very quickly.[49]

Later, when CCA wanted to open a new 1,540-bed facility in Tennessee, there was a problem. The state already had a private prison and a law that did not allow more than one such prison to operate in the state at any given time. Enter special access. State senator Robert Rochelle, who had received at least $1,000 in campaign funds from various CCA board members and who had previously sponsored legislation on behalf of the company, put forward a bill to allow CCA to open its prison despite the law.[50]

Like an octopus's tentacles, CCA's political connections in Tennessee in the 1990s seem to reach everywhere. According to journalist Alex Friedmann, "Peaches Simkins, Governor Sundquist's former chief of staff, reportedly owned CCA stock while she was advising the governor on prison privatization. And the speaker of the House in Tennessee's General Assembly, Jimmy Naifeh, is married to CCA political lobbyist Betty Anderson."[51]

And then there are the campaign contributions. Between 1994 and 1996, CCA chief executive officer Dr. Robert Crants, along with Beasily and his wife, donated at least $60,491 to forty-six Tennessee politicians, among them Governor Sundquist and Senator Jim Kyle, the chairman of the Select Oversight Committee on Corrections.[52] In recent years, the prison company's executives have further escalated their efforts to build financial and political ties to members of both parties in the state. As a result, the company's attempt to take over Tennessee's prison system just won't go away.

In spring 1997, CCA's political allies once again began to push for the company to take over the state's prisons, only this time the opposition came from an unexpected direction. Wackenhut, CCA's chief competition, hired former senator Howard Baker's law firm to lobby against the proposed sale, on the grounds that if Tennessee were to privatize its entire system, Wackenhut should get a sizable portion of the prisoner pie. As a result of this lobbying battle between the private-prison firms, turning over the state's prison system to private companies is still on hold, but it would seem that the question is more one of how to divvy up the booty than of whether to give the for-profit prison companies that have filled Tennessee's campaign coffers for years what they want.

The private-prison corporations are spending considerable money on politicians in many states in an effort to get their share of prisoners and to make sure that the prisoners keep coming. And the money appears to be working. In 1998, when the state of Oklahoma was threatening to cancel a contract with CCA, Governor Frank Keating stepped in to prevent the termination. The press wasted little time before questioning whether the governor's actions might have been motivated by the sizable sum of money that CCA had pumped into his campaign coffers. Even money spent at the lowest levels of government can pay big dividends.

The passage of the legislation that initially allowed private prisons in the states of Texas and New Mexico has been attributed to heavy lobbying efforts on the part of law-enforcement organizations in those states. Not surprisingly, as soon as the prisons became legal, members of law enforcement were the first to quit their jobs, form private-prison companies, and then sign lucrative contracts with their friends and former colleagues.

The Bobby Ross Group, one of the private-prison companies started by a former sheriff, was running seven facilities in Texas that housed inmates from six different states. The company was doing quite well on its profit margin—the difference between the daily per-head fee paid by the states and the actual expense to house the prisoners—until September 1997, that is, when three Montana inmates escaped from the company's Dickens County facility. In fact, the company was apparently doing too well on its profit margin. Montana investigators sent to the prison found that the inmates were literally going hungry, a condition that naturally tends to increase a company's profits substantially by cutting expenses.[53]

One might think that Texas would have shut down such a for-profit prison under the circumstances, but that is not what happened. A month after the Montana investigators had found the disturbing conditions at the prison, the Texas Commission on Jail Standards gave the facility its highest possible rating. A few weeks later, the inspector who had written the glowing report acknowledged that besides his job as a prison inspector for the state, he also worked as a "consultant" to the Bobby Ross Group, which paid him $42,000 a year.[54]

In recent years, riots and escapes have plagued the prisons run by the Bobby Ross Group. It's enough to make a person wonder why any jurisdiction would continue to place their prisoners in the company's care. One explanation is that they have a top-drawer lobbyist. The company hired William Sessions, the former head of the FBI, as an adviser. Reportedly, one of Sessions's jobs was to go on sales calls with company execs[55]—which brings us to that other form of political influence, the revolving door between government and industry.

We have seen this revolving door in action for years in other government sectors. The Environmental Protection Agency has become a training ground for employees who eventually wind up making more money in the employ of industries that pollute. Chemical, mining, oil, and manufacturing corporations are constantly hiring former EPA employees who can show them how to get around the agency's regulations or help the companies cut sweetheart deals with their new employee's old friends at the agency. Similarly, defense contractors have long done their employee recruiting at the Pentagon or in Congress, a practice that gives them access to the decisionmakers who hand out multibillion-dollar contracts. But since the mid-1980s, it is corrections that has become the new springboard to lucrative private-sector employment.

For example, like other corporations in the complex in the 1990s, the management for CCA and Wackenhut is largely composed of former high-ranking corrections and law-enforcement officials—including a former head of the FBI, a former CIA director, a former CIA deputy director, a previous head of the Secret Service, a former attorney general, a former head of the Federal Bureau of Prisons, the former chairman of the Tennessee Republican Party, and the former director of the Virginia Department of Corrections, to name a few.[56] As a result, it's fair to say that private-prison companies tend to do their business with their employees' former friends and colleagues at the taxpayer's expense.

The director of the Federal Bureau of Prisons makes $125,000 a year. Although that's a great deal of money, compared to the $350,000 that the chief executive of Wackenhut makes, it's chump change. This revolving door can serve the prison-industrial complex in a couple of ways. First, it allows those who have left government for the private sector to solicit business from their friends and former colleagues. Second, high-paying prison-industrial complex jobs can be dangled like carrots—or as Jimmy Carter might put it, "bribes"—before current government employees. The idea is that cooperation on the part of the government employee today means a high-paying job with the company tomorrow.

Again, this method of doing business works at all levels of government. Not surprisingly, I have found a strong correlation between former state DOC employees who now work for private prisons and which states put their prisoners in what private facilities. For instance, when the private prison in Appleton, Minnesota, needed inmates to fill its empty beds, the company hired a former prison official from Colorado as the private prison's warden. Lo and behold, shortly thereafter Appleton ended up housing 500 Colorado inmates at a price of more than $750,000 a month.[57]

Remember that $34-million-a-year contract for soy products between VitaPro and the state of Texas prison system? At one point, the state was investigating possible improprieties in the signing of the contract resulting from a connection between a private-prison developer, who also turned out to be a VitaPro sales rep on occasion, and the state's purchasing director.[58] No criminal charges were ever filed in the matter, yet the state did eventually cancel the contract because it had not gone through the proper channels.

This is how phase two's "special access" works. There is nothing illegal about it in most instances—immoral, maybe, but not illegal. I say immoral because lobbying for more prisons and hard-on-crime legislation in order to increase profits is not like lobbying for tax exemptions, trade agreements, or less government regulation, or at least it shouldn't be. Although the goals are the same—to improve the bottom line for corporations or unions—there is something disturbing about pushing for legislation to incarcerate more human beings for longer periods of time in order to achieve what is obviously a purely financial objective. But these are the kinds of conflicts that are now unavoidable in light of our decision to turn justice into an industry where hundreds of billions of dollars are up for grabs every year.

6

The Weapons of War

I think I am in agreement with most of the judges in the federal system that mandatory minimums are an imprudent, unwise and often unjust mechanism for sentencing.

—Supreme Court Justice Anthony Kennedy, 1994[1]

The reason we went to mandatory sentencing was because of these "soft-on-crime" judges.

—Senator Orrin Hatch, Frontline, March 9, 1999[2]

We've examined the influence exerted on electoral politics during the last two decades by the media, the consultants, and those who make up the political money supply. This chapter will focus on some of the policies that have resulted from that influence, namely, a variety of predetermined sentencing structures as well as a renewed enthusiasm for capital punishment.

By the beginning of the 1970s, most states had begun to build at least a few new prisons, and state legislatures were strengthening their sentencing guidelines in response to an increase in crime that had occurred during the 1960s. These early anticrime measures increased the nation's prison population by approximately 200,000 by 1980. Although they seemed impressive at the time, compared with what was to transpire in the mid-1980s, these early measures paled in significance.

In response to public opinion polls, which by 1983 had begun to reflect a societal crime anxiety due to "crime-gap" myths and the media's violent content, politicians set about to create legislation that would turn this public fear into votes. They succeeded in 1984 with the passage of the Sentencing Reform Act, which was the most significant salvo fired in the modern war on crime to date. David Kopel, respected author and research director of the Independence Institute, has called this piece of hard-on-crime legislation "the most significant change in sentencing policy in American history."[3]

The 1984 act abolished parole in the federal system and allowed the Sentencing Commission to radically alter the established sentencing guidelines in favor of much harsher and longer sentences that the federal courts were then required to follow without exception. The 700 pages of guidelines created as a result of the act effectively returned America to the same type of long and certain sentences that it had abandoned nearly 100 years earlier because they were found to be ineffective, overly costly, and unjust and made prisons extremely dangerous places for both inmates and guards.

Subsequent to the abandonment of sentences with a predetermined length in the late 1800s, the United States had avoided mandatory sentences, with the exception of those enacted in the 1950s as a means to combat narcotics. But by 1970, even these few remaining mandatory sentences had been found to be quite flawed and were repealed by Congress. As a portent of the manner in which the rise in influence of the consultants would alter politics in the last two decades of the twentieth century, then congressman George Bush—who, at the urging of his hired handlers, would later use the hard-on-crime Willie Horton ads to defeat Michael Dukakis in the 1988 presidential election—adamantly opposed mandatory sentencing.

In 1970, Bush described his reasons for voting for the bill that eliminated such sentences.

> Contrary to what one might imagine, however, this bill will result in better justice and more appropriate sentences. . . . Federal judges are almost unanimously opposed to mandatory minimums, because they remove a great deal of the court's discretion. . . . As a result [of repealing mandatory minimums] we will undoubtedly have more equitable action by the courts, with actually more convictions where they are called for, and fewer disproportionate sentences.[4]

Just eighteen years after uttering these words in opposition to mandatory minimums, Bush would conveniently reshape his political ideology to public opinion so thoroughly as to lead the way in establishing new mandatory sentences while simultaneously declaring his opponent, Dukakis, to be a "soft-on-crime" liberal, even though Dukakis, in essence, had put forward a position on crime that was very similar to the one Bush himself had claimed to hold prior to his presidential aspirations.

With the ability of judges to determine sentences greatly impaired by the passage of the 1984 Sentencing Reform Act, the prison population began to swell at a rate never before seen. Despite its being hailed as a tool to combat violent crime, in reality, the 700 pages of new sentencing guidelines turned out to be primarily aimed at minor regulatory offenses. In his writings, Kopel has used several examples to illustrate this last point, including the fact that under the new sentencing structure, some types of gambling drew longer prison terms than manslaughter; a person entering the United States illegally was punished with the same sentence as a person convicted of abusive sexual assault that puts a child in fear; and aggravated assault had the same sentence as smuggling a certain dollar value of fish.[5] The illogical guidelines created by the Sentencing Reform Act are rife with such disparities between violent and nonviolent crimes, and as a result, they are much more efficient at filling our prisons with nonviolent offenders than they are at taking violent predators off the street. For the first time since our poorly thought out attempt at prohibition, there are now more nonviolent criminals in our prisons than violent ones.

Despite the obvious flaws of these sentence reforms, Congress wasn't about to back away from its new creation. It had found a powerful campaign tool in the Sentencing Reform Act. Everyone who even remotely questioned the wisdom of the new guidelines or the resulting explosion in the nonviolent prison population was quickly labeled "soft on crime." Judges, the vast majority of whom, as noted by Congressman Bush in 1970, opposed the guidelines for a number of valid reasons, were quickly saddled with the "soft-on-crime" moniker, as illustrated in the statement by Senator Orrin Hatch at the beginning of this chapter.

By the late 1980s, thanks largely to "crime-gap" propaganda and increasingly violent TV content, the public began to show overwhelming support for tough-talking politicians who promised them more public safety. They also exhibited an equal disdain for the judges and elected leaders who had been branded by the new "soft-on-crime" McCarthyism. And if there were any who still doubted the career-ending power of the "soft-on-crime" label, Dukakis's destruction at the hands of the Bush consultants in 1988 would erase that doubt for years to come.

Consider these remarks in 1992 by Bruce Sundlun, a Democrat from Rhode Island.

> These programs [prison alternatives] are clearly the right thing to do, no question. But I want to know what it will take to sell these programs because they might leave you open to political potshots from people who would say you're soft on crime. I'm up for reelection this year, and Willie Horton is as well known in Rhode Island as is Michael Dukakis.[6]

As a result of the political success of the Sentencing Reform Act, Congress decided to turn the anticriminal rhetoric up a few notches in the form of congressional mandatory sentences that would allow politicians to take still more credit for fighting violent crime, a handy claim come election time. Not only has Congress passed more than a hundred of these mandatory sentences, but it has made sure that the new sentencing structure supersedes all other sentencing guidelines. Based on the manner in which many current policy decisions regarding crime are being made—namely, through polling and campaign finance—it is fair to say that concerning the sentencing process, thanks to Congress, judges have all but been replaced by the public's exaggerated perception of being victimized by crime and the desires of corporations that wish to profit from a growing prison population.

Like the 700 pages of guidelines established as a result of the 1984 Sentencing Reform Act, these new, even harsher, mandatory sentences passed by Congress have been touted as a tool to fight the violent crime that is supposedly overwhelming our communities as a result of drug use. But in application, Congress's new sentences, like those created in 1984, have resulted in the incarceration of hundreds of thousands of nonviolent offenders but have had little or no effect on those who commit violent acts. In fact, many observers of the criminal-justice system now believe that Congress's tinkering with sentencing standards has made it increasingly difficult to find room in our overcrowded prison system for the violent offenders the public is truly concerned about.

Three Strikes and We're Out

Michael Riggs was homeless and broke, and his health was failing. Lacking the financial resources to seek the medical attention he needed,

Riggs made a decision he now regrets. He walked into a supermarket and stole a bottle of vitamins. Unfortunately for Riggs, he lived in California and had been previously convicted of several other nonviolent crimes.

Riggs is now one of the 40,000 inmates—one-fourth of California's entire prison population—who have been sentenced under that state's three-strikes law.[7] I use Riggs as an example not because his situation is uniquely pathetic but rather because his self-prepared appeal of the three-strikes law was the first to make it to the Supreme Court, or at least to almost make it. On January 18, 1999, despite the fact that four of the justices described Riggs's case as "obviously substantial" with regard to the constitutionality of the three-strikes law, the court decided not to hear his arguments. In the end, only Justice Stephen Breyer voted in favor of hearing the case.[8] For now, the twenty-three states, as well as the federal government, that have enacted a three-strikes law are free to continue to dole out incredibly harsh sentences to repeat offenders.[9]

California's three-strikes law is a perfect illustration of how the perpetual prisoner machine has changed the face of America's justice system. In the early 1990s, Fresno, California photographer Mike Reynolds, whose daughter had been murdered by a parolee, was working to secure signatures for a citizens' initiative that would greatly increase the sentences of repeat violent offenders. Reynolds wasn't having much success, however. Several of his attempts had died in legislative committees, and in general, politicians did not support his attempts. But thanks to the media, things were about to change.

In 1993, a terrible tragedy occurred. It was one of those sensational crimes that serves the media in its effort to boost profits. Polly Klaas, a twelve-year-old girl, was abducted during a slumber party at her suburban home in Petaluma, California. Klaas was eventually found murdered, but not before the local and national media had thrown the story into the spotlight. Night after night, week after week, Californians and the rest of America watched as Polly's father made emotional pleas for information on his daughter's whereabouts. Eventually, a man named Richard Allen Davis was arrested and admitted to the kidnapping and murder. Davis had been previously arrested for burglary and kidnapping, so the stage was now set for Mike Reynolds and his citizens' initiative.

Prior to the Klaas murder, then California governor Pete Wilson had refused to support Reynolds's initiative, now known by the name "three strikes and you're out," but that was before the Klaas case had worked the electorate into an anticriminal lather. Wilson and a senior California senator both spoke at the little girl's funeral. They turned the Klaas case into an example of everything that was supposedly wrong with the justice system. Even President Clinton singled out the Klaas case in his State of the Union Address, blaming leniency and softheadedness on crime as the cause for Polly's death.

Within a few weeks of Polly's murder, nearly every candidate running for a major California office, regardless of party affiliation, had endorsed Reynolds's three-strikes initiative. And why not? Due to the massive media exposure in the Klaas case, polls showed that California voters believed that crime was the state's single biggest problem and that they were now in favor of the three-strikes initiative by an astounding margin of eight to one—and 88-percent support for anything is the kind of poll results that get the attention of politicians and their consultants.[10] It was clear that not supporting three strikes had become a recipe for electoral defeat. And just in case the polls weren't enough political incentive to back Reynolds's measure, as I mentioned earlier, the National Rifle Association and the prison guards' union began to pump money to candidates willing to support the harshest proposed version of the law.

On March 9, 1994, Wilson signed Assembly Bill 971—three strikes—into law. Shortly thereafter, the identically worded Proposition 184 was placed on the ballot by citizens and passed. Three strikes had become a reality. In a knee-jerk reaction to a horrible tragedy, Californians would now lead the way in what they believed would be a war on violent crime. They would do it for Polly Klaas.

Most Californians were under the impression that the new law would ensure that repeat violent offenders would be permanently removed from society, but few apparently read the law's fine print. Three strikes was not reserved for violent offenders alone. It could be applied to a wide variety of offenses such as stealing vitamins. As a result of three strikes, California has been forced to embark on a massive prison expansion—an expansion that has served well the biggest financial backer of the law, the prison guards' union, in the form of major salary increases for its members and the hiring of thousands of new guards.

In the 132 years between 1852 and 1984, the state of California only built a total of twelve prisons. In the eleven-year period between 1985 and 1996, the state built sixteen more. And some experts predict that three strikes could eventually require that state to build as many as twenty to fifty more prisons just to house the new wave of life sentences being created by the law.[11] So has this hard-on-crime response to repeat offenders taken dangerous violent criminals off the street? Absolutely. Unfortunately, however, three strikes is like using a sawed-off shotgun to shoot the bad guy in a crowded room. You may get him, but at what cost?

Dale Broyles, a man who had previously been convicted as an ex-felon in possession of a firearm is now doing life in California. Broyles drank too much one night and was thrown into the back seat of a parked car by friends at a party he was attending. The car was illegally parked and was subsequently towed away with the intoxicated Broyles still in the back seat. The tow-truck owner called the cops, who found the passed-out man still in the car. They also found a handgun in the glove box. Despite testimony by several people that neither the gun nor the car belonged to Broyles, he received life under the three strikes law.

Edward Morrison is a mentally disturbed man with a drug addiction. Morrison was on parole when he tested positive for drugs and was sentenced to six months in a minimum-security facility. With less than one month to go on his sentence, Morrison walked away from the prison. He was arrested shortly thereafter when he stopped at a gas station to apply for a job. Morrison's escape resulted in his being sentenced under three strikes.

Duane Silva has been diagnosed as having schizoaffective disorder and being bipolar, with an Axis II diagnosis of mild mental retardation. Silva has an IQ of 71. The young man's first run-in with the law stemmed from setting two trash cans on fire. Once he had lit the fires, Silva himself called the fire department. He later told the firefighters he had been working for the sheriff's department and had been given the job of walking the streets and burning down the businesses that belonged to dope dealers. He pleaded guilty and was found incompetent to stand trial. Silva was sentenced to a year of mental treatment. Strike one.

Silva's next run-in with the law was similar. He started two small fires in pickup trucks. This time Silva claimed that he was working undercover for the fire department. Strike two. Silva's third encounter with law enforcement was no less bizarre. It came when he burglarized a friend's house and stole a VCR and some jewelry. After the family returned home, Silva told his friend that he knew where a VCR like the one that had been stolen was located. Silva then called 911 to report that he had located the stolen VCR. When the police interrogated the man in possession of the VCR, they discovered that he had bought it from Silva for $40. Strike three.

Unfortunately for the clearly troubled Silva, this last brush with the law happened a few weeks after the passage of three strikes. Over the broken-English pleas of Silva's mother, who repeatedly tried to tell the judge that her son was "not right in the head," Silva was sentenced to life in prison.

The stories go on and on. A man steals a $5.62 chuck steak to feed his mentally retarded brother and mother after his mom's Social Security check was lost in the mail. He gets life. In Washington state, the first state to pass a three-strikes law—thanks to the financial backing of the NRA—a thirty-five-year-old homeless man robbed $135 from a sandwich shop by putting his finger in his pocket and claiming to have a gun. It was his third petty theft, and he is now doing life without parole.[12]

The Center on Juvenile and Criminal Justice has documented many other disturbing cases where the three-strikes laws have been applied to nonviolent offenders. And as much as we would like to think that such cases are the rare exception to the rule, they aren't. A full 70 percent of all three-strikes prosecutions in California have been for nonviolent and nonserious offenses. In Los Angeles County, it's even worse. Only 4 percent of those convicted under the three-strikes law have committed a crime of violence.[13]

When faced with the reality of how three strikes was being applied, prosecutor David T. Bristow, deputy district attorney for San Bernardino County, California, refused to apply the three-strikes law to nonviolent crimes. Bristow told his superiors that based on moral and ethical grounds, he could not do so. Not wanting to appear "soft on crime," District Attorney Dennis Stout, Bristow's boss, asked for and received the conscientious prosecutor's resignation.[14] If ethical and moral objections aren't enough to raise concerns over the three-strikes laws, then the economic implications should be.

The fiscal realities of three strikes are only now beginning to sink in on the politicians and voters who jumped on the hard-on-crime bandwagon following the Klaas murder. It costs $25,000 a year to incarcerate a young inmate. As a prisoner sentenced to life ages, the price tag increases, nearly tripling to $70,000 a year for inmates over the age of fifty-five. A Stanford University study estimates that the total cost for an average life sentence in California is around $1.5 million. That's a lot of taxpayer money when you consider that 70 percent of those life sentences are being doled out for nonviolent offenses such as a man stealing a $5 piece of meat to feed his hungry dependents. The study predicted that if the prison population increases as expected for the next twenty years or so, California's three-strikes law will cost that state's taxpayers hundreds of billions—not millions, but billions—of dollars.[15]

California has become the case study for three strikes because it has implemented its three-strikes law more liberally than those jurisdictions that have followed in its hard-on-crime footsteps. The California Department of Corrections estimates that California will be forced to spend $6.7 billion a year to fully implement the three-strikes law.[16] This is more than five times the original estimate that was presented to taxpayers. And as we will see later in the book, such incredible expenditures by California's Department of Corrections have devastated the rest of the state's budget, including the areas of education and other crime-preventing social programs.

As I mentioned earlier, there are now twenty-three states as well as the federal government with some version of the three-strikes laws on their books. But aside from California, Georgia, Nevada, Florida, and Washington, most states have rarely used their new law for putting away repeat offenders.[17] One reason for this lack of use is that other harsh adjustments to the sentencing guidelines, such as mandatory sentencing and truth in sentencing, have already left most states building prisons as fast as they can in a futile effort to catch up with their booming nonviolent prison populations. Since these states cannot keep up with their prisoner population as it is, using their three-strikes laws would be budgetary suicide. With that being the case, why have so many states passed a law that they know they cannot implement? The answer to this question is very telling. I believe that most three-strikes laws have been passed for no other reason than that they allow politicians to make a public display of their electorate-pleasing commitment to all that is hard on crime. And I am certainly not alone in this view.

U.S. Supreme Court Justice William H. Rehnquist had this to say about such mandatory sentencing practices as three strikes:

> Mandatory minimums . . . [a]re frequently the result of floor amendments to demonstrate emphatically that legislators want "to get tough on crime." Just as frequently they do not involve any careful consideration of the effect they might have on sentencing guidelines, as a whole. Indeed, it seems to me that one of the best arguments against any more manda-

tory minimums, and perhaps against some of those we already have, is that they frustrate the careful calibration of sentences, from one end of the spectrum to the other, which the sentencing guidelines were intended to accomplish.[18]

The same politicians who hype the fact that they have voted for three-strikes laws must realize that these laws are fiscally irresponsible and that if they were to be put into widespread practice, their state would wind up with the same horrific budgetary problems as those now being experienced in California. According to the National Association of Criminal Defense Lawyers (NACDL):

> States such as California that rushed to enact broad "three strikes" laws, are now finding that their judicial and prison systems—to say nothing of their state and local budgets—are being strained past the breaking point by the huge volume of cases resulting from these laws . . . we caution state legislators and voters against hastily adopting broad "three strikes" laws without carefully examining their inherently debilitating impact on courts, prisons, budgets, law-enforcement and prison officials, and particularly on nonviolent offenders for whom life in prison would be a profoundly unfair punishment.[19]

As noted in the defense attorney's warning, the impact of three strikes on a state's court system can also be quite significant. Since being convicted three times equals a potential life sentence, suspects are no longer willing to accept plea bargains in exchange for a guilty plea. They now prefer to take their chances in front of a jury. Prior to three strikes, 94 percent of all cases in California were handled through plea bargaining. After three strikes, only 14 percent of those faced with a second strike and only 6 percent of those facing a third strike have sought a plea agreement. According to California's Legislative Analyst's Office, jury trials in that state have increased by 150 to 300 percent in most counties as a result of three strikes.[20] Not only does this radically increase the court cost to taxpayers, but it has also resulted in extreme overcrowding in the county jail systems, where suspects are held awaiting their trial.

Jails such as those in Santa Clara, San Diego, and Los Angeles Counties will need to add a significant number of beds as a result of three strikes.[21] These and other counties are now considering using private for-profit facilities to take over their new overflow of inmates. Due to the fact that 70 percent of California's total jail beds are currently capped under court orders to prevent overcrowding, many counties have been forced either to stop prosecuting some cases or to release already sentenced criminals early.[22]

In Los Angeles County, for example, thanks to the influx of those awaiting trial under three-strikes charges, the average inmate is now serving only 45 percent of the sentence before being released.[23] Once again, it's ironic that a law born out of public concern over the premature release of prisoners would, in fact, cause that very scenario to unfold. But it's like Justice Rehnquist said, these hard-on-crime sentencing measures often "do not involve any careful consideration of the effect they might have on sentencing guidelines, as a whole."

Even though most states and even the federal government have had the good sense not to use their three-strikes laws to a significant degree, this does not mean that they never will. There is still a grave danger lurking on the horizon simply because these laws are on the books. As we have seen, all it takes is the media saturation from one sensationalized Polly Klaas-type case to cause politicians to hit the "on" switch on their three-strikes laws. For instance, I have little doubt that if Eric Harris or Dylan Klebold, the gunmen in the Columbine school shooting, had had any type of violent criminal history prior to the 1999 tragedy, there would have been politicians in twenty-three states scrambling to aggressively enforce their three-strikes laws. And there is yet another threat from the fact that these laws are on the books at a time when our system of government is becoming more and more influenced by the will of the market every day. Clearly, the powerful prison-industrial complex lobby and other hard-on-crime special interests such as the NRA—entities that pushed hard for the creation of such laws in the first place—will continue to use campaign financing as a means to exert pressure on politicians for the increasing use of their three-strikes laws. After all, what good is a law with the potential to pump billions of dollars into the prison-industrial complex if nobody is willing to use it?

Mandatory Sentencing

One way to tell which direction the political winds are blowing on any particular issue is to watch the president's State of the Union Address. Sometimes the Democrats leap to their feet to show support for their agenda, and sometimes the Republicans do the same. More and more often these days, as a result of the blending of the two parties' platforms to match public opinion, members of both parties can be found springing out of their seats in a fit of camera-conscious applause to show bipartisan support for something the president says.

Ever since 1980, when Ronald Reagan announced that America was no longer going to coddle criminals, virtually every State of the Union Address has emptied the leather seats whenever a new hard-on-crime policy, particularly a new round of mandatory sentences, is mentioned. Even during the address of 1999, at a time of extreme partisan bickering over the president's impeachment, Clinton was able to obtain a brief moment of enthusiastic congressional support when he alluded to once again increasing the prison sentences of those who break the drug laws. But over the years, not every seat in the chamber has been emptied by the annual dose of hard-on-crime rhetoric. The seats occupied by the members of the Supreme Court have always remained occupied.

Now we all know that the members of the Supreme Court are not allowed to stand, applaud, or even display positive or negative facial expressions during the address, the idea being that they must appear impartial on all issues at all times. But this picture of a Congress wildly applauding hard-on-crime rhetoric while the justices sit emotionless in their chairs would likely not change even if the members of our country's highest court were allowed to express their opinions during the address.

It seems the justices understand something that our congressional representatives apparently don't: The hard-on-crime changes to the sentencing guidelines being pushed into law by Congress are destroying the nation's criminal-justice system and causing our prisons to overflow while accomplishing nothing beneficial to Americans. These sentencing changes are, as put so eloquently by Supreme Court Justice Stephen Breyer, "very rotten bananas."[24]

It is hardly an exaggeration to say that no one thinks that mandatory sentences are a good idea—no one, that is, except the public, which has been presented a distorted image of crime by the media and those putting forward the crime-gap myths, the politicians who cash in on that distortion, a few prosecutors with political aspirations, and the companies that profit from a growing prison population. Judges, attorneys, the Federal Courts Study Committee, the Federal Judicial Center, the National Association of Criminal Defense Lawyers, the Sentencing Commission, and even Attorney General Janet Reno have all voiced their opposition to these predetermined sentencing guidelines. With so many knowledgeable sources in the justice system opposed to them, why have mandatory sentences proliferated at such a staggering pace? The answer is: because of "the politics of public opinion." From the wars on drugs and crime to the Contract with America put forward during the short-lived "Republican revolution" of the mid-1990s, mandatory sentencing is largely the result of vote-seeking politicians meddling in the judicial system for their own gain.

In the 1970s, New York launched the modern round of mandatory sentencing with the passage of the Rockefeller drug laws. Since then, most states have implemented some form of predetermined sentencing, as has the federal government. It is estimated that the additional costs to taxpayers for prisoners receiving mandatory sentences in the year 1990 alone was $91 million. It is also estimated that if these mandatory sentences were to be reduced by only 20 percent, taxpayers would save $200 million per year. Yet despite such facts, it appears that the 1999 Congress has every intention of passing a new round of mandatory sentences.

Numerous studies on the impact of mandatory sentencing have been conducted. Almost all have reached the same conclusions. Mandatory sentencing is unduly expensive. It has no demonstrable effect as a deterrent. It has not lowered the crime rate. It has no effect on the rate of recidivism. It has radically increased the prison population, which has resulted in severe overcrowding and increased costs to taxpayers. And it has eliminated the ability of judges to use their discretion in matters of sentencing—arguably their main purpose for existing.

In describing mandatory sentencing, a December 1993 Department of Justice report titled *An Analysis of Nonviolent Drug Offenders with Minimal Criminal Histories* referred to these sentences as an ineffective punishment philosophy because they don't account for individual characteristics.[25] In other words, a person's criminal history, arguably the single most important element in traditional sentencing decisions, no longer matters. All that is taken into account are the details of a crime such as the amount of drugs a person had in possession at the time of arrest—5.0 ounces gets a five-year sentence, 5.1 ounces gets ten. Period.

In commenting on the rigidity of mandatory sentences during a court hearing, U.S. District Court judge Spencer Letts said,

Congress decided to hit the problem of drugs, as they saw it, with a sledgehammer, making no allowance for the circumstances of any particular case. . . . Under the statutory minimum, it can make no difference whether he is a lifetime criminal or a first-time offender. Indeed, under this sledgehammer approach, it could make no difference if the day before making this one slip in an otherwise unblemished life, the defendant had rescued fifteen children from a burning building, or had won the Congressional Medal of Honor while defending his country.[26]

In his testimony before Congress in 1993, Judge Vincent L. Broderick, speaking on behalf of the Judicial Conference of the United States, conveyed "the complete and unmitigated opposition of the federal judges of this country to mandatory minimums."[27] As a result of such opposition to mandatory sentencing, a number of judges have actually stepped down, and many senior justices now refuse to hear the drug cases where these unfair sentencing guidelines are most often applied. Even America's "top cop" finds such sentencing practices to be inappropriate.

Attorney General Janet Reno has voiced grave concern over mandatory sentencing. Reno believes that such sentencing should be restricted to violent criminals only and points out that most individuals receiving mandatory sentences are nonviolent, low-level drug defendants.[28] In commenting on this trend, a report by the NACDL states, "Regrettably, Attorney General Janet Reno's wisdom [mandatory sentences should only be applied to violent offenders] has been overridden to date by an administration all too eager to flex its 'tough on crime' political bona fides."[29]

As we have seen, this predetermined sentencing structure has severely tied the hands of both the judicial system and the nation's pardon and parole boards. Judges can no longer take into account the particulars of individual cases. In a very real way, our judges have been turned into little more than courtroom props. It is now the adversarial prosecutors, by way of their authority to decide whether or not to charge a defendant under a statute that is subject to a mandatory minimum, who have assumed the power to determine the length of sentences. This is hardly the system of checks and balances envisioned by those who established our criminal-justice system.

The increasing power of prosecutors is a particularly disturbing evolution in our courts when you consider that many prosecutors are simply using their offices as a political stepping-stone. In our current political environment, a former prosecutor with a particularly hard-on-crime record has been proven to have a very good chance of reaching the next level of elected office. As of 1999, there were no less than fifty congressmen who had reached their position by way of the Prosecutor's Office.[30]

For this reason, I believe that it is accurate to say that many of the mandatory sentences being doled out—particularly those going to first-time nonviolent offenders—are more the result of the political aspirations of prosecutors than an attempt to reflect some sense of justice. I say this because prosecutors, of all people, should be aware that their heavy use of mandatory sentencing for nonviolent offenders is on occasion causing the early release of violent inmates.

Not only does occasionally granting early release to a violent inmate to make room for nonviolent offenders serving mandatory sentences pose a potential danger to the public—albeit a greatly exaggerated one in the press—it also feeds the propaganda that gave birth to hard-on-crime sentencing in the first place. Every time a parolee with a violent history commits a new violent crime, the media go overboard with their sensationalized coverage, and the public winds up demanding still harsher mandatory sentences. It is a repetitive and destructive cycle.

Once again we are using a scattergun approach to criminal-justice policy. Politicians exploit the anticriminal feeding frenzy that occurs every time the media hype the rarest of events—a violent offender released early who commits a subsequent violent crime—to push the creation of sentencing policies that may indeed stop a handful of violent crimes but do irreparable harm to hundreds of thousands of nonviolent offenders in the process at an astronomical cost to the public. I am not implying that stopping a few violent crimes is not important. I am simply pointing out that if politicians would take a more responsible approach to mandatory sentences—for instance, limiting them to violent offenders, as has been suggested by so many in the judicial system—there would be plenty of room in our existing prisons to assure that violent offenders are never released prematurely.

In a 1994 report, the Federal Judicial Center summed up its view of mandatory sentences by quoting Professor Michael Tonry, who said, "Basic new insights concerning application of mandatory penalties are not likely to emerge. . . . We now know what we are likely to know, and what our predecessors knew, about mandatory penalties. As instruments of public policy, they do little good and much harm."[31]

Truth in Sentencing

This weapon of the war on crime is simply more of the same. I will not bother to once again describe the ineffectiveness of this policy as regards the crime rate. It suffices to say that it has had no more effect than the other examples of political tinkering with the sentencing guidelines. It increases the prison population. It increases the expense of the prison system to taxpayers. It plays well to those entering the voting booth. And in the end, it accomplishes more harm than good, particularly when it comes to the 500,000 men and women who are employed in our prisons.

To understand the absurdity of "truth in sentencing," we have to take a brief look at the history of penology. In the first hundred years of our nation's existence, prison sentences were long and sure. A ten-year sentence meant that an inmate would serve ten years. And though this may sound like a good idea, in application it created a dangerous environment for both prisoners and those charged with their care.

Prisoners who know that they will have to serve every day of their sentence regardless of their actions while in prison have no incentive for good behavior or for making an attempt at rehabilitation. In the late 1800s, after having had eighty years of failed efforts at reform and after conducting a number of studies aimed at improving the prison system, the United States adopted the practice of assigning inmates indeterminate sentences. Instead of telling prisoners that they would serve five years, a judge would hand down a sentence of five to ten years. If an inmate behaved properly and exhibited signs of being reformed, release would be possible after five years. Failure to abide by the rules or show progress would result in the prisoner's serving all or a part of the additional five years of the sentence. Although it can be argued that this two-tiered sentencing structure has never accomplished much in the area of reform—largely due to the prisonization effect—few penologists would dispute that it greatly improved the ability of those who run our prisons to control prisoners and thereby keep their employees safe.

Judges understand the importance of incentive-oriented sentencing. Prison administrators and guards understand its importance. Only our representatives in Congress are apparently ignorant of its advantages, having shown no regard for the lessons of history. Politicians have apparently misinterpreted the current sentencing practices as somehow being "soft on crime," and as a result, they have set about to turn back the penology clock to that time in our history when sentences were certain and prisons were a dangerous place to be, regardless of which side of the bars you were on.

The idea behind truth in sentencing is to require that an inmate serve at least 85 percent of the maximum sentence that was originally handed down. In other words, under truth in sentencing, inmates sentenced to five to ten years are forced to serve at least $8^{1}/_{2}$ years, regardless of their behavior. Prison officials have continuously raised objections to this plan, stating that such a small sentencing span does not offer inmates a practical incentive for complying to the prison rules. Despite these objections from those who know what they are talking about, Congress has used every means available to push their truth-in-sentencing agenda.

As with the other sentencing modifications created out of the public opinion polls that reflect society's twisted impression of crime, supporters of truth in sentencing claim that it is needed to keep violent criminals off the street. But just as with three strikes and mandatory sentences, no less than 75 percent of those affected by truth in sentencing are nonviolent offenders, whose cost of additional incarceration under this sentencing structure can hardly be justified. And truth be known, the whole explanation being offered to the public regarding the need for truth in sentencing is based on a completely flawed interpretation of the facts.

When politicians hear that an inmate serving a two-to-five-year sentence is getting out after only two years, they interpret it as meaning that the inmate served less than half of the sentence. But this is not the case at all. When judges use the indeterminate sentencing structure, they generally dole out much longer sentences than they would otherwise. They do not intend for inmates to serve the latter part of their sentence unless they prove to be a disciplinary problem. In this example, the last three years of the sentence is issued in order to give those who run our prisons some form of nonviolent leverage over their charges. It is a tool of the system to help ensure compliance to the rules of prison life.

I must admit that I find it hard to believe that the politicians who are removing this valuable tool from the hands of prison administrators are really ignorant of its importance. It seems more likely that in our present political state, where the appearance of being hard on crime translates into votes and campaign funds, ambitious politicians are intentionally painting an inaccurate portrait of indiscriminate sentencing because it helps their political cause. For example, many politicians get a good deal of mileage out of pointing to crimes committed by released prisoners, arguing that they would still be in jail if they were serving their maximum sentences.

Of course such crimes do occur, but even if every state adopted truth in sentencing tomorrow, this mechanism's ability to stop such crimes would be short-lived indeed, limited to a one- or two-year window at best. As a result of the prisonization process, many of those who enter the prison system will reoffend once released, whether it's after two years of a five-year sentence or after four years of a five-year sentence. This means that a crime prevented in 1995 by truth in sentencing becomes a crime committed 1997 that might not have happened otherwise. At best, truth in sentencing is an expensive tool in the war on crime that offers a temporary illusion of safer streets.

Consider this example, pointed out by the National Criminal Justice Commission in its 1995 report, released in book form as *The Real War on Crime*. When the state of Virginia was considering the adoption of truth in sentencing, its plan to abandon parole called for the construction of twenty-five new prisons at a cost of $2 billion. In addition, state accountants estimated that it would take $500 million per year to run the new truth-in-sentencing prison system—double the cost of the old system. Not only was truth in sentencing expensive, but adopting it meant that money from other programs would have to be diverted into corrections. Virginia governor George Allen Jr. admitted he was looking to parks and schools as possible sources for the increased prison costs.

In his attempt to sell the electorate on this new hard-on-crime measure, Governor Allen turned to the same old clichés we hear from our elected officials every day. First, he claimed that the state needed truth in sentencing because of the "rapid rise of violent crime," an intriguing claim, considering that violent crime in Virginia had actually been falling in the two years prior to Allen's making his pitch.

Next, Allen told his constituents that "putting dangerous predators back on the streets" was one of the main causes of criminal victimization. This was also wrong. In Virginia, only 9 percent of robberies, 2 percent of rapes, 4 percent of murders, and 2 percent of aggravated assaults were being committed by people who had been paroled.[32]

Finally, the governor told the state's voters that his new plan for corrections would target "violent career criminals." The presence of this completely false statement can be chalked up to politics as usual. Allen's own projections for Virginia's conformity to truth in sentencing showed that it would impact four times as many nonviolent offenders as violent ones. Unfortunately, voters in nearly every part of the country have been equally misled about the need for truth in sentencing.[33]

The only data that seem to support the implementation of truth in sentencing are the polls that continue to show that the public will embrace almost anything if it's packaged under the guise of offering them safety from violent criminals. Apparently, that's enough for most of our elected officials in Washington, as evidenced by the extreme pressure that they have put on the states to force them to comply with their hard-on-crime initiatives.

The 1994 crime bill created a $10-billion pool of money to be allocated to the states for new prison construction. But in an effort to push its crime agenda on the states, Congress held the badly needed funds hostage, as it had with highway funds when it demanded state compliance with the speed limit of fifty-five miles per hour. Only those states demonstrating a hard-on-crime resolve, including the adoption of truth-in-sentencing, would get access to the money. This was bad news for most states, considering that their prisons were bursting at the seams due to the effects of nearly two decades of mandatory sentences. The money was sorely needed. But as is often the case with the dangling-carrot incentive, the states should have thought twice before accepting the offer.[34]

The General Accounting Office reported that, to their credit, sixteen states refused the federal government's offer of money, each of them citing the fact that "truth in sentencing" would eventually cost more to implement than the federal government was offering in return. Still, many states made the shortsighted decision to adopt this latest hard-on-crime measure in order to secure the badly needed dollars for prison construction. As a result, their already unmanageable prison populations have done nothing but grow far beyond the temporary relief offered by the federal government's money.

The Death Penalty

In 1976, the Supreme Court decided that after decades of living without capital punishment, which had been found to be a cruel and unusual punishment, the United States could once again begin executing criminals. The return to the death penalty is perhaps the least logical of all hard-on-crime policies. Study after study has shown that it does not work as a deterrent to murder; that it has resulted in extradition problems, as most civilized nations will not extradite individuals accused of murder to the United States because their laws prohibit turning over suspects who might be put to death; and that with a price tag of a couple of million dollars per execution, it would be far more economical to use life without parole as the "ultimate" sentence.[35] These are the most basic arguments against the death penalty. They do not even take into consideration the morality of execution or the fact that we occasionally kill innocent people or that we tend to only execute poor people, mostly blacks, or that some executions are more driven by polls than by the quest for justice.

Yes, "driven by polls." In the broadest sense, this is true because, as we have seen, our hard-on-crime policies have their roots in public opinion polls, but it is also true in the most specific, grotesque sense as well. In an article titled "Judges and the Politics of Death: Deciding Between the Bill of Rights and the Next Election in Capital Cases," which appeared in the 1995 *Boston University Law Review*, authors Stephen Bright and Patrick Keenan described how in most states that have the death penalty, judges must stand for reelection. The two went on to clearly demonstrate that death sentences are often doled out as a means of achieving political popularity.[36]

Writing for the *Atlantic Monthly* in 1998, Christopher Hitchens concurred with this opinion, noting that judges around the country make some of their capital-punishment decisions in the same manner that Bill Clinton made his mind up about the execution of Ricky Ray Rector, an inmate who had been sentenced to death despite the fact that he was severely retarded. Clinton refused to commute Rector's sentence after poll results showed that it would be more politically expedient to allow the execution to continue, regardless of Rector's mental disability.[37]

Such a reality becomes all the more disturbing when one starts to examine the demographics of execution. It's fair to say that our ultimate penalty has been reserved almost exclusively for the poor and primarily for those of color.[38] In places like Harris County, Texas, one young black man after another is being put down as if an epidemic had broken out in a livestock pen. This single county that contains most of Houston executed more than thirty people in 1997 alone. Across the nation, seventy-four people were executed in that same year. Ironically, that's almost the exact number of innocent people—seventy-seven, as of February 1999—who have been released from death row since 1976.[39]

So just how sure are we that those whom we execute are guilty? Not very. The state of Illinois, for instance, is only batting 500. Since 1976, that state has executed twelve, while being forced to release twelve innocent men from death row.[40] The average length of time needed for a person to be proven innocent on death row is between six and ten years, but many cases take considerably longer.[41] It took Hayes Williams thirty years to finally prove his innocence in Louisiana in 1997. Dennis Fritz sat on death row in Oklahoma for twelve years before being released after DNA testing linked another man to the murder he had been found guilty of committing. Other such stories are similar—fifteen years here, a dozen there.

The only chance that most death-row inmates have to prove their innocence is habeas corpus. As I said, this process usually takes around six years. But even this relief for the innocent has been rendered impotent by hard-on-crime proponents whose polls tell them that Americans want to speed up the execution process. In response to such polls, Bill Clinton has given us the Counter-Terrorism and Effective Death Penalty Act, which practically eliminates the right of habeas corpus by shortening the process to one year. Gene Nichol, dean of the University of Colorado Law School, calls the act "the most serious restriction on habeas corpus protections in half a century."[42] Had Clinton's "hard-on-habeas" act been in place since 1976, seventy innocent men would now likely have been put to death rather than having been set free.

We have been told that shortening the period for habeas corpus will stamp the word "reduced" on the $2 million price tag for snuffing a criminal. Several states, including Florida and Texas, have passed legislation to speed up the execution process because they claim that in its current condition, it costs too much to implement.[43] In fact, saving money, not justice, seems to be at the heart of most of the current death-penalty decisions.

The number-one reason that innocent people have been freed from death row in recent years is DNA testing. Unfortunately, DNA testing cost about $10,000 a pop, a price apparently too high for the justice system. Even though states are willing to spend millions to execute an inmate, most requests by the condemned for DNA testing are refused because of the costs. So just at the time when technology is making it possible to find some of those on death row who are innocent, the government is hell-bent on killing them before their innocence can be established.

In this same save-money, forget-justice vein, in May 1999, Nebraska governor Mike Johanns vetoed a measure that would have placed a two-year moratorium on that state's executions, pending an investigation into allegations that the death penalty is being applied unfairly to a disproportionate number of poor and minority offenders. Johanns said that he vetoed the measure because it could have been used as a basis for unnecessary appeals that are time-consuming and expensive.[44] What is troubling here is that such appeals would only have come about if the allegation were proven to be true by the research that would have been conducted during the moratorium, and if that were the case, then the new round of appeals would hardly be "unnecessary." Once again, saving money on the death penalty seems to have trumped the concept of justice. And if we take a step backward, we can see that economics also plays an important role during the trial of those who find themselves on death row.

Sadly, to get to death row, it seems that you have to go through a court-appointed attorney. As I mentioned earlier, low-income defendants are twice as likely to be found guilty as defendants with high incomes. This is not a knock on public defenders, but rather on the system itself. Low-income suspects who can't afford an attorney get one appointed by the courts, but that's about all they get. The courts rarely supply enough money for the appointed defense attorney to properly investigate the crime or to spend the necessary amount of time on the case to adequately represent a client. It's not unusual for a public defender to handle about four times the case load recommended by the bar.[45]

Experience is another factor with public defenders. In Harris County, Texas, for example, death-penalty cases—which any attorney worth his or her salt will tell you require a specific expertise—are assigned to whatever public defender is available. In a Harris County murder case I was reviewing in 1996, it turned out that the court-appointed attorney had never handled a murder case. In fact, the attorney had been practicing contract law prior to being assigned this death-penalty case. Let's just say he did a less than stellar job with the defense and that his client is now on death row, despite substantial evidence of police wrongdoing.

The economics of such cases is the reason that in recent years, law students working on class projects at universities have been able to show that several death-row inmates were indeed innocent. The students have been able to go back to the crime scene and find witnesses whom the police apparently overlooked. If adequate funding for investigators had been made available to experienced lawyers at the time of the trial, the innocent defendants, who have been freed years after their arrests, would likely never have been incarcerated in the first place. It is exactly because low-income suspects get such poor representation at the time of their trial that the appeals process is so important. And now our hard-on-crime politicians are streamlining the appeals process in the name of saving money. It's no wonder that civilized nations refuse to turn over murder suspects to the United States.

It suffices to say that if the death penalty cannot be dispensed with equity and absolute certainty of guilt, it should not be dispensed at all. I believe that most Americans would agree with this principle. Then why do polls continue to show support for the death penalty in light of the fact that these basic parameters are clearly not being met? It's simple: Americans only hear one side of the story. The media and our elected officials rarely discuss the inequalities between rich and poor within our justice system. In fact, less than 3 percent of all crime coverage ever examines the court proceedings in a case.[46] Instead, the media choose to focus nearly entirely on the sensational aspects of a murder that generate profit. Obviously, after being bombarded with one emotional bloody image after another, coupled with heart-wrenching testimonies by a victim's loved ones, it is nearly impossible for the public to be in any way concerned about those accused of such heinous crimes, even if it means that innocent people are occasionally executed.

The death penalty, three strikes, mandatory sentences, truth in sentencing—these are only some of the weapons in the war on crime, a war that most Americans believe is being waged against violent crime. But if stopping violent crime is truly the goal of this war, then those in charge are using the wrong weapons to fight it. You would think that if the military can go out of its way to target a foreign enemy like Iraq with "smart bombs" in an effort to cut down on collateral damage, our elected officials would have the wisdom to do the same in their domestic war on violent crime. But today's weapons, which our leaders have told us were designed to combat violent crime, are anything but "smart." They destroy entire demographic groups with the lack of discernment of a nuclear blast.

7

Collateral Damage

In the last fifteen years, American elected officials have required prisons to engage in a bold social experiment. The historical prison policy—the incarceration of violent criminals—has been replaced with a policy of using prisons mainly to punish drug offenders with increasingly severe, mandatory terms in increasingly overcrowded prisons. The social experiment has been a failure.

—**David B. Kopel**, Prison Blues:
How America's Foolish Sentencing
Policies Endanger Public Safety,
May 17, 1994[1]

To borrow a term from criminologists Franklin Zimring and Gordon Hawkins, American voters have fallen prey to the old "bait-and-switch" routine. When politicians take their public opinion polls, they see that the electorate has an exaggerated concern about being victimized by violent crime—the type of crime they see on their TVs nightly. As a result, politicians promise their constituents that they will wage a war against this violent crime, but this is where the switch comes into play.

In their attempt to appear as though they are following through on their campaign promises, politicians have enacted one impressive-sounding draconian sentencing measure after another—three strikes, hundreds of mandatory sentences, and truth in sentencing. Subsequently, they have reported to their constituents that they have tripled the prison population. People naturally assume that this means that there are a million fewer violent criminals on the streets, but they are wrong. The truth is that 70 to 80 percent of all of those being affected by these incredibly harsh sentencing measures are nonviolent offenders—many of them first-time, low-level drug offenders, and most of them low-income minority citizens whose rehabilitation could be safely and more effectively accomplished outside the prison structure for a small fraction of the current cost to taxpayers.

By 1990, 88.9 percent of first-time drug offenders with no prior record were being sentenced to prison for an average term of 68.4 months by the federal courts. Only 79.4 percent of first-time violent offenders were sentenced to prison by the same courts, and those who had committed violent crimes were serving on average less than fifty-seven months behind bars.[2] By 1997, Justice Department figures showed that the average time served by individuals convicted of murder, rape, robbery, and aggravated assault had dropped to only forty-nine months.[3]

Such statistics make perfect sense when you consider that even with the amazing growth in the number of prison beds in the United States since 1980, if mandatory minimum sentences are being applied disproportionately to nonviolent crimes such as drug cases, there simply isn't enough prison space to hold violent offenders not covered by the mandatory sentences. As a result, it can, and has been, argued that we are actually replacing violent offenders with nonviolent criminals in our prisons.

Such is the position taken by sociologist Robert Figlio, who suggests that most violent crimes are committed by a few sociopaths. Figlio believes that if these few repeat offenders were taken off the street for long periods of time, violent crime would be dealt a substantial blow. Figlio also believes that this has not been accomplished because of the lack of prison space, a result of the massive incarceration of nonviolent drug offenders.[4]

David Kopel also holds this view. In his policy analysis for the CATO Institute titled *Prison Blues,* Kopel uses Department of Justice statistics to convincingly demonstrate that the actual sentences being served by those convicted of violent crime have been decreasing since 1980 as a result of the increasing sentences being served for nonviolent crimes.[5] Likewise, a study conducted in Illinois found that incidents of violent crime in that state actually rose as a result of increased drug enforcement. The report found that the incarceration of nonviolent drug offenders was forcing the early release of violent prisoners.[6]

Although it may be true that violent criminals are being released to make room for nonviolent offenders sentenced under mandatory minimums, I believe that the overall danger to the public from such early releases has been greatly exaggerated by the media and law enforcement. Still, it is somewhat ironic that the war on violent crime, which we are told is being waged because the public wants it, has turned out to be a conflict that fills our prisons with so many nonviolent offenders that it is forcing the release of those whom the public rightfully fears the most. Clearly, those who have established these misguided policies must do everything within their power to conceal the realities of their actions from the public. Failure to do so would likely put an end to using crime as a campaign tool, and in the end, it would significantly threaten the new multibillion-dollar industry that now revolves around prisons. As a result, a good deal of statistical spin has been generated to obscure the truth.

Establishing the public misperception that the war on crime is being waged primarily against *violent* offenders has not simply been left to chance. The government has deliberately released misleading information to justify its current crime policies and garner continuing support from the targeted electorate. Here are a couple of examples of such spin turned up by the National Criminal Justice Commission.

In 1991, the Justice Department completed an analysis of the prison population being held in state facilities. The analysis offered this conclusion to the public: "Ninety-four percent of inmates [held in state prisons] had been convicted of a violent crime or had a previous sentence to probation or incarceration."[7] According to the NCJC, "This statistic has been cited by journalists, think tanks, and politicians at every level of government to justify the rapid expansion of the prison population."[8]

Such use of this statistic is understandable. After all, it seems to indicate that the vast majority of prisoners are being held because they have committed violent acts against the public. That is clearly what this statistic was designed to imply. But consider this statistic: Ninety-four percent of all Americans are millionaires or have worked at some time in their lives. It sounds as though there are a lot of millionaires, but the truth is, this statement tells you nothing about the number of millionaires, and so it is with the Justice Department's 94-percent statistic on violent criminals.

In both of the above examples, the operative word is "or," which in effect renders the statistics meaningless. In reality, at the time of the

Justice Department's analysis, there were nearly three times as many offenders being held in state prisons who had never been convicted of a violent crime as there were prisoners who had. The NCJC came to this conclusion regarding this piece of Justice Department hard-on-crime propaganda:

> The perception of the violent recidivist stalking the public provides a misguided view of the true repeat offender and plays into the "bait and switch" aspect of crime policy. People on probation and parole in any given year account for only 3 percent to 5 percent of all violent offenses known to police that occur each year. A Justice Department study found that only 17.9 percent of state inmates are violent recidivists. . . . There is a huge difference between 94 percent and 17.9 percent.[9]

The next example of misleading statistics designed for the bait-and-switch routine comes compliments of the FBI. In their 1994 Uniform Crime Report, the FBI concluded that "something has changed in the constitution of murder to bring about the unparalleled level of concern and fear confronting the nation."[10] The FBI was referring to its conclusion that murder had become much more random and as a result had greatly increased the chances that anyone, anywhere, anytime could be a victim. In response to this conclusion, the press did its part to disseminate this new and terrifying message to the public. *USA Today* actually ran a headline over the report's figures that read, "All Have 'Realistic' Chance of Being Victim, Says FBI."[11]

So was this FBI report accurate? Hardly. It was simply more statistical propaganda designed to push the hard-on-crime agenda that increases law-enforcement budgets via the fear caused by the public's belief in the existence of the "crime gap." Members of the NCJC, using the FBI's own data, dispelled this myth of the increasing randomness of murders in their 1995 report titled *The Real War on Crime*. In 1976, there were 8.8 murders per 100,000 people. In 1980, there were 10.2. And in 1993, the number was 9.5. As you can see, the murder rate was reasonably flat during this seventeen-year period. Likewise, the percentage of people known to have been murdered randomly by a stranger was relatively flat: 13.8 percent in 1976, 13.3 percent in 1980, and 14 percent in 1993. So where did the FBI get the idea that random murders had skyrocketed?

There is one more category for murder that comes into play here: the percentage of murders where the killer's identity is unknown to police.

In other words, unsolved murders. In 1976, 24 percent of murders fell into this category. By 1993, 39.3 percent of murders were by killers whose identity was unknown to police. Then what does this statistic have to do with the FBI's dramatic conclusion that random murder was escalating out of control? Although the answer should have been "nothing," in reality the answer was "everything."

In an effort to reaffirm the public's fear of being victimized by violent crime and to garner further support for crime policies that increase law-enforcement budgets, officials at the FBI added random murders to the number of murders in which they didn't know who the killer was. Instead of reporting to the public that 14 percent of murders were random, they reported that 53.3 percent of murders were random. It's another example of adding together two sets of statistics that have nothing to do with one another. Experts point out that the majority of the murders where the killer's identity was not known to police were drug related, so even though the cops don't know who the perpetrator was, chances are that the victim knew the killer.[12] There are countless other examples of such statistical voodoo designed to put forward the illusion that *violent* crime is out of control and that the war on crime is being primarily waged against violent criminals.

The media also helps with this deception. I can't even count the number of clips from newspapers in my files that use the phrases "war on violent crime" and "Congress's fight against violent crime." Considering this bombardment of misinformation being unleashed by the media, politicians, and law enforcement, it's no wonder that the public's perception regarding the composition of the prison population is so far off base.

The Faces Behind the Bars

As a result of declaring a politically expedient war on primarily nonviolent crime as opposed to the promised war on violent crime, I believe that it is safe to say that the approximately 2 million people who now fill our prisons and jails are not who we think they are. As opposed to the public's perception of a prison system spilling over with repeat violent offenders, the single largest prison expansion in history has resulted in the majority of our prison space being taken up by nonviolent offenders.

In 1983, U.S. prisons held 660,800 inmates. Of those, approximately one in twelve, or 57,975, inmates were locked up on drug charges. By

1993, only ten years later, 353,564 people—more than one out of every four inmates—were doing time as a result of drug infractions.[13] Between 1985 and 1994, 71 percent of prisoners added to the federal prison system were imprisoned on drug charges, and the incarceration of one out of every three state prisoners added during this same period stemmed from drug arrests.[14] Not only were most new prisoners doing time for drugs, they were doing more time than violent criminals, thanks to the mandatory sentences being dictated by Congress.

America's prison population is 94 percent male, even though women are now the fastest growing sector of those imprisoned. A full 65 percent of our prisoners never completed high school, which helps to explain why so many of them are illiterate. Thirty-three percent were unemployed and another 32 percent were making less than $5,000 per year at the time of their arrest. These last statistics clearly support the opinion that poverty is the single greatest influence over criminal behavior. Seventy-one percent of all prisoners have been convicted of nonviolent crimes, mostly for drug-related and property-offense violations. Nearly 60 percent of all those in prison or jail claim that they were under the influence of drugs or alcohol at the time they committed their crime. Studies conducted in 1999 found that between 16 percent and 24 percent of all inmates are suffering from "extreme mental problems." And finally, in the 1990s, the majority of all prisoners are minority citizens.[15]

Since 1984, as a result of what has been described as "the discriminatory nature" of the Sentencing Reform Act, in addition to the mandatory sentences established by Congress and the racially defined law-enforcement practices now being applied in jurisdictions all across the country, the black and Hispanic prison populations have exploded. Between 1986 and 1991, the number of black males imprisoned for drug offenses increased by 429 percent. The number for black females incarcerated for drugs during this same period skyrocketed by 828 percent, and the number of Hispanic drug offenders in prison swelled by 320 percent. In contrast, the number of white drug offenders being imprisoned during this same period barely doubled, despite the fact that the majority of U.S. drug users are white.[16]

According to The Sentencing Project, an independent source of policy analysis and data established in 1986 and widely used by both news media and policymakers, African Americans constitute only 13 percent of all monthly drug users, yet they account for 35 percent of all arrests for the possession of drugs, 55 percent of all drug convictions, and a shocking 74 percent of all those receiving drug-related prison sentences.[17] Because of this multiple, which logic tells us has its roots in race-biased actions on the part of law enforcement, the courts, and those who write the laws, thirty-eight state prison systems reported significant increases in the racial disparity of their prison populations between 1988 and 1994. By the end of this period, the incarceration of blacks in all state prisons combined was 7.66 times that of whites. Twelve states and the District of Columbia reported that black incarceration was running at more than ten to one compared to whites.[18]

Like other aspects of the bait-and-switch approach to fighting crime, this disparity in incarceration rates of different racial groups has nothing to do with the commission rates of violent crimes. The imprisonment of black violent offenders increased at a nearly identical rate to that of white violent offenders during this same period, which means that the 7.66 to 1 differential in black and white incarceration has most likely resulted from nonviolent drug convictions.

There is no better or more damning example of racist sentencing practices than the well-publicized crack versus powder cocaine mandatory sentences. These two forms of the same drug have been treated in wildly differing fashions by Congress, even though the only major difference in these two types of cocaine—despite media hype to the contrary—is in the color of the hands they are most often found at the time of arrest—crack in brown, powder in white.[19] This is not to say that more blacks than whites use crack but rather that more blacks are arrested for crack than whites. In fact, according to the Department of Health and Human Services, 64.4 percent of crack users are white and only 26.6 percent are black. Even so, a study conducted in 1992 by the U.S. Sentencing Commission found that 91.3 percent of the people who were sentenced under the federal crack laws were black. Only 3 percent of those sentenced for federal crack offenses were white.[20] These lopsided statistics become even more alarming when you realize that the crack cocaine sentencing guidelines that have been established by Congress are 100 times more severe than those for powdered cocaine.

Since the passage of the 1986 Crime Bill, a person caught with only 5 grams of crack receives a mandatory sentence of five years, and 5.1 grams draws a ten-year sentence. With regard to powdered cocaine, the same bill required the possession of 500 grams to trigger an equal sentence. Crack cocaine is more prevalent in low-income communities because it is considerably cheaper than the powdered version of the drug, which tends to be a fashionable high among people who more closely resemble the appearance and status of those in Congress—wealthy and white.

In America in the 1990s, black families continue to be more likely than whites to live in poverty. In fact, they are approximately seven times as likely as whites to be impoverished.[21] If we consider the disproportionate number of minorities living in poverty in conjunction with the fact that low-income defendants are twice as likely to receive a prison sentence as those in higher income brackets and that once sentenced, blacks on average serve terms 20 percent longer than whites, it only stands to reason that the two-tiered cocaine sentencing statutes would have a devastating impact on the black community.[22]

Since the 1980s, the law-enforcement presence in communities of color has been increased sharply, as has the law-enforcement practice of racial profiling. This increase in street cops and random searches has not transpired to the same degree in the areas where impoverished whites live. In 1997 and 1998, the New York City Police Department's street crimes unit stopped and frisked more than 45,000 people it claimed were suspected of carrying weapons. The unit was wrong 35,000 times, but it did manage to make numerous drug busts as a result of this "searching for guns." In describing such random searches, Ira Glasser, the executive director of the American Civil Liberties Union (ACLU), said, "When you rely on hunches, you rely on prejudices, and the people most likely to be stopped are black or Hispanic."[23] As a result of such race-biased law enforcement, African-American crack users are several times more likely to get arrested than white crack users.

Research has also demonstrated that law enforcement's policy of arresting small-time dealers as opposed to those making crack purchases has also created a racial imbalance in crack sentences. In many neighborhoods where crack is sold by African Americans, the vast majority of crack buyers are white, but rather than arresting the hundreds of white buyers, law enforcement chooses to only arrest the handful of black sellers.

So why has Congress put such a law on the books? It would be nice if this discriminatory sentencing policy could be explained away as the result of some political oversight, but it can't. Since shortly after the passage of the 1986 Crime Bill, Washington politicians have been made well aware of the fact that their sentencing guidelines for crack are having a devastating impact on our minority population in the form of mass imprisonment. There have even been a number of attempts to level the cocaine playing field, but each has gone down in flames at the hands of hard-on-crime politicians, or more accurately, "hard on minority crime" politicians.

In 1995, even the Sentencing Commission, the government body that gave us 700 pages of sentencing guidelines designed to imprison an unparalleled number of nonviolent offenders, attempted to rectify this disparity in the sentencing structure by suggesting that the amount of crack required to trigger a mandatory sentence should be matched to powder's 500 grams. But Congress, which has all but taken control of sentencing from the commission, said no. In 1997, the commission tried again to lower the disparity to a still-racist level of five to one. Once again, our elected officials would have none of it. In 1997, Bill Clinton, bowing to pressure from the minority lobby that stuck by him through his impeachment problems, suggested creating a ten-to-one disparity between crack and powder. But at the writing of this book, even this watered-down version of reforming the cocaine laws appears destined for defeat at the hands of a Congress that doesn't dare to do anything that could be construed as soft on crime.

What this means is that our elected officials have been made well aware that their mandatory cocaine sentences are racially biased and are resulting in the incarceration of tens of thousands of nonviolent, low-income, minority drug users while simultaneously providing only a slap on the wrist to white cocaine abusers. It is difficult to find an explanation for continuing to allow such culturally destructive political behavior outside of the fact that Congress's actions seem designed to appeal to the targeted electorate—white suburbanites who tend to fear urban blacks—by promising to be hard on crime in a manner that will most affect those in the nontargeted minority community. In other words, the current cocaine laws are a useful tool for the consultants and their political clients.

As a result of establishing sentencing guidelines and law-enforcement practices that prey upon those living in poverty while tending to allow the wealthy to avoid prison, nearly one in three of all black American men between the ages of twenty and twenty-nine are now under the supervision of the criminal-justice system on any given day.[24] And as I mentioned previously, if the current race-biased trends in our justice system continue, it is estimated that by the year 2020, two out of three

African-American men between the ages of eighteen and thirty-four will be in prison, at which time we will find ourselves incarcerating 6.9 million of our minority citizens.[25] Is it any wonder that some critics of our current criminal-justice policies have once again begun to use the "S" word—"slavery"?

A Rose by Any Other Name

The race card has changed the whole playing field. Because the prison system doesn't affect a significant percentage of young white men, we'll increasingly see prisoners treated as commodities. For now the situation is a bit more benign than it was back in the nineteenth century, but I'm not sure it will stay that way for long.

—*Jerome Miller, former youth corrections officer*
in Pennsylvania, 1997[26]

The reality that the current prison expansion is financially benefiting investors in the upper one-third of the economy, a demographic group that is overwhelmingly white, is made all the more disturbing by the fact that impoverished blacks, Hispanics, and other ethnic minorities are being incarcerated at greatly disproportionate rates to whites. In the past, I have been critical of those who insisted upon defining the shortcomings of the justice system in terms of black versus white, not because they were necessarily wrong in their assessment but because I believed that the argument could be more accurately framed in economic terms.

But I now believe that it is impossible to ignore recent statistics that reflect the fact that the combining of high poverty rates among ethnic minorities with increasingly race-biased law-enforcement and court-system practices is causing a criminal-justice genocide concerning certain of our minority populations, particularly black Americans. The evidence is in. It is overwhelming. And it is irrefutable. If we do not stop the growth of the prison system, two out of every three black men will be in prison in the not-too-distant future, and no "civilized" nation can sport such a demographic chink in its armor.

So does the term "slavery" really apply to what is taking place in today's prison system? Although it's true that people are being held in chains as a means to profit and that a disproportionate number of the imprisoned are black and Hispanic while a disproportionate number of those who are benefiting from the situation are white, is it actually possible to apply such a powerful term to the current situation without somehow diminishing its meaning? After all, today's prisoners are criminals, whereas yesterday's slaves were innocent victims plucked from their African homeland at gunpoint and sold like cattle in the market.

Even so, I believe that there are some important similarities between our current prison industry and historical slavery. This is not to say that there is any comparison between the conditions of then and now or that the absolute injustice of historical slavery is being repeated today, but there are aspects of this comparison, which is being made more and more often, that demand examination.

As I said, individuals being incarcerated for profit today have been found guilty of a crime. This single factor, above all else, is our society's foremost rationalization for allowing wealthy individuals to gain financially from the incarceration of prisoners culled largely from impoverished minority neighborhoods. But is the nature of the crime really enough to justify our current actions? I think not.

America's current economic policies, including the diversion of funds from social programs into corrections, which we will explore in more detail later, fosters an environment that guarantees that a disproportionately large segment of the minority population will continue to live under the crime-enhancing power of poverty, and in a democracy, we must all share the responsibility for such policies. Since to some degree it is our shortsighted political actions on the economic front that are exposing certain individuals to the temptation of the criminal lifestyle, I believe that it is somewhat accurate to describe the current mass imprisonment of our low-income minority population as having resulted from a sort of race-based cultural "sting operation."

In other words, we have created political and economic circumstances that guarantee that a large number of people of color will live in an environment that we know breeds crime. We have then surrounded these same people with an overwhelming police presence far beyond what exists in other, lighter-skinned communities. And finally, when the citizens in these occupied neighborhoods succumb to the temptation dangled before them, we lock them away for incredibly long periods of time—periods much longer than those prescribed for white people who commit the same crimes. I understand that we cannot discount the concept of personal responsibility, but neither can we continue to overlook the politically manipulated forces that do play an important role in determining who will and who won't live in poverty, get arrested, and be sentenced to prison.

Through the refinement of the behavioral sciences, we now have a better understanding of criminal behavior than ever before. We now know that poverty, lack of education, and a single-parent family structure all play an important role in determining who will eventually find their way into prison. Since the destruction caused by each of these forces is, to some degree, within the control of our democratic system to relieve, if not eliminate, we can therefore assume that our current circumstance with regard to minority imprisonment rates is the result of voters having *chosen* a course of action that does not seek to undermine these crime-enhancing forces. This lack of democratic action when it comes to crime prevention is one of the reasons that I do not believe that the practice of profiting through imprisonment can be justified by the single fact that a person has been convicted of breaking a law.

After all, if criminal behavior is the only litmus test for becoming a commodity, we're all in trouble. Research has found that the vast majority of Americans, over 70 percent of us, have committed at least one imprisonable offense such as illegal drug use, driving while intoxicated, shoplifting, and so forth at some point in our lives. This is as true of George W. Bush and William Jefferson Clinton as it is of myself. When this statistic pertaining to the general population is compared to the racial composition of the current prison population, it becomes clear that it is not the commission of crimes that determines who goes to prison in the 1980s and 90s but rather who gets caught. And this is where the deck is clearly stacked against nonwhites.

With regard to this last point, the NCJC noted that

> since the mid-70s, African-Americans have consistently accounted for 45 percent of those arrested for murder, rape, robbery, and aggravated assault. These numbers tell us that the proportion of overall crime committed by African-Americans has not increased for several years. Yet since 1980, the African-American prison population has increased dramatically while the white prison population has increased far less. . . . Something more is at work than changes in crime patterns.[27]

I believe that the differential of 7.66 blacks to 1 white in who goes to prison is largely attributable to the racially biased law-enforcement practices that now permeate the whole of society. In *No Equal Justice: Race and Class in the American Criminal Justice System,* Georgetown

University law professor David Cole uses a number of examples to demonstrate just how race-biased law enforcement has become. For instance, he has noted that a black driver on the New Jersey Turnpike is three times as likely as a white driver to be stopped for a traffic violation. This means that blacks on the New Jersey turnpike are also three times as likely to be sent to prison as whites for a more serious crime discovered during a traffic stop, as many crimes are.

Such racial profiling is being practiced by law-enforcement agencies from coast to coast. In May 1999, the ACLU filed a lawsuit against the Oklahoma Highway Patrol alleging that the organization intentionally targeted nonwhite motorists and subjected them to illegal searches and harassment.[28] The Colorado Highway Patrol has also come under fire in recent years for targeting Hispanic drivers for random stops. The San Jose, California, police department is currently conducting a study to determine the degree to which its officers are using racial profiling in their decisions on which motorists to stop and search. As previously mentioned, since the election of hard-on-crime Mayor Rudolph Giuliani, New York City's police department has stopped, frisked, and harassed literally tens of thousands of young blacks and Hispanics without probable cause. In Chicago, 42,000 mostly black and Hispanic citizens were arrested between 1995 and 1998 under a race-biased "no-loitering" law that was eventually found to be unconstitutional by the Supreme Court in 1999.[29] Unfortunately, the examples go on and on.

As a means of fighting the war on drugs, U.S. customs officers now detain and search thousands of U.S. citizens every year. But not all citizens are being targeted for these "random" searches equally. Evidence surfaced in 1998 that indicates that black women returning from trips abroad are statistically eight times as likely to be forced to submit to a body search by customs officers than are white males returning from similar trips. Customs has been unable to explain this racial bias because its own data demonstrate that black women are actually less likely to be smuggling drugs than white men.[30] Even so, such racial disparity in who gets searched guarantees that a disproportionate number of black women will get caught and sent to prison and a disproportionate number of white smugglers will remain free. Charles Ogletree, a black professor of law at Harvard University, has bluntly summed up this type of racial profiling by law enforcement: "If I'm dressed in a knit cap and a hooded jacket, I'm probable cause."[31]

Understanding how racial profiling impacts the composition of the prison population is not that complicated. Let's say that there are two demographically similar neighborhoods, the only difference between them being racial composition—one is predominantly white, the other black. Now you take a hundred cops and put them into these two neighborhoods, but instead of putting fifty into each community, you put eighty into the white neighborhood and twenty in the black. The twenty cops in the black community are told that they can only search a person if there is a strong reason to believe that they have broken the law. The eighty cops in the white neighborhood, by contrast, are allowed to search anyone at any time if they feel a person "looks suspicious." So which neighborhood will supply the most people to the prison system in the long run? All other things being equal, obviously the white one.

As simplistic as this example is, if you reverse the police presence and the definition of probable cause in the two neighborhoods, you are basically describing the world in which low-income blacks and Hispanics now live. At the end of the twentieth century, who goes to prison is as much about whom we "expect" to commit crime as it is about who commits crime.

Under such circumstances, it seems difficult at best to rationalize the practice of upper-class whites profiting from the imprisonment of impoverished minority citizens. Yet, regrettably, this significant ethical dilemma has sparked little public debate outside of minority communities. I believe this lack of dialogue explains why most of the people who are profiting from the current prison expansion have felt no need to justify their investment in the human commodity. They are simply never made to consider the humans-as-chattel aspect of their business dealings.

Although it's true that we still have to provide housing, food, and guards for our charges in today's version of the human trade, the prisoners-for-profit business differs from historical slavery in that we never actually have to see the human beings from whom our profits are being derived. We no longer need to subject ourselves to the cries of the men, women, and children whose families have been ripped apart by the process that creates our dividend checks—which is not to say that the anguish and tears no longer exist. We just can't hear them or see them from our broker's office.

Today's prison investors buy and sell their interest in the human cargo by way of invisible electronic bits and bytes that fly through Wall Street computers often thousands of miles away. It seems that to a large degree we have made this new business of imprisonment culturally acceptable by making the process indirect. For example, in today's investment world, millions of would-be shareholders simply hand over their money to a mutual fund. They don't care where the money is ultimately invested. As a result of this increasingly opaque process, today's investors are never made to contemplate, let alone confront, whether owning shares in the modern plantation overseen by the prison-industrial complex is significantly different from owning a bill of sale for a human being—albeit a human being that broke at least one statute. Although I do, indeed, acknowledge that the prison business is quite different from historical slavery, I can't help but wonder if it is *different enough*.

In early 1999, I was flipping channels one night at two in the morning when I more or less stumbled across the old Clark Gable film *Band of Angels*. In this 1957 film, Gable portrays a Southern plantation owner living in New Orleans and a young Sidney Poitier plays Gable's highest-ranking slave, a sort of right-hand man whom Gable owns. But Gable isn't like the other slave owners in the film who are always shown to be beating, raping, and otherwise abusing their slaves. On the contrary, aside from the fact that he has purchased his black workers and doesn't pay them and occasionally has affairs with his female charges, who of course are at least half white, Gable is shown to treat his slaves basically as equals—albeit in that same sort of twisted way that the clichéd 1950s man treated his wife as an equal.

Just as I was about to turn off the tube and hit the hay, one of the subplots took an unexpected turn toward deep water. An angry Poitier was being questioned by a half-white, half-black, sex-kitten slave, who had become the object of Gable's affection; her questioning concerned Poitier's seemingly unwarranted bitter attitude toward Gable. The mixed-blood slave reminded Poitier of how well Gable treated the people he owned. And finally, she went so far as to tell Poitier that he should be grateful for his circumstances. At that moment, Poitier delivered a powerful dialogue about how he hated and despised Gable far more than any of the other slave owners for exactly that reason. "I hate him for his kindness," raged Poitier, "it's worse than the rawhide." The point being made by Poitier's character was that in comparison to other owners' practices, Gable's kind, sanitized, even lofty-minded treatment of his slaves had made slavery seem more innocent and, therefore, more acceptable. From Poitier's character's perspective, this made Gable the worst of the slave owners, not the best of his kind.

Like Gable's fictional slave owner, we have made profiting from people in cages seem innocent, acceptable, lofty-minded, and even beneficial to society. We have gone so far as to try and morally rationalize our dividend checks by making them subject to a simplistic litmus test: We cannot profit from anyone in shackles unless they have broken at least one law. But all things considered—those things being that our fear of crime is media-driven and unwarranted; our hard-on-crime policies are poll-driven and unnecessary; our law-enforcement practices and our court system are racially biased; and the ever-widening economic gap is within the control of voters to bridge if they so choose—I believe that the billions of dollars in profit being generated as a result of the current explosion in the prison population demands that we reexamine the path we are on. All of us, especially the millions among us whose bank accounts are being swelled by the growing prison system, must ask ourselves this question: Are we really different enough from our ancestors, or has our sanitized, indirect, Wall Street approach to imprisonment for profit somehow made us the worst of our kind?

The War on Logic

The issue of race is not the only reason that turning prisoners into an avenue for profit bears reexamining. Much of the decisionmaking that guides today's justice system clearly flies in the face of common sense and fiscal responsibility. For instance, many of our nation's 810,000 opiate addicts are turned away each year by drug-treatment programs because there is no room for them due to a chronic lack of funding. There is currently only room for about 115,000 people in the treatment system. In 1998, drug czar Barry McCaffrey asked Congress to change the methadone treatment system in such a way as to allow access to all addicts.[32] Ironically, while Congress was explaining that it couldn't find the funds to implement McCaffrey's treatment proposal, the House passed a new mandatory sentence for methamphetamine, making the punishment for its possession very similar to that of crack cocaine—five grams equals five years, fifty grams equals a ten-year sentence. This one new mandatory sentence will cost many times more to implement than McCaffrey's entire drug treatment plan. This decision on the part of Congress is shown to be all the more unreasonable in light of research by the Rand Corporation that has shown that drug treatment would have fifteen times more impact on reducing crime than mandatory sentences, and at a small fraction of the cost.

This type of illogical reasoning permeates the wars on crime and drugs. The government claims that it can't shake loose the $4,000 it takes to treat a drug addict, yet it willingly spends a quarter of a million dollars of taxpayer money to incarcerate just one nonviolent addict for a ten-year mandatory sentence. All the while, it claims that such sentencing will somehow reduce violent crime, which in reality isn't being affected at all by this silly fiscal behavior.

The economic impact of this shortsighted bait-and-switch trickery is astounding. In 1997, the *Washington Post* reported that the war on drugs had cost Americans $290 billion.[33] That's as much as the current defense budget and more than the 1998 trade deficit, and despite the hard-on-crime rhetoric to the contrary, the vast majority of this expense had nothing to do with fighting violent crime. For instance, politicians are doling out billions for antidrug commercials on television that several studies have found may well cause more drug use than they prevent. Critics of these slick TV spots argue that the "peripheral" message being conveyed by the commercials is that drug use will make you thin, attractive, and wealthy—a wrongheaded message that may help to account for why drug use is on the rise among teenagers, the commercial's targeted audience.

Other illogical drug policies include spending an estimated $10 billion a year, one-fourth of the annual budget for the war on drugs, to combat the use of marijuana.[34] There is now a congressional mandatory sentence requiring that people growing a certain number of pot plants (1,000) must be sentenced to life without parole, and even more disturbing, the 1994 Crime Bill created a death sentence for certain pot transgressions. Fifteen states likewise have now passed laws creating life sentences for nonviolent marijuana offenses. Such legislation means a $1.5-million prison tab to taxpayers for one pot infraction. This is despite the fact that research has shown that pot users (prior to experiencing the prisonization effect) are no more likely to commit other types of crimes than the general population.[35] As of 1999, one out of every six federal prisoners is incarcerated as a result of sentences pertaining to pot.[36] That means there are now more people in federal prison as a result of having broken the marijuana laws than there are because of having committed a violent crime.

If the real goal of Congress's fixation with passing mandatory sentences is to fight violent crime as it claims, then politicians should be establishing ten-year predetermined sentences for those who consume alcohol, not those who use drugs. According to a study by the National Institute on Drug Abuse titled *The Economic Costs of Alcohol and Drug Abuse in the United States, 1992*, drugs are responsible for approximately 25 to 35 percent of property crimes but only 4 to 5 percent of violent crimes. Alcohol, in comparison, accounts for 3 to 4 percent of property crimes and a staggering 25 to 30 percent of all violent crimes.[37] Yet we tax alcohol and create decade-long sentences for drug abusers. I'm not actually advocating a new round of mandatory sentences aimed at drinkers, just pointing out the illogical nature of mandatory sentences aimed at drug use as a means to fight violent crime.

Let's face it, if politicians were out there telling us the truth about their war on crime, particularly how they are wasting hundreds of billions of dollars to lock up nonviolent criminals who could be dealt with for pennies on the dollar with alternatives to prison that would not put the public at risk, they probably wouldn't be getting our votes. The only way that the war on crime can maintain its political appeal to the targeted electorate is if it continues to be masked in the illusion that it is being waged primarily against the violent criminals whose actions are greatly exaggerated by their sensationalized depiction on TV and in the movies.

In short, we have been sold a war against *violent* crime, but the government has delivered something else—a war with its roots in race and class, a war that has resulted in the imprisonment of millions of low-income citizens for *nonviolent* offenses, 60 percent of whom would not even have received a stay in prison for their actions prior to Congress's meddling with the sentencing guidelines. Those who have sought our votes have promised us that they would make us safer from crime by increasing the prison population, even though research tells us incarceration has little or no effect on the rate of crime.

The truth is, our elected leaders are engaging in a *Wag the Dog* crime war with a cruel twist. Just as in the 1998 movie, where a filmmaker is hired to create an imaginary war to distract the public's attention away from a presidential scandal, the war on crime is a conflict equally designed for voter consumption. The main difference here is that in the crime war, the props are real, the props are human beings, and, more accurately, the vast majority of the props are nonwhite human beings. Sadly, this is not the first time in our history that we have allowed our criminal-justice policies to decimate certain segments of our population. There was another time.

A Return to the "Dark Ages"

History has a way of repeating itself, and our current sentencing policies and the resulting impact they are having on our prison system is a perfect example. Between 1850 and 1900, America experienced what is now known as the "Dark Ages" of penology. There were a number of factors that led to this terrible time in our prison history. As I mentioned earlier, the mandatory sentences of nineteenth-century America left prison officials with but one means of controlling their inmate population—corporal punishment. Without the mechanism of indeterminate sentencing, the tools that ensured that the prison rules would be followed became whippings, water torture, total isolation, and hanging by the thumbs.

Just as today, over 90 percent of those sentenced into the prison system of the "Dark Ages" were eventually released back into the public domain. To say that they had not been rehabilitated by their cruel treatment is an understatement. The men and women being released from these early institutions of torture had been turned into something less. Many were virtually incapable of adjusting to everyday life on the outside and soon found themselves back behind bars. Unfortunately, the public didn't seem to care about the plight of prisoners between 1850 and 1900. Historians tell us that there was a reason for the general population's indifference toward its system of justice at this time.

In the thirty years prior to the Civil War, the role of prisons in the United States had undergone a substantial transformation under the guidance of the Jacksonian reformers, who believed that prisons could be used as a means of rehabilitation and not just for dispensing punishment, as had been the case during the first forty-five years of the nation's existence. This notion of rehabilitation was enthusiastically embraced by the public for most of the antebellum period. Spurred on by the reformers' well-meaning, yet naive, dream of curing crime once and for all and buoyed by a healthy economy that was creating economic opportunity throughout all strata of society, Americans living between 1820 and 1845 proved more than willing to spend their tax dollars to create a new and enlightened prison system based on the vision of rehabilitation.

Unfortunately for these Jacksonian do-gooders, the behavioral sciences had not yet been discovered, and the attempts of the day to cure the criminal mind were rooted almost exclusively in harsh discipline and were therefore predestined to fail. As a result of the prison system's inability to cure crime with discipline over a thirty-year period, the public's support for building prisons and running them with the goal of rehabilitating criminals had already begun to diminish in the decade prior to the Civil War. Then, with the onset of war and its subsequent devastation of the overall health of the economy, particularly in the South, what little public enthusiasm for spending money on prisons that existed prior to the conflict quickly evaporated.

To compound this already decaying situation, America's postwar prisons—which had previously held mostly lower-class whites—were now being filled to the brim with recently freed black slaves and newly arrived Irish immigrants. Both of these segments of society were more or less despised by the general population, a reality that would largely account for the final demise of the reform-minded, antebellum-period prison system. Historians believe that these three factors—a declining economy, the realization that discipline as a means of reform was a failed concept, and the increasing black and Irish composition of the prison population—all worked in conjunction to set the stage for the terrible things that followed.

It would be nearly fifty years before the emergence of the behavioral sciences would once again energize the public's enthusiasm for prison as a means of reform. In the interim between the Civil War and the end of the nineteenth century, the only thing that would matter to the general population or to the government, for that matter, would be cutting the cost of the prison system by any means possible. And just as today, the private sector claimed that it could save the nation money through prison privatization.

At first, entrepreneurs convinced legislatures in Louisiana and New York that they could make the prisons pay for themselves by contracting out prisoners as laborers to private interests.[38] The recently freed blacks in the South soon found themselves once again working the same plantations, only this time under worse circumstances than their former slavery. Unlike the pre–Civil War slave owners, those who contracted prison labor no longer had a vested interest in keeping their workers alive. If the new prison slaves fell dead in the fields, they were replaced at no charge by the justice system.

Soon prison systems across the nation turned to the leasing of convicts to corporations and wealthy individuals as a means of cutting costs or, in some instances, actually generating profits. Historians have noted

that as the market gained control of the prison system, corruption became endemic to this new business as companies and individuals paid
off wardens, guards, and politicians to ensure that they would look the
other way as prisoner abuse became increasingly rampant. It would only
be a short time before profit-seeking corporations would take the privatization concept a step further.

In Texas, corporations completely took over the care of prisoners at
no cost to the state.[39] Once a company had a prisoner in its possession, it
could do pretty much whatever it wanted with its new human chattel. It
could beat these unfortunates, starve them, work them to death, or
shoot them on the spot; it didn't really matter to anyone, because the
state had relinquished its control and oversight of prisoners to the companies, and the public was more or less nonplussed by the abuse of the
mostly black prison population in the South.

In 1886, Mississippi leased its state penitentiary—lock, stock, and
barrel—to J. W. Young and Company for fourteen years. However, two
years later, that contract was canceled, and a rich plantation owner
named Edmund Richardson worked out an even better deal with the
state. Mississippi agreed to pay Richardson $18,000 a year to take its
prison off its hands. In addition to receiving the money, the planter was
given complete control of the prison and its inhabitants to do with as he
pleased.[40]

Louisiana followed the Mississippi model and in 1868 leased its entire Baton Rouge Penitentiary to a private firm that turned around and
sold the lease for a large profit to a corporation run by one Major
Samuel James. For the next thirty-three years, James ran what historians have called the "most cynical, profit-oriented, and brutal prison
regime in Louisiana history."[41] Other state prisons were turned over to
private corporations for a symbolic $1 fee, making it clear that the only
interest that states had in their prison systems during this time was to
economically wash their hands of the whole situation. The privateers
had promised to save the states money, and they had, but at what cost?
It would be nearly five decades before anyone would bother to tally the
human toll of this privatization experiment.

By the early 1900s, three things brought an end to the "Dark Ages."
First, the development of the behavioral sciences sparked a new opti-
mism in the general population that crime could be treated as a disease
and cured. In addition, reformers began to report on the horrendous
conditions within the privately run prisons, and their stories of abuse

were so shocking that even a public seemingly indifferent to the adverse treatment of blacks and immigrants began to question the conditions within the private system. And finally, workers began to complain that the unpaid prison workforce was creating unfair competition within the labor market. As a result, the government finally launched a number of investigations to determine the effectiveness of the increasingly privatized prison system. What investigators found spelled the end of privatized incarceration.

The most famous of these investigations was the Wines and Dwight Report. In 1867, the New York Prison Association commissioned Enoch Wines and Theodore Dwight to conduct a nationwide survey of penal methods and evaluate their efficiency. The resulting paper, *Report on the Prisons and Reformatories of the United States and Canada*, was most disturbing. Wines and Dwight reported that not one institution in the United States was operating on the premise that rehabilitation was a priority. The report stated that prison conditions were atrocious and unacceptable. Crowded, rat-infested cells; decaying buildings; poorly trained and corrupt guards; horrifying working conditions; and abusive punishments had become the norm in public and private facilities. America's attempt to save money on its prison system had created a level of abuse so abominable that the general population, which had previously pushed its elected leaders to cut costs by all means available, now demanded a stop to the practice of prison privatization.

As a result of the inmate abuses during the "Dark Ages," many things were changed. Indeterminate sentencing was created to restore order inside the walls. Private prisons were outlawed. And the idea that prison could serve as a pathway to reform was given a new lease on life by the arrival on the scene of the behavioral sciences. America had learned an important lesson the hard way. It was not to forget this ugly chapter in history for nearly a century.

Same Old Logic, Same Old Problems

As technology has become more hyperactive, we, the people have become more laid-back; as the deposits in its memory banks have
become more fat, the deposits in man's memory bank have become
more lean. Like Harold Pinter's servant, the machine has assumed
the responsibilities that were once the master's. The latter has become the shell of a once thoughtful, though indolent, being. It is the
Law of Diminishing Enlightenment at work.

—*Studs Terkel*, **The Great Divide, 1988**[1]

The inmates had barely gotten off the bus when it started. They were
still handcuffed and shackled as the guards that they had never seen before that moment began to beat them. According to reports by arriving
inmates, several prisoners were hog-tied and pepper sprayed—the
painful mixture shot into their eyes as their new keepers pried them
open to worsen the effect. "That's so you boys remember you're not in
Colorado anymore," said one of the guards. "You're in Texas now."

After their violent introduction was over, the still-stunned prisoners
were led into an aging warehouse that had once been used to store mail.
The building had been retrofitted with bars over the old storage bays to
create crude cells. The inmates were massed twenty-six to a cell with little regard for prisoner classification—murderers and rapists claimed

their bunks beside nonviolent forgers and drug users. The long narrow cells had only one bathroom, and in almost no time, the ancient plumbing at the old warehouse exhibited its inadequacy. The cells began to stink as feces and toilet paper spilled onto the cold concrete floor. But not all of the prison's inhabitants were disappointed with the conditions. The swarms of cockroaches that had invaded the cells seemed to enjoy their new digs.

It was midsummer in East Texas, and the temperature was rocketing above 105° every day. Inside the warehouse turned prison, inmates crowded close to windows in their attempt to escape the sweltering stuffiness that was greatly amplified by the relentless East Texas humidity. What little relief the outside air offered was frequently overpowered when the trains came. The old warehouse had been constructed nearly on top of the train tracks that had once been used to deliver its bags of letters and packages. But now, the trains passed slowly by the prison, pouring thick diesel fumes into the already barely breathable air.

The inmates were forced to stay in their bug- and excrement-infested cells for twenty-three hours out of each day. They were even forced to eat unsanitary food from crusty plates within the confines of these same dung-laden cargo bays. At night, supposedly to better monitor their charges, the guards refused to turn off the lights, making sleep more of a memory than a reality for the prisoners, who, as a result, couldn't even escape the nightmare of their new surroundings in their dreams. According to the inmates, those who tried to use their blankets to block out the perpetual light were beaten. When the men caged in the warehouse complained about anything, they were beaten. If the complaints persisted, the entire cell would be gassed into silent submission. And for this, the state of Colorado was paying approximately $20,000 a day.

Although this description of a "warehouse turned prison facility" may sound like a historical depiction of prison conditions from the "Dark Ages," it isn't. This description of conditions is based on several articles I wrote in 1995 when 500 Colorado inmates were placed into a private prison in Texarkana, Texas. As the stories ran, officials from the Colorado Department of Corrections and the county that operated the for-profit prison denied the accuracy of my reports. Eventually, an enlightened federal judge in Denver ordered all payments to the private prison suspended until an independent expert could determine conditions within the "warehouse." Fortunately for the Texas-né-Colorado inmates, a surprise inspection of the facility revealed that the conditions at the for-profit prison were at least as bad as what I had reported. In the end, Colorado terminated its contract and moved the inmates out of the Texas hellhole.

Incredibly, many of the same forces that created the dreadful conditions in our prisons a hundred years ago are also responsible for the increasing number of problems in our modern prison system. We are once again writing our statutes and conducting our law-enforcement practices in such a way that our prisons are overflowing with those Americans whom society cares the least about—and this time around it's low-income blacks and Hispanics. Just as was true a century ago, Americans today rarely exhibit any desire to rehabilitate "those" criminals. Such lofty notions have been replaced by public demands for a return to mandatory sentences, chain gangs, hard labor, and the death penalty. And finally, just as in our past, we have again become infatuated with the promises of private corporations that tell us that they can lock away these undesirable criminals more cheaply than the state.

We have truly come full circle and have forgotten the wisdom of Harry Truman, who said, "The only thing new is the history we don't know."[2] I believe that the similarities between our treatment of "justice" at the end of this century and the end of the last is evidence that the concept of "progress" tends to be little more than a myth that rattles around in the heads of those who cannot discern the difference between technology and enlightenment.

The Conflicts of Shareholder Primacy

When it comes right down to it, the explanations being offered for a return to privatized incarceration today are no different than they were for our initial failed experiment with for-profit justice 100 years ago. Corporate America and the politicians it financially supports claim that by allowing the competition of the marketplace to govern the prison system, the United States will realize improved prison conditions at a reduced price. But just as a century ago, what isn't being discussed is the inevitable and unavoidable conflict between shareholder and public interests, a conflict that, according to corporate law, the shareholders must win.

Although the stated motives for privatizing haven't changed, the conditions have. There is an important difference between most modern private prisons and those of their "Dark Ages" predecessors. In the past, private prisons represented the most decrepit facilities, physically speaking, within the system. Today, private prisons, with the exception of facilities like the one in Texarkana, tend to provide inmates with the most modern, the cleanest, and the most physically attractive conditions of incarceration available within the prison system. As one might expect, this fact is often put forward by the prison industry as proof that for-profit justice is superior to that dispensed in the public sector. The industry is quick to point to surveys of inmates that it has conducted that show that the majority of prisoners being moved from overcrowded public prisons into new private facilities prefer the latter. Still, I don't believe that this argument of better physical conditions is a valid reason to support privatization.

First of all, turning the comparison of private versus public prisons into a comparison of physical structures makes little sense. It is like making an argument to let corporations take over the legislative process (more than they already have) because the World Trade Center is a far more modern building than our nation's capitol building. Many public prisons are decades old, some more than a century. Many of these decaying public facilities were built at a time when prison architects were told to design cold stone fortresses that would create the sensory deprivation that was mistakenly thought to lead to rehabilitation. We now know that such conditions work against reform, yet for most of the twentieth century, America has failed to reinvest in new prisons whose design features are based on a modern understanding of criminal behavior.

Consequently, newly constructed private facilities are, in fact, warmer, cleaner, and generally more comfortable than their aging public counterparts. And prisoners do prefer these new facilities, as well they should. But the difference in the physical plants, which is being touted as proof of superiority by privately funded prisons, is misleading. The real argument here is that *new* prisons are preferable to *old* prisons, not that *private* prisons are preferable to *public* institutions. Modern prisons constructed by government have conditions equal to or superior to those created in the private sector. With a million more prisoners in the system this decade than last, modern facilities would be coming on line with or without the participation of private-prison corporations. For this reason, I believe that physical structures should have no bearing on the private versus public prison debate.

What *should* be a part of the discussion is a comparison of how private prisons are operated, as opposed to how public facilities are operated. I believe that an examination of private-prison operations during the last fifteen years clearly demonstrates that the conflict between shareholder demands for profit and the care of inmates puts both the public and prisoners at risk. What is most disturbing about the examples of shareholder primacy we will examine momentarily is that the private-prison industry is admittedly in a phase of development where it is striving to create model institutions in its effort to convince politicians and the public that it can outperform the public sector at imprisonment. If it is failing now during this period of courtship, one can only guess how bad things will likely become when the industry is no longer on its best behavior.

According to Dr. Russell Clemens, economist with the Department of Research for the American Federation of State, County, and Federal Employees, "[P]roblems regarding security, staffing, and quality of services have plagued prison privatization from its inception." The economist has also pointed out that "[e]scapes and problems pertaining to health care and food service have characterized the low quality of services in privately operated prisons."[3] Although most of the problems listed by Clemens plague all prison systems, public or private, to some degree, it is the way that these problems are handled by private prisons that demonstrates the conflict between the public's interests and the corporation's commitment to its shareholders.

For instance, Esmor Corrections used to run an Immigration and Naturalization Service detention center in Elizabeth, New Jersey. In 1994, the detention center erupted in a massive riot, and more important to the prison corporation, the riot resulted in significant media coverage. The riot at Esmor's facility is important for two reasons. First, it confirmed that the private-prison corporation had, indeed, placed shareholder interest above the interest of the prisoners. A federal investigation into the cause of the riot determined that the prisoners had revolted because the company had continuously skimped on food, on upkeep of the facility, and on guard salaries, all of which padded the corporation's bottom line at the expense of those behind the razor wire. The description of conditions in Esmor's New Jersey facility sound similar to those discovered by Montana inspectors when they arrived at the private prison operated by the Bobby Ross Group in Dickens County, Texas. In both situations the prisoners were literally going hungry.

Second, the riot at Esmor's New Jersey facility sent a chilling message to the rest of the prison industry, a message it has clearly not forgotten. Following the publicity from the riot, Esmor's stock price plummeted from $20 a share to $7.[4] As we will see, the reality that riots, escapes, and other bad news such as prisoner abuse can greatly affect stock value in the private-prison business has placed the shareholder's interests in direct conflict with both public and prisoner safety.

Since the Esmor riots, one private-prison corporation after another has been caught failing to report problems within its facilities. One explanation for this fact is that it protects the shareholders from the adverse market reactions that would likely occur if a problem were to be reported. At Correction Corporation of America's facility in Youngstown, Ohio—the same prison that quotes the company's stock price on a sign next to the road that runs past its complex—the conflict between what that sign stands for and the public interests has become all too clear in recent years.

In 1994, Youngstown needed jobs. In its effort to lure employers to the economically depressed city, officials began courting CCA in hopes of landing a private prison and the jobs that come with such an enterprise. In 1995, the city got its wish. CCA opened a 1,700 capacity medium-security prison and created 450 new jobs.[5] From the very beginning, it was CCA's intention to fill its new facility with inmates from the overflowing prisons in Washington, D.C. Youngstown officials were understandably concerned about who would be held in the new prison, so they sought and received assurances from the company that only inmates suitable to a medium-security facility would be moved to Ohio—but Youngstown was in for a surprise.

The financial success of private prisons is largely determined by one factor; a facility must be at least 90 percent occupied to turn a profit. In this respect, private prisons are a business similar to the hotel industry. As a result of their responsibility to shareholders, private-prison corporations have been known to do what they have to in order to fill their beds, including seeking prisoners from out of state and housing dangerous violent inmates in facilities inadequate for such prisoners.[6] CCA's Youngstown facility was no exception. Despite its promises and contractual obligations to only imprison inmates appropriate to a medium-security facility, CCA began to take in a variety of murderers and other violent offenders who should not have been held in a medium-security institution. It's likely that Ohio officials would never have discovered the presence of these inmates if not for an escape in July 1998. Much to the dismay of Youngstown's residents and its civic leaders, of the six inmates who escaped from the corporation, five were murderers.

Even prior to the escape, the composition of CCA's Youngstown prison population had come into question following an opinion piece in the *Washington Post* by Margaret Moore, the director of the Washington, D.C., corrections department. In the article, Moore claimed that the Youngstown facility was housing some of D.C.'s "most violent and recalcitrant inmates," including murderers.[7] As a result of the article, Youngstown joined in a lawsuit filed by prisoners from the for-profit prison that claimed that the inmates' lives were in danger because of having maximum-security prisoners housed in the general population at a medium-security prison. The lawsuit sought to remove the violent inmates from the Youngstown population.

The *Wall Street Journal* reported that as a result of the suit, the court ordered CCA to hire an outside expert to classify the Youngstown inmates. The consultant determined that 113 prisoners were, in fact, maximum-security level and that an additional 201 inmates should be classified as "close security," a classification usually reserved for violent offenders. In addition, the consultant reported to the court that CCA's staff had not even been qualified to classify prisoners. Then how did CCA expect to screen its prisoners, if no one at the company was qualified to do so? One explanation is that the company's contract with D.C. gave it five days to examine an inmate's transfer file and reject any prisoners deemed inappropriate for the medium-security facility, but even this basic safeguard was apparently ignored. Robert Adams, CCA's chief of security at the Youngstown prison, told the court that he had never seen a transfer file and that he didn't know of anyone at his company who had examined such a file.[8] This is not to say that the company didn't know it was taking in maximum-security inmates. Consider the case of inmate Richard Johnson.

Johnson is a convicted murderer with a violent history behind bars, including the 1995 stabbing of a guard in the Washington, D.C., prison system. Washington's files classified Johnson as a maximum-security inmate. Despite being a convicted murderer, CCA moved Johnson to Youngstown. Shortly after his arrival, Johnson attacked a guard and stabbed a fellow inmate. CCA's own file stated that Johnson was dangerous and not suited for the general population. Still, the company did not send Johnson back to D.C., and it eventually put him back in with the inmate population. On February 28, 1998, according to police reports, Johnson was seen leaving the cell of inmate Derrick Davis, holding a bloody knife. Davis was later found dead in his cell. He had been stabbed fifteen times. Johnson has been charged with aggravated murder in the Davis case and has pled not guilty. But the Johnson saga doesn't end here.

Shortly after the Davis murder, a court affidavit claims that inmate Bryson Chilsey told CCA officials that his life was in danger. Chilsey's wife claims that she wrote to both the mayor and city council of Washington, D.C., pleading for help for her husband. But their requests for assistance fell on deaf ears. According to a Youngstown police report, a month after the Davis murder, Johnson and another inmate, Alphonso White, chased Chilsey up a flight of stairs; then Johnson held him as White stabbed him to death. White has pled guilty to the murder of Chilsey. Johnson has once again entered a plea of not guilty.

Youngstown is not the only example of the private-prison industry's questionable handling of prisoner classification. In Santa Fe County, New Mexico, CCA brought in murderers and rapists from Oregon to fill its private jail cells. It has been reported, though denied by the company, that CCA failed to notify the Sheriff's Department that it was housing inmates who posed a danger to the public and that only after county officials threatened to cancel their contract with the company were the Oregon prisoners removed from the jail.[9]

In Houston, Texas, CCA was running a facility designed to hold illegal aliens until they could be deported. Unbeknownst to the Texas Board of Criminal Justice, CCA had placed 200 sex offenders from Oregon in the facility. Once again, Texas authorities would likely never have known that the Oregon prisoners were at the Houston facility if not for the fact that two of the prisoners, including a man serving nineteen years for raping, robbing, and assaulting an eighty-eight-year-old woman, escaped. Following the escape, one member of the Texas board told the *Wall Street Journal* that the CCA facility "was in no way designed for individuals with a violent criminal history." The company responded by claiming that the Houston facility was a good match for the Oregon sex offenders and that it had no responsibility to notify Texas officials as to whom it was holding in its private institutions.[10]

The belief on the part of prison corporations that they have no obligation to keep local authorities or the public informed as to the makeup of their out-of-state inmate populations is clearly a widely held philosophy. A drug rehabilitation program in Denver was accepting 70 percent of its clients, convicted felons, from places like Maryland and Washington, D.C. The out-of-state jurisdictions used Denver because they had no place on the East Coast to put the men in need of drug treatment. The few existing programs back East were full, so the courts simply gave the felons bus tickets to Denver. Once again, local authorities had no idea that these men were in their area until tragedy struck. Only after one of the men was kicked out of the program and then allegedly raped and murdered a young woman living near the residence that housed the addicts did authorities discover the practice of bringing in out-of-state felons.[11] Clearly, this "none-of-your-business" attitude on the part of prison profiteers is not in the best interest of the public, but as we will see, it is in the best interests of the prison company's shareholders.

At the Texarkana private prison I described earlier, murderers and other violent offenders from Colorado were likewise housed in the general population, despite the facility not being rated for maximum-security inmates. I spoke to a man convicted of forgery who had been moved to this Texas facility, and he told me that he and other nonviolent offenders were terrified for their lives. Even more disturbing, I spoke to a convicted murderer in the warehouse who confirmed that the other inmates *should* fear him and the other violent inmates. After noting he had nothing to lose, as he was already going to spend his life in prison anyway, he told me that he wouldn't hesitate to kill another inmate if the person did something to "get on his nerves." And statistics seem to justify this inmate fear over the private-prison industry's habit of mixing prisoners of varying classifications.

Tennessee officials claim that the rate of serious incidents at CCA's medium-security prison in Clifton, Tennessee, ran some 28 percent higher than the overall rate for such incidents in that state's publicly run prisons.[12] And then there's the inmate-to-inmate violence at CCA's Youngstown prison. In its first fourteen months of operation, the Youngstown facility, which holds a mere 1,700 inmates, had thirteen stabbings that resulted in two deaths. Compare this to the fact that the entire Ohio prison system with 49,000 inmates only had twelve assaults with deadly weapons and no fatalities during all of 1997.[13]

During the first fifteen years of the new experiment with privatization, violence, escapes, and riots have repeatedly plagued the private prisons. Considering the often mixed-classification composition of the private-prison population, one could certainly argue that the public is being placed at risk by the companies' practice of accepting criminals into lower-security facilities than their classifications or records might indicate to be prudent. This dangerous practice could not likely exist if the private prisons were required to provide their prisoners' background files to local authorities. But such reporting isn't likely to happen because it would work against the corporations' ability to generate profits. A filled bed is a profitable bed, and all indications are that the companies will continue to do whatever it takes to keep occupancy high, including the mixing of inmates of varying classifications and the importing of prisoners from out of state.

The practice of moving inmates across state lines makes it more likely that prisoners of mixed classifications will be thrown together behind the same prison walls. Hypothetically speaking, when North Carolina sends 500 inmates to a private prison in Texas, Texas government officials have no idea who is being held in the private facility, and often, due to serious lapses in protocol, even the corporation that owns the prison doesn't know the background of the inmates it accepts.

Further exacerbating the problem is the fact that many private prisons hold inmates from several different states simultaneously, making it nearly impossible for even the prisoners' home states to know with whom their inmates are being housed. Murderers from Oregon could be housed with marijuana violators from Tennessee. It's a dangerous business practice that would not occur in a public facility. As we have seen, it is often only after escapes, riots, or other problems transpire that communities, local law-enforcement agencies, and various departments of corrections find out just who it is that is filling the beds in a private prison. This serious lack of government oversight at private facilities is another manifestation of the conflicts that arise between profit and public safety. And there is yet another such conflict of interest that arises from the practice of moving prisoners from state to state to fill beds.

Rehabilitating prisoners is always in the public interest. It both prevents the public from being further victimized by a criminal upon his or her release and saves taxpayers money by preventing the future incarceration of the individual. I have interviewed several prison counselors who have told me of the importance of maintaining the family structure while an inmate is incarcerated. Inmates who receive frequent visits and support from parents, spouses, and children are much more likely to make it on the outside once released. When jurisdictions ship inmates halfway across the country to a private prison, this reform-aiding family support is destroyed.

Since the vast majority of prisoners are from low-income demographic groups, their families cannot possibly afford to travel great distances to maintain this vital contact. After years of being held in out-of-state private prisons, many inmates are returned to their home-state facilities or are released only to find that their loved ones have remarried or no longer desire to maintain contact. Once this occurs, the chances that someone else will eventually be victimized by the inmate are increased dramatically.

Private prisons also use loopholes created by moving prisoners across state lines to increase profits by avoiding state requirements to provide acceptable conditions or expensive programs such as sex-offender and drug-rehabilitation training that greatly increase the chances for a prisoner's reform. For example, when I was doing research in 1995, I found that Colorado statutes required that any private prisons in Colorado that held Colorado inmates must provide equal to or better conditions than institutions operated by the state, including providing prisoners with access to the same programs offered in state facilities. Clearly, based on the intention of this statute, housing Colorado inmates in a private facility in Colorado would make it difficult for a corporation to turn a profit. So what's a prison company to do? The answer is to transport Colorado prisoners over state lines.

Consider the Texarkana warehouse. Colorado could never have legally placed its prisoners into this dreadful facility had it been located in Colorado. But by crossing state lines, the statutes no longer applied. Instead of the two-to-a-cell housing that would have been required if the private prison had been located in Colorado, the Texarkana warehouse-turned-prison used this loophole to cram twenty-six inmates into a cell with one bathroom. Instead of having to offer expensive treatment programs, Texarkana could leave prisoners locked down for twenty-three hours out of every day without providing any programs. The prison did provide a Bible study.

Many states have requirements similar to those of Colorado, which explains why even though some thirty states are home to private prisons, many of those states are forced to place their inmates in private facilities outside of their own jurisdictions in order to sidestep their own laws designed to prevent prisoner exploitation. As a result, North Carolina prisoners might wind up being shipped to Oklahoma, and Oklahoma prisoners might be shipped to Texas. Colorado inmates go north to Minnesota, while Minnesota prisoners might get shipped to private prisons in the South. This is only one of the profit-enhancing, reform-harming loopholes created by the interstate prisoner trade.

In addition to causing inmates to lose critical family support and access to rehabilitative programs, housing prisoners out of state is also responsible for many of the riots and escape attempts in private facilities—that's to say, unhappy prisoners shipped far from family and friends are often unruly prisoners. These riots and escapes bring up yet another conflict between shareholder interests and those of the public. For example, let's go back to CCA's Youngstown prison and the escape of five murderers in 1998. Remember the stock quote in front of the Youngstown prison? Remember what happened to Esmor's stock price following the press coverage of its riot? One could certainly argue that CCA clearly recalled both at the time of the Youngstown breakout.

"The facts [concerning the escape] lead one to believe there was an attempt to deceive the police or cover up the event," Youngstown mayor George McKelvy told the *Wall Street Journal*. CCA has denied the mayor's claim, stating that the idea of a cover-up is ridiculous and that the company is "a victim of a political witch hunt in Ohio."[14] The controversy surrounding the escape was centered on just when CCA decided to notify authorities that the murderers were on the loose in the community. All parties agree that such notification should have been immediate. Youngstown officials have accused the company of dragging its feet when it came to telling the world that five murderers had escaped from its prison.

According to CCA's own records, the first alarm from an outdoor motion detector went off at 1:06 P.M. on the night of the escape. More than two hours passed before a call was finally placed to local authorities, which claimed that there had been an escape. Despite this call, when police arrived at the prison, CCA guards told them that there was no problem. This denial was being put forward even though the police claim that they could see guards running through the woods around the prison. Even after a siren began to sound, police say that the CCA guards maintained their story that there had been no escape. The company denies that its guards told police that an escape hadn't occurred once the alarm sounded. "In my opinion," said Captain Kane of the Youngstown Police, "the escape was not reported promptly or properly." Youngstown mayor McKelvy is even more harsh in his assessment of the corporation. As the mayor put it, CCA is the "most deceitful, dishonest corporation I have ever dealt with."[15]

If CCA did, in fact, delay reporting the escape, what motive could there be for such an action that clearly endangers the public? Hypothetically speaking, of course, if a private-prison company could manage to recapture its own escaped inmates and thereby avoid the bad publicity that follows such a breakout—especially one involving murderers being held in a medium-security facility—it could be worth millions of dollars to the corporation in its stock value. Consider that following the publicity regarding the escape and other problems at the Youngstown prison, CCA's stock hit a new fifty-two-week low.

Once again, CCA's Youngstown facility is not the only private prison to be accused of failing to report problems. At a Bobby Ross Group facility in Karnes County, Texas, two Colorado inmates escaped and a full day passed before the incident was reported to state authorities.[16] A riot at the Texarkana warehouse also demonstrates this hesitation to be upfront with bad news. In 1995, I reported that a riot had broken out in the Texarkana facility. Much to my dismay, the private prison responded that there had been no riot. Then the head of the Colorado Department of Corrections made the same claim. I later learned that when it comes to state corrections looking into incidents concerning their inmates being held in out-of-state private prisons, the word "investigate" tends to mean that someone had placed a phone call to the corporation, only to be told that things are fine.

Unfortunately for the private prison and the CDOC, I wasn't writing from the prisoner rumor mill. When the riot broke out in Texarkana, two other reporters from my paper and I were tape-recording the riots as they happened. Several inmates had called my office from the pay phones in their cells when the riot started. When the guards started spraying gas, the prisoners were forced to retreat, but they left the phones off the hook so we could hear and record the whole ordeal. Eventually, the state was forced to admit that the riot had occurred, but it still tried to downplay the eruption's significance. Once again, bad news proved to be an economic disaster for the prison. As I mentioned earlier, Colorado was forced in the end to cancel its $20,000-per-day contract. I refer to this tendency to hide bad news in an effort to prevent shareholder losses as the "Esmor effect."

Another area where shareholder primacy comes into play is that of prisoner abuse at the hands of corporation guards or due to chronic understaffing. One of the best examples of this problem I have seen was uncovered at a privately run youth facility in Brush, Colorado, by *Rocky Mountain News* reporter Ann Imse, whose impressive series of articles on the facility eventually led to its closing.

At one time, the High Plains Juvenile Facility, which was owned and operated by Rebound, Inc., was housing serious youth offenders from twenty-one states and charging prices that ranged from $52,000 to $65,000 per youth per year.[17] Then in 1998, Matt Maloney, a mentally disturbed thirteen-year-old who had been sent to the facility by Utah authorities, committed suicide. The investigation surrounding Maloney's death would reveal an institution out of control.

High Plains was suffering from one of the prison industry's biggest problems, inadequate staffing. The single most important area for making profit from private prisons is in cutting labor costs. As a result of low pay, poor training, and a stressful work environment, it is often difficult for private prisons to hire enough employees and to keep those employees on board once they are hired.[18] For several years leading up to the Maloney suicide, state inspections at High Plains, rare though they were, had repeatedly found inadequate personnel to carry out the specific tasks contractually guaranteed by the company. One inspection after another found that the numbers of required staff for educational, medical, and counseling purposes were not present at the facility. Each time, the corporation would claim that the lack of employees was a temporary shortage, but each subsequent inspection would show the same lack of trained personnel in one or more of the areas.[19] Despite this fact, Rebound, Inc. continued to charge the states $142 to $180 per day per child.

Less than half the number of staff required by law to be present in the units at the institution were on duty the night the thirteen-year-old Maloney died. Employees at High Plains were expected to run group-therapy sessions after just one week of in-house training and another week of observation. Despite the chronic lack of skilled medical staff—records reveal that a psychiatrist spent only six hours on site each month at the 184-bed facility—High Plains had been advertising itself as a facility appropriate to house inmates with serious mental disorders. That's why Utah authorities had sent the disturbed Maloney to the Colorado institution.

Gary Dalton, head of Utah's youth corrections program, told the *News* with regard to the suicidal young inmate, "[W]e thought it had a treatment program to handle a boy who'd been so abused that he had turned violent to himself. We expected someone trained in therapy . . . more of a psychologist or social worker. We weren't getting the service we were paying for."[20] At the time of Maloney's death, there were a substantial number of youths at the facility who were being administered powerful psychotropic drugs. Based on the lack of mental health staff, Betty Marler, director of Colorado Youth Services, whose department had placed ten mentally ill clients in High Plains, said, "They clearly did not have enough psychiatric hours to adequately evaluate the use of those psychotropic drugs."[21] Other Colorado officials agreed that High Plains was at fault, going so far as to claim that failure to prevent Maloney from killing himself on a day when he had told High Plain's staff that he intended to do so amounted to child neglect. The state may have been concerned with abuse in the Maloney case, but apparently it hadn't been all that concerned with High Plain's abuses prior to this incident.

In all, there had been an incredible seventy allegations of abuse at High Plains since 1993. Social services reported twenty-three substantiated cases of abuse just since 1997. Of the twenty-three cases turned over to local and state authorities, only one was investigated prior to the Imse articles. State inspectors found that High Plains staff had seriously overused physical restraints. Inadequate staffing often made it necessary for teenage inmates with no training at all to help place other inmates in the restraints. In addition, many of the abuse cases had to do with staff having sexual relations with the young offenders. But rather than prosecute those cases at the time, which would have resulted in bad press for both the state and the private facility, a decision was made to quietly fire employees caught having sex with the underage teens.[22]

Although the problems with staffing at the High Plains youth prison were obviously severe, finding and keeping well-trained employees has been nearly as problematic for most prison corporations. Sixty percent of the cost of incarceration is labor. Considering that expenses such as food and health care are more or less fixed, labor is clearly the area where private prisons must cut costs in order to be profitable, but such skimping on employee paychecks creates a serious problem. In Florida, for example, that state's auditor found that the personnel turnover at Gadsden Correctional Facility for Women, a for-profit prison run by U.S. Corrections Corporation, was 200 percent annually, a rate ten times more severe than at Florida's state-run institutions.[23] Considering the extensive training required to create a staff capable of running a prison responsibly, 200-percent turnover translates into a staff ill pre-pared for the difficult task of running a prison. The minutes from a CCA administrative meeting at a Tennessee facility show the "chief" stating, "We all know that we have lots of new staff and are constantly in the training mode. . . . Many employees [are] totally lost and had never worked in corrections."[24]

Most guards at state and federal facilities earn union-scale wages and receive both retirement benefits and health insurance. They also re-ceive hundreds more hours of training than their counterparts at private prisons, who often earn as little as $7.00 an hour, with little or no bene-fits. Some private corporations do offer their employees stock in the prison company in an effort to reduce turnover. But critics of this prac-tice point out that giving guards and wardens a piece of the profits also gives such employees a strong incentive to conceal problems that, as we have seen due to the Esmor effect, can have a devastating effect on a company's stock price. Remember how the police in Youngstown claimed that the CCA guards told them that there had been no escape. CCA guards are shareholders, and following the reports of the escape, their stock did, in fact, hit a fifty-two-week low.

As a result of all the problems coming to light at the High Plains facil-ity, most states pulled their youths from the complex, and Colorado eventually pulled the license from the owner, Rebound, Inc. Incredibly, seven months later, a "different" company, Youth Education, applied for a new license to run the High Plains facility under a new name, Salt Creek School. Youth Education had the same address as Rebound, Inc. It also had the same chief executive and chief operating officer, and it planned to use the same contract medical personnel including doctor, psychologist, and psychiatrist as had been used at High Plains. The biggest difference between the two companies seemed to be the fact that Youth Education only wanted to house "out-of-state" youths, not inmates from Colorado.

Longtime Rebound critic John Dicke, a lawyer and psychologist, told the *Rocky Mountain News* that he believed that the reason for the com-pany wanting to avoid the housing of Colorado offenders in the Youth Education facility demonstrated that the new company simply wanted to avoid serious scrutiny from Colorado officials, the only officials lo-cated geographically close enough to monitor the facility with any con-sistency.[25] Dicke makes a valid point, considering that most states rarely, if ever, send inspectors to the out-of-state private prisons holding their inmates unless they have been made aware that there is some kind of trouble. And generally, knowledge of such problems can only come from the company whose commitment to shareholders makes it in its best interest not to notify anyone when things go wrong.

This is yet another loophole created by moving prisoners across state lines. Most states admittedly have an inadequate number of inspectors to oversee their own institutions. A state with 50,000 inmates can hardly be expected to fly one of its handful of prison inspectors halfway across the country on a regular basis to check on a couple of hundred inmates being held in a for-profit facility. Concerns regarding such problems with the oversight of inmates held in out-of-state private prisons sparked a heated debate in Wisconsin in early 1996 when Governor Tommy Thompson laid out a plan to ship inmates to Texas.

"How are you going to make them accountable?" queried Christopher Ahmuty, then executive director of the ACLU in Wisconsin, in regard to Thompson's plan. "Send state inspectors down there? They barely have time and resources to inspect jails in Wisconsin."[26] Corrections secretary Michael Sullivan answered Ahmuty's questions, though I suspect his responses offered little comfort. Sullivan explained that Wisconsin correctional personnel could keep track of the inmates they had shipped some 2,000 miles away by the use of computers while they were figuring out how to do inspections—as if a computer at the northern extreme of the nation can tell if an inmate at the southern limit is being starved or beaten, getting access to rehabilitative programs, or being denied proper health care.[27]

I've talked with several prison inspectors who have told me that they are counting on inspectors from the states with private prisons holding their inmates to make sure that the facilities are being responsibly managed. I have also talked to the inspectors where the private prisons are located, who tell me that they don't regularly inspect any facility unless it holds inmates from their state. In other words, a private-prison company that only holds inmates from a state or states other than its own is basically able to avoid most government oversight. I certainly believe that the lack of oversight that results from the interstate prisoner trade helps to account for why private prisons so often choose to house prisoners from anywhere except the state where their prisons-for-profit are located. Why else would they develop a business plan requiring expensive prisoner transportation, when there are generally plenty of prisoners in need of beds in the state where the facility is located? And if avoiding oversight is the goal here, what is it that the private prisons are afraid regulators might find?

Further adding to this problem of overseeing private prisons that house only out-of-state inmates is the fact that prison corporations are not subject to the freedom-of-information process that exists in public institutions. With government oversight greatly impaired by distance, manpower, and jurisdictional problems, the only remaining avenue for substantive oversight falls to journalists, activists, and family members of the prisoners themselves. In a publicly run institution, it is possible to review internal documents that may well reveal the evidence needed to write a story or bring a lawsuit in situations of abuse. But corporate prisons can simply deny that anything is wrong and then refuse to provide documentation to back up their claims. For example, I have been seeking documents under the Freedom of Information Act concerning potential fiscal improprieties between the state of Colorado and a private prison in Appleton, Minnesota, for three years. The state continues to claim that the documents I've requested are in the possession of the corporation and that the corporation doesn't have to comply with my FOIA request.

As a result of this near total lack of accountability, private-prison corporations are operating more or less under the same flawed self-reporting structure that has been such a dismal failure for the Environmental Protection Agency. The EPA admits that it doesn't have enough inspectors to check up on corporate polluters, so it has developed a laughable system in which, for the most part, it only investigates those environmental violations that are self-reported by the polluting corporations themselves. And so it has largely become within a private-prison industry that often cleverly chooses to house only prisoners from out of state. Unless an escape, the death or serious injury of a prisoner, or a riot becomes known to the public or the prison company chooses to turn itself in for violations—an unlikely scenario in light of the Esmor effect—no one is monitoring, to any responsible degree, what is happening behind the walls of private prisons.

On those rare occasions when a state does bother to investigate private facilities, what they find is often shocking. For example, when Oklahoma finally bothered to send a representative to inspect one of the five private facilities in Texas where it was housing inmates, it discovered some inmates being confined naked in their cells and complaining of freezing. The inspection also revealed that the company hadn't even bothered to clean up the blood spilled from previous stabbings. A video that captured guards physically abusing inmates eventually surfaced, finally forcing Oklahoma authorities to move their prisoners into a different for-profit prison. The original facility remains in business.

When Colorado authorities finally took a hard look at yet another privately owned youth facility, the Rocky Mountain Boys Ranch, they found files containing the details of 163 critical incidents that had occurred in 1998 alone but that the owner of the facility had inappropriately failed to report to state officials. The incidents included sexual assault and violent attacks. A closer examination uncovered numerous other violations, including accusations that the director-psychologist for the facility had shown up drunk at work and verbally abused the residents. At one point, the director failed to be present on the property for a five-month stretch, even though he was required to be present at least half of the time.[28]

As disturbing as the thought may be, from a profit perspective, covering up these problems made perfect sense in light of the Esmor effect. When the hidden incident reports were found, the ranch was closed by state officials, and the owner lost the contracts that were paying as much as $40,000 per year per resident. Think about the unintended message this sends to private institutions everywhere. Such conflicts of interest are simply impossible to avoid in a privatized corrections system.

Apples and Apples

So has free-market competition in the prison industry given the public a product superior to that provided by the public sector? I don't believe that it has. I am not implying that all private prisons and treatment programs are substandard in comparison with all those in the public sector. Although shareholder primacy makes it impossible to know for sure, it may well be that many private facilities are offering an equal or in some instances a superior product, compared to certain public-sector prisons at this time. I am simply stating that it is not free-market competition that is determining prison quality.

New private-prison facilities are not superior to aging public prisons because they are privatized; they are better only because they are newer, just as new public facilities are superior to old public facilities. The industry would ask that we compare the cold stone fortress of Leavenworth to the new privatized Leavenworth facility operated by CCA, which has been recently erected near the aging publicly operated prison, but this is an inaccurate assessment of the two products. We should compare new public facilities with new private facilities to determine which are best.

When we make this apples-and-apples comparison, we see two physical structures equal in quality in some instances, with new public-sector prisons showing great superiority over some new private institutions such as the converted warehouse in Texarkana. This comparison of new facilities also reveals comparable rehabilitative programs in some cases, but once again, many new private prisons have greatly inferior programs or, in some cases, none at all. And this is where the similarities end. As a rule, we find a better-trained, better-paid workforce with lower turnover in public-sector prisons. We find superior government oversight in public institutions and, therefore, a stricter adherence to prisoner classification in the public prisons. We find inmates in the public prisons to be better able to maintain contact with their families, a fact that cuts down on recidivism. And most significant, all private prisons—all of them—suffer from the influence of the Esmor effect, which is caused by the unavoidable and ever-present conflict between shareholder primacy and public interests.

This conflict of interests still exists even in those private prisons where it has yet to rear its ugly head, and eventually, when something does go wrong, as it will in all prison settings, it will come into play. That being the case, it seems to me that new public-sector prisons are significantly superior to new private facilities.

In reality, the very idea of a competitive market in the prison industry is nothing short of corporate spin designed to convince the public that privatizing the justice system is in the public's best interests. Stock analysts have already begun to steer their clients into the half dozen or so companies that are expected to emerge as the only prison corporations, following the consolidation that is currently underway in the industry. Wackenhut and CCA already control over half the entire prison market, which makes the concept of free-market competition as much a myth in the prison business as it is within the military-industrial complex.

If the competitive market forces that prison corporations and politicians would have us believe existed were truly in effect, then governments would be making their determinations on which prison companies to use in what locations based entirely upon which facilities offered the best conditions at the best value, but this is not the situation at all. Free-market forces as a determinant cannot exist in the current environment, where only a handful of companies are "competing" and hard-on-crime policies are creating prisoners much more rapidly than the system—public or private, or some mix of the two—can handle.

For example, did the state of Colorado decide to use the High Plains facility because it was the best facility at the best value? No. According to state officials, "Colorado needed Rebound as much as Rebound needed Colorado." The state has admitted that it knew that the private facility was understaffed, abusing the young inmates, and providing inadequate services at an exorbitant price for several years, and yet it still used the facility. Colorado Youth Services claims that it had no choice but to use High Plains because the lack of room in the state system demanded out-placement and the state couldn't find a better situation. The chief of Colorado Youth Services put it this way: "What's your bargaining power? You either pay the price, or you have nothing."[29]

Did judges in Maryland and Washington, D.C., send felons in need of drug treatment to Denver because it offered the addicts their best chance for rehabilitation at the best price? No. According to officials in those two jurisdictions, they used the Denver treatment program because it was the only place with beds available, and they used it despite their concerns that the program was providing an inadequate product.

The head of the Colorado Department of Corrections told me that he did not want to send prisoners to the Texarkana warehouse or to a private prison in Appleton, Minnesota. He told me that he knew that shipping prisoners out of state was bad for the inmates. He eventually admitted that he knew that the Texarkana conditions were inadequate compared to the state's prisons, and his department finally acknowledged that the Minnesota facility was actually costing taxpayers more, not less, than incarceration in public prisons.

In other words, Colorado was not using these private prisons because market forces made them the logical or preferable choice, as the industry would have you believe. It was using them because it had no choice at all. The Colorado public-prison system was overflowing with nonviolent drug offenders serving incredibly long mandatory sentences, which forced the state to pay whatever the private prisons demanded for whatever conditions they were offering no matter how inadequate or expensive.

In a truly competitive market, would CCA build three new prisons, one costing more than $100 million, in California, even though it does not have a contract with that state? It seems unlikely, but CCA knows that the three-strikes law and other mandatory sentences have created far more prisoners than California's system can handle and that eventually that state will be forced to pay the company for its beds because it is under a court order to reduce overcrowding and the voters have refused to increase their tax burden with bonds to build still more prisons. California will use CCA, but not because of free-market competition. It will use the company because it has no choice in light of the increasing prisoner population wrought by the media and political components of the perpetual prisoner machine. In short, the forces guiding the use of private prisons at the end of the twentieth century are more akin to extortion guided by nepotism than to those of free-market competition.

And what of the conflicts of interest resulting from shareholder primacy? As we have seen, private-prison corporations are clearly willing to put the public and those sentenced into their care at risk in their effort to fill their beds and make more money for their shareholders. Even in this period when the industry is on its best behavior, we have seen repeated examples of not reporting escapes, riots, and other problems in a timely fashion. We have seen the companies charge taxpayers for services that were not being provided. We have heard the corporations claim that they have no legal responsibility to the public to tell citizens when dangerous prisoners have been moved into their communities. We have seen these prison profiteers cut staffing to the bone and provide substandard training for their employees, a practice that endangers both the public and the prisoners in the name of profit. We have found prisoners in these private facilities literally going hungry, being denied adequate health care, and being forced to live in overcrowded, unsanitary conditions as if they were so much beef. We have seen time after time how nonviolent and nonserious offenders are being forced to live in the same space as murderers with records of preying on their fellow inmates. Citizens, journalists, and family members have repeatedly sought information regarding purported abuses and potential financial improprieties, only to be told that private-prison corporations are allowed to keep their records secret from the public even though it is the public that pays for their services. We have watched as these corporations have taken prisoners across state lines, far away from their families, a practice that allows the companies to avoid a good deal of government oversight and to bypass laws specifically written to protect inmates from being caged in substandard housing or denied needed rehabilitative programs. We have seen these problems, which arise from the conflict between shareholder interest and that of the public, and we will see much more of the same in the future when this honeymoon period is over.

How does the prison industry explain away its problems? It explains them the same way that the defense industry explains excessively priced toilet seats and wrenches or the way politicians dispatch the issue of illegal campaign contributions when they get caught, meaning that the prison corporations brush aside these problems as the rare exception to the rule, while continuing to claim that all the other private prisons—the ones that have not been caught—are being operated in a stellar, cost-saving fashion. Is this claim true, though? It seems doubtful to me, but who knows? That's the problem. Unless a corporation decides to commit financial suicide and self-report its deficiencies as they occur, there is little means to accurately gauge the performance of these for-profit institutions. The one thing we do know is that these prison corporations have a legal obligation to their shareholders to protect their stock value, which translates into an obligation to prevent bad press. Does this mean that we should expect private-prison corporations to cover up problems? If I'm a shareholder, which as you'll recall I reluctantly am, I would expect nothing less.

Consider the Esmor effect that followed in each of the circumstances discussed in this chapter. Esmor had a riot; its stock value fell by two-thirds. The Texarkana warehouse received bad press for riots and poor conditions; it lost its only contract, a $20,000-a-day contract with Colorado. Rebound, Inc. had a suicide that sparked an investigation by a reporter; it went out of business in Brush, Colorado. CCA had an escape and other violence in its Youngstown facility; its stock hit a fifty-two-week low.

These examples clearly demonstrate that there is a considerable incentive for private-prison corporations to be less than forthcoming with bad news concerning their operations, even if such hesitation to report problems risks the public safety and that of the prisoners. In fact, I'll go one step further: I believe that private-prison corporations have a legal obligation to their shareholders to put the public and their prisoners at risk when such conflicts of interest do arise. This is the problem with privatizing the prison system. Despite industry rhetoric to the contrary, it is impossible for corporations to fulfill both their obligation to shareholders and their obligation to the public. These responsibilities are mutually exclusive.

Since we know from hundreds of years of experience that the shareholder will always win out in the end, it would seem that we are foolishly pushing for a privatized prison system that cannot work. It did not work 100 years ago. It is not working now. So why on earth would we think that it will work in the future? Analysts tell us that in the future, there will be even less competition than there is now, and the government will have become so dependent on the prisons owned by the corporations that America will not be able to reverse its course, even if it should decide it needs to. That being the case, we should ask ourselves: Why are we engaging in a policy seemingly predestined for failure? I believe the answer to this question is the same now as it was during the "Dark Ages" of penology: Those who are charting this privatized course for our future are also those who are benefiting from the journey.

9

The Hidden Costs of Private Prisons

Since profits depend on the existence and expansion of the prison population, corporations will attempt to increase both the number of prisoners and the length of their stay.

　　　—Shaheen Borna, "Free Enterprise Goes to Prison," 1986[1]

I did a little experimenting with the information contained in the last chapter. I asked a number of people to read about the problems occurring in private prisons and then asked them whether they would prefer a public- or private-prison system. Almost without exception their answer was "public." I then suggested to these same readers that private prisons cost taxpayers much less to operate than their public counterparts. I asked them again which they preferred. Not surprisingly, considering the current atmosphere regarding crime and criminals, when the majority of the people who had said that they preferred public prisons were told that private prisons would save them considerable money, they changed their opinion in favor of a privatized system, noting that although shareholder primacy creates the potential for problems, a substantial cost savings would more than offset such potential.

　　I believe that the real power of the pro-privatization argument can be found herein. The bottom line is this: If it costs less or if the industry can convince people that it costs less, the majority of Americans will think privatization a good idea. For that reason, I will use this chapter to examine the private-prison industry's claim that it is saving America money when it comes to the justice system, a claim that I believe the evidence shows to be false.

There are a couple of ways to compare the costs of private versus public prisons, through an individual comparison of facilities and through an examination of the overall long-term impact of private industry's funding of prisons on the cost of corrections. In this chapter, we will look at the industry's claim that it can operate individual prisons at a lower cost to taxpayers than the government can.

Efficiency Versus Bureaucracy

Let's start by dissecting the old standby industry argument that corporations have been using to wrestle traditionally operated government functions into corporate hands for decades, namely, that private corporations can perform tasks more quickly and efficiently and, therefore, at a reduced price. Industries that have used this argument are quick to point out that bureaucracy makes government efficiency an impossibility and that market competition makes a public-private merger the only logical course of action. This "efficient corporation" versus "inefficient bureaucratic government" argument has been put forward so many times that few of us ever question its accuracy, whether it's being applied to building tanks, the proposed private management of the social security system, or privatizing our prisons.

I must admit that on its surface this simple industry claim seems to make sense. After all, who in their right mind would argue that our mammoth government even remotely exhibits any attribute similar to efficiency? But still, is the industry's explanation for why we should privatize matters of public responsibility really as simple as it is being made out to be? I think not.

Take, for instance, the assertion that "bureaucracy" will prevent the government from being able to perform the task at hand efficiently. This assessment plays well to a public conditioned to view "bureaucracy" in only negative terms. But what is bureaucracy? The dictionary defines it as "government by officials; the routine world of regulations."[2] Granted, it's not an exciting definition, but neither is it an overly sinister one.

What proponents of privatization are really saying is that official oversight and regulations get in the way of efficiency. So the question becomes: efficiency at doing what? In most instances, this government oversight and regulation has been put in place to protect the public interest from those who would exploit it for their own gain. Admittedly, today's government is composed of layer upon layer of regulatory redundancy, which often results in more carbon copies than productive oversight. But even so, is our best alternative to ineffective, redundant government regulation to throw out the baby with the bathwater, so to speak? Must we discard our government's ability to protect our interests because it has grown inefficient?

Let's assume for the sake of argument that the corporate assertion that bureaucracy must, in all cases, prevent efficiency is correct. What does this really mean when it comes to privatizing the prison system? Once again, I believe this is to some degree a case of comparing apples and oranges. Implying that we can compare corporate efficiency to government efficiency as if the two are interchangeable opens the door for many abuses. Ask yourself this: What is the primary goal of a corporation? The answer is: to make as much money as possible for its shareholders. Now ask yourself: What is the primary goal of government? The answer is: to serve the interests of the people. So what happens when we act as if these two goals are exchangeable? Nothing that could be described as beneficial to the noninvesting public.

The corporations claim that they are highly efficient entities, and I agree. That means that in the case of the prison-industrial complex, we should assume that the corporate goal of making as much profit as possible through the funding of prison construction, the housing and care of inmates, prison labor, and the providing of essential prisoner services will be efficiently accomplished. Next, corporations claim that the government is inefficient. Once again, in its current bloated state, I would have to agree. Since the government's role in this privatized prison scenario is to spend taxpayer money as responsibly as possible in order to incarcerate inmates under acceptable conditions, including providing them with avenues to rehabilitation, we should assume that the government will do a less than stellar job with this task.

Are you beginning to see the problem with this picture? Creating public-private hybrids under these conditions is paramount to asking a three-year-old to change a $20 bill for a polished con artist and not get taken to the cleaners. It simply can't be done. A public-private hybrid—

comprised of an efficient profit-seeking corporation and an inefficient government payer and overseer—is a public disaster waiting to happen.

We've seen this scenario played out a thousand times, and yet we never seem to learn our lesson. It has come in a multitude of shapes and sizes, from well-publicized defense-industry fiascoes to even more ludicrous examples such as the construction of an unnecessary, federally funded airport being built in the middle of a cornfield in the middle of nowhere and left to decay unused. We saw it in 1998 when health-care giants Quarum Health Group and Columbia/HCA were accused of falsifying claims to inflate their hospital reimbursements from Medicare, Medicaid, and the Civilian Health and Medical Program of the Uniformed Services.[3] In fact, as of 1999, 2,550 hospitals have been caught inflating their billings to Medicare.[4] And then there is the nursing-home industry, a business similar in some ways to private prisons in that the corporations have nearly total control over a captive audience. So how has free-market competition worked in the nursing-home industry? Nearly one-fourth of the 17,000 nursing homes have been caught providing inadequate care or overbilling their clients.[5] There is literally no limit to how much money an "efficient" private corporation can suck out of an "inefficient" government payer. And the prison system is proving to be no exception.

A Lack of Evidence

Let's revisit the High Plains Juvenile Facility in Brush, Colorado, and examine the economics surrounding that privatized institution. First of all, it would appear that the company's lobbying efforts paid off big. In its attempt to reduce spending on corrections or, as some have argued, as a payback for campaign-finance support, the conservative Colorado legislature actually inserted the privately owned High Plains facility into its 1988 budget, making it impossible for Colorado Youth Corrections not to use the institution. Enter the inefficient government payer. For nearly a decade, no one bothered to examine whether the High Plains deal was actually saving money, which was the reason originally touted for using the facility. Colorado officials have actually acknowledged that they assumed the youth prison was less expensive simply because it was privatized. Obviously, the old efficiency-versus-bureaucracy argument worked to perfection in the High Plains case. As a part of her investigation, reporter Ann Imse looked into the company's billing records, only to find that the private facility wasn't efficient at all—unless of course the object of its efficiency was to bilk money out of taxpayers, in which case it was doing a spectacular job.

We have previously discussed the fact that High Plains was billing its clients for services that weren't being adequately provided, but this was nothing compared to what was happening on the real-estate side of the business. As a part of its contract, the state of Colorado had agreed to pay Rebound, Inc., the High Plains owner, $3 million a year in rent for the facility. This agreement turned out to be quite a deal for the corporation. Rebound had only spent approximately $9 million to build High Plains. By the time of the Imse investigation, Colorado had already paid the company $20 million in rent on the $9 million facility in less than ten years.[6] How could such a ridiculous contract have ever made its way through the system?

According to Youth Services spokesman Dwight Eisnach, corrections simply wasn't prepared to handle a contract like the one with High Plains. According to Eisnach, "We didn't have anyone on our staff who could even analyze these things."[7] This response to the High Plains contract sparked an editorial in the *Rocky Mountain News* that asked the questions "How long would the state have continued to pay this $3 million a year to High Plains had the deal not been exposed?" and, perhaps more pointedly, "Are there other contracts the division of Youth Services won't want to defend once they become public knowledge?"[8] This is just the kind of thing that all too often happens when we privatize government works. But are private prisons more cost-efficient than public prisons? As you might expect, it depends on who you ask.

As a rule, the private-prison industry claims that its facilities cost at least 10 percent less to taxpayers than do public prisons. Some private prisons claim much higher savings somewhere in the 20 to 50 percent range. Texas private-prison contracts actually go so far as to require a 10 percent savings, and Florida contracts require at least a 7 percent savings.[9] But based on what the corporations themselves claim—"government is inefficient"—why should we assume that Texas, Florida, or any other state's bureaucrats, for that matter, are any better equipped to keep track of prison costs than those in Colorado? And if they aren't, why should we assume that other prison corporations, whose goal is to maximize profits, won't likewise take advantage of this inefficiency? We'll come back to these questions in a moment. For now, let's examine just how these private corporations supposedly incarcerate prisoners for less.

As I mentioned earlier, costs such as food, health care, alarm systems, and so on are relatively fixed. Private prisons and public facilities both attempt to cut these costs as far as possible. Both systems spend between $1 and $1.50 per day per inmate on food, and both have been found guilty in recent years of providing their inmates with inadequate calories and limited health care. I would put this abuse found in both public and private prisons forward as evidence that both systems are equally motivated to do whatever it takes—including jeopardizing the health of their charges—in their effort to cut costs. Other services are also comparable in expense because both systems use a similar bidding process to choose between the same companies seeking contracts. That being the case, the ability to cut the cost of imprisonment basically boils down to reducing costs associated with labor, training, and benefits, which, as I mentioned earlier, represent 60 percent of the overall expense of incarceration.[10]

In their effort to save on labor expense, prison corporations pay as little as $7 to $10 an hour and often give no benefits to guards and pay even less to other staff.[11] If for no other reason than this low pay for frontline employees, one would assume that private-prison budgets would be at least 10 percent below those of their public counterparts. However, even the industry must admit that not all of this savings on labor will make its way to the taxpayer. The first billion or so dollars in this pile of cash that isn't being paid in employee salaries has to go to the corporation and its shareholders as profit, and that's certainly an expense the government doesn't have to pay. Another portion of the pile goes to corporate managers, who pay themselves six-figure incomes that are often three times higher than their public-sector counterparts. Still, the private-prison companies tell us that their facilities cost at least 7 to 10 percent less to operate, and they claim to have the evidence to prove it.

According to privatization proponents, a 1991 study by the Texas Sunset Advisory Commission said private prisons cost 15 percent less to operate than public prisons; a 1991 study published in the *Journal of Contemporary Criminal Justice* said that private facilities save taxpayers money; the fact that the Auditor General's Office in Florida and Texas requires savings and that private prisons are still being used in those states also proves that the corporations must be meeting this goal; and an official report by the Texas Criminal Justice Policy Council stated that private prisons cost less than public prisons.[12]

These are the studies that seem to turn up again and again when someone is trying to push for the use of private prisons. Despite the fact that these examples do say at some point that private prisons save money or rather that that the private prison studied saved money over the public prison studied, I do not believe that there has ever been a government function privatized—let alone one of such a controversial nature as private prisons, where corporations are given complete control over U.S. citizens, including the right to physically punish and even kill them if need be—that has come into existence as a result of so little empirical data. And just how good is this "proof" that private prisons cost less for equal or better services, anyway? Apparently not very.

According to Dr. Russell Clemens, the labor economist with the Department of Research for the American Federation of State, County, and Federal Employees, there have only been three studies pertaining to prison privatization that can be viewed as impartial. One was completed under the supervision of the National Institute of Corrections, another by the National Institute of Justice, and the third by the General Accounting Office (GAO). The first two found "no cost savings associated with prison privatization."[13]

The third and most comprehensive study to date was the one conducted by the GAO in 1996. The reason I say this was the most "comprehensive" study is that the purpose of the GAO research was to examine every other study comparing public to private prisons that had been conducted between 1991 and 1996, including most of the studies I have already mentioned as well as others conducted by the states of Tennessee, California, and Washington. This report by the GAO was prepared for and presented to the Subcommittee on Crime, Committee on the Judiciary, House of Representatives.

In its final report, the GAO concluded that after examining the entire body of research comparing public to private prisons, "it could not draw any conclusions about cost savings or quality of service" because all of the studies comparing private to public institutions to date have had mixed results or have showed no difference between public and private institutions.[14] Laurie E. Ekstrand, associate director for the GAO's Administration of Justice Issues, summed up the GAO's findings by saying, "The bottom line of the report is that although private prisons are touted as a way to save money, the five studies we reviewed provide no evidence that they save money."[15]

These revelations by the GAO should be very disturbing indeed. Not only is America racing ahead with prison privatization based on almost no data to support such a monumental decision, but the federal government itself, through the GAO, admits that even the small amount of data that does exist doesn't clearly demonstrate that private prisons are less costly or offer equal or better services than public institutions. This finding is made even more remarkable by the fact that these existing studies of cost comparison did not even take into consideration the massive hidden costs of private prisons. If they had, I believe that public institutions would have shown themselves to be far less expensive than private prisons, as opposed to just being comparable.

Hollywood Accounting

Red tape, in a lot of cases, is there to protect the public.

*—M. Wayne Huggins, spokesman for
the National Sheriffs' Group, 1986*[16]

In writing for the *British Journal of Criminology*, Shaheen Borna has described a belief shared by many criminologists that government bureaucracy will actually be increased by the use of private prisons—an increase that will add still more cost to the taxpayers even though this "hidden cost" will never show up in the comparative studies. According to Borna:

> The efficiency argument ignores several points. First, the perceived need to regulate private prisons may in fact *add* another layer to government bureaucracy rather than reducing it. It is not to difficult to imagine a group of government employees writing and updating regulations for the private prisons, with a second group hired for the purpose of on-site inspections, and a third group processing the paperwork generated by the other two.[17]

Not only would *proper* oversight demand additional levels of bureaucracy and inspection, but the fact that private prisons hold out-of-state prisoners would dictate that millions of extra dollars per year would be spent on travel-related expenses by the inspectors and others. The only alternative to increasing government expense to regulate the private-prison industry would be to allow the industry to regulate itself for the most part, but this is what is more or less happening today, and it is already abundantly clear that under such slack oversight, at least some of the prison corporations will succumb to the temptation to abuse inmates and taxpayers in their pursuit of greater profits. Many critics of privatizing the prison system argue that most of the cost savings being claimed by private prisons, such as this example of oversight and inspections illustrates, are, in fact, only the result of cost shifting on paper. The complaint is that for every dollar claimed as savings in the private sector, an extra dollar is being spent in the public realm. James Moran touched on this point in his article for the Office of International Criminal Justice. As Moran put it:

> Public officials who advocate privatization point to the reduction in costs, which appeals to city managers responsible for providing services on limited budgets. Contracting for a service may reduce overhead cost, but will not necessarily provide more efficient or better service. The saving of overhead expenses might require increased insurance coverage, and does not eliminate the need to monitor the contract agency, to ensure that the obligations of the contract are being fulfilled. Dissenters are concerned that the cost savings in subcontracting is in actuality a cost transfer to another expense.[18]

In addition to the economic arguments, the corporate assertion that privatizing our prisons will save money by lessening bureaucracy flies in the face of past experiences as well. The public-private hybrid created by the defense industry is a perfect example. In January 1999, President Clinton asked Congress for an additional $110 billion for defense spending over the next six years. One of the reasons the money was needed—as pointed out by a general in the Pentagon—was that the added layers of bureaucracy and paperwork created by the need to oversee the privatized defense industry is wasting between $20 to $30 billion a year.[19] Experience should be telling us that when we privatize a function of government, bureaucracy and its associated costs increase, not decrease. And even if the privatization of prisons could somehow avoid this bureaucratic pitfall, there are still plenty more hidden costs that must be taken into consideration.

In the beginning of the privatization debate, prison corporations argued that one positive aspect of privatizing the system was that for-profit prison corporations, unlike their public counterparts, would be good neighbors—taxpaying entities that returned a portion of their revenues to the various levels of government in the form of taxes. But this claim has proven to be false for the most part. First of all, in an effort to bring in jobs to economically struggling communities, rural counties are offering private prisons sweetheart tax breaks on property taxes. And second, the prison industry leaders, CCA and Wackenhut, which control the vast majority of the nation's private prisons, have structured their prison businesses in the form of real-estate investment trusts (REITs), a move that allows the corporations to avoid virtually all of their tax burden.[20]

In fact, private prisons are actually removing tax dollars from the system, which represents another hidden cost. Since 60 percent of the cost of incarceration is represented by employee salaries and since the main means of reducing expenditures for the prison corporations is to reduce those salaries, it stands to reason that this process would have to be resulting in a substantial loss in state and federal income taxes. For example, a unionized prison guard in California making $45,000 annually can be expected to pay somewhere in the area of $8,000 to $10,000 a year in taxes. A private-prison guard making $7 an hour will only pay around $2,000 in taxes. Much of this $6,000 to $8,000 difference per guard per year winds up as corporation profits, which, as just mentioned, are often untaxed. When you consider that the United States has a half-million prison guards, not to mention other corrections employees, the potential lost tax revenues of a privatized prison system are enormous. Some estimates have placed the lost tax revenue associated with just CCA's being structured as a REIT at $50 million a year.[21]

Prisoner labor presents yet another serious problem for the industry's claim of saving the taxpayer money. Most people want prisoners to work because they want prisoners to have to pay for as much of their own cost of incarceration as possible. To this end, most states have passed legislation that requires a large portion of all the money paid to prisoners who work to go either toward offsetting their cost of incarceration or to victim restitution, or both. But once again, private prisons are using the out-of state loophole to pad their own pockets with the money generated by prisoner labor that should be going to reimburse taxpayers.

For example, Colorado has laws requiring that much of the money coming from inmate labor must go to offset the taxpayers' expense and to repay victims. But consider what happened when Colorado inmates were shipped to a private prison in Appleton, Minnesota, and were put to work in a variety of industries. At one point, Colorado citizens were paying $26,000 a day to the private prison to house 500 inmates; this number was eventually doubled. Many of the prisoners—I can't report an exact figure because the state and the private-prison claim that my FOIA request doesn't entitle me to such information from a private corporation—were earning money by working for several private enterprises that had contracted for prison labor with the facilities owner. Had the working inmates been in the public system in Colorado, taxpayers would have been saving potentially millions of dollars on the cost of incarceration as a result of this labor. But because the prisoners had been moved across state lines, the labor earnings, aside from the few cents an hour paid to the inmates, were kept by the private prison's owner.

This can be a very significant loophole when you do the math. Private prisons are often paid $5 to $7 an hour per prisoner by companies who use inmate labor. Of this hourly fee, the prison corporations often pay the inmates as little as $.23 to $1.15 an hour.[22] As I said, I have been trying to get the exact figures on the Appleton labor for years, only to be refused, so here is a theoretical estimate of the kind of potential loss to taxpayers that we're talking about. Let's say that 500 prisoners are working six hours a day, five days a week for companies that are paying the prison corporation $5 an hour per inmate. The prison then pays the inmates an average of $.35 an hour. In this scenario, the private prison would be pocketing $3.62 million a year minus any expenses associated with overseeing the labor environment that would have gone to offset the taxpayers' bill for incarceration had the inmates been housed in a public prison in the state of Colorado.

And Colorado is not alone. As already noted, most states have legislation authorizing the use of money earned by prisoners to reimburse taxpayers. A source at the National Institute of Justice who didn't wish to be identified told me that as of 1999, only six states had passed laws to close this loophole. It should come as no surprise, considering the amount of potential dollars at stake, that when I attempted—through industry organizations and the Department of Justice—to verify the number of prison industries in private prisons that were not returning money to the taxpayers of the inmates' home states, I was stonewalled or told that no one is keeping track of such information.

Personally, I have no trouble believing that no one within the government—the same government that the prison industry tells us is "inefficient"—has been monitoring this clear abuse of the private-prison system. It just makes me wonder how many other loopholes that we don't know about are being used by the "efficient" prison corporations to exploit taxpayers and prisoners.

These are only some of the hidden costs of private prisons. Critics of the industry point to still more areas of cost shifting, such as insurance, legal fees, and higher interest rates and other increased costs associated with the lease-revenue bonds sometimes sold to fund the construction of prisons.

As a result of these hidden expenses, the evidence suggests that if a comparison between public and private prisons were to be conducted—a truly comprehensive comparison that took into account all of the cost shifting, out-of-state loopholes, lost tax due to reduced salaries, and so forth—the private prisons would not be able to demonstrate any cost savings over their public-sector counterparts. In fact, such a study would most likely find that the private prisons are more expensive than public prisons. I can say this with confidence because according to the GAO and the several states that have done comparison studies—studies that did not even take these hidden costs into account—the research to date has not been able to demonstrate that private prisons are saving the public money. The one study that did claim to find an absolute cost savings in the private sector, which was conducted by the Texas Sunset Advisory Commission in 1991, has been found to be sorely deficient. According to the GAO, the Sunset study compared one private prison to an "imaginary" public facility. Such industry-friendly number crunching can hardly be considered relevant to the debate.[23]

Simple logic would also seem to show that prison corporations may not be saving the money that they claim. Ask yourself this: If you owned a private-prison corporation and you knew that you could produce a comprehensive multistate comparison that took into account the hidden costs we've just discussed and that such research would prove your claims of saving taxpayers at least 10 percent over public institutions, then why wouldn't you have conducted such a comparison sometime during the last fifteen years? Such a report would likely result in entire state prison systems being privatized as well as that of the federal government. Such hard data would likely cause the private-prison industry to grow exponentially almost overnight. In other words, such a study would be worth many billions of dollars to the industry.

The logical explanation for why no such study exists is that such a comprehensive comparison would demonstrate once and for all that the private-prison industry's claim that it is saving taxpayers money is, in fact, false. If this is the case, and I believe that it is, then the industry has wisely chosen to pursue its growth and profits by other means, namely, by espousing poorly supported claims of cost savings, by using influence over politicians purchased through campaign financing to bring pressure on governments to privatize the system, and by exploiting the connections achieved through crossover (public to private) employment.

This business plan helps to explain why—despite the obvious lack of empirical data to support the position that private prisons cost less for an equal product—one jurisdiction after another has nonetheless been moving full speed ahead with privatization, despite the government's obvious shortcomings when it comes to being able to adequately monitor the cost-effectiveness of the private system. Below are some examples that illustrate why it is irresponsible for the government to be pushing the privatization of the prison system at this time.

In 1998, when the state of Virginia decided it should determine how cost-efficient its use of private prisons had been before committing more prisoners to them, it quickly hit a roadblock. Ron Jordon, a staff analyst on Virginia's House of Delegates Budget Committee, was forced to admit that the Virginia Department of Corrections currently has no way of even measuring whether private-prison contracts are saving taxpayers money or costing them more.[24]

The states of Tennessee, California, and Washington continue to use private prisons—with Tennessee even considering selling its entire prison system to CCA and then paying the corporation to house its inmates—even though all three of these states have conducted cost-comparison studies between public and private prisons and concluded that, at best, there is no consistent difference in quality or costs. According to the GAO, these studies found that some private prisons seemed to cost less, some more, and others the same. And what of the other thirty-odd states now using private prisons that have never even bothered to investigate the difference in cost between public and private prisons? Why are these jurisdictions using more and more private prisons even though they admittedly have no idea of whether such prisons are costing their citizens more or less money?

For six years, Colorado shipped a portion of its prison population to out-of-state private prisons. During this time, I was told repeatedly by CDOC officials that using these private prisons was saving the taxpayers money. I do think that the officials I was dealing with thought this was true. Yet in 1998, as the state prepared to bring back the last of its out-of-state prisoners, the CDOC suddenly admitted that the out-of-state private prisons had, in fact, been costing more, not less, than public-sector incarceration.[25] This inability to do the math for six years clearly demonstrates why states should not be pushing ahead with private incarceration at a time when they are obviously ill prepared to determine the value of such a decision.

This same "blind faith in the market" approach is also being pursued by the federal government, which is moving toward the privatization of its prisons even though it is equally in the dark about whether private prisons save money. A five-year test project is now underway at a prison facility in Taft, California. This federally funded private-prison experiment is being managed by Wackenhut Corrections Corporation. Three years ago, the government claimed that it would use the findings from the Taft study to determine whether it should privatize a good deal of the federal prison system, but instead of waiting for the results of its own test, the government has been going ahead with using an increasing number of private prisons and at one point even admitted its intention to move toward privatizing the majority of the system. After federal corrections employees took offense at the sudden appearance of this "plan to privatize," the Clinton administration quickly backpedaled, claiming that it had meant to say that it was simply studying the plan.[26]

Too Late to Turn Back—a Corporate Strategy

To those not familiar with the questionable process that tends to take place when government responsibilities are handed over to profit-seeking corporations, it might seem odd that our local, state, and federal governments would wait until *after* they have already become completely and irreversibly dependent on the private-prison industry before finally taking steps to determine whether using such prisons is a good idea. But in truth, this is par for the course. We've seen it happen in the defense industry and with Medicare, and it's about to happen again with Social Security. I believe that such poorly timed and poorly thought out political action is attributable to the awesome power wielded by those who hold the political money supply.

It is estimated that by the time the federal government's Taft study is completed, private prisons may already be holding as many as 200,000 of our nation's prisoners, and this figure could be much higher if entire systems were to privatize in bulk, as is being contemplated in Tennessee.[27] Even if the Taft study or other, more comprehensive research by state or federal authorities that might be done someday should indicate that our public-sector prisons are cheaper and provide a higher quality of service than those of the corporations, it will likely already be too late to reverse course and bring such a large number of prisoners back into the public domain. It will have become nearly economically impossible to do so.

With court-mandated limits on prison overcrowding, federal, state, and local governments would be forced to simultaneously drain their budgets in an effort to build the many new prisons that would be needed to hold the recalled inmates or would be forced to pay premium prices to the prison companies to acquire their facilities. Either way, the effect on governments would be similar to what happens to individuals when the bank suddenly calls in the mortgage on their homes or farms. In other words, we would experience an economic "prison crisis," whose shock waves, including tax increases and a massive diversion of funds from other areas into prisons, would quickly devastate public education, infrastructures, child welfare, and other important programs even more so than the substantial diversion that is already taking place. The only alternative to this scenario would be to suddenly release a few hundred thousand inmates, but that option is clearly political suicide in the current hard-on-crime environment.

Based on what has transpired to date, I believe that by the time our elected officials have actually determined whether private prisons are cost-effective—this statement optimistically assumes that they will eventually bother to pursue this information in earnest—the prison-industrial complex will already be holding the mortgage on our children's future. At some point, a point that is only a few years away at best or may already have arrived, we will have little choice but to play by the prison-industrial complex's rules when it comes to paying for prisons.

Just as with the military-industrial complex, once we are fully dependent upon the few prison corporations that remain following the industry's consolidation, there is every reason to assume that we will find ourselves paying a price for prison space and related services many times higher than the amount they should cost or would have cost had incarceration remained the exclusive responsibility of government. I suspect that the industry's desire to reach this "point of no return" threshold explains why prison corporations and the politicians that they lobby are in such a hurry to increase the use of private prisons yet seem to be in no rush at all to create the data that would either confirm as true or expose as false the economic rhetoric surrounding the use of their prisons-for-profit.

Sidestepping
the Restraints
of Democracy

Man's capacity for justice makes democracy possible, but man's inclination to injustice makes democracy necessary.

—*Reinhold Niebuhr,* **Children of Light and Children of Darkness, 1944**[1]

Just as today, a time when our media-induced crime anxiety has brought the issue of lawlessness to the forefront of public concern, there have been periods in our past when America has been consumed with the issue of crime out of an unwarranted fear that criminals were somehow pushing society to the brink of collapse. Such an exaggerated fear of crime existed during the antebellum period, following the Civil War, in the midst of Prohibition, during the Great Depression, and in the politically tumultuous 1960s. In each of these periods, our society was, indeed, in a state of disconcerting flux. But viewing these times with the advantage of hindsight, we can now see that crime was merely a scapegoat for other political and economic forces that were the real culprits behind the turmoil.

For instance, consider what was happening in the United States just prior to and during the antebellum period, which began around 1820.

Citizens during this era believed that crime was radically escalating and that as a result, the social structure was collapsing. One noteworthy reformer of the day, Dorothea Dix, summed up what many people saw as the problem when she said, "It is to the defects of our social organization, to the multiplied and multiplying temptations to crime that we chiefly owe the increase of evil doers."[2]

With regard to the questions of whether antebellum society's fear of crime was justified or whether the perceived social crisis was real or imagined, historian David J. Rothman has written:

> [T]he likelihood is that the preoccupation with crime [during the antebellum period] has less to do with the real incidence of crime and more to do with general social attitudes about a society in change. Whatever the reality, there was a subjective vision of disorder. Indeed, it is this perspective that is most helpful in enabling us to understand the resulting form of the public response to crime.[3]

The real roots of this perceived disorder were likely twofold. First, there was a general anxiety attributable to the growing understanding that the slavery issue would likely lead to war. The Abolitionist movement had divided society into three opposing camps: those who wanted a multicultural society of citizens, those who wanted free blacks but not black citizens, and those who wanted to maintain slavery.

Strangely enough, the second cause for the perception of disorder can be found in the economic success of the New World, which was providing never before seen opportunities to all strata of the population. As a result of this unprecedented economic opportunity, parents became more preoccupied with bettering their financial standing than with family matters; children dropped out of school and left home at a younger age because they desired to seek their own fortune; and families became separated by great distances at a time when communication under such circumstances was nearly impossible.

The Oxford History of the Prison states that these circumstances created a general perception that children no longer obeyed their parents or their teachers and that the role of the family was diminishing. The church too believed that it was losing its influence over society. Advice books of the day reflected this feeling of lost order. The best-sellers at the time, *The Father's Book* and *The Rollo Code of Morals*, offered instruction on how to raise an obedient child. Teachers put forth an organized effort to make school a more important component in the lives of America's youth. Churches tried to regain control by inventing the structure of Sunday school.[4] And perhaps most important, the Jacksonian reformers decided that more prisons could return order to a society that was seemingly spinning out of control. All in all, observers of American culture at the time made it known that the United States was going to hell and that crime was responsible for a good portion of the ride.

So in a very real sense, the importance of the school, family, and church structures of the antebellum world were diminishing, but it was the birth pangs of a new culture that idealized capitalism above all else and a political landscape cluttered by slavery that were the cause for this decline in influence—not crime. In the end, however, as a consequence of their misperception that crime was the biggest threat to their way of life, those in antebellum society decided to greatly expand the prison system as a cure-all. To their credit, as the system grew under the guidance of the Jacksonian reformers, the first penal system in the world based on the concept of reform as opposed to punishment and incapacitation alone was created. We now know that prison as a means to reform is a failed idea, particularly this early attempt that did not have the advantage of the yet-undiscovered behavioral sciences, but still it was an enlightened effort at the time and likely accounted for the large degree of public support that existed for this brainchild of the reformers.

Historians have noted that state after state began to spend more tax dollars on prisons precisely because the expansion was being enthusiastically embraced by a general population that naively believed it would eventually lead to the elimination of crime. In other words, the U.S. prison system was growing in the 1820s and 1830s because it was the desire of the majority of voters that it do so, but by the mid-1840s, things were beginning to change. The public's enthusiasm for financially supporting a growing prison population had begun to wane.

There were a number of reasons for this change of heart on the part of taxpaying voters at the end of the antebellum period, including the realization that isolation and discipline—the only techniques being employed at the time to rehabilitate inmates—were not going to lead to a crime-free society as had been promised. Also important was the fact that the economy was worsening on the doorstep of civil war, which made spending money on criminals seem ill-advised. Whatever the reasons for the public's decision to stop funding the growth of the system, the end of the antebellum expansion should be viewed as having resulted from democracy in action, just as the decision to expand the system had been some twenty years earlier. It is here—in the concept of the electorate being able to exercise a certain control over the prison system via its willingness or refusal to fund the system's growth—that the prison expansions of the past part ways with today's inflating inmate population.

In nearly every facet of American democracy, we can find a set of checks and balances built into the system. Criminal justice has historically been no exception to this rule. In most of the periods previously mentioned (except for the 1960s, which ushered in the current expansion, and the post–Civil War era, which led to the failed privatization experiment of the "Dark Ages"), it would be accurate to say that the prison population only grew to the extent that voters were willing to pay for the cost of the added incarceration. At some point, regardless of their level of anxiety over crime, the built-in safeguards of our political system—in particular the requirement that state and local governments need voter approval in order to create debt in the public's name—have always forced Americans to choose between halting any crackdown on crime or having to increase their own tax burden to build more prisons or house more prisoners as a result of their anticrime efforts.

This is the democratic restraint that has heretofore existed over criminal justice and that has always served to counterbalance any overzealous, fear-induced push to wildly expand the prison population. But beginning around 1980, a change in the manner in which we fund prison construction and operations created an opportunity to circumvent this historically effective barrier to mass imprisonment. The tenfold increase in the U.S. prison population is ample proof that the opportunity was seized upon.

At some point during the 1980s, nearly every state in the union began to reach the economic limits of its ability to build new prisons. Hard-on-crime changes to the sentencing guidelines had filled prisons and jails to overflowing, even though states had exhausted their corrections budgets to build and operate nearly 600 new facilities.[5] It was at this point that the checks and balances of our democracy should have come into play. Just as in the past, the expanding prison population of the 1980s would require voters in nearly every part of the nation to choose between continuing with hard-on-crime policies as they were structured or having to pay for still more prisons. It was the moment of truth for the war on crime—or at least it should have been.

All across the nation, bond issues earmarked for prison construction were being placed on the ballots. In the early 1980s, some of these bond issues passed and some failed, but as the decade rolled on, voters in one jurisdiction after another began to make it clear that the expansion would have to be greatly curtailed or even stopped. They made their opinion known by defeating an ever-increasing number of the prison bond issues at the polls. In writing for the *British Journal of Criminology* in 1986, Shaheen Borna described this critical point in the expansion:

> Though they must reduce already overcrowded prisons and accommodate new inmates, public officials are having a difficult time raising sufficient funds to build and operate additional facilities. . . . Facing current trends in tax-limiting legislation, uncertain aid programs, and *difficulty in passing bond referenda*, financially strapped state and local governments are increasingly turning to the private sector to build and run the prisons. (emphasis added)[6]

The majority of Americans may still have been emotionally, even intellectually, supportive of hard-on-crime measures, as evidenced by their continued backing of politicians espousing such a platform, but concern over their pocketbooks had apparently become an equal or even more important priority. Schizophrenic voting behavior aside, the defeat of the bond issues, coupled with court-imposed limits on prison overcrowding, should have spelled the end of the expansion and forced revisions to the sentencing guidelines for nonviolent offenders as a means of controlling the number of incoming prisoners.

The electorate had exercised its power to limit government spending on prisons just as it had at the end of the antebellum period and at other times in our past, but this time things would be different. This time the politicians and corporations that had begun to benefit from the expanding prison population had a "plan B" up their sleeve. Instead of rethinking the sentencing guidelines in order to reduce the influx of prisoners to a number that would work with the existing number of prison beds, they chose instead to implement what I refer to as the "prison-industrial credit-card plan"—a scheme of sorts that allowed, and continues to allow, our elected officials to keep the prison population and its corresponding diversion of tax dollars into the private sector growing despite the lack of will by voters to fund the process.

The plan is simple enough: If the states can't afford to continue to build new prisons because the majority of their taxpaying voters are unwilling to support the sale of bonds for that purpose, then the prison-industrial complex will keep the expansion going by paying to construct the new facilities itself. This comes about in the form of private prisons or by the underwriting of prison construction through the sale of bond-like financial instruments that don't require voter approval, namely, through lease-revenue, a.k.a. lease-payment, bonds. Here's how the plan works.

Let's say, for example, that in order to keep up with its growing inmate population, a state needs to build six new prisons at a cost of $1.4 billion. This is far more money than almost any state would likely be able to funnel into corrections from its general fund at any one time. That being the case, historically a state finding itself in this circumstance would have only two options: to get voters to approve the sale of general obligation bonds to raise the $1.4 billion needed to build the new prisons or, in lieu of the passage of such a bond issue, to take measures to shrink the number of inmates entering the system.

This requirement of voter approval for bonds creating debt in the public's name has always offered citizens a means of reining in those in government who might otherwise be tempted to overextend themselves when it comes to spending other people's money. But in a less obvious fashion, this same fiscal control by voters should also be viewed as a democratic tool designed to enable the electorate to have a direct say over more specific policies such as those relating to criminal justice. For instance, if voters in our example refuse to approve the sale of bonds to build the new prisons, then they have, in effect, directed state officials to amend sentencing policies as assuredly as if the question of sentencing had been placed on the ballot itself. Unfortunately, this financial oversight of government spending has been rendered nearly meaningless by the market's participation in the prison-building process.

First of all, let's look at how private-prison corporations are impacting this equation. As I said, $1.4 billion is far more money than a state can practically divert at any given time out of other programs and into corrections. This inability to come up with such a massive amount of funds for a onetime expenditure is the very "problem" that has always allowed voters to maintain control over the size of the prison population by controlling the bonding process. But what happens to this voter control if CCA, Wackenhut, and other private-prison companies use their investors' money to step in and construct the six new prisons that the voters refused to bankroll? The answer is this: It ceases to exist.

And so it is with privatization, which is allowing politicians to bypass much of the fiscal control heretofore exercised by voters. In addition, using private prisons instead of increasing the voters' tax burden through bonds allows politicians to avoid being tagged by the old "tax-and-spend" moniker in the next election. "When you're looking at having to build a new facility and having to float bonds," observed Adrian Moore, director of economic studies at the Reason Foundation, "there is a greater interest [for politicians] in letting the private sector do it."[7] But don't get the wrong idea. Even when politicians use private prisons as a politically preferable alternative to floating bonds, it's still the taxpayers who wind up picking up the tab, and the tab will eventually be even bigger than it would have been for the bonds.

Once the corporations have spent their own money to build the prisons, they then charge a hefty daily fee per inmate in exchange for allowing a jurisdiction to use their facilities and thereby comply with court-ordered limits on overcrowding. Some contractual arrangements also obligate a state or county to pay an additional lease payment, such as was the situation with the state of Colorado during the High Plains fiasco. What's important to note here is that in one way or another, the corporations charge enough to the jurisdictions to quickly recoup their capital outlay for the construction of the prisons while simultaneously making a nice profit along the way and for decades to come. In the end, it is a sort of credit-card mentality brought about by this private financing of prisons—get what you want now and then make payments forever.

Although it's true that it is financially impossible for our state to divert $1.4 billion out of other programs and into corrections all at once in order to build the six prisons, it is quite possible—though still extremely damaging to programs such as education and child welfare—for the state to divert millions of dollars into corrections on a regular basis so that it can make what really amount to credit payments to the private-prison companies who laid out the money to construct the facilities. Most important to the continuance of the expansion, this ongoing diversion of funds out of social programs into corrections and ultimately into the private-prison corporations isn't like issuing general obligation bonds to build prisons. It can be authorized by politicians who never have to seek the approval of the voters to spend their money.

Thus, the use of private prisons in our example not only renders voters incapable of stopping the flow of their tax dollars into the prison expansion, but it also depletes the social wealth of their state, and in the end, just as with most credit-card purchases, the whole mess will eventually wind up costing taxpayers considerably more than the original $1.4 billion sticker price. The end result of using private prisons in the real world of concrete and razor wire is that it allows governments to continue to increase the prison population despite the fact that in many jurisdictions throughout the country, voters have made their desire to stop paying for more prisons known by defeating bond issues. In just the last fifteen years, private-prison corporations have allowed the prison and jail system to grow by more than 150 facilities.[8] And private prisons are only one of the methods being employed by politicians to get around the fiscal constraints that the electorate has attempted to place upon them when it comes to increasing the prison population.

Lease-Payment Bonds

Lease-backed bonds continue to be the preferred means of financing prisons. Because they do not require voter approval, issuing lease revenue bonds allows states and localities to save their general obligation bond capacity for more popular projects.

—Reuters, "Crowded U.S. Jails Mean More Bonds, Privatization," August 14, 1998[9]

The prison-funding ploy most often used these days to fill the gap left by reluctant taxpayers involves using Wall Street giants like Merrill Lynch, Allstate, Shearson Lehman, Smith Barney, and Goldman Sachs and Company to underwrite the costs of prison construction by selling tax-exempt, high-interest, non-voter-approved, lease-revenue, a.k.a. lease-payment, bonds to institutional and individual investors. This prison "bond" business is now a $2.3 billion industry, whose impact on the electorate's ability to control the prison expansion is even greater than that of the use of private prisons.[10]

As the name implies, lease-revenue bonds were originally intended only to be used to finance projects that generated a revenue stream such as convention centers, toll roads, or stadiums. Because the revenue stream was to be used to repay the lease-revenue bondholders, many states made it legal for their legislatures to issue these bonds without voter approval. Obviously, this type of bond was never envisioned as a method for funding prison construction because prisons consume rather than generate revenue. But in the 1980s, some imaginative politicians would change all that, at least on paper, and as a result, Americans would lose virtually all of their control of the size and expense of their prison systems.

In the 1980s, after demanding harsher punishments for criminals such as mandatory sentences, California voters began to get cold feet when it came to picking up the ever-growing tab for incarceration. After voting to approve the initial round of general-obligation bonds used to build the first batch of new prisons the state needed due to its new hard-on-crime policies, the California electorate did an about-face, refusing to approve billions more in prison bonds just a few years later. I suspect the voters' logic was simple: They had built more prisons, locked up an unprecedented number of their fellow citizens at an astronomical cost, and yet the crime rate hadn't changed. This refusal by California voters to issue more bonds to build still more prisons—a decision that historically would have curtailed the growth of California's prison population due to court-ordered restrictions on overcrowding—was rendered meaningless by a little political sleight-of-hand.

To the delight of powerful lobbyists from law enforcement, the guards' union, private-prison companies, Wall Street investment firms, and other special interests, California's government did an end run on the voters and issued *lease-revenue* bonds, which did not require voter approval to build the prisons that the electorate had made clear it did not wish to fund. Although it's true that lease-revenue bonds are supposed to be used only for projects that generate a revenue stream, politicians faced with the politically difficult choice of having to eat a healthy portion of hard-on-crime crow or overriding the will of California voters chose the latter and devised a way to sidestep the revenue requirement. They did this by building the new prisons in the name of the Department of Public Works, which then turned around and leased the prisons back to the Department of Corrections, creating the legally required revenue stream—at least on paper. In reality, the "revenue" consisted entirely of tax dollars being diverted from the general fund through corrections and into public works. It was contrived at best, illegal at worst.

Not only did this questionable use of non-voter approved bonds eliminate the electorate's control over how big California's prison population could grow—the state can now build prisons anytime it wants using lease-backed bonds—it did so in a manner that will eventually cost taxpayers much more than if they had simply passed the general-obligation bonds in the first place. It is estimated that this one round of lease-revenue bonds in California will eventually cost that state's taxpayers $800 million more in debt service costs than would have been required had the prisons been built using general-obligation bonds.[11] There are a number of reasons that lease-revenue bonds, or "lease-payment bonds," as they are more accurately referred to when misused for prison construction, are so much more expensive than their voter-approved cousins.

First of all, general-obligation bonds are backed by the full faith and credit of the state (entire taxing power) and therefore will usually carry the highest rating and lowest possible interest rates. The only security pledged to bondholders for lease-payment bonds is the annual debt-service appropriations required for lease payments. As a result, lease bonds generally carry a lower rating, are considered a riskier investment, and therefore must pay higher interest rates to lure investors. In addition, the underwriting process for general-obligation bonds requires competitive bidding, whereas the underwriting for lease-payment bonds can be negotiated directly by politicians. This questionable practice leaves the door wide open for underwriters to get better deals due to influence they have gained by way of their financing of campaigns. Another added expense of lease-payment bonds is the requirement that a reserve fund must be established in order to market the bonds. In addition, property and liability insurance do not have to be purchased when general-obligation bonds are used, but they are required in the case of lease-payment bonds. And finally, prisons funded by voter-approved general-obligation bonds need issue only enough bonds to cover the cost of the project plus 1 percent for issuance costs, whereas prisons funded with lease-payment instruments must issue enough bonds to cover the project costs, underwriting fees, debt service during the construction period, insurance costs, and the reserve fund. Over the life of the instruments, the California Legislative Analyst's Office estimates that lease-payment bonds will cost taxpayers an average of 15 to 20 percent more than general-obligation bonds would. That's an additional cost of $275 million to $370 million for every $1 billion in capital projects funded by lease-payment bonds with a twenty-five-year maturity.[12]

Not only are California voters being made to pay for prison construction they refused to authorize at the polls, but they are having to pay

much more because of their refusal. This antidemocratic and excessively expensive scenario is being repeated in jurisdictions from coast to
coast.

In the mid-1970s, New York passed the Rockefeller drug laws, which
required the first new mandatory drug sentences since the federal
mandatory sentences had been voted out in 1970 by George Bush and
company. As a result of these mandatory minimum sentences, New
York's prison population had doubled in size, and its prisons were extremely overcrowded when Mario Cuomo became New York's governor.[13] The hard-on-crime atmosphere at the time made it politically impossible for Cuomo, a self-proclaimed liberal, to repeal the Rockefeller
laws, so the governor decided instead to follow in his predecessor Governor Hugh Carey's footsteps and build the necessary prisons to hold
the inmates. Cuomo also decided to continue to fund the construction
on these prisons in the same "creative" fashion employed by the more
conservative Carey.

In 1981, New York's voters had been asked to approve a $500-million
bond issue to build new prisons. They voted down the bond issue, once
again demonstrating the political schizophrenia that is rampant in a society that fears criminals but doesn't want to provide the taxes to imprison them.[14] This refusal by the voters to pay for building more prisons should have served to greatly limit the growth of New York's prison
population, and it should also have become the catalyst to force a debate regarding the application of mandatory minimum sentences to
nonviolent drug offenders. But the debate never happened. Instead,
New York, like California, would turn to investor money raised through
the sale of bonds that the electorate would never get the chance to vote
down.

Cuomo decided to continue Carey's practice of using the state's Urban Development Corporation as the mechanism to build the prisons.
Ironically, the UDC had originally been created in the 1960s as an
agency designed to build housing for the poor, and under the guidance
of New York's governors in the 1980s and 1990s, it would certainly be
doing that, though hardly as envisioned by its original architects. The
UDC was chosen to build the prisons because unlike the state's Department of Corrections, the agency was allowed to issue state bonds without voter approval. Once again, as with California, the prisons being
built by one government agency were then leased to another, making
the bonds at least appear to be in accordance with the statutes. In all,

Cuomo built more prison cells in ten years at a cost of $7 billion using a low-income housing agency than all of his predecessors combined in New York's history had built with voter-approved bonds.[15]

As with all bonds that don't carry the blessing of the electorate, the instruments issued by the UDC carried much higher interest rates. For example, in 1991, New York's Department of Corrections sold its Attica prison to the UDC for $200 million, which had been raised by selling bonds without voter approval. The prison was then leased back to the DOC. This arm's-length transaction was used to generate money for other areas of New York's budget. Because of the high interest on the bonds sold to do this one prison deal, it is estimated that New York taxpayers will eventually pay close to $700 million for the Attica paper shuffle. That's $200 million more than the entire prison bond issue voted down in 1981, and voters didn't even get a chance to veto the costly Attica transaction.[16]

Despite the enormous number of prisons added by Cuomo, the state's prison system was more overcrowded in 1995 when Cuomo left office than it was at the beginning of his prison-building spree. And the taxpayers who said "no" to $500 million in prison bonds are now saddled with billions in prison debt they never approved. As of 1999, New York's prison system is cramming approximately 70,000 inmates into facilities designed to hold only 52,400.[17]

Things have changed very little in the Empire State since Cuomo's departure. As of 1999, current governor George Pataki is pursuing yet another ambitious $650-million prison construction program that would once again use the Urban Development Corporation to both raise the funds and sidestep the voters. This time around, however, a taxpayer group calling itself CHANGE-NY has joined forces with the state's Conservative Party in a call for New York lawmakers to put the prison-construction project to a vote by the people in the form of a bond issue. Ironically, both of the groups demanding voter approval for the sale of these bonds support building more prisons. Their only reason for demanding that New York voters have a say in raising the prison construction funds is that voter approval would save a minimum of $100 million in interest alone over the life of the bonds.[18]

New York Democrats who oppose more prisons, as well as the League of Women Voters, the Citizens Budget Committee, and the Fiscal Policy Institute, have all joined in the push to put the prison-construction bonds on the ballot. Despite this pressure, it appears that the conservative Pataki administration is afraid that such democracy might throw a wrench into the governor's hard-on-crime policies. Administration spokesman Patrick McCarthy has been quoted as saying that the governor's plan to use non-voter-approved bonds is "legal" and that Pataki has every intention of pushing ahead with his plan because "this is a public safety issue, not a political issue."[19]

I'm not sure how to translate this last statement. It would seem to be implying that in issues concerning criminal justice, politicians are endowed with some special authority that allows them to strip the electorate of its right to approve debt being created in its name and thereby also to strip the voters of their ability to affect policy changes through such funding decisions—an alarming interpretation of the laws.

It is estimated that by the time Pataki adds his prisons, which will take three years to build, New York's prison system will already have added more new inmates than the 7,000 that the new prisons will hold. Even if New York didn't increase its number of inmates at all during this construction period, the new prisons would still leave the state system holding some 10,600 more prisoners than it can adequately house. Both California and New York are perfect examples of what happens when we try to out-build crime.

Criminologists have long argued that the U.S. prison population will always grow to fit the number of beds available and that prison construction is therefore an important component in determining the nation's justice policies. As simplistic as this observation sounds, it has proven to be quite accurate. If voters refuse to pay for more prisons, the prison system becomes full and law enforcement and the courts are more or less forced to implement alternative measures to deal with criminals. Historically, this has resulted in reduced prison sentences or probation for nonviolent first-time offenders. But in the 1980s and 1990s, the market's involvement in funding the construction of public and private prisons has helped the system to grow by nearly 100,000 beds every year, despite the electorate's refusal to fund much of this new prison construction.[20] And just as the criminologists suggested would happen, the prison population has continued to expand at approximately the same rate as that of bed space—leaving the system just as overcrowded as when the buildup began.

This connection has led to several attempts over the past twenty-five years to place a moratorium on prison construction. The most recent attempt was in Colorado in 1999 when Representative Dorothy Rupert proposed legislation that would have halted prison construction until a study researching less expensive alternatives to prison could be conducted. Even though Rupert's attempt to halt the construction of new prisons was inspired by the fact that Colorado's Department of Corrections budget had jumped 1,200 percent since 1990, though not by any desire to give criminals a break, her moratorium proposal was quickly labeled "soft on crime" by its critics. As a result, the idea failed to garner significant support and never made it out of committee. Instead, Colorado lawmakers passed a 1999 crime bill doling out yet another round of increased sentences for crimes such as auto theft.[21]

The correlation between the size of the prison system and the number of prisoners it holds also provides a strong argument for those who believe that privatization is costing taxpayers more, not less. Even if the prison corporations were saving the 10 percent over public-sector prisons that they claim—which as we have seen is hardly a given—their constant adding of cells to the system guarantees that the overall price tag on corrections will go up instead of down. It's like this. Which is least expensive: to pay 90 percent of a $50-billion corrections tab to lock up 2 million people or to pay 100 percent of a $25-billion bill for 1 million prisoners? The prison-industrial complex and hard-on-crime politicians would ask us to believe that the former is saving us $5 billion a year, but the reality is that this larger system, created by way of the prison-industrial credit-card plan, is costing us $20 billion a year more. This points to yet another important issue.

The only way to expand the prison system without raising taxes as we are currently doing is by diverting a larger and larger portion of the tax money already being collected and used for other programs into prisons. This means that since the cost of corrections has gone up $20 billion a year, we can assume that a good portion of this $20-billion annual expenditure is being culled from the social wealth. When we examine which programs get cut to fund prisons, who profits from this diversion, and who it harms, we can begin to see how incarceration is increasingly pitting the interests of the underclass against those of the targeted suburban voters who also happen to compose the majority of America's investor class.

The Diversion of Funds

The art of government is to make two-thirds of a nation pay all it possibly can pay for the benefit of the other third.

—***Voltaire***[22]

There are two ways to view the massive diversion of funds to pay for the prison expansion that is now taking place in local, state, and federal budgets, meaning that tax revenues are being diverted from left to right and from bottom to top. "Left to right" represents the political aspect of this shift in funding. Social programs, many of which came into existence in the liberal political atmosphere of the 1960s, have been the hardest hit. There is no question that education, welfare, affordable housing, drug rehabilitation, mental-health care, and other programs designed to level the economic playing field for Americans living at the bottom of our economy are being diminished by ever-growing prison expenditures. In a political sense, it appears that the diversion of funds from "liberal" programs into corrections, a historically "conservative" program, mirrors the political shift to the right that has occurred in American politics in general as a result of the "blending" of the parties wrought by the rise in influence of the political consultants and their public opinion polls.

When we analyze this diversion of funds from an economic standpoint, it can be seen as a shift of resources from bottom to top. When the market took control of prison construction and management in order to fill the gap left by the electorate's regular refusal to authorize the issuance of general-obligation bonds for prison construction, corrections expenditures became free of their democratic restraints for the first time this century. As a result, they have increased seven times over in less than twenty years. Although all taxpayers, rich and poor, are paying their share of this massive increase in expenditures in proportion to their overall tax bill, those who constitute the upper third of the economy, a.k.a. the investor class, are having their tax burden more or less subsidized by their ability to profit as shareholders in corporations that are pocketing much of the money represented by this expenditure or as purchasers of the lease-payment bonds being sold to fund prison construction.

For instance, let's look back at New York's paper shuffle of Attica prison. New York's Department of Corrections sold Attica to the UDC for $200 million. Because the bonds sold to raise the money for this transaction were not voter approved, New York taxpayers, rich and poor, will eventually have to spend $700 million to repay the bondholders. So who are these bondholders who are going to put $500 million of taxpayer money in their pockets as profit? The answer is: the investors who for the most part compose the upper one-third of the economy. Now transfer this upward diversion concept to the overall correctional picture.

Both through their shares in the multitude of corporations that now comprise the prison-industrial complex and through their ownership of prison bonds, America's investor class is actually benefiting economically from the growth in the prison system. Consider the message conveyed by a recent article that ran in Denver's largest daily newspaper in 1999 under the enthusiastically worded headline "Residents Have First Crack at Bond Sale to Expand Jail." The article's opening sentence stated, "Arapahoe County residents will have a chance to make a little profit while helping build a 450-bed expansion of the county jail."[23] Although such a statement may sound innocent enough on the surface, the underlying implications of its message are enormous. What does this article really mean when it says "residents?" Although it's true that each and every Arapahoe County "resident" will have an increased tax burden in order to pay for the jail expansion, it is not true by any stretch that each and every "resident" has the opportunity to "make a little profit." We must read between the lines here. In the context of this article, the term "residents" is only referring to the small minority of Arapaho County citizens who could afford to invest the minimum requirement of $5,000 to purchase one of the jail bonds.

Arapahoe County is a snapshot of the American prison and jail system in the 1990s. The wealthiest of Americans are funding the prison expansion in exchange for profit, while the middle and lower classes are left to provide the prisoners and the majority of the tax dollars that eventually wind up in the investors' bank accounts. The infusion of private money into the prison-building process has basically rendered voters powerless to stop the prison expansion or its resulting diversion of funds.

Not only is the investor class benefiting financially from the prison expansion, but it represents that portion of the electorate that is least affected by the diversion of tax dollars out of social programs and into corrections budgets. All across America, public education is being gutted to fund prisons. But more and more often these days, those at the top of the economy don't send their children to public schools anyway, and if they do, they likely attend class in the suburbs, where bonds for additional educational spending are routinely passed, easily replacing what has been diverted into prisons. Consequently, the decay of public education resulting from increased corrections spending is occurring most rapidly in urban districts and has virtually no impact on those benefiting from the prison expansion. Similarly, how many of those in the investor class have ever been dependent upon government programs for housing, food, or health care?

It seems that every year I read a headline referring to the fact that the gap between rich and poor in the United States is constantly widening. The year 1999 was no exception, with a May wire story reporting that despite years of a robust economy, the chasm is now bigger than ever, with one out of every three American children living at or near the poverty level.[24] There are an infinite number of explanations for why such a large segment of the population has not benefited from America's current economic boom, and though the diversion of funds out of social programs aimed at relieving poverty and into prisons is just one of these explanations, it is more significant than most.

This diversion goes far beyond simply shuffling dollars from the pockets of the poor into the investment funds of the wealthy. It greatly impacts the health care, education, housing, and even nutrition of the 90 million Americans living at the bottom. As a result, it can single-handedly all but guarantee that a steady supply of people will turn to a life of crime either as a matter of survival or to support their drug or alcohol habit, the means they use to escape the harsh reality of their circumstances.

It is this cycle of "prisons begetting poverty begetting crime begetting prisoners" that makes the prisoner machine seem "perpetual." Today's criminal-justice system is like the E. C. Escher drawing where the staircase descends downward only to end up back at its beginning. In other words, though the diversion system may appear to be working to the casual observer, logic should be telling us that it is badly flawed and has no place in the real world.

The Machine in Action

It troubles the Commission that the size of the American prison population and the number of people living in poverty both increased dramatically in the 1980s. Worse, the growth of each seemed to feed off of the growth of the other. This is because funding for prison expansion came largely at the expense of programs designed to alleviate poverty.

—National Criminal Justice Commission, 1995[25]

Even justice-system insiders acknowledge the shortcomings of the contrived circular pattern that is emerging in the prison business. "The people in Congress and the state legislatures only hear from the people with a fear of crime who have the attitude that that if we lock people up we don't have to worry about them anymore," said Benjamin Baer, chairman of the U.S. Parole Commission. "But sooner or later," he continued, "you have to ask whether you are willing to let your kid have a mediocre education in order to send a few more people to prison."[26] Perhaps there is no better example of Baer's point, or of the perpetual prisoner machine in action for that matter, than the state of California, which incarcerates one out of every eight prisoners in the United States.

As a result of spending increases in its Department of Corrections, increases opposed by the majority of voters, California's university system has seen its share of public funds slashed by over $250 million. Between 1983 and 1995, California was forced to reduce its higher-education workforce by 8,100 people. At the same time, mind you, the corrections department was increasing its number of employees by a whopping 169 percent and a prison guard now makes more than a tenured professor.[27]

According to Vincent Schiraldi of the Center on Juvenile and Criminal Justice, the war on crime has devastated the state's education system. The CJCJ reports that in fiscal year 1995–1996, California student fee increases generated $85 million, while the three-strikes law alone cost taxpayers $75 million. In Schiraldi's view, "As students pay those increases, they should be aware that they are not paying for better educations, they are paying for prisons."[28] Schiraldi's belief that prisons have eclipsed education as the top fiscal priority in California is well founded.

In 1995, at the same time University of California regents were lamenting the fact that they could not build their tenth campus because the necessary $600 million would be unavailable in the foreseeable future, California's government was busy pouring billions into the first six of the estimated thirty to fifty new prisons the state will eventually need to accommodate the influx of bodies created by mandatory sentencing, stiffer enforcement of parole violations, and the three-strikes law. California's Department of Corrections now estimates that by the year 2000, the number of persons in the state's prison system will have increased to over ten times the size it was in 1980. CDOC also estimates that at full impact, three strikes will increase the annual costs of the system by $6.7 billion.[29]

That's an astounding figure when you consider the damage to California's overall budget caused by the comparatively paltry $2.8 billion worth of corrections expenditures in 1995, which was considered a watershed year because it marked the first time in California's history that the corrections budget was larger than that of the university system ($2.6 billion).[30] And it's not just higher education that's having its resources diverted into the prison-industrial complex.

Welfare aid to families with dependent children has been cut by $225 million. As a result of this diversion of funds, by 1994, a mother with two small kids was expected to live on $631 a month—this at the same time that California was spending $2,000 a month to incarcerate one inmate.[31] A 1991 report from CJCJ stated, "The siphoning off of monies which could be put to Welfare, Education, Health and Prevention . . . are issues that policy-makers must address. The system fails to rehabilitate those it incarcerates and in many ways breeds its future 'clients.'"[32] Unfortunately, what is happening in California is happening everywhere.

"When I'm writing a tuition check for my daughter at the University of Michigan, I feel I am in part subsidizing the corrections system," says Dr. John Schwarz, and he ought to know. Schwarz is a state senator in Michigan and has watched the budget for the university slashed to free up money for prisons ever since 1979. Since then, that state has spent billions of dollars to add more than thirty new prisons to its system. When the buildup began, one out of every fourteen state employees worked for the prison system. By 1995, one out of every four was a DOC employee. As a result of Michigan's diversion of funds into corrections, the ability of the poor to survive in places like Detroit and Flint has been made much more difficult. Consequently, the low-income urban neighborhoods in these cities have become the main supplier of inmates to the new investor-funded prisons.[33]

In 1998, Colorado governor Roy Romer found himself in the middle of a prison-expansion crisis. Colorado has legislated a 6-percent growth limit on department funding increases from year to year, and the corrections department needed a 15.8 percent increase just to keep its doors open. The law would only allow the increase to corrections if the money could be cut from other areas of the budget such as education, infrastructure, and programs aimed at relieving poverty. Colorado was forced to make the cuts, and 1998 looks like it's only the beginning. According to Ari Zavaras, the director of Colorado prisons at the time,

"[U]ntil populations of state prisoners sentenced to the Department of Corrections stabilize, this budgetary growth can be expected to continue into the future."[34]

The diversion of revenues has been devastating on the county level as well. Jefferson County, Colorado, has been diverting millions of dollars out of its general fund and into an 800-bed expansion to its jail complex since 1998. While more and more tax dollars are going toward corrections, the county is being forced to cut its education budget by as much as $12 million for the 1999–2000 school session.[35] Following the 1999 Columbine school shooting that took place in Jefferson County, angry residents questioned authorities as to why students who showed obvious signs of mental dysfunction were not getting the counseling and health care they clearly needed. Officials explained that there wasn't enough money in the budget for counselors and that the Jefferson County school system couldn't afford to get saddled with psychiatric bills if it recommended treatment.[36]

Despite these budget shortfalls, Jefferson County is taking still further steps that will ensure that the "perpetual" aspect of the prisoner machine continues. Sheriff John Stone is moving forward with a plan that will require inmates in the newly enlarged jail to pay for their stay as if the jail were a hotel. According to county officials, the public is showing great enthusiasm for the plan. I have spoken to a number of residents of the county, however, who have told me that they support the plan because it will offer relief from the expense of the growing jail system. This belief makes it clear that they haven't read the proposal's fine print.

The money being charged to prisoners won't offset the taxpayers' expense for the jail; rather, it will be used to pay for additional sheriff's deputies.[37] This means that prisoners will be required to pay for more deputies, which in turn will mean more arrests, which will mean more prisoners; and in the end, that will result in the need for yet another jail expansion down the road, which will likely lead to further cuts in education and mental health programs. It's an illogical pattern that is emerging all across the nation.

Since 1980, Minnesota's prison spending has quadrupled to $234 million, and by 1999, MDOC spending is expected to see another 45 percent increase, much of it lacking the support of the electorate.[38] In Minnesota, as with the rest of the nation, an increasing corrections budget seems to be more about image than crime. "Nobody wants to look weak," said Orville Pung, former corrections commissioner for Minnesota. "Nobody wants to be accused of being a wimp. Everybody wants to get tough, and toughness is translated into longer sentences."[39]

A 1996 study of the Minnesota system found that the expansion of its prison population was due to increasingly longer sentences for youth offenders arrested on drug charges and the implementation of "dozens of new and enhanced criminal penalties." The study concluded that the prison system had grown because of hard-on-crime adjustments to the sentencing structure, not because crime had increased. The report went on to warn that "[w]ithout a change in policy direction, corrections spending will consume a larger share of the state's budget and crowd out other priorities such as education and health."[40]

By 1996, Minnesota governor Arne Carlson had done an about-face from Orville Pung's position—at least in his rhetoric. Carlson commented, "Minnesota simply cannot pour dollar after dollar into prisons without first finding a responsible way to pay for them. We need to stop lurching from budget to budget and take a look at the big picture. We do not want to mortgage our children's future by committing hundreds of millions in taxpayer dollars to more prisons."[41]

In Alabama, the prison expansion of the last twenty years has seen ADOC spending increase by nineteen times over. In 1976, corrections spending required approximately 4 cents out of each general fund dollar. By 1995, Alabama was spending 16 cents out of each tax dollar for corrections.[42] In a state where programs for the poor have historically been inadequate to deal with the high level of poverty that exists, this diversion of funds has been devastating.

Even though recent studies have found that it is hard-on-crime's longer mandatory sentences and adjustments to the drug laws that are causing the budgetary problems, Alabama's politicians are continuing to support still more hard-on-crime measures. State prison commissioner Ron Jones is touting chain gangs and the elimination of "frills" such as coffee and TV as a cure-all for Alabama's prison problems—as if it's the cost of coffee that has caused the prison price tag to increase nineteen times over at the expense of social programs.[43]

Oklahoma, too, has been on a major incarceration push for the last four years. During this short span, corrections spending has increased by 50 percent and now consumes approximately 6 percent of the overall state budget, as compared to less than 4 percent in 1995. Even though Oklahoma's crime rate has been falling for twenty years, the state has been steadily moving up in the national standings when it comes to rates of imprisonment. Four years ago, the state's prisons held 14,000 inmates. Today, Oklahoma's 21,000 inmates place it third in the nation in rate of incarceration. At the same time its ranking in prisoners has been rocketing upward, its ranking in spending on teachers' salaries has been going down. Oklahoma now ranks dead last in this education category. Sue Hinton, the chair of Oklahoma's Justice Fellowship Task Force, has described this increasing prison–decreasing education trend as the kind of thing that only makes sense in a state that wants to limit its economic development to "companies that run private prisons or raise pigs."[44]

In Connecticut, where the state has spent some $400 million on new prison cells in recent years, it has been reported that almost every city and town is now facing cuts in school budgets as a direct result.[45] Prisons have become the fastest-growing area of expenditures in Texas, at a time when it cannot find the money to fight urban poverty in places like Houston and Dallas, the places that are supplying the majority of the system's prisoners. As early as 1991, following a decade that saw the Texas penitentiary system swell by 475 percent, a prison reform group calling itself Citizens United for the Rehabilitation of Errants (CURE) joined the ACLU in lobbying the legislature to halt the Texas prison expansion.

CURE's reasoning was simple. The group believed that a good portion of the hundreds of millions of dollars being funneled into prisons was coming out of rehabilitation programs. CURE thought that this diversion explained why during the previous five years, while the number of prison cells in the state doubled, crime had gone up by 30 percent.[46] Unfortunately, the same scenario is being repeated nearly everywhere in the country to one degree or another these days.

A 1994 George Washington University study found that per capita expenditures for corrections had exceeded those for education nationwide for the first time in U.S. history. In discussing the findings of his study, William Chambliss, a sociologist at the university and the former president of the American Society of Criminology, said, "At this rate, we will be seeing an even greater increase in the number of people in prison and a higher incidence of illiteracy. We're trading textbooks for prison cells."[47]

For the foreseeable future, the eight states I have mentioned and the forty-two that I haven't will have little choice but to continue to divert funds away from their health care, education, child welfare, housing, and other poverty- and thus crime-combating programs and into their prison budgets. Such fiscal action is basically unavoidable so long as investors and corporations continue to fill the prison-construction void left behind by a schizophrenic electorate that continues to elect hard-on-crime politicians while being simultaneously unwilling to increase its tax burden to pay for the resulting growth in the prison population.

Opponents of the ongoing prison expansion argue that these conflicting positions among voters regarding their prison system could not have coexisted, as they currently do, had the dispensing of punishment remained within the exclusive domain of government. The idea here is that the electorate's refusal to pay for prisons would have brought an end to the expansion nearly a decade ago, regardless of the level of voter support for politicians espousing hard-on-crime rhetoric. As one might surmise, this argument has given rise to a heated constitutional debate as to whether private corporations can legally punish citizens found guilty by the state.

Maybe in a Democracy

The United States' global industrial pre-eminence may be slipping, but the domestic output and international sale of one of its manufacturers is booming—packaged consciousness. Packaged consciousness—a one-dimensional, smooth-edged cultural product—is made by the ever expanding goliaths of the message and image business. Gigantic entertainment- information complexes exercise a near-seamless and unified private corporate control over what we think, and think about.

—Herbert I. Schiller, Information Inequality, 1996[48]

Although I oppose the current prison expansion for the reasons set out in this book, in all fairness I must confess that there are several sound arguments as to why privatizing the prison system may, in fact, be a constitutionally legal alternative to maintaining the system as an exclusive responsibility of the state. This is not to say that I think privatization should be allowed. My problem with the arguments surrounding corporate America's involvement in dispensing punishment stems from the fact these arguments are predicated upon what I believe to be a badly flawed presupposition, namely, that we live in a properly functioning democracy.

In a healthy democracy where all authority is considered to have been granted to the state from the majority of individuals, it could be argued that citizens therefore have the right to empower the state to transfer certain elements of its authority into the private sector provided that the majority view this transfer as beneficial.

Charles H. Logan, professor of sociology at the University of Connecticut in Storrs and author of the book *Private Prisons: Cons and Pros*, is one of the experts who believes that privatization does not necessarily conflict with the American concept of justice. Writing for the Opposing Viewpoints Series on American Prisons, Logan made the following argument:

> The most principled objection to the propriety of Commercial prisons is the claim that imprisonment is an inherently and exclusively governmental function and therefore should not be performed by the private sector at all, even under contract to the government. How can it be proper for anyone other than the state to imprison criminals? Perhaps the place to start is by asking what makes it proper for the state itself. By what right does the state imprison?
>
> In the classical liberal tradition on which the American system of government is founded, all rights are individual, not collective. The state is artificial and has no authority, legitimate power, or rights of its own other than those transferred to it by individuals. .... Thus, the power and authority to imprison does not originate with the state, but is granted to it. Moreover, this grant is a conditional one. Citizens reserve the right to revoke any of the powers of the state, or indeed, the entire charter of the state, if necessary.[49]

Logan further argued that since the state's power to punish is delegated to it by the citizenry, "those same citizens, if they wish, can specify that certain powers be further delegated by the state, in turn, to private agencies."[50] As I said, I believe that this is a valid argument in support of the position that privatizing punishment could be a constitutionally legal option in a properly functioning democracy. We must therefore ask ourselves if America at the end of the twentieth century is, in fact, such a democracy.

At its most basic level, a healthy democracy must be the result of an informed electorate selecting representatives whose loyalty is wholly to those same citizens. Under such circumstances, our elected leaders could be expected to make decisions like "privatizing punishment," based upon what is in the best interest of the majority of their constituents. But, as we have already discussed, modern communications technology, primarily television, and our process for funding political campaigns have made this foundational element of a democracy increasingly difficult to attain.

In a nation where the first priority of the news media is profit, not the public's right to know, and where reelection has clearly replaced governance as the first priority among many politicians, can a real democracy even exist, let alone flourish? Most of us now form our impression of American democracy primarily through the same reality-distorting television window that we have relied upon for our perspective on crime—the same portal of illusion that has wrongly convinced the majority of Americans that the imaginary "crime gap" actually exists. This being the case, then it could be well argued that we are no longer living in a democracy at all but rather in a technologically created illusion of a democracy or, as described by Nolan Bowie when he was a visiting lecturer in public policy at Harvard University in 1996, a place where "the legitimate consent necessary for representative democracy is manufactured."[51]

This, I'm afraid, is the world in which we now live. Modern technology has not only made it possible for the powers-to-be to know what we are thinking, it has made it possible for the powers-to-be to determine, to a frightening degree, what we think about. Rather than enhancing democracy as some have argued, I believe that today's communications technology, coupled with advances in our understanding of polling and persuasion techniques, has undermined the credibility of our political system. A true representative government cannot survive long in a nation where the controlled images flowing from the microchips owned by a handful of powerful corporations have become a more important determinant to our attitudes and behavior than reality itself.

Economist John Kenneth Galbraith has written, "Wants can be synthesized . . . shaped by the discreet manipulations of the persuaders."[52] If Galbraith is correct, then we should be asking ourselves whether we are being hard on crime because we have reasoned that it is the right thing to do. Or is it possible that we are being hard on crime because those with a vested interest in fighting the war on crime, marketing images of violence, and increasing the prison population desire for us to be so? This question would demand considerable attention even if our criminal-justice system were still wholly a function of government. But now that the system is rapidly being turned into a multibillion-dollar private industry that can directly benefit from such technological manipulation, the future of our justice system and even our democracy may well depend upon our answering questions such as this both quickly and accurately.

Pulling the Plug

He that will not apply new remedies must expect new evils; for time is the greatest innovator.

—*Francis Bacon, "Of Innovations," 1625*[1]

Along the Connecticut River near the town of Northfield, Massachusetts, an amazing example of modern engineering can be found in the form of the Northfield Mountain hydroelectric dam. What makes this dam and other "pump-back" dams different from their traditional counterparts is their ability to reuse the same water over and over again for the purposes of generating electricity. Those who designed this marvel figured out a way to use the power generated by the dam to pump the water that turns its turbines back uphill so that the process can be repeated daily. Although this dam may sound like a "perpetual" power-generating machine, it is not. It requires more electricity to move the water back uphill than the amount the process actually generates in return. So why would a power company spend millions to build such a model of inefficiency? Because it makes good economic sense. The dam may not be a perpetual power machine, but it is a perpetual profit machine.

There is one more part to this power-generating equation. The price of electricity varies at different times of the day. During peak daylight hours and in the early evening, the power company is paid a premium for its electricity. In the off-hours such as midnight to 4 A.M., the price paid for electricity drops significantly. This variance allows the company to use cheap electricity in the middle of the night to pump the water back uphill so that it can be released during the day to generate a higher-priced commodity. So it is this dual-pricing scenario that over-rides the dam's flawed design of diminishing returns and justifies its existence and continued operation.

Thanks to the recidivism-breeding prisonization effect and the diversion of funds out of crime-preventing social programs and into corrections, the prisoner machine tends to function something like this "pump-back" dam. It expends taxpayer money to create a looped process wherein it fuels itself by reusing the same prisoners over and over again or by creating new ones as a result of its ability to divert the social wealth through its crime-furthering turbines. Like the Northfield Dam, the machine's initial appearance of being a self-sustaining mechanism is also a bit deceptive. Although our prisoner machine does have the ability to create a seemingly endless supply of prisoners and thereby seemingly endless revenues, in order to accomplish this feat, it must continuously consume an ever-growing stream of tax dollars that are not being replenished and are finite. This is the prisoner machine's Achilles' heel. Lacking anything similar to the dam's dual-pricing scenario to override this flaw in design, the prisoner machine will eventually consume itself out of existence. The only questions are when, and at what cost?

As I stated in the introduction to this book, I don't believe that the current prison expansion can continue for another twenty years at its same rate because in order for this to happen, the prisoner machine would have to be fueled by the incarceration of the majority of African-American males, along with a substantial percentage of the nation's black female, Hispanic, and Native American populations. Such a level of imprisonment would simultaneously result in the machine's consumption of most of the tax dollars now being collected by our state governments. Despite the targeted electorate's discouraging track record when it comes to overlooking the human toll being paid for the machine's continued operation, experience tells us that the fiscal downside to this whole prison process for taxpayers will eventually result in voters rebelling against the idea of a constantly growing prison system.

But can we afford to simply wait for this taxpayer rebellion to pull the plug on the prisoner machine? With the inmate population doubling in size every few years—the next plateau will be 4 million mostly low-income minority prisoners—the answer is: absolutely not. To wait would be to condone a humanitarian and cultural disaster of massive proportion. Even if we stopped the prison expansion today, the damage it has already done—particularly to the black community—will require decades to repair, if it can be fixed at all.

Some states already have as many as five black males in prison for every one in college, and this differential is constantly increasing. Reversing such trends will not be easy, considering factors such as recidivism and the increased odds that the children of a prisoner will turn to crime themselves someday due to their having been raised in a one-parent home in poverty, as most are. So long as black families constitute a disproportionately high percentage of the impoverished households in our country, they will continue to be sucked into the prisoner machine's turbines at a disproportionately high rate.

Making matters worse, the democratic process that could be used to slow the current that is pulling America's low-income communities into the machine has already been badly weakened by the fact that a nearly inconceivable 4 million mostly poor U.S. citizens have already lost their right to vote due to a felony conviction. This includes 1.5 million African Americans, including 14 percent of all black males.[2] This stripping of voting rights is seriously impacting the very urban areas where a healthy electorate is most needed in order to effect change quickly, and the number of low-income minority citizens losing their right to self-determination is continuing to grow like the number of hamburgers sold at McDonald's. If this trend continues at the current rate, it is estimated that 40 percent of the next generation of black men will not have the right to vote.[3] They will truly have achieved commodity status.

So how do we pull the plug on the perpetual prisoner machine now, as opposed to waiting for the tax dollars to dry up? I think the first step is to identify who it is that has their hands on the machine's controls, including its off switch. Based on the discussion thus far, it would be easy to assume that such control rests solely with the media owners, the politicians, and the executives who run the corporations of the prison-industrial complex. Certainly these people do have great say over the machine's operation, but even they are simply following orders.

On a certain level, assigning responsibility to these individuals for the creation and control of the prisoner machine is like attributing responsibility for the Northfield Dam's construction and operation to its concrete and water—which is to say that being an integral component of a mechanism does not the architect make. Whether it's media corporations, politicians, or the prison-industrial complex, these components of the perpetual prisoner machine exploit crime as they do for one reason and one reason only—we reward them for doing so. It is therefore our hands that are ultimately resting upon the off switch.

Hopes Versus Rewards

It would be easy to end this book with a plea to implement all the obvious cures for what ails our criminal-justice system, with policies that would spell the end for the prisoner machine such as: eliminating mandatory sentences for nonviolent offenders; returning to the use of less expensive and more effective prison alternatives such as substance-abuse programs, well-supervised probation, and community service when dealing with nonviolent offenders; putting a stop to the law-enforcement practice of racial profiling; leveling the racial playing field in areas such as cocaine sentencing; waging wars on poverty, illiteracy, and addiction, not drugs; establishing at least a temporary moratorium on prison construction; eliminating the use of private prisons; passing statutes at every level of government that would require the sale of all bonds to be used for prison and jail construction to be subject to voter approval; establishing serious campaign finance reform; forcing the breakup of the media monopolies; and so on and so forth. These remedies are easy to suggest, but they are not particularly realistic solutions under our current circumstances.

Don't get me wrong, these are the right steps for pulling the plug on the prisoner machine. If we were to suddenly do any of the things suggested in this list, let alone all of them, the prison population would start shrinking, which would free up tax dollars for crime-preventing social programs such as education and welfare aid to children, and that would eventually halt the ongoing annihilation of Americans who live in poverty. And in general, the world would be a better place. But people have been trying to bring about these policy changes for decades and have not been particularly successful.

So I have chosen instead to end this book by addressing what I believe is the underlying reason for the creation of the prisoner machine in the first place and for our continuing failure when it comes to the implementation of the needed changes on this list—namely, the existence of several wrongheaded reward systems that must be corrected before any progress on the prison front is likely to be made.

As renowned management specialist Steven Kerr put it:

> Whether dealing with monkeys, rats, or human beings, it is hardly controversial to state that most organisms seek information concerning what activities are rewarded, and then seek to do (or at least pretend to do) those things, often to the virtual exclusion of activities not rewarded. The extent to which this occurs of course will depend on the perceived attractiveness of the rewards offered, but neither operant nor expectancy theorists would quarrel with the essence of this notion. . . . Nevertheless, numerous examples exist of reward systems that are fouled up in that behaviors which are rewarded are those which the rewarder is trying to discourage, while the behavior he desires is not being rewarded at all.[4]

Kerr has described this process of establishing misguided reward systems as "the folly of rewarding A, while hoping for B."[5]

It is to this "folly" on a number of fronts that we owe the creation and continued operation of the perpetual prisoner machine. Without intending to do so, we have made the launching and maintenance of the largest prison expansion in history a very rational and, one could even argue, proper (on certain levels) decision by those who are now exerting influence over the dispensing of justice in this country—the media, politicians, the prison-industrial complex, and investors.

Most Americans *hope* that the media, in particular the television and movie industries, will behave responsibly and limit the number of violent images that they send into our homes. We *hope* that news organizations will put their commitment to the public ahead of their quest for profits. We *hope* that politicians will honestly tell us what they believe, not what they think we want to hear. We *hope* that political candidates will engage in meaningful debates about important issues and that they won't become compromised by campaign donations. We *hope* that our laws and those who enforce them will be fair and racially unbiased. We *hope* that our courts will offer every citizen, regardless of economic status or race, equal access to justice. And finally, we *hope* that corporations will not put their bottom line ahead of the public's well-being. This is the behavior we *hope* for—but it is not the behavior that we reward.

For instance, the media gear of the machine dispenses an excessive amount of violent, crime-oriented content that creates the by-product of societal anxiety over crime. Media corporations disseminate mayhem because we reward them for doing so, not because they are particularly fascinated with violent subject matter. As discussed previously, when it comes to determining the content of movies and television programming, media corporations rely on a simple formula to guide their decisions. They divide the cost of production by the size of the audience the production will draw. Based upon this formula, the owners of the media have determined that inundating us with violent images of crime will cause their profits to rise. In order to see how this content decision fits the "rewarding A, while hoping for B" model, we must examine the public's stated desires regarding what content it hopes to see on TV and movie-theater screens.

In 1998, CNN and *Time* joined forces on a new television news magazine. In preparation for the inaugural show, they polled the public about its news preferences. The poll found that most people complained about a lack of investigative stories and other hard news. They also bemoaned being inundated with celebrity-driven features and stories about violent crimes.[6] Similarly, a 1993 poll found that 57 percent of respondents believed that news programs devoted too much attention to violent crime.[7] In 1996, *U.S. News & World Report* conducted another poll that was aimed at the entertainment rather than the news side of the business. This poll showed that 90 percent of all Americans think that TV shows have a negative impact on the country because they are too violent.[8] Americans told the pollsters that they believed TV content leads to violence, divorce, and the break-up of the family. A 1985 Harris survey found that 78 percent of Americans disapprove of the violence they see on television.[9] A 1992 Associated Press poll found that 82 percent of the public thinks that movies are too violent.[10] And finally, a 1993 *Times-Mirror* poll found that 72 percent of respondents think that entertainment television contains too much violence, and 59 percent claimed that they were "personally bothered" by violence in entertainment content.[11] Based upon these poll results, it is clear that the public is *hoping* that the media companies will give them less sensationalized and violent content in both the news and entertainment genres. In fact, even this "hope" has been measured by a poll that found that 81 percent of Americans want the media to voluntarily limit their output of sex and violence.[12]

One would think that if media owners really wanted to maximize their profits, they would give the public what it wants—less violence.

But truth be known, media corporations *are* giving the "public" what it wants. It's just that the companies realize that what the public says it wants and what it is willing to read and watch are two different things, and when media owners talk about the "public," they are generally thinking in global, not domestic, terms. To know what kind of content the public is willing to reward, just do what the television owners, movie studios, and newspapers do; look at the ratings, the box office, and pickup rates, not the polls.

Remember which type of "news" reports have been the most watched and read by the public in recent years and therefore have generated the most profit—Princess Diana's fatal car crash; the murder of JonBenet Ramsey; the Columbine school shooting; O. J.; the Bobbitts; Fisher and Buttafuoco; and the like. And what of those investigative stories and in-depth reports on important issues like campaign finance reform, the subjects we tell pollsters that we *hope* to see more of? They continue to cost more to produce and draw smaller audiences than sensationalized violence.[13]

When it comes to entertaining ourselves, we can't get to the theater fast enough to plop down a ten spot to watch some guy in dark glasses use his big gun to blow the brains of some poor slob onto the white wall behind him. All the while, of course, our hero never misses a beat in the consumption of his jelly doughnut or his conversation regarding the kinky sexual encounter he had the previous night. Whether it's Schwarzenegger, Van Damme, Tarantino, Willis, Eastwood, or Seagal, the bloodier the carnage, the bigger the financial reward from many of the same people who tell pollsters that violent entertainment content is ruining the country. Polls, it would seem, reflect our *hopes*, whereas ratings and the box office reflect what we *reward*. Americans are indeed sending two opposite messages to media corporations, but only one is wrapped around hundreds of billions of dollars—and that one is "Give us more violence."

So put yourself in the shoes of a CEO at a media corporation. For good or bad, such an executive's first responsibility is to the shareholders, who expect one thing from the company—maximum return on their investment. The CEO may be well aware that the public believes that saturating the airways with images of sensationalized violent crime is bad for the country and may even be sympathetic to and in agreement with the public's concerns. But our CEO also knows that the same people who are *hoping* that the network will disseminate less sensationalized vi-

olent news content wouldn't hesitate to click away from an in-depth report on government corruption in favor of a rival network that leads its
news programming with coverage of a gruesome murder involving a former nude model-turned-mud wrestler, a pickax, and a ferret.

So what's our CEO to do? Take the moral high ground to low ratings,
low profits, and the swift termination of a seven-figure salary? Our misguided reward system for both the newsroom and entertainment programming has left our exec and media company little alternative but to
continue to produce and even increase the company's use of culturally
destructive violent images in exchange for profit. And so it is that the
public's propensity for rewarding the very behavior that we are trying to
discourage, while failing to reward the behavior we actually desire, has
made the decision by media corporations to increase the amount of violent content they disseminate a very rational, even economically responsible, course of action. And this is only one misguided reward system.
What we've done for the media, we've done twice over for our politicians.

In describing one of our misguided reward systems for politicians,
Kerr noted that there are two types of goals in the world of politics: "official" goals and "operative" goals. He has described official goals, which
represent "A" in his formula, as those that are "purposely vague and
general and do not indicate . . . the host of decisions that must be made
among alternative ways of achieving official goals and the priority of
multiple goals. They usually may be relied on to offend absolutely no
one, and in this sense can be considered high acceptance, low quality
goals."[14]

For our purposes, the "official" goal of the hard-on-crime policies being put forward by politicians is their claim that such policies will make
us safer. A perfect example of putting forward this "official" goal can be
found in the final sentence of the crime section in the Republican
Party's Contract with America, which states that the purpose of more
prisons, longer sentences, and increased law enforcement is "to keep
people secure in their neighborhoods and kids safe in their schools."
Just as Kerr has suggestd, such a political position is put forward to offend absolutely no one while finding ready acceptance. It provides no
details of how this proposed feat will be accomplished, nor does it take
into consideration any alternative methods for making us safe that
might, in fact, be much less expensive and more effective than prisons,
cops, and longer sentences.

However, "operative" goals—which represent "B," or what we *hope* for in the formula—are described as "higher in quality but lower in acceptance" because they tend to set out specifics. In the case of fighting crime, operative goals would, for instance, set out where the money for more prisons and law enforcement would come from (increasing taxes or diverting funds from the social wealth) as well as what alternative means of reducing crime and increasing public safety will be ignored in order to pursue the course of building more prisons and using more cops.

In poll after poll, we claim that we want our politicians to provide us with operative goals—the real facts and figures behind the rhetoric. We want to know where the money for prisons is going to come from, exactly how it will be spent, and exactly what will be accomplished because we spent it. This is the stated desire of the electorate.

Now imagine yourself to be a politician. You know that the public wants detailed *operative* goals, but you also know that vague *official* goals are more readily accepted by voters. This discrepancy likely stems from the fact that talking about the details of a position allows the voter to actually formulate a position more readily and that position may turn out to be in opposition to that of the candidate. If all candidates in an election were to put forward operative goals, this would not be such a problem. But what happens if one candidate gives the public what it *hopes* for, details, and another sticks to the low-quality, highly acceptable official goals, a.k.a. rhetoric, such as "prisons will keep your children safe in their schools"?

Experience tells us that the politician who sticks to rhetoric will win. As Kerr put it: "[T]he American voter typically punishes (withholds support from) candidates who frankly discuss where the money will come from, rewards politicians who speak only of official goals, but hopes that candidates (despite the reward system) will discuss the issues operatively."[15]

In light of the fouled-up reward system we have created for politicians, we must once again, just as with the media executives, accept much of the responsibility for their socially irresponsible behavior. Politicians spout their hard-on-crime rhetoric and pass their counterproductive mandatory sentences because we reward them for doing so and punish them when they don't. Once again, it is naive to expect politicians to take the moral high road and do what's right when we have made it perfectly clear that their doing so will most likely result in their defeat come election time. In effect, we have made the politicians' decision to pursue the expedient hard-on-crime course of action—a course that feeds the public's unwarranted fear of crime through rhetoric rather than seeking to assuage its fear with the real facts about crime—a very rational choice. And this is only one of the backward reward systems we have established for politicians. Consider the issue of campaign finance.

We say that we are tired of politicians accepting money from special interest groups such as the prison-industrial complex in exchange for access and a certain degree of influence over the policymaking process. We *hope* that politicians will voluntarily limit this practice, yet we continue to nearly exclusively *reward* the candidates who purchase the most television time with the same special interest money that we *hope* they will voluntarily spurn. The fact that the politician who raises the most money wins more than 90 percent of the time has, yet again, made it a rational, if not moral, decision on the part of those who govern us to do the wrong thing—in this instance, to trade influence for campaign funds.

As a result of this misguided reward system, we have turned our democracy into what former president Jimmy Carter has referred to as a political system based on legalized bribery.[16] Hardly the kind of government we should expect to turn its back on the desires of a rich and powerful lobby such as the prison-industrial complex—a lobby that wants to see the prison system grow.

As for the prison-industrial complex itself, it too is awash with problems stemming from an inconsistent reward system. I won't rehash all of them here, but the conflicts of interest related to shareholder primacy as discussed in Chapter 8 are the result of *hoping* that prison corporations will put their responsibility to the public and the prisoners ahead of their responsibility to shareholders, yet financially *rewarding* the corporations that do just the opposite.

And, of course, there is the issue of reform in a privatized prison system. This may be the most absurd reward system of all. We *hope* that all prisons will strive to rehabilitate an inmate as quickly as possible, if not for humanitarian reasons then as a means of reducing the expense of the inmate's current and future incarceration. But do we financially reward private prisons based upon their ability to rehabilitate prisoners, a practice that would clearly establish a proper reward system? No, we do the opposite.

The longer a prison corporation holds an inmate, the more money the company makes. The worse they do the job of reforming the inmate, the more likely the prisoner will continue to recidivate and produce future profits for the company. This backward reward system for the corporations of the prison-industrial complex has turned the prisonization effect into a windfall, a valuable process that transforms prisoners serving a short sentence into annuities.

Once again, as with the earlier examples of media executives and politicians, I'm not implying that the men and women who run the companies within the prison-industrial complex are bad people. I'm simply pointing out that because we financially reward long sentences that do not reform while punishing short stays that end in rehabilitation, we have put them in an awkward position where in order to behave in the fashion *hoped for* by the public, they would literally have to strive every day to lower their profits in the hopes of one day going completely out of business. It just isn't going to happen.

So how do we turn off the perpetual prisoner machine in light of our having inadvertently established these mixed-up reward systems for media owners, politicians, and the corporations of the prison-industrial complex? Before we discuss what we can do, we should take a moment to talk about what we shouldn't do.

Before anyone jumps to the wrong conclusion, let me assure you that this discussion is not leading to a call for censorship or any other type of government restrictions as a means of controlling the media's exaggerated use of violent content. As a journalist and author, and as an American, for that matter, I am adamantly opposed to censorship for the usual reasons. Namely, it is an encroachment upon our right to free speech, and in the end, no matter how well intentioned its application might be, history tells us that its use always winds up enhancing the ability of one segment of the population to control another, making censorship mutually exclusive with a democracy such as ours, theoretically designed to protect the rights of the minority. Censorship is a Pandora's box we dare not open.

As for other types of government or even self-imposed industry regulations aimed at controlling content, unless we reform the underlying misguided reward system that we have established for the media when it comes to violence, they simply cannot work. And if we should manage to establish a proper reward system, they are not necessary. For instance, the understanding that television violence is having a negative impact on our children has led to the establishment of a complicated ratings system that is difficult for even parents to decipher. But is this ratings solution really a victory over violent content? At the same time media corporations were being made to rate their programs for violence, among other things, they were also busy tripling the overall amount of violent content they dispense. I suspect that only a politician or a media executive would claim such a result a victory.

The idea of looking to government to control the media's exploitation of violence is predicated upon the belief that the majority of us are either too lazy or too stupid to make our own decisions over what we read and watch. Imposing censorship is like asking the government to take control of our remotes because we are too intellectually weak to change the channel. Call me an optimist, but I don't think that the vast majority of us are that inept.

If we want to counter the media's ability to create a widespread and unjustified fear of crime, a move that would greatly retard the chain reaction that *is* the prisoner machine, then there are a couple of things that we can realistically do. The first, and I believe the most practical and proper solution, is to simply educate ourselves and our neighbors about media content.

It is important for the public to understand that to a large degree, the role of the press in the United States has changed from that of fourth estate to purveyor of morbid entertainment. Understanding this fact will allow people to see that the world shown on the nightly news is not our world at all but rather the image of a fictional world a hundred times more violent and crime-laden than reality. Viewers may still choose to watch the same sensationalized newscasts, but at least they will be knowingly doing so more for the program's tasteless entertainment value than for its informational worth. Viewing television news through this protective lens will help decrease the ability of its violent content to act as a powerful persuader steering the viewer in an unwarranted hard-on-crime direction.

Creating public awareness as to the persuasive, anxiety-causing capabilities of violent entertainment content is also an important factor that, along with a better understanding of news content, will help at least some people to escape the influence of the politically destructive "mean world syndrome." In short, I believe it is easier and more democratically correct to change the way we view the violent images of television and movies than it is to try to cause these violent images to be taken from our view.

Another path to decreasing the amount of violence in both news and entertainment content would be to put forward a concerted effort to alter our reward system for media owners by changing our viewing habits. We must remember that executives at media corporations are not sadistic psychopaths out to inflict pain on the world. These people only assault us with violent content because we are masochists who indirectly—through ratings and advertising—pay them to do so. If we begin to reward them for not bombarding us with violent images, they will stop. Here's a practical example of how we could begin to correct our faulty reward system.

Television viewers may soon have the opportunity to choose between our current "body-bag journalism" and something more akin to news as a foundational element of democracy. As of June 1999, Robert MacNeil and several other high-profile journalists who have grown frustrated with the dismal state of television news are pushing for the creation of a late-night newscast to be aired on PBS that would run opposite local nightly news programs. This new program would reportedly skip the sensational while providing hard news to open the program, followed by business and economic news, in-depth background reports, and, finally, commentary.[17]

I'm not pushing this PBS show in particular as some cure-all for the plague of market-driven journalism. After all, PBS has certainly come under fire in recent years for its increasing dependence on corporate sponsorship. The importance of the emergence of news programming like that proposed by MacNeil rests in its ability to give us the opportunity to choose between a newscast offering only news and the existing newscasts that offer morbid entertainment mixed with a little news; in choosing the former, we would be given the opportunity to send an important message to those who own the media.

If enough people begin to watch and thereby reward this or any other responsible news programming—which also happens to be the very type of programming that we have repeatedly told the pollsters that we have been *hoping* would appear on the scene—then we will have replaced one of our misguided reward systems with a healthy one. The other news programs will then have little choice but to follow suit or risk losing market share.

Obviously, the same "voting with your viewing minutes" approach can apply to entertainment content as well. If enough people stop watching violent TV programs and going to the movie theater to see violent films, then advertisers will stop purchasing commercial space during those programs, and even with the influence of the global market, that will force media owners to rethink their content strategy. I must confess that I'm more than a little skeptical that this "just say 'no' to violence" approach can actually be effective. I suspect a lot more people enjoy getting their daily dose of violent entertainment than would ever admit to it in a poll.

One last method worth discussing as concerns limiting the use of violent content, particularly in entertainment programming, would be to get Washington to enforce the antitrust laws that are already on the books and to amend or eliminate the global trade agreements that have cleared the way for the formation of the worldwide media monopolies such as Disney and Time Warner—the same corporations that are now dictating our dangerously unbalanced diet of mayhem, mayhem, and more mayhem, based upon what best nourishes their shareholders.

Unfortunately, this approach to tossing a wrench into the media gear of the prisoner machine will likely prove difficult, perhaps even impossible, to accomplish, thanks to those other misguided reward systems on the political front. Remember, media corporations pump tens of millions of dollars into campaign coffers every year to make sure they get what they want from our elected leaders. It would take one massive citizens' movement pushing the antitrust issue to offset the influence purchased by media dollars, not to mention that special media influence created by the news media's capacity to reward or destroy a politician's career.

With regard to our backward reward system for politicians, we cannot change them unless the majority of us are willing to shape our voting behavior to our stated beliefs. For instance, we can demand yet another round of campaign finance reform. But as long as those who must write and pass this reform know that we will vote for the candidate who raises the most money and not the candidate who does the right thing, politicians will continue to build loopholes such as "soft money" into any future reform efforts. In short, as long as we refuse to reward any candidate but the one who spends the most, there will be no legitimate and substantial campaign finance reform.

And it's the same for other issues as well. We claim that we want our candidates to speak "operatively" on the issues. Yet in election after election, third-party candidates do this very important thing that we are asking, and we reward them by voting for the guy with the really white teeth who ran that wholesome ad where he was playing with the golden retriever and his little girl while saying something about the new millennium being the sunrise for a better America.

It's important to talk about doing away with mandatory sentences, changing the cocaine sentencing guidelines, ending racial profiling, breaking up the media trust, prison-building moratoriums, prison bonds, the constitutionality of corporate owned prisons, and the criminal-justice genocide of blacks in America. But it seems that every year we "talk," and every year the prison population grows.

Nothing can change until we, meaning all of us, or at least the majority of us, find the wherewithal to make our actions—whether they are watching TV, voting, or investing—a manifestation of our ideals. At some point, if our justice system and our nation are to have any chance of being healed, we will have to start rewarding "B," not just hoping for "B." Today would be a good time to implement our new and healthy reward systems—because it's almost election time, and it looks like the boys are at it again.

New Century, More Powerful Machine

As this book goes to press, we have reached the end of the twentieth century, and so it is time to look forward instead of back. What will the year 2000 elections—the first political step into the new millennium—reveal to us about the future of our criminal-justice system? Apparently, the answer is: more of the same.

As of June 1999, John Zogby, arguably the nation's hottest new pollster, and his fellow demographers have once again begun the task of taking the pulse of Americans in an attempt to determine the trends that will weigh on the outcome of upcoming national elections. What Zogby and his fellow pollsters find will likely set the agenda for the 2000 presidential race as well as other congressional contests. Preliminary reports from the polling front lines indicate that the hot campaign issues for the first elections of the new millennium will not be as originally expected.

Zogby's most recent polls have found that many Americans have given up on the American Dream—an interesting finding in the middle of an economic boom—and that as a result, the economic issues such as Social Security and Medicare, which are the issues that were predicted to be the center of attention in the 2000 elections, have fallen in importance to the electorate. In fact, according to a wire service report, when

Zogby listed the order of public concerns as determined by his polls, Social Security was at the very bottom, along with other unimportant issues like poverty, homelessness, and hunger.[18]

So what issue is the public most concerned about heading into the century's first elections? The not-so-surprising answer is none other than "crime." Unfortunately, this does not mean "crime" in the sense of "Isn't it great that it's falling?" or "Oh my gosh, we've actually locked up 2 million people and most of them are black." But rather, it means that the elections will once again be about "crime" as a contest to see which party and which candidates can be the "hardest on it." Even now, the political consultants are gathering around tables dreaming up ways to make their clients sound tougher on criminals than their opponents without ever having to discuss the issue of crime or prisons "operatively." Production companies are already springing to action to provide us with the new century's version of the "Willie Horton" ad. All this, and more, is happening, and we have only the perpetual prisoner machine to thank. In fact, what is happening in 1999 may be the best example of the destructive potential of the prisoner machine in action since the tragic Polly Klaas murder led to the passage of California's three-strikes law.

Considering the timing of the polls by Zogby and others, it is obvious to most observers that the explanation for the public's hyperconcern over crime and violence at a time when both had been decreasing for several years can be found in the media's unprecedented saturation coverage of the Columbine school shootings in Littleton, Colorado. Even though the shootings took place nearly three months prior to the time the polls were conducted, the Columbine incident was still getting substantial minutes and column inches in the national press at the time of the polls. As mentioned in Chapter 3, another national poll taken only a few weeks after the school shootings found that the public's outlook for America's future had gone from positive just six months prior to the shooting to negative as a result of the media's overkill coverage of this single event.

The media's use of the Columbine incident as a means to generate profits resulted in a truly staggering and, I think, unparalleled quantity of emotional coverage regarding the tragedy. And just as the experts have warned, lots of violent content means lots of public anxiety. This particular massive dose of sensationalized news coverage has caused a spike in America's crime anxiety large enough to push the issues of crime and violence to the very pinnacle of public concern. Unfortunately, the timing could not have been worse, as the poll taking for the 2000 elections was just getting underway and quickly picked up on this increasing fear-of-crime trend. As a result, political consultants have already begun shaping their election-2000 clients' platforms, intending to turn this completely unwarranted media-derived crime fear into political capital by further feeding the fear through rhetoric rather than by attempting to dispel the fear with facts—such facts as those reported in a study conducted by the Centers for Disease Control and Prevention and released in August 1999, which demonstrated that despite a rare incidence like Columbine, violence among high-school students has declined significantly since 1991,[19] or the facts in a U.S. Department of Education study also released in August 1999, showing that there had been a 30-percent decline between 1997 and 1998 in the number of students carrying guns at school.[20]

This means that instead of using the year-2000 elections to address important issues including the prison expansion, both in terms of its economic cost and its genocidal effect on our minority populations, politicians will instead once again be scrambling to get their names attached to new bills creating still more mandatory sentences, less probation and parole, and more laws on everything ranging from gun control to ratings on video games to restricting speech over the internet to allowing the Ten Commandments to be posted in schools. All of which, of course, will sound good to an electorate riddled with crime anxiety but will do nothing to lower the rate of crime or to stop future school shootings. This is not to say that such political posturing will not have an effect. It will most certainly cause the prison population to continue to swell and will further escalate the diversion of the social wealth into the bank accounts of the prison-industrial complex and its investors.

At this point, it is impossible to estimate what the final fallout from the prisoner machine's treatment of the Columbine incident will be. It certainly has the potential to influence our justice policies at least to the extent of the 1993 Klaas murder, whose media treatment similarly resulted in polls reflecting an exaggerated fear of crime throughout the California electorate. As you'll recall, the opinion polls following the Klaas tragedy eventually influenced nearly every candidate running for elected office in California to jump on the hard-on-crime bandwagon, which included throwing their support behind an obscure citizens' initiative known as "three strikes and you're out." To date, passage of the three-strikes law has added more than 40,000 inmates serving sentences of twenty-five years to life to California's prison rolls, and it's estimated that the cost to California taxpayers for three strikes will eventually top $6 billion a year, most of which, in light of California voters' refusal to pass new bond issues, will have to be diverted from other parts of the budget, including education and welfare aid to children.

All of this has resulted in less than six years from the prisoner machine's exploitation of one twelve-year-old's tragic murder. Obviously, this does not bode well for the future, when you consider that the Klaas incident received only a small fraction of the sensationalized hype afforded to the Columbine shootings and that the Columbine incident is quickly becoming a major factor in an upcoming national, not state, election cycle. Only time will reveal the overall impact the prisoner machine's exploitation of Columbine will have on the criminal-justice system, but all indications are that it will be significant. And what about the next sensational tragedy, and the one after that?

News coverage of violent crimes that seemed terribly overhyped just a couple of years ago now looks tame and responsible compared to the sensationalized circus of mayhem that so often passes for news these days. With more and more news-type programs turning to violent content in their battle for ratings, it is hard to guess just how far this tabloidization of the media will go. But this you can bet on: The next time a tragedy like Columbine strikes, the coverage will be even more sensational and saturating, which means that the public's anxiety over crime will increase even more.

Again, it's hard to predict the future impact that this ever-growing societal fear of crime will have in the political realm, because every year, politicians escalate their use and dependence upon polling to guide their decisions, which means that the overall efficiency of the prisoner machine is being constantly improved. Considering the way that the gears of the machine feed off one another, I believe that it is certainly safe to predict that unless we take serious measures to stop this chain reaction soon, the overall negative impact of the perpetual prisoner machine on our society will become continuously more pronounced with every passing year, and that will make for a very long century.

Notes

Introduction

1. Eric Schlosser, "The Prison-Industrial Complex," *Atlantic Monthly* 282 (6) (December 1998):52; U.S. Department of Justice, Bureau of Justice Statistics, various reports issued in 1999, including *Prisoners in 1998* and *Jails and Jail Inmates* (Washington, DC: U.S. Government Printing Office, 1999), <http://www.ojp.usdoj.gov/bjs>.

2. U.S. Department of Justice, Bureau of Justice Statistics, *Historical Corrections Statistics in the United States, 1850–1984* (Washington, DC: U.S. Government Printing Office, December 1986), <http://www.ojp.usdoj.gov/bjs>.

3. Steven R. Donziger, ed., *The Real War on Crime: The Report of the National Criminal Justice Commission* (New York: HarperPerennial, 1996), p. 37.

4. U.S. Department of Justice, Bureau of Justice Statistics, *Criminal Victimization in the United States: 1973–1992 Trends* (Washington, DC: U.S. Government Printing Office, 1994), p. 9.

5. U.S. Department of Justice, Bureau of Justice Statistics, *Direct Expenditure by Criminal Justice Function, 1982–1992* (Washington, DC: U.S. Government Printing Office, 1999), <http://www.ojp.usdoj.gov/bjs>; U.S. Department of Justice, Bureau of Justice Statistics, *Justice Employment and Expenditure Extracts, 1992*, table F (Washington, DC: U.S. Government Printing Office, 1999), p. 6, <http://www.ojp.usdoj.gov/bjs>; various interviews with individuals at the National Institute of Justice and the U.S. Department of Justice in 1999 regarding estimated rate of growth of criminal justice expenditures between 1992 and 1999. The most recent available statistics for criminal justice expenditures are for 1992. The $150-billion figure is an estimate based on the belief of those interviewed who said expenditures grew as rapidly between 1992 and 1999 as they did between 1982 and 1992.

6. Cheryl Russell, "True Crime," *American Demographics*, August 1995, p. 2, <http://www.demogrphics.com/publications/AD/>; Donziger, *The Real War on Crime*, p. 9.

7. Camille G. Camp and George M. Camp, *The Corrections Yearbook: Adult Corrections* (South Salem, NY: Criminal Justice Institute, various years, 1981 through 1997);

Tracy Sacco, "Crowded U.S. Jails Mean More Bonds, Privatizations," Reuters, August 14, 1998. See also Project South staff, *Crime, Injustice, and Genocide Quiz* (Atlanta: Project South National Office, October 1996), <http://www.projectsouth.org/html/crimequiz.html>.

8. Center for the Study of the States at the Rockefeller Institute of Government, "State and Local Criminal Justice Spending: Recent Trends and Outlook for the Future," *Highlights* (February 1999), p. 3, <http://rockinst.org/csshigh.htm>.

9. Jerome G. Miller, *Hobbling a Generation: Young African-American Males in the Criminal Justice System of America's Cities* (Baltimore: National Center on Institutions and Alternatives, 1992); Marc Mauer and Tracy Huling, *Young Black Americans and the Criminal Justice System: Five Years Later* (Washington, DC: The Sentencing Project, October 1995); U.S. Department of Justice, Bureau of Justice Statistics, *National Corrections Reporting Program—1992*, p. 12, <http://www.ojp.usdoj.gov/bjs>.

10. Mauer and Huling, *Young Black Americans and the Criminal Justice System*, <http://www.sproject.com>; Karyl Kristine Kicenski, "The Corporate Prison: The Production of Crime and the Sale of Discipline," George Mason University, 1998, research paper published at <http://speech.csun.edu/ben/news/kessay.html>.

11. Donziger, *The Real War on Crime*, p. 106.

Chapter 1

1. E. F. Schumacher, *Small Is Beautiful* (New York: HarperCollins, 1973), quoted in *The Oxford Dictionary of Phrase, Saying, and Quotation,* ed. Elizabeth Knowles (New York: Oxford University Press, 1997), p. 139.

2. Daniel Burton-Rose, "Prison Profits," *Cleveland Free Times*, November 19, 1997; Angela Y. Davis, "Masked Racism: Reflections on the Prison Industrial Complex," *Colorlines*, Alternet, downloaded November 1998 from <http://www.igc.apc.org/an/>, or see *Colorlines*'s web site at <http://www.arc.org/CLArchive/past.html>; "Present Market Share of Private Prison Corporations," January 1999, <http://web.crim.ufl.edu/pcp/census/1999/Market.html>.

3. U.S. Department of Justice, Bureau of Justice Statistics, *Direct Expenditure by Criminal Justice Function, 1982–1992* (Washington, DC: U.S. Government Printing Office, 1999), <http://www.ojp.usdoj.gov/bjs>; U.S. Department of Justice, Bureau of Justice Statistics, *Justice Employment and Expenditure Extracts, 1992*, table F (Washington, DC: U.S. Government Printing Office, 1999), p. 6, <http://www.ojp.usdoj.gov/bjs>; various interviews with individuals at the National Institute of Justice and the U.S. Department of Justice in 1999 regarding estimated rate of growth of criminal justice expenditures between 1992 and 1999. Most recent available statistics for criminal justice expenditures are for 1992. The $150-billion figure is an estimate based on the belief of individuals interviewed who said expenditures grew as rapidly between 1992 and 1999 as they did between 1982 and 1992.

4. Kristin Bloomer, "America's Newest Growth Industry," *In These Times*, March 17, 1997, p. 14.

5. Corrections Yellow Pages web site, accessed February 24, 1999, at <http://www.correctionsyellow.com>.

6. Project South staff, *Crime, Injustice, and Genocide Quiz* (Atlanta: Project South National Office, October 1996), <http://www.projectsouth.org/html/crimequiz.html>.

7. New York Times Syndicate, "Prison Products, Services Attract Merchants, Wardens," *Palm Beach Post*, August 25, 1996; this article used a $26-billion figure for prison product sales. Steven R. Donziger, ed., *The Real War on Crime: The Report of the National Criminal Justice Commission* (New York: HarperPerennial, 1996), p. 93; this source quotes literature from the American Jail Association Convention, which states that the local-jail market alone is $65 billion. The $100-billion figure is based on adding these two figures together and adjusting for growth to the prison and jail system in recent years as determined from interviews with various Justice Department employees. See also footnote 3, this chapter.

8. *State Farm Road Atlas* (Bloomington, IN: State Farm Insurance Companies, 1998).

9. U.S. Department of Justice, Bureau of Justice Statistics, *Changes in the Number of Criminal Justice Employees* (Washington, DC: U.S. Government Printing Office, 1999), <http://www.ojp.usdoj.gov/bjs>; James Austin, "America's Growing Correctional-Industrial Complex," *Focus* (The National Council on Crime and Delinquency), December 1990, p. 4; James Moran, "Privatizing Criminal Justice," paper presented at Crime and Justice in the Americas Conference, Office of International Criminal Justice (Chicago), March 13, 1995, pp. 2–3, <http://www.acsp.uic.edu/iocj/pubs/cja/080315./html>.

10. Interview with Eric Butterfield, editor of *Construction Report,* published by *Correctional Building News* on March 14, 1999. Original source for Butterfield material is *The Corrections Yearbook* (South Salem, NY: Criminal Justice Institute, 1998).

11. Construction Report web site, visited February 24, 1999, <http://www.correctionalnews.com>; Deeann Glamser, "Towns Now Welcoming Prisons," *USA Today*, March 13, 1996.

12. Ken Silverstein, "America's Private Gulag," originally appeared in *CounterPunch*, November 14, 1997, <http://www.loompanics.com/Articles/America.html>.

13. Kevin Helliker, "Expanding Prison Population Captivates Marketers," *Wall Street Journal*, January 20, 1995.

14. Kathy Walt, "State Wants Judge to Pull Plug on $34 Million Prison Food Deal," *Houston Chronicle*, October 16, 1996.

15. Eric Schlosser, "The Prison-Industrial Complex," *Atlantic Monthly*, December 1998, vol. 282, no. 6, pp. 51–77; Helliker, "Expanding Prison Population Captivates Marketers."

16. Helliker, "Expanding Prison Population Captivates Marketers."

17. Interviews with various personnel employed by Colorado Department of Corrections and with private-prison employees in Texarkana, Texas, during 1995; Schlosser, "The Prison-Industrial Complex."

18. Ann Carnahan, "Prisoner Assaulted, Suit Says," *Rocky Mountain News*, March 2, 1999.

19. David Lamb, "Main Street Finds Gold in Urban Crime Wave," *Los Angeles Times*, October 9, 1996.

20. Jennifer Gonnerman, "Portrait of a Prison Town," *Village Voice*, March 11, 1997; Schlosser, "The Prison-Industrial Complex."

21. Alex Friedmann, "Juvenile Crime Pays," *Prison Legal News* (9) (2) (February 1998):1.

22. "Present Market Share of Private Prison Corporations," January 1999.

23. Sandra Block, "Everybody's Doin' the Jailhouse Stock," *USA Today*, June 5, 1996; "Present Market Share of Private Prison Corporations," January 1999; Cathy Lazere, "Privatizing Prisons: Finance Chiefs Face a Peculiar Lineup of Problems Helping Move a Business out of the Public Sector," *CFO Magazine*, February 1997, <http://www.cfonet.com/html/Articles/CFO/1997/97Fepris.html>; Project South staff, *Crime, Injustice, and Genocide Quiz.*

24. Jeremy Quittner, correspondent, "The Incarceration Industry: Teeming Prison Rolls Bode Well for Private Jails," aired on *Fox News* at 3:12 P.M., April 22, 1998, <http://www.prisonactivist.org/news/5–98/The-Incarceration-Industry-Teaming-Prison.html>; Schlosser, "The Prison-Industrial Complex."

25. Block, "Everybody's Doin' the Jailhouse Stock"; "Present Market Share of Private Prison Corporations," January 1999.

26. Linda Seebach, "The White House Hypes Its New Crime-Fighting Bill," *Rocky Mountain News*, May 23, 1999.

27. Notes from CBS *60 Minutes* segment aired October 20, 1996: Correspondent Leslie Stahl interviewing spokesman for Unicor, Mr. Schwab.

28. "P.I.E. Programs," *1998 C.I.A. Directory* (Baltimore, MD: Correctional Industries Association, 1998), pp. 100–108; interview with Rod Miller of Jail Industries Association, March 16, 1999; U.S. Department of Justice, National Institute of Justice, *Work in American Prisons: Joint Ventures with the Private Sector* (Washington, DC: U.S. Goverment Printing Office, Office of Justice Programs, 1995).

29. Dan Pens, "Microsoft 'Outcells' Competition: A Captive Labor Force at Washington's Twin Rivers Corrections Center," *Z Magazine*, May 1996, pp. 47–49; C. Brown Stone, "The Economics of Crime and Punishment," *San Francisco Bay Guardian*, circa 1994; Peter Gilmore, "Made in the U.S.A. . . . by Convicts," *Labor Party Press*, July 1997; Davis, "Masked Racism"; Kyung Sun Yu, "High Tech, Hard Labor: The Global Economy Behind Bars," *Texas Observer*, May 5, 1995, pp. 9–11.

30. "P.I.E. Programs," *1998 C.I.A. Directory*, pp. 100–108; interview with Rod Miller of Jail Industries Association, March 16, 1999.

31. Project South staff, *Crime, Injustice, and Genocide Quiz*, projected that the labor figure of $8.9 billion is attributed to Corrections Industries Association.

32. "P.I.E. Programs," *1998 C.I.A. Directory*, p. 108.

33. Gilmore, "Made in the U.S.A. . . . by Convicts"; Silverstein, "America's Private Gulag."

34. Karyl Kristine Kicenski, "The Corporate Prison, The Production of Crime, and the Sale of Discipline," George Mason University, 1998, research paper published at <http://speech.csun.edu/ben/news/kessay.html>, p. 9.

35. James Hansen, "When It Comes to Working Conditions, Nike Is No Sport," *Rocky Mountain News*, February 1997.

36. Robert W. McChesney, "The Global Media Giants: The Nine Firms That Dominate the World," *Extra* (November–December 1997), <http://www.fair.org/extra/9711/gmg.html>.

37. Lance Gay, "Bad Guys Getting Away with Violence Even More Frequently, TV Survey Claims," Scripps Howard News Service, *Rocky Mountain News*, April 17, 1998; MediaScope staff, *National Television Violence Profile, 1994–1995: Analysis of Violence in Television Programming* (1996), at <http://www.mediascope.org/ntvssmfn.html>.

38. Michael F. Jacobson and Laurie Ann Mazur, *Marketing Madness: A Survival Guide for a Consumer Society* (Boulder, San Francisco, Oxford: Westview Press, 1995), pp. 188, 195.

39. McChesney, "The Global Media Giants."

40. Robert J. Samuelson, "Why We're Married to the Market," *Newsweek*, April 27, 1988, p. 51. A figure of 2,008 mutual funds in the United States was quoted on the program *9 News*, an NBC affiliate in Denver, Colorado, at 5:00 P.M., March 12, 1999.

41. Block, "Everybody's Doin' the Jailhouse Stock."

Chapter 2

1. U.S. Department of Justice, Bureau of Justice Statistics, *Criminal Victimization in the United States: 1973–1992 Trends* (Washington, DC: U.S. Government Printing Office, 1994), p. 9; Fox Butterfield, "Crime Tumbles Again," *New York Times*, June 10, 1999.

2. David B. Kopel, *Prison Blues: How America's Foolish Sentencing Policies Endanger Public Safety*, Policy Analysis No. 208 (Washington, DC: Cato Institute, May 17, 1994), p. 2.

3. William J. Chambliss, *Power, Politics, and Crime* (Boulder: Westview Press, 1999), p. 16; Robert James Bidinotto, *Criminal Justice? The Legal System Versus Individual Responsibility*, special ed. for Law Enforcement Alliance of America (Irvington-on-Hudson, NY: The Foundation for Economic Education, Inc., 1994), p. 1.

4. Jan Van Dijk, *Criminal Victimization in the Industrialized World* (The Hague, Netherlands: Ministry of Justice, 1992), pp. 10, 24, 33, 57; Steven R. Donziger, ed., *The Real War on Crime: The Report of the National Criminal Justice Commission* (New York: HarperPerennial, 1996), pp. 9, 12.

5. Cheryl Russell, "True Crime," *American Demographics* (August 1995), <http://www.demogrphics.com/publications/AD/>.

6. David Westphal, "Despite Declines in Serious Crimes, Prisons Filling Up," Scripps Howard News Service, *Rocky Mountain News*, February 8, 1999.

7. Eric Schlosser, "The Prison-Industrial Complex," *Atlantic Monthly* 282 (6) (December 1998):51–77.

8. Donziger, *The Real War on Crime*, p. 48.

9. Ibid., p. 4.

10. Albert J. Reiss Jr. and Jeffrey A. Roth, eds., *Understanding and Preventing Violence* (Washington, DC: National Academy Press, 1993), p. 414; Donziger, *The Real War on Crime*, p. 4.

11. Steven Chermak, *Victims in the News: Crime and the American News Media* (Boulder, San Francisco, Oxford: Westview Press, 1995), p. 55.

12. Schlosser, "The Prison-Industrial Complex," pp. 51–77.

13. Fox Butterfield, "Police React to Pressure for 'Improved' Statistics," *New York Times*, *Rocky Mountain News*, February 16, 1999.

14. Ibid.

15. Ibid.

16. U.S. Department of Justice, Bureau of Justice Statistics, *Making Confinement Decisions* (Washington, DC: U.S. Government Printing Office, 1987).

17. Barrett and Greene, "Prisons," p. 19.

18. Johnny McGaha et al., "Felony Probation: A Re-examination of Public Risk," *American Journal of Criminal Justice* 11 (1) (1987):1–9; Genneard F. Vito, "Felony Probation and Recidivism: Replication and Response," *Federal Probation* 50 (4) (1986):17–25; M. A. Cuniff, *A Sentencing Postscript: Felony Probationers Under Supervision in the Community* (Washington, DC: National Association of Criminal Justice Planners, 1986).

19. Barrett and Greene, "Prisons," p. 19.

20. Donziger, *The Real War on Crime*, p. 58.

21. Barrett and Greene, "Prisons," p. 19.

22. U.S. Department of Justice, Bureau of Justice Statistics, *Direct Expenditure by Criminal Justice Function, 1982–1992* (Washington, DC: U.S. Government Printing Office, 1999), <http://www.ojp.usdoj.gov/bjs>; U.S. Department of Justice, Bureau of Justice Statistics, *Justice Employment and Expenditure Extracts, 1992*, table F (Washington, DC: U.S. Government Printing Office, 1999), p. 6, <http://www.ojp.usdoj.gov/bjs>; various interviews with individuals at the National Institute of Justice and the U.S. Department of Justice in 1999 regarding estimated rate of growth of corrections expenditures between 1992 and 1999. Most recent available statistics for criminal justice expenditures are for 1992. The $50-billion figure is an estimate based on the belief of those interviewed who said expenditures grew at approximately the same rate between 1992 and 1999 as they did between 1982 and 1992.

23. Barrett and Greene, "Prisons," p. 20.

24. Donziger, *The Real War on Crime*, pp. 31–32.

25. Peter Sleeth and Jeffrey A. Roberts, "Unaffected by Longer Terms," *Denver Post*, circa 1993.

26. John Sanko, "$500 Million for Prisons?" *Rocky Mountain News*, January 8, 1999; John C. Ensslin, "Colo. Inmates to Stay in State," *Rocky Mountain News*, December 12, 1998.

27. Schlosser, "The Prison-Industrial Complex," pp. 51–77.

28. David J. Rothman, "The American Way of Jail," *New York Times*, March 1, 1998.

29. U.S. Department of Justice, Bureau of Justice Statistics, *Prisoners in 1994, U.S.* (Washington, DC: U.S. Government Printing Office, 1995).

30. Marc Mauer, *Americans Behind Bars: The International Use of Incarceration, 1992–1993* (Washington, DC: The Sentencing Project, 1994), <http://www.sproject.com/test/pubs/tsppubs/sumpolicy.html>.

31. Donziger, *The Real War on Crime*, p. 42.

32. Sue Hinton, "Prison Law Moving in Right Direction," *Daily Oklahoman*, May 22, 1999.

33. The Sentencing Project, *Facts About Prisons and Prisoners* (1997), <http://www.sproject.com/test/pubs/tsppubs/1035bs.html>.

34. Fox Butterfield, "Drug Tied to Drop in Crime: Crack Epidemic's Rise and Fall Reflected as Crime Numbers Decline Drastically," *New York Times, Rocky Mountain News*, December 28, 1998.

35. Ibid.

36. Thomas Mathiesen, "Prisons Cannot Rehabilitate," *America's Prisons: Opposing Viewpoints,* Opposing Viewpoints Series, 5th rev. ed., ed. Stacy L. Tipp (San Diego: Greenhaven Press, 1991), pp. 38–44.

37. David P. Syang, "The Inability of Corrections to Correct," *Prisons, Protest, and Politics*, ed. Burton M. Atkins and Henry R. Glick (Englewood Cliffs, NJ: Prentice-Hall, 1972), pp. 25–39.

38. Ibid.

39. Ibid.

40. "Inside the Nation's Largest Private Prison Chain: Guards Rape at Will, Victims Scoffed At," *CounterPunch*, November 16, 1998, p. 1.

41. James Gilligan, *Violence: Reflections on a National Epidemic* (New York: Vintage Books, 1996), p. 175.

42. Ibid.

43. Stan Bailey, "Cons: 'Hitching Post' Humiliating," *Birmingham News*, October 8, 1996.

44. Associated Press, "Homegrown Monster Disturbs Town," *Rocky Mountain News*, February 24, 1999.

45. Mathiesen, "Prisons Cannot Rehabilitate."

46. Mauer, *Americans Behind Bars*, p. 8.

47. Schlosser, "The Prison-Industrial Complex," pp. 51–77.

48. Kopel, "Prison Blues," p. 2.

49. Sleeth and Roberts, "Unaffected by Longer Terms."

Chapter Three

1. D. Graber, *Crime News and the Public* (New York: Praeger Publishers, 1980), pp. 49–50; Steven R. Donziger, ed., *The Real War on Crime: The Report of the National Criminal Justice Commission* (New York: HarperPerennial, 1996), p. 69.

2. Lance Gay, "Bad Guys Getting Away with Violence Even More Frequently, TV Survey Claims," Scripps Howard News Service, *Rocky Mountain News*, April 17, 1998; Associated Press, "Studies Link Fear, Cynicism to Crime Coverage in TV News," *Minnesota Daily*, May 12, 1997; Alexis M. Durham et al., "Images of Crime and Justice: Murder and the 'True Crime' Genre," University of Tampa, Tampa, Florida, p. 8, cited in Donziger, *The Real War on Crime*, p. 69.

3. Donziger, *The Real War on Crime*, p. 66.

4. Cheryl Russell, "True Crime," *American Demographics* (August 1995), <http://www.demogrphics.com/publications/AD/>.

5. Ibid., p. 2.

6. Durham et al., "Images of Crime and Justice," in Donziger, *The Real War on Crime*, p. 69; Vincent Schiraldi, *The People Behind the Headlines* (San Francisco: Center for Juvenile and Criminal Justice, October 1994).

7. Joseph Angotti, *Consortium for Local Television News Surveys*, survey collection, University of Miami, May 6, 1997; Associated Press, "Studies Link Fear, Cynicism to Crime Coverage in TV News."

8. Dusty Saunders, "MacNeil Eyes Serious Late-Night Newscast," *Rocky Mountain News*, June 15, 1999.

9. F. Davis, "Crime News in Colorado Newspapers," *American Journal of Sociology* 57 (1951):325–330, cited in Donziger, *The Real War on Crime*, p. 71.

10. J. Sheley and C. Atkins, "Crime, Crime News, and Crime Views," *Public Opinion Quarterly* (45) (2) (1981):492–506.

11. Center for Media and Public Affairs, "Study Finds Rise in TV, Guns, and Violence," executive summary, September 11, 1996, <http://www.cmpa.com/archive/viol95.html>.

12. Gay, "Bad Guys Getting Away with Violence."

13. Louise Parker, Mary Deen, and Mary H. Lees, "Television Violence," *Research Review* (Washington State University) 3 (whole issue, Fall 1994).

14. Scott Stossel, "The Man Who Counts the Killings," *Atlantic Monthly* 279 (5) (May 1997):86–104.

15. American Pediatric Association, "Policy Statement: Children, Adolescents and Television," *Pediatric* 85 (1990):643.

16. Center for Media and Public Affairs, "Study Finds Rise in TV, Guns, and Violence."

17. Stossel, "The Man Who Counts the Killings."

18. George Seldes, *The George Seldes Reader*, ed. Randolph T. Hunt (Brunswick, Melbourne, Australia: Barricade Books, 1994), cited in "Is the Entire Press Corrupt?" *Extra*, November 12, 1994, <http://www.fair.org/extra/9411/george-seldes.html>.

19. Walter Cronkite, "On That Chart," *Nation* 262 (22), June 3, 1996, p. 22.

20. Lawrence K. Grossman, "On That Chart," *Nation* 262 (22), June 3, 1996, p. 28.

21. Jim Naureckas, attributed to Ken Auletta, *Three Bind Mice*, cited in "Media Monopoly: Long History, Short Memory," *Extra* (November–December 1995), p. 64.

22. Mark Crispin Miller, "Free the Media," *Nation* 262 (22), June 3, 1996, p. 10.

23. Interview with Paul Klite of Rocky Mountain Media Watch, February 1999. Rocky Mountain Media Watch conducted the study in 1997.

24. Stossel, "The Man Who Counts the Killings."

25. Associated Press, "Networks Bow to Viewer's Perceived Apathy," circa 1999.

26. Stossel, "The Man Who Counts the Killings."

27. Steven M. Chermak, *Victims in the News: Crime and the American News Media* (Boulder, San Francisco, Oxford: Westview Press, 1995), p. 22.

28. Phyliss Kaniss, *Making Local News* (Chicago: University of Chicago Press, 1991), cited in Chermak, *Victims in the News*, p. 23.

29. A. Friendly and R. L. Goldfarb, *Crime and Publicity: The Impact of News on the Administration of Justice* (New York: Twentieth Century Fund, 1967).

30. Chermak, *Victims in the News*, p. 23.

31. Donziger, *The Real War on Crime*, p. 9; Chermak, *Victims in the News*, pp. 47–57.

32. W. Wilson, *Good Murders and Bad Murders: A Consumer's Guide in the Age of Information* (New York: University Press of America, 1991), pp. 4–5.

33. Chermak, *Victims in the News*, pp. 38–39.

34. Dusty Saunders, "TV Coverage of Rampage Lifts News Audience Ratings," *Rocky Mountain News*, April 30, 1999.

35. Chermak, *Victims in the News*, p. 21.

36. Ibid., p. 22.

37. *New York Times Co. v. Sullivan*, 376 U.S. 254, 1964.

38. Ronald Collins, *Dictating Content* (Washington, DC: Center for the Study of Commercialism, 1992), p. 20, cited in Michael F. Jacobson and Laurie Ann Mazur, *Marketing Madness: A Survival Guide for Consumer Society* (Boulder, San Francisco, Oxford: Westview Press, 1995), p. 206.

39. Bernard Weinraub, "Paramount Withdraws Its Ads After a Bad Review in Variety," *New York Times*, June 10, 1992.

40. Jacobson and Mazur, *Marketing Madness*, p. 207.

41. Scott Donaton, "Mercedes in Full Retreat on Ad Placement Order," *Advertising Age*, September 20, 1993, p. B8, cited in Jacobson and Mazur, *Marketing Madness*, p. 207.

42. Peg Masterson, "Many Editors Report Advertiser Pressure," *Advertising Age*, January 11, 1993, p. 22.

43. Anne Marie Kerwin, "Behind the Waltzing," *Editor and Publisher*, June 13, 1992, p. 18.

44. Miller, "Free the Media," p. 10.

45. Robert W. McChesney, "The Global Media Giants," *Extra* (November–December 1997), <http://www.fair.org/extra/9711/gmg.html>.

46. Noelle Knox, "Mergers and Acquisitions Total $1.61 Trillion in 1998," Associated Press, *Rocky Mountain News*, January, 14, 1999.

47. Naureckas, "Media Monopoly: Long History, Short Memory."

48. Ben Bagdikian, "The 50, 26, 20 . . . Corporations That Own Our Media," *Extra* (June 1987), <http://www.fair.org/extra/best-of-extra/corporate-ownership.html>.

49. Ibid.

50. Ibid.

51. McChesney, "The Global Media Giants."

52. Ibid.

53. Ibid.

54. Oliver Stone, "On That Chart," *Nation* 262 (22), June 3, 1996, p. 18.

55. Gay, "Bad Guys Getting Away with Violence"; Center for Media and Public Affairs, "Study Finds Rise in TV, Guns, and Violence."

56. McChesney, "The Global Media Giants."

57. Ibid.

58. Ibid.

59. Stossel, "The Man Who Counts the Killings."

60. George Gerbner, "Rethinking Media Violence," *Gerbner Series Study Guide, Part II: The Killing Screens: Media and the Culture of Violence* (Northampton, MA: Media Education Foundation, 1998), <http://www.mediaed.org/guides/gssg2.html>.

61. George Gerbner, "Why So Much Violence?" *Gerbner Series Study Guide, Part II: The Killing Screens: Media and the Culture of Violence* (Northampton, MA: Media Education Foundation, 1998), adapted from *Television Violence Profile No. 16* (Philadelphia: Annenberg School for Communication, 1994), p. 6, <http://www.mediaed.org/guides/gssg2.html>.

62. Ibid.

63. Ibid.

64. Stossel, "The Man Who Counts the Killings."

65. Todd Gitlin, "Imagebusters," *American Prospect* 16 (Winter 1994):113.

66. Stossel, "The Man Who Counts the Killings"; Gerbner, "Why So Much Violence?" p. 6.

67. Stossel, "The Man Who Counts the Killings."

68. McChesney, "The Global Media Giants."

69. Short Takes staff, "Bernstein Laments State of Journalism," *Rocky Mountain News*, February 24, 1999.

70. Jim Naureckas, "Corporate Ownership Matters: The Case of NBC," *Extra* (November–December 1995), <http://www.fair.org/extra/9511/nbc/html>.

71. Ibid.

72. See <http://www.gannett.com>.

73. Miller, "Free the Media," p. 10.

74. Todd Gitlin, "Brain Tennis," *Hotwired* (1997), <http://vip.hotwired.com/synapse/braintennis/97/27/right3.html>.

75. Jacobson and Mazur, *Marketing Madness*, p. 208.

76. Alison Leigh Cowan, "Magazine Dropping Column by Expert on Executive Pay," *New York Times*, February 25, 1992.

77. Jacobson and Mazur, *Marketing Madness,* p. 208.

Chapter 4

1. Jerry Mander, *Four Arguments for the Elimination of Television* (New York: Quill, 1978), p. 24.

2. Scott Stossel, "The Man Who Counts the Killings," *Atlantic Monthly* 279 (5) (May 1997):86–104.

3. H. W. Stanley and G. G. Niemi, *Vital Statistics on American Politics* (Washington, DC: Congressional Quarterly, 1985), cited in Steven M. Chermak, *Victims in the News: Crime and the American News Media* (Boulder, San Francisco, Oxford: Westview Press, 1995), p. 4.

4. Ibid., p. 3.

5. Ibid.

6. Stossel, "The Man Who Counts the Killings."

7. Ibid.

8. L. R. Huesman and Leonard Eron, *Television and the Aggressive Child: A Cross-National Comparison* (Hillside, NJ: Lawrence Erlbaum Associates, 1986); Kevin Szaflik, "Violence on TV: The Desensitizing of America," Ridgewood High School Online (1998), <http://www.ridgenet.org/szaflik/tvrating.html>.

9. John Lang, "Experts Spread the Copycat Blame," Scripps Howard News Service, *Rocky Mountain News*, May 21, 1999.

10. Plato, *Dialogues*, cited in Richard E. Petty and John T. Cacioppo, *Attitudes and Persuasion: Classic and Contemporary Approaches* (Dubuque, IA: Wm. C. Brown Company Publishers, 1981), p. 69 (from Jowett [1937], p. 511).

11. Petty and Cacioppo, *Attitudes and Persuasion*, p. 7.

12. Steven R. Donziger, ed., *The Real War on Crime: The Report of the National Criminal Justice Commission* (New York: HarperPerennial, 1996), p. 69.

13. This is a paraphrased recreation of an actual news report aired on the local news in Denver, Colorado, following the shooting deaths of three individuals in Aurora, Colorado, in September 1998. The subject matter and the gist of the quotes are accurate. I wrote this description the following morning after watching the actual newscast.

14. D. Graber, *Crime News and the Public* (New York: Praeger Publishers, 1980), pp. 49–50.

15. Michael F. Jacobson and Laurie Ann Mazur, *Marketing Madness: A Survival Guide for Consumer Society* (Boulder, San Francisco, Oxford: Westview Press, 1995), p.

195; U.S. Census Bureau, "Up to the Minute U.S. Population Meter," March 12, 1999, <http://www.census.gov/main/www/popclock.html>.

16. Chermak, *Victims in the News*, pp. 25, 45.

17. Ibid., p. 37.

18. George Gerbner, *Women and Minorities on Television*, American Federation of Television and Radio Artists, Screen Actors Guild (Philadelphia: Annenberg School for Communication, University of Pennsylvania, 1993).

19. Petty and Cacioppo, *Attitudes and Persuasion*.

20. S. M. Berger, "Conditioning Through Vicarious Instigation," *Psychology Review* (69) (1962):450–466.

21. Center for Media and Public Affairs, "Study Finds Rise in TV, Guns, and Violence," executive summary, September 11, 1996, <http://www.cmpa.com/archive/viol95.html>.

22. Petty and Cacioppo, *Attitudes and Persuasion*, p. 73.

23. Donziger, *The Real War on Crime*, p. 2.

24. Ibid., p. 76.

25. Petty and Cacioppo, *Attitudes and Persuasion*, p. 236.

26. Ibid., pp. 87–92.

27. "Busted: America's War on Marijuana," PBS documentary aired on *Frontline*, March 16, 1999.

28. Johnny McGaha et al., "Felony Probation: A Re-examination of Public Risk," *American Journal of Criminal Justice* 11 (1) (1987):1–9; Genneard F. Vito, "Felony Probation and Recidivism: Replication and Response," *Federal Probation* 50 (4) (1986):17–25; M. A. Cuniff, *A Sentencing Postscript: Felony Probationers Under Supervision in the Community* (Washington, DC: National Association of Criminal Justice Planners, 1986); Thomas Mathiesen, "Prisons Cannot Rehabilitate," *America's Prisons: Opposing Viewpoints*, Opposing Viewpoints Series, 5th rev. ed., ed. Stacy L. Tipp (San Diego: Greenhaven Press, 1991), pp. 38–44.

29. *National Television Violence Profile, 1994–1995*, Summary of Findings and Recommendations, Media Scope, <http://www.mediascope.org/ntvssmfn.html>.

30. Ibid.

31. Debra Seagal, "Tales from the Cutting-Room Floor: The Reality of Reality-Based Television," *Harper's Magazine*, November 1993, p. 51.

32. Donziger, *The Real War on Crime*, p. 70.

33. Report aired on *NBC Nightly News*, 6:00 P.M., October 15, 1998. Report was attributed to the U.S. Department of Education.

34. Dan Freedman, "Voters Say U.S. Spirit Is Deflated: Shootings, War, Have Group Members Glum About Present, Future," Hearst Newspapers, *Rocky Mountain News*, May 8, 1999.

35. Ibid.

36. Donziger, *The Real War on Crime*, pp. 65–66.

37. Ibid., p. 66.

38. Dan Thomasson, "Broadcasters Need Self-Policing," *Scripps Howard News Service*, June 15, 1999.

39. George Gerbner, "Reclaiming Our Cultural Mythology," *In Context* (Spring 1994):40.

40. George Gerbner, "Rethinking Media Violence," *Gerbner Series Study Guide, Part II: The Killing Screens: Media and the Culture of Violence* (Northampton, MA: Media Education Foundation, 1998), p. 4, <http://www.mediaed.org/guides/gssg2.html>.

41. Associated Press, "Studies Link Fear, Cynicism to Crime Coverage in TV News," *Minnesota Daily*, May 12, 1997.

42. Ibid.

43. *National Television Violence Profile Scientific Papers, 1994–1995* (Studio City, CA: Mediascope, 1996).

44. Todd Gitlin, "Brain Tennis," *Hotwired* (1997), <http://vip.hotwired.com/synapse/braintennis/97/27/right1.html>.

45. Gerbner, "Rethinking Media Violence," pp. 4–5.

46. Ibid., p. 4; Gitlin, "Brain Tennis."

47. Gerbner, "Reclaiming Our Cultural Mythology," p. 40.

48. Grace Ferrari Levine, "Learned Helplessness in Local TV News," *Journalism Quarterly* 3 (1) (Spring 1986):12–18, 23.

49. Ibid.

50. Martin E.P. Seligman, *Helplessness: On Depression, Development, and Death* (San Francisco: Freeman, p. 44).

51. Benneth Roth, "Court Deals Blow to Media Ride-Alongs," *Houston Chronicle, Rocky Mountain News*, May 25, 1999.

52. Ibid.

53. Ron Rosenbaum, "The Man Who Married Dan Rather," *Esquire* (November 1982), p. 40.

54. Sam Husseini, "Felons on the Air: Does GE's Ownership of NBC Violate the Law?" *Extra* (November–December 1994), <http://www.fair.org/extra/9411/ge-felon.html>; Jim Naureckas, "Corporate Ownership Matters: The Case of NBC," *Extra* (November–December 1995), <http://www.fair.org/extra/9511/nbc/html>.

Chapter 5

1. Richard E. Petty and John T. Cacioppo, *Attitudes and Persuasion: Classic and Contemporary Approaches* (Dubuque, IA: Wm. C. Brown Company Publishers, 1981), p. 73.

2. Seabach, "The White House Hypes Its New Crime-Fighting Bill," *Rocky Mountain News*, May 23, 1999.

3. Peter Carlson, "Corrections Trends for the Twenty-First Century: Our Future Behind the Walls and Wire," *Keeper's Voice*, downloaded January 20, 1999, <http://www.acsp.uic.edu/iaco/kv170105.html>.

4. Larry J. Sabato, *The Rise of the Political Consultant* (New York: Basic Books, 1981).

5. Ibid., p. 12.

6. Ibid., p. 37.

7. Ibid., p. 7.

8. Dick Morris, *The New Prince* (New York: St. Martin's Press), 1999; Duane Davis, "How to Win at Politics," *Rocky Mountain News*, June 13, 1999.

9. Bob Herbert, "Casket in the Sea Fuels Myths of Conspiracy Buffs," *New York Times*, *Rocky Mountain News*, June 18, 1999.

10. Sabato, *The Rise of the Political Consultant*, p. 36.

11. Ibid., p. 12.

12. Alan Baron, "The Slippery Art of Polls," as cited in ibid., p. 21.

13. *60 Minutes*, CBS report aired December 13, 1998 (off-camera interviews had been conducted with Dick Morris and Larry J. Sabato).

14. *National Journal*, May 1, 1976, p. 575–576, cited in Sabato, *The Rise of the Political Consultant*, p. 37.

15. Michael de Courcy Hinds, "Felling Prisons' Costs," *New York Times*, August 17, 1992.

16. John Nichols, "Apathy, Inc.: Republicans Aim to Drive Down Voter Turnout," *Progressive* (October 1998), <http://www.progressive.org/nichols9810.html>.

17. Ibid.

18. Jon Arthur and Amy Shapiro, eds., *Color Class Identity: The New Politics of Race* (Boulder: Westview Press, 1996), pp. 144–146.

19. Nichols, "Apathy, Inc."

20. Ibid.

21. Kelli Arena, "For Whom the Polls Toll," aired on CNN 9:43 P.M. EST, October 15, 1996; *60 Minutes*, CBS report aired December 13, 1998.

22. Bob Herbert, "Donor Class Calls the Big Shots," *New York Times*, *Rocky Mountain News*, July 21, 1998.

23. Ibid.

24. Center for Responsive Politics, *Money and Incumbency Win Big on Election Day*, November 4, 1998, <http://www.crp.org>.

25. Ibid.

26. Howard Kurtz, "Ads Use Crimes' Pain for Candidates' Gain," *Washington Post*, November 2, 1994; Howard Kurtz, "In 1994 Political Ads, Crime Is the Weapon of Choice," *Washington Post*, September 9, 1994.

27. Carlson, "Corrections Trends for the Twenty-First Century."

28. Center for Responsive Politics, "The Clockwork Green," *Speaking Freely*, downloaded November 13, 1998, <http://www.crp.org>.

29. Ibid.

30. Ibid.

31. Ibid.

32. Associated Press, "Working the Phones," Washington bureau, October 27, 1998.

33. Center for Responsive Politics, "Money Begets Access, Access Begets Action," *Speaking Freely*, downloaded November 13, 1998, <http://www.crp.org>.

34. Ibid.

35. Center for Responsive Politics, "When Appearance Becomes Actuality," *Speaking Freely,* downloaded November 13, 1998, <http://www.crp.org>.

36. Bill Moyers and Sherry Jones, "Washington's Other Scandal," cited in Jim Hightower, "Political Bribery: The American Way," *Boulder Weekly* (November 1998).

37. Alice Ann Love, "'Legal Bribes' Embarrassing, Carter Says," Associated Press, *Rocky Mountain News*, October 20, 1997.

38. Center for Responsive Politics, *Serious Money: The Top 100 Overall Contributors*, downloaded November 13, 1998, <http://www.crp.org>.

39. Center for Responsive Politics, *Million Dollar Spenders, Jan. 1–June 30, 1997*, downloaded November 13, 1998, <http://www.crp.org>.

40. Center for Responsive Politics, *Top 50 Soft Money Contributors*, downloaded November 13, 1998, <http://www.crp.org>.

41. Frank Rich, "Wasting Time and Money on an Anti-Drug Message," *New York Times*, July 16, 1998.

42. Steven R. Donziger, ed., *The Real War on Crime: The Report of the National Criminal Justice Commission* (New York: HarperPerennial, 1996), pp. 81–82; Center for Responsive Politics, *Serious Money.*

43. Caleb Foote, *The Prison Population Explosion: California's Rogue Elephant* (San Francisco: Center on Juvenile and Criminal Justice, June 1993), p. 12.

44. Ibid., p. 12.

45. Eric Schlosser, "The Prison-Industrial Complex," *Atlantic Monthly* 282 (6) (December 1998):51–77.

46. *Trading Books for Bars: The Lopsided Funding Battle Between Prisons and Universities* (San Francisco: Center on Juvenile and Criminal Justice, June 1993), p. 12.

47. Schlosser, "The Prison-Industrial Complex."

48. Anthony Ramirez, "Upsizing America's Prisons, Slowly: Despite a Checkered Past, the Future Is Looking Brighter for the Private Prison Industry," *New York Times*, August 14, 1994; Schlosser, "The Prison-Industrial Complex."

49. Schlosser, "The Prison-Industrial Complex"; Alex Friedmann, "Strange Bedfellows: CCA's Political Connections," *Loompanics* (1998), <http://www.loompanics.com/Articles/America.html>.

50. Alex Friedmann, "Strange Bedfellows."

51. Ibid.

52. Ibid.

53. Schlosser, "The Prison-Industrial Complex."

54. Ibid.

55. Ibid.

56. Ibid.

57. Contract executed between the State of Colorado and Prairie Correctional Facility in 1996 agreeing to pay $52 per head per day to Prairie.

58. Associated Press, "Prisoners No Longer Have Beef with Meat Substitute, *Lubbock Avalanche-Journal,* November 5, 1995; Associated Press, "State Examines Purchasing Scrutiny," *Austin American–Statesman*, circa January 1996; Clay Robinson, "Ex-Official's Ties to Firm Investigated: Prison Board Studies Food Company Pact," *Houston Chronicle*, January 10, 1996.

Chapter 6

1. Anthony Kennedy, testimony before U.S. House Appropriations Subcommittee, cited in "Mandatory Sentencing Is Criticized by Justice," *New York Times*, March 10, 1994.

2. "Busted: America's War on Marijuana," PBS documentary aired on *Frontline,* March 16, 1999.

3. David B. Kopel, *Prison Blues: How America's Foolish Sentencing Policies Endanger Public Safety*, Policy Analysis No. 208 (Washington, DC: CATO Institute, May 17, 1994), p. 10.

4. Ibid., p. 12.

5. Ibid., p. 11.

6. Michael de Courcy Hinds, "Felling Prisons' Costs," *New York Times*, August 17, 1992.

7. Associated Press, "Is 'Three Strikes' Out?" *Daily Times-Call*, December 10, 1998.

8. Richard Carelli, "25 to Life for Stealing Vitamins," Associated Press, *Rocky Mountain News*, January 20, 1999.

9. Associated Press, "Is 'Three Strikes' Out?"

10. Vincent Schiraldi, *The People Behind the Headlines* (San Francisco: Center for Juvenile and Criminal Justice, October 1994).

11. *Trading Books for Bars: The Lopsided Funding Battle Between Prisons and Universities* (San Francisco: Center for Juvenile and Criminal Justice, June 1993), p. 1; Schiraldi, *The People Behind the Headlines.*

12. Schiraldi, *The People Behind the Headlines;* Steven R. Donziger, ed., *The Real War on Crime: The Report of the National Criminal Justice Commission* (New York: HarperPerennial, 1996), pp. 19–20.

13. David Esparza et al., "The 'Three Strikes and You're Out' Law: A Preliminary Assessment," *Status*, Legislative Analyst's Office, State of California, summary, January 6, 1995, p. 7; Schiraldi, *The People Behind the Headlines.*

14. "Mandatory Minimum Sentences and 'Three Strikes,'" *NACDL Legislative Policies* (Washington, DC: National Association of Criminal Defense Lawyers, 1997), downloaded January 27, 1999, <http://www.criminaljustice.org/LEGIS/leg15.html>.

15. *Trading Books for Bars.*

16. Ibid., p. 1.

17. Associated Press, "Is 'Three Strikes' Out?"

18. William H. Rehnquist, "Luncheon Address," in U.S. Sentencing Commission, *Drugs and Violence* (Washington, DC: U.S. Government Printing Office, 1994), pp. 286–287, cited in Kopel, *Prison Blues,* pp. 18–19.

19. "Mandatory Minimum Sentences and 'Three Strikes,' p. 13.

20. Esparza et al., "The 'Three Strikes and You're Out' Law," pp. 4–7.

21. Ibid., p. 5.

22. Ibid., p. 6.

23. Ibid.

24. "Mandatory Minimum Sentences and 'Three Strikes,' p. 13.

25. Department of Justice, Bureau of Justice Statistics, *An Analysis of Nonviolent Drug Offenders with Minimal Criminal Histories*, December 1993, p. 41.

26. "Mandatory Minimum Sentences and 'Three Strikes,' p. 5.

27. Ibid.

28. Ibid.

29. Ibid.

30. Alexander Cockburn, "U.S. Has Become Prosecutorial State, *Creators' Syndicate, Rocky Mountain News*, February 6, 1999.

31. Michael Tonry, "Mandatory Penalties," *Crime and Justice: A Review of Research*, vol. 16, ed. Michael Tonry (Chicago: University of Chicago Press, 1990), pp. 243–244.

32. Donziger, *The Real War on Crime*, p. 24.

33. Ibid.

34. Ted Gest, "A War on Crime or a Feud in Congress: An Anticrime Program Smells a Lot Like Pork," *U.S. News and World Report*, May 20, 1995.

35. "Tab for Death Penalty: $2.5 Million," *Rocky Mountain News*, August 15, 1999.

36. Stephen Bright and Patrick Keenan, "Judges and the Politics of Death: Deciding Between the Bill of Rights and the Next Election in Capital Cases," *Boston University Law Review* (1995), cited in Christopher Hitchens, "Scenes from an Execution," *Atlantic Monthly* (January 1998):42.

37. Hitchens, "Scenes from an Execution," p. 42.

38. Stephanie Nebehay, "U.N. Urges U.S. to Cease Executions," Reuters, *Rocky Mountain News*, April 4, 1998.

39. Richard Carelli, "'Execution Train' Picks Up Speed," Associated Press, December 28, 1997; Paul Haven, "Debate on Executions Heats Up," Associated Press, *Rocky Mountain News,* May 31, 1999; Clarence Page, "Sense of Decency in Jeopardy," *Tribune Media Services*, February 11, 1999.

40. CBS *Nightly News*, report aired November 10, 1998; also see Associated Press, "DNA Testing Saving Condemned Illinois Inmates," *Rocky Mountain News*, August 16, 1999.

41. Nat Hentoff, "Constitution's Greatest Enemy," Newspaper Enterprise Association, *Rocky Mountain News*, Febrary 16, 1998.

42. Gene Nichol, "Clinton's Lousy Civil Rights Record," *Rocky Mountain News*, February 5, 1999; Nat Hentoff, "Constitution's Greatest Enemy."

43. Carelli, "'Execution Train' Picks Up Speed"; CBS *Nightly News*, report aired November 10, 1998.

44. Kevin O'Hanlon, "Execution Moratorium Rejected," Associated Press, *Rocky Mountain News,* May 27, 1999.

45. Interview with defense attorney and former prosecutor Lee Hill, conducted March 13, 1999.

46. Steven Chermak, *Victims in the News: Crime and the American News Media* (Boulder, San Francisco, Oxford: Westview Press, 1995), p. 21.

Chapter 7

1. David B. Kopel, *Prison Blues: How America's Foolish Sentencing Policies Endanger Public Safety,* Policy Analysis No. 208 (Washington, DC: CATO Institute, May 17, 1994), p. 10.

2. U.S. Department of Justice, Bureau of Justice Statistics, *Compendium of Federal Justice Statistics, 1990* (Washington: U.S. Department of Justice, September 1993), p. 42; Kopel, *Prison Blues,* p. 21.

3. National News Briefing section, "Inmates in Prison Longer," *Rocky Mountain News,* January 11, 1999.

4. Robert M. Figlio, "Self-Reported and Officially Defined Offenses in the 1958 Philadelphia Birth Cohort," in *Cross-National Longitudinal Research on Human Development and Criminal Behavior,* ed. Elmer G.M. Weitekamp and Hans-Jurgen Kerner (Dordecht, Boston, London: Kluwer Academic Press, 1994).

5. Kopel, *Prison Blues,* pp. 25–28.

6. Bruce L. Benson and David W. Rasmussen, *Illinois' War on Drugs: Some Unintended Consequences,* Heartland Policy Study No. 48 (Chicago: Heartland Institute, 1992).

7. U.S. Department of Justice, Bureau of Justice Statistics, *Survey of State Prison Inmates* (Washington, DC: U.S. Government Printing Office, 1991).

8. Steven R. Donziger, ed., *The Real War on Crime: The Report of the National Criminal Justice Commission* (New York: HarperPerennial, 1996), p. 74.

9. Ibid., pp. 74–75.

10. U.S. Department of Justice, Federal Bureau of Investigation, *Crime in the United States—1993* (Washington, DC: U.S. Government Printing office, December 4, 1994), section 5.

11. Robert Davis and Sam Vincent Meddis, "Random Killings Hit a High," *USA Today,* December 5, 1994.

12. Donziger, *The Real War on Crime,* pp. 76–78.

13. *War on Drugs: Racial Impact of a Failed Policy* (Washington, DC: The Sentencing Project, 1997), <http://www.sproject.com>.

14. Marc Mauer, *Americans Behind Bars: U.S. and International Use of Incarceration, 1995* (Washington, DC: The Sentencing Project, 1997).

15. *Facts About Prisons and Prisoners* (Washington, DC: The Sentencing Project, 1997), <http://www.sproject.com>.

16. *War on Drugs: Racial Impact of a Failed Policy*.

17. Karyl Kristine Kicenski, "The Corporate Prison, the Production of Crime, and the Sale of Discipline," George Mason University, 1998, research paper published at <http://www.speech.csun.edu/ben/news/kessay.html>, p. 9; Marc Mauer and Tracy Huling, *Young Black Americans and the Criminal Justice System: Five Years Later* (Washington, DC: The Sentencing Project, 1995).

18. Marc Mauer, *Intended and Unintended Consequences: State Racial Disparities in Imprisonment* (Washington, DC: The Sentencing Project, 1997).

19. Craig Reinarman and Harry G. Levine, "Crack in Context: Politics and Media in Making of a Drug Scare," *Contemporary Drug Problems* (Winter 1989):38–62.

20. C. Stone Brown, "The Economics of Crime and Capitalism," *San Francisco Bay Guardian*, circa 1994.

21. Thomas W. Hale, *A Profile of the Working Poor*, U.S. Department of Labor, Bureau of Labor Statistics, Report 914 (Washington, DC: U.S. Department of Labor, August 1997).

22. H. Sklar, "Reinforcing Racism with the War on Drugs," *Z Magazine*, December 1995, p. 20.

23. Frank Bruni, "Public Assent Behind Crimes of the War on Crime," *Wall Street Journal*, February 21, 1999.

24. Mauer and Huling, *Young Black Americans and the Criminal Justice System*.

25. Donziger, *The Real War on Crime*, p. 106.

26. Ken Silverstein, "America's Private Gulag," originally appeared in *CounterPunch*, November 14, 1997, <http://www.loompanics.com/Articles/America.html>.

27. Donziger, *The Real War on Crime*, p. 14.

28. *CNN News*, report aired May 20, 1999.

29. Bob Herbert, "High Court Howls at Ethnic Profiling," *New York Times, Rocky Mountain News*, June 15, 1999.

30. *Dateline NBC*, report aired April 27, 1999.

31. David Cole, *No Equal Justice: Race and Class in the American Criminal Justice System* (New York: New Press, 1999), cited in Stephen Gillers, "The Double Standard," *New York Times on the Web*, March 28, 1999, <http://www.nytimes.com/books/99/03/21/reviews>.

32. Christopher S. Wren, "Drug Czar McCaffrey Urges Wider Access to Methadone for Addicts," *New York Times, Rocky Mountain News*, circa December 1998.

33. *Washington Post*, June 8, 1997, cited in *War on Drugs: Racial Impact of a Failed Policy*.

34. "Busted: America's War on Marijuana," PBS documentary aired on *Frontline*, March 16, 1999.

35. Ibid.

36. Ibid.

37. National Institute on Drug Abuse, National Institute on Alcohol Abuse and Alcoholism, *The Economic Costs of Alcohhol and Drug Abuse in the United States—1992* (Rockville, MD: Lewin Group, 1998), section 6.1 synopsis, p. 2.

38. Phil Smith, "Private Prisons: Profits of Crime," *Covert Action Quarterly* (Fall 1993):42–49.

39. Ibid.

40. Shaheen Borna, "Free Enterprise Goes to Prison," *British Journal of Criminology* 26 (4) (October 1986):324.

41. Ibid., p. 325.

Chapter 8

1. Studs Terkel, *The Great Divide: Second Thoughts on the American Dream* (New York: Avon, 1988), p. 1.

2. Harry Truman, cited in Joel Dyer, *Harvest of Rage* (Boulder: Westview Press, 1997), p. 11.

3. Russell Clemens, "Privatizing Criminal Justice: The Corrections Debate: Con," paper presented at Crime and Justice in the Americas Conference, Office of International Criminal Justice (Chicago), March 13, 1995, <http://www.acsp.uic.edu/iocj/pubs/cja/080315.html>.

4. Sandra Block, "Everybody's Doin' the Jailhouse Stock," *USA Today*, June 5, 1996.

5. Greg Jaffe and Rick Brooks, "Hard Time: Violence at Prison Run by Corrections Corp Irks Youngstown, Ohio," *Wall Street Journal,* August 5, 1998.

6. *Lessons and Cautions for Carnac: Privatization of Prisons Brings Both Big Business and Mixed Results*, Department of Foreign Affairs and International Trade, Canada, report downloaded August 4, 1998, <http://www.canada.dallas.org/english/esw2001/esw5004.html>.

7. Jaffe and Brooks, "Hard Time."

8. Ibid.

9. Clemens, "Privatizing Criminal Justice."

10. Jaffe and Brooks, "Hard Time."

11. Hector Gutierrez, "Escapee Once in Drug Rehab Program," *Rocky Mountain News*, June 2, 1999; John Sanko, "Owens to Write Maryland's Governor About Prisoners," *Rocky Mountain News*, June 6, 1999.

12. Jaffe and Brooks, "Hard Time."

13. Ibid.

14. Ibid.

15. Ibid.

16. Eric Schlosser, "The Prison-Industrial Complex," *Atlantic Monthly* 282 (6) (December 1998):51–77.

17. Ann Imse, "Child Abuse, Suicide Investigated at Private Prison," *Rocky Mountain News*, April 4, 1998.

18. Ann Imse, "Report Shows Chaotic Staffing at Rebound," *Rocky Mountain News*, April 20, 1998.

19. Ann Imse, "State Yanks Kids from Prison," *Rocky Mountain News*, April 2, 1998.

20. Ann Imse, "Utah Expected Better from Prison," *Rocky Mountain News*, April 16, 1998.

21. Ann Imse, "Abuse Cases at Prison Not Fully Investigated," *Rocky Mountain News*, April 17, 1998.

22. Ann Imse, "Staff-Youth Prison Sex Under Fire," *Rocky Mountain News*, April 13, 1998.

23. Ken Silverstein, "America's Private Gulag," originally appeared in *CounterPunch*, November 14, 1997, <http://www.loompanics.com/Articles/America.html>.

24. Ibid.

25. Ann Imse, "Former High Plains Officials Regroup," *Rocky Mountain News*, November 8, 1998.

26. Sharon Theimer, "Long-Term Problems in Moving Inmates," Associated Press, February 2, 1996.

27. Ibid.

28. Hector Gutierrez and Ann Imse, "State Closes Youth Ranch," *Rocky Mountain News*, June 12, 1999; Ann Imse, "Youth Home Director Troubled," *Rocky Mountain News*, June 15, 1999; Ann Imse, "Director of Boys' Ranch Misled State, Report Says," *Rocky Mountain News*, June 12, 1999.

29. Ann Imse, "Youth Prison Chief Surprised at High Cost," *Rocky Mountain News*, April 14, 1998.

Chapter 9

1. Shaheen Borna, "Free Enterprise Goes to Prison," *British Journal of Criminology* 26 (4) (October 1996):331.

2. *The New Lexicon Webster's Dictionary of the English Language* (New York: Lexicon Publications, 1988).

3. Anne Marie Squeo, "Justice Joins Whistle-Blower Suit," *Bloomberg News*, October 6, 1998.

4. *CNN News*, report aired March 3, 1999.

5. *CNN News*, report aired March 22, 1999.

6. Ann Imse, "Auditors: Jail Rent Too High," *Rocky Mountain News*, May 26, 1998.

7. Staff editorial, "High Finance at High Plains," *Rocky Mountain News*, May 29, 1998.

8. Ibid.

9. Charles H. Logan, *Prison Privatization: Objections and Refutations*, University of Connecticut, downloaded January 20, 1999, <http://www.ucc.uconn.edu/~wwwsoci/fraser.html>.

10. Cathy Lazere, "Privatizing Prisons: Finance Chiefs Face a Peculiar Lineup of Problems Helping Move a Business out of the Public Sector," *CFO Magazine*, February 1997, <http://www.cfonet.com/html/Articles/CFO/1997/97Fepris.html>.

11. Ken Silverstein, "America's Private Gulag," originally appeared in *CounterPunch*, November 14, 1997, <http://www.loompanics.com/Articles/America.html>.

12. Charles W. Thomas, "Privatizing Criminal Justice: The Corrections Debate: Pro," paper presented at Crime and Justice in the Americas Conference, Office of International Criminal Justice (Chicago), March 13, 1995, <http://www.acsp.uic.edu/iocj/pubs/cja/080315.html>.

13. Russell Clemens, "Privatizing Criminal Justice: The Corrections Debate: Con," paper presented at Crime and Justice in the Americas Conference, Office of International Criminal Justice (Chicago), March 13, 1995, <http://www.acsp.uic.edu/iocj/pubs/cja/080315.html>.

14. *Private and Public Prisons: Studies Comparing Operational Costs and/or Quality of Service*, letter report (Washington, DC: U.S. General Accounting Office, August 16, 1996), p. 1.

15. Tami Lubby, "Private Prison Industry," *Keeper's Voice* 18 (1) (1997), <http://www.acsp.uic.edu/iaco/kv1801/180125.html>.

16. T. Bivens, "Can Prisons for Profit Work?" *Philadelphia Inquirer Magazine*, August 12, 1986, p. 15, cited in Christine Bowditch and Ronald S. Everett, "Private Prisons: Problems with the Solution, *Justice Quarterly* 4 (3) (September 1987):447.

17. Borna, "Free Enterprise Goes to Prison," p. 332.

18. James Moran, "Privatizing Criminal Justice," paper presented at Crime and Justice in the Americas Conference, Office of International Criminal Justice (Chicago), March 13, 1995, <http://www.acsp.uic.edu/iocj/pubs/cja/080315.html>.

19. *NBC Nightly News*, report aired January 4, 1999.

20. Jeremy Quittner, correspondent, "The Incarceration Industry: Teeming Prison Rolls Bode Well for Private Jails," aired on *Fox News* at 3:12 P.M., April 22, 1998, <http://www.prisonactivist.org/news/5–98/The-Incarceration-Industry-Teaming-Prison.html>.

21. Ibid.

22. Karyl Kristine Kicenski, "The Corporate Prison: The Production of Crime and the Sale of Discipline," George Mason University, 1993, research paper published at <http://speech.csun.edu/ben/news/kessay.html>, p. 4; Silverstein, "America's Private Gulag."

23. *Private and Public Prisons*, p. 4.

24. Reuters, "Analysts Want Prison Costs Measured," State's News Service, September 22, 1998.

25. John C. Ensslin, "Colo. Inmates to Stay in State," *Rocky Mountain News*, December 26, 1998.

26. Associated Press, "Contracting with Private Firms Helped Fulfill Political Promise," *Denver Post,* January 19, 1996.

27. Lazere, "Privatizing Prisons."

Chapter 10

1. Reinhold Niebuhr, *Children of Light and the Children of Darkness*, 1944, in *The Oxford Dictionary of Phrase, Saying, and Quotation,* ed. Elizabeth Knowles (New York: Oxford University Press, 1997), p. 123.

2. David J. Rothman, *The Oxford History of the Prison: The Practice of Punishment in Western Society*, ed. Norval Morris and David J. Rothman (New York, Oxford: Oxford University Press, 1995), p. 116.

3. Ibid.

4. Ibid., pp. 116–118.

5. Camille G. Camp and George M. Camp, *The Corrections Yearbook: Adult Corrections* (South Salem, NY: Criminal Justice Institute, various years 1981 through 1990).

6. Shaheen Borna, "Free Enterprise Goes to Prison," *British Journal of Criminology* 26 (4) (October 1986):323.

7. Tracy Sacco, "Crowded U.S. Jails Mean More Bonds, Privatizations," Reuters, August 14, 1998.

8. Ibid.

9. Ibid.

10. Ken Silverstein, "America's Private Gulag," originally appeared in *CounterPunch,* November 14, 1997, <http://www.loompanics.com/Articles/America.html>.

11. Tom Maurer, "Backdoor Bonds: Lawmakers Levy Prison Debt Rejected by Voters," *Bakersfield Californian*, January 16, 1994; staff, "Billions in Bond Sales Sidestep Voters: State Uses Alternate Means to Get What Agencies Want, at Higher Cost to Tax Payers," *San Jose Mercury News,* August 17, 1993.

12. Legislative Analyst's Office for the State of California, "Uses and Costs of Lease-Payment Bonds," *Status*, May 3, 1995.

13. Eric Schlosser, "The Prison-Industrial Complex," *Atlantic Monthly* 282 (6) (December 1998):51–77.

14. Kenneth Lovett, "Prison-Bond Vote Gets Support," Ottaway News Service, *Prison News and News Articles for Corrections Officers in New York State* (June 1999):19.

15. Schlosser, "The Prison-Industrial Complex."

16. Ibid.

17. Lovett, "Prison-Bond Vote Gets Support," p. 19; Schlosser, "The Prison-Industrial Complex."

18. Lovett, "Prison-Bond Vote Gets Support," p. 19.

19. Ibid., p. 20.

20. Interview with Eric Butterfield, editor of *Construction Report,* published by *Correctional Building News* on March 14, 1999. Original source for the Butterfield material is *The Corrections Yearbook* (South Salem, NY: Criminal Justice Institute, various years).

21. Ann Imse, "Lawmaker Wants to Stop Adding Prisons for 3 Years," *Rocky Mountain News,* January 28, 1999.

22. Voltaire attributed; Walter Bagehot, *The English Constitution*, 1867, in *The Oxford Dictionary of Phrase, Saying, and Quotation*, p. 196.

23. Marlys Duran, "Residents Have First Crack at Bond Sale to Expand Jail," *Rocky Mountain News*, March 16, 1999.

24. Ann McFeatters, "Rich Get Richer, Poor Get Poorer," Scripps Howard News Service, *Rocky Mountain News*, May 24, 1999.

25. Steven R. Donziger, ed., *The Real War on Crime: The Report of the National Criminal Justice Commission* (New York: HarperPerennial, 1996), p. 28.

26. Katherine Barrett and Richard Greene, "Prisons: The Punishing Cost," *Financial World*, April 18, 1989.

27. Center on Juvenile and Criminal Justice, *Trading Books for Bars: The Lopsided Funding Battle Between Prisons and Universities* (San Francisco: Center on Juvenile and Criminal Justice, 1995).

28. Vincent Schiraldi, "More Cells Than Classrooms in State's Future," *San Jose Mercury News*, May 29, 1995.

29. Center on Juvenile and Criminal Justice, *Trading Books for Bars.*

30. Schiraldi, "More Cells Than Classrooms in State's Future."

31. Caleb Foote, *The Prison Population Explosion: California's Rogue Elephant*, (San Francisco: Center on Juvenile and Criminal Justice, special report, June 1993).

32. Ibid.

33. Joe Hallinan, "Prisons: A Growth Industry: Some States Assign More Importance to Corrections Than Education," *Star-Ledger*, March 19, 1995.

34. John Sanko, "$500 Million for Prisons?" *Rocky Mountain News*, January 8, 1998.

35. Reported on *9 News*, Denver, Colorado's NBC affiliate during the 5:00 P.M. newscast, May 9, 1999.

36. Ann Imse, "Roadblocks Keep Mentally Ill Kids from Getting Treatment," *Rocky Mountain News*, May 11, 1999.

37. Charley Able, "Jeffco Eyes Billing Inmates," *Rocky Mountain News*, May 10, 1999.

38. Minnesota Planning Department, *Paying the Price: The Rising Cost of Prison; Minnesota Planning Outlines Options to Costly Prison-Building Cycle*, news release, March 14, 1996.

39. Barrett and Greene, "Prisons," p. 18.

40. Minnesota Planning Department, *Paying the Price.*

41. Ibid.

42. Stan Bailey, "Prison Costs Pinching: System Is Growing by 100 Convicts Monthly, Eating 16 Cents of Each General Fund Dollar," *Birmingham News*, March 12, 1995.

43. Ibid.

44. Sue Hinton, "Prison Law Moving in Right Direction," *Daily Oklahoman*, May 22, 1999.

45. Barrett and Greene, "Prisons," p. 18; Michael Kroll, "Prisons: Rural America's Growth Industry," *PNS*, March 19, 1989.

46. Jennifer Wong, "Prison Sell: Cashing In on Incarceration," *Texas Observer*, May 3, 1991, pp. 4, 8.

47. Arlene Levinson, "Prisons Booming: Increase at Expense of Schools' No Guarantee Crime Will Fall," Associated Press, *San Francisco Examiner*, July 3, 1994.

48. Herbert I. Schiller, "On That Chart," *Nation* 262 (22), June 3, 1996, p. 16.

49. Charles H. Logan, "Private Prisons Are Just," in *America's Prisons: Opposing Viewpoints*, 5th rev. ed., ed. Stacy L. Tipp (San Diego: Greenhaven Press, 1991), p. 161.

50. Ibid., p. 162.

51. Nolan A. Bowie, "On That Chart," *Nation* 262 (22), June 3, 1996, p. 20.

52. John Kenneth Galbraith, *The Affluent Society* (Cambridge, MA: Riverside Press, 1958), pp. 156–158.

Chapter 11

1. Francis Bacon, "Of Innovations," *Essays*, 1625, in *The Oxford Dictionary of Phrase, Saying, and Quotation*, ed. Elizabeth Knowles (New York: Oxford University Press, 1997), p. 64.

2. Andrew Shapiro, "Challenging Criminal Disenfranchisement Under the Voting Rights Act: A New Strategy," *Yale Law Journal* (103) (1993):537; National Public Radio, report aired October 22, 1998; *CBS Nightly News*, report aired October 22, 1998.

3. National Public Radio, report aired October 22, 1998; *CBS Nightly News*, report aired October 22, 1998; Marc Mauer, *Intended and Unintended Consequences: State Racial Disparities in Imprisonment* (Washington, DC: The Sentencing Project, 1997), p. l, <http://www.sproject.com/test/pubs/tsppubs/sumpolicy.html>.

4. Steven Kerr, "On the Folly of Rewarding A, While Hoping for B," *Academy of Management Journal* 18 (1975):769–783.

5. Ibid.

6. Inaugural episode of *CNN/Time NewsStand*, aired on CNN network, poll results reported by correspondent Jeff Greenfield.

7. "TV Violence: More Objectionable in Entertainment Than in Newscasts," *Times Mirror Media Monitor*, March 24, 1993.

8. Scott Stossel, "The Man Who Counts the Killings," *Atlantic Monthly* 279 (5) (May 1997):86–104.

9. Highlights synopsis of the Sixteenth Television Violence Profile, as previewed by George Gerbner on January 27, 1994, before the National Association of Television Program Executives Annual Conference, Miami Beach, Florida, <http://www.cemnet.org/news/highlights.txt>.

10. Associated Press, cited in Pierce O'Donnell, "Killing the Golden Goose: Hollywood's Death Wish," *Beverly Hills Bar Journal* (Summer 1992):14–17.

11. "TV Violence: More Objectionable in Entertainment Than in Newscasts."

12. "Are Music and Movies Killing America's Soul?" *Time*, June 12, 1995, cited in *Mediascope*, "American Public Opinion on Media Violence," <http://www.mediascope.org/fopinion.html>.

13. *1997: Year-End Survey on the People and the Press*, Pew Research Center, cited in Christopher Matthews, "Faith Tempers Anger over Injustice," Tribune Media Services, February 12, 1998; inaugural episode of *CNN/Time NewsStand*.

14. Kerr, "On the Folly of Rewarding A, While Hoping for B."

15. Ibid.

16. Alice Ann Love, "'Legal Bribes' Embarrassing, Carter Says," Associated Press, *Rocky Mountain News*, October 20, 1997.

17. Dusty Saunders, "MacNeil Eyes Serious Late-Night Newscast," *Rocky Mountain News*, June 15, 1999.

18. Dan Thomasson, "Despite Good Times, Dreams Fade," Scripps Howard News Service, *Rocky Mountain News*, June 26, 1999.

19. Associated Press, "Report: Violence Among High-School Students Declining," *Rocky Mountain News*, August 15, 1999.

20. June Kronholz, "School Firearm Expulsions Dropped in 97–98," *Wall Street Journal*, August 11, 1999.

Index

Access, special, and campaign financing, 141–142
Adams, Robert, 205
Advertising
    as a science, 84
    and media content control, 67–70, 80
    and persuasion methods, 90, 91, 94
Ahmuty, Christopher, 215
Alcohol and violent offenses, 193–194
Alderman, Jeffrey D., 55
Alexander, Lamar and Honey, 147
Allen, George, 170
Allstate, 5, 246
Alternatives to incarceration, 2, 37–38
American Civil Liberties Union (ACLU), 184
American Detective, 104
Amplifier effect, 103–107
Analysis of Nonviolent Drug Offenders with Minimal Criminal History, An, 165
Annenberg School of Communications, 74, 108, 109, 111
Aryan Brotherhood, 48
Attica prison, 250, 253
Attitudes, 90–91
Attitudes and Persuasion: Classic and Contemporary Approaches, 95, 96, 97, 98, 117

Baby-boomers, maturing of and effect on crime rate, 43
Bacon, Francis, 265
Baer, Benjamin, 256
Bagdikian, Ben, 71
"Balance," 99–100
Band of Angels, 191
Baron, Alan, 124
Bart, Peter, 68
Baxter, Leone Smith, 120
Baywatch, 74, 75
Beasily, Thomas, 147, 148
Beck, Allen, 29
Behavioral Science Corporation, 121
Behind the Oval Office, 123
Beliefs, 90–91
Benchmark poll, 124
Bensky, Larry, 78
Bernstein, Carl, 77
Big One, The, 19
Blacks
    and the death penalty, 172
    disproportionate population in prisons, 6–7, 182–192, 266–267
    and television depiction of crime, 93–94
    women and drug searches, 189
    See also Race
Bobbitt, John Wayne, 60–61, 271

Bobby Ross Group, The, 149, 203, 211

Boca Raton, crime reporting in, 33–34

Bond issues, for prison construction, 4–5

Bonds
  lease-payment as means to bypass
    voters, 4–5, 244–252
  state, as check on prison expansion,
    4–5, 242–245, 247

Borna, Shaheen, 223, 230, 243

Bowie, Nolan, 263

Brennan, William, 67

Breyer, Stephen, 157, 164

Bright, Stephen, 172

Bristow, David T., 160

Broderick, Vincent L., 166

Brokers, prisoner, 15

Brown & Williamson, 69

Broyles, Dan, 159

Buffett, Warren, 70

Bush, George, and mandatory sentencing,
  154–155, 249

Bush, George W., 131

Buttafuoco, Joey and Mary Jo, 104, 271

Byrd, James, 48

Cable television, 105

Cacioppo, John T., 95, 96, 97, 98, 117

California
  and building of new prisons, 158–159
  and diversion of money from
    education, 256–257
  and lease-revenue bonds, 247–249
  prison system, 145–146
  and "three-strikes" law, 145–146,
    156–161, 256

California Correctional Peace Officers
  Associations, 145, 158

California Teachers' Union, 24

Campaign financing, 131–139
  and hard-on-crime policy, 137–138
  and post-election "special access,"
    138–142

Carey, Hugh, 249

Carlson, Arne, 259

Carlson, Peter, 119, 135

Carter, Jimmy, 142, 150, 274

Carville, James, 131

CATO Institute, 50, 178

Census Bureau, 2, 35–36

Center for Media and Public Affairs
  (CMPA), 55, 56, 57

Center for Responsive Politics, 139, 140

Center for the Study of Commercialism,
  67–68

Center on Hate and Extremism, 48

Center on Juvenile and Criminal Justice,
  160

Central Valley Project, 120

Chambliss, William, 260

Chermak, Steven, 32–33, 64, 65–66, 67

Children
  and education from television, 85
  and television violence, 56–57

Chilsey, Bryson, 206

Citizens United for the Rehabilitation of
  Errants (CURE), 260

Clemens, Russell, 203, 229

Clemmer, Donald, 44

Clinton, Bill
  and access for contributions, 142
  and cocaine sentencing, 185
  and corporate mergers, 70
  and focus groups, 126
  and growth of police, 18, 117
  impeachment trial of, 86
  and public opinion polls, 131, 172
  and purported leniency on crime, 158
  as television politician, 122–123
  and traditional Democratic issues, 136
  and Twenty-First Century Law
    Enforcement and Public Safety Act,
    117

Clinton, Hillary, 131, 147

Clinton Correctional Facility, 16–17

Cocaine, 42–43, 183–185

Cold War, preoccupation with, 28, 29–30

Cole, David, 188–189
Colorado Department of Corrections, 51,
    252
    and effect of prisons on crime rate, 40
    and private prisons, 235–236
Colorado Youth Services, 213, 219,
    226–227
Columbine High School shooting, 61,
    64–65, 89, 163, 271
    and effects on America's psyche,
    105–106, 280–282
Communist China, numbers of prisoners,
    1
Competitive market in prison industry,
    218–222
Computers and crime record keeping, 31
Conditioning, vicarious classic, 95–96
Construction Report, 13
Contract with America, 115–117, 165
Corporal punishment, 196
Corporations
    and growth of prison population, 21
    growth of prison related, 10–11
    mergers of, 70–71
    underwriting of prison facilities, 4–5,
    244–246
Corrections Corporation of America, 5,
    10, 17–18, 46, 214, 218
    and California, 146, 219–220
    political contributions of, 147–148
    and prisoner classification, 204–207
    and real-estate investment trusts, 13,
    232
    and Tennessee, 147–148
    Youngstown facility, 1–2, 204–205, 207,
    210–211, 221
Corrections Yellow Pages, 11
Cost
    of alternatives to incarceration, 2,
    37–38
    of correction institutions, 38
    of criminal justice system, 2, 5–6, 11,
    36–38, 283(n5)

of imprisonment for drug offenders
    rather than imprisonment, 1
    92–194
of mandatory sentencing, 165
of prisoners, 160–161
prison expansion, taxpayers concerns
    of, 4
of prison housing, 12–13
of privatization of prisons to taxpayers,
    5, 223–237
See also Bonds
Council for Excellence in Government,
    107
Counter-Terrorism and Effective Death
    Penalty Act, 173
Crack cocaine
    and crime rate, 42–43
    sentencing for, 183–185
Crants, Robert, 148
Cribbs, C. Hadden "Sonny," 48
Crime
    as a profit source, 22–26
    belief of it as biggest problem, 89, 91,
    97
    history of exaggerated fear of, 239–242
    media created fear of, 3–4, 88–89,
    91–95
    myths about to support hard-on-crime
    policies, 30–52
    myth that it is decreased by prisons,
    38–42
    myth that it is on the rise, 31–33
    public anxiety about, 28–29
    reporting of, 31–36
    See also Street crime; War on Crime
Crime and Publicity, 63
Crime bill of 1994, 171
Crime gap, 27–53
Crime rate
    and Canada, 41
    and crack cocaine culture, 42–43
    and employment, 42
    and maturing of baby-boomers, 43

and prison population growth, 27
and public anxiety about crime, 28–29
Criminal history, 165
Cronkite, Walter, 58, 79
Crystal, Graef, 80
Cuomo, Mario, 249–250

Dahmer, Jeffrey, 101
Daily Variety, 68
Dalton, Gary, 212–213
"Dark Ages" of penology, 195–198, 242
Davis, Derrick, 206
Davis, Richard Allen, 157
Death penalty, 171–175
DeConcini, Dennis, 139, 140
Democracy and prison expansion,
    261–264
Democratic Party, 129, 130, 135–136
Details, 101
Dialogues, 90
Dial Soap, 14
Dicke, John, 214–215
Dictating Content, 67–68
Disney Corporation, 69, 70, 143, 278
Dix, Dorothea, 240
DNA testing, 173
Dole, Bob, 131, 136
Dominion Management, 15
Donors, campaign, 132–134
Downey, Thomas, 141
Drug offenders
    and imprisonment rather than
        treatment, 192–194
    mandatory sentences for, 249
    sentencing of, 166, 178, 181–182
Drug rehabilitation programs, 2, 192–193
Drugs, War on, 189
Dukakis, Michael, 96, 136, 154–155, 156
Dwight, Theodore, 198

Earl Warren Legal Justice Institute, 36
Early release of prisoners, 163, 167, 179
Education, diversion of funds from,
    254–255, 256–257, 259, 260

Eisenhower, Dwight, 29, 120
Eisnach, Dwight, 227
Ekstrand, Laurie E., 229
Employment and the crime rate, 42
Esmor Corrections, 203–204
Esmor effect, 211, 214, 216, 217, 218,
    221
    See also Private-prison corporations,
        and non-reporting of problems

Father's Book, The, 240
Fear as byproduct of television violence,
    88–89, 103, 109
Federal Bureau of Investigation (FBI)
    and crime reporting, 34
    and misleading statistics, 180–181
    and Uniform Crime Report, 31–32
Federal Bureau of Prisons, 150
Federal Judicial Center, 167
Figlio, Robert, 176
Fisher, Amy, 104, 271
Focus groups, 125–126, 130
Ford, Gerald, 122
Fountain, Tony, 45–46
*Four Arguments for the Elimination of
    Television*, 83
Fowler, Wyche, 141–142
Fox, Alan, 43
Freedom of Information Act, 216
Friedmann, Alex, 148
Friendly, A., 63
Fritz, Dennis, 173
Future predictions of prison expansion, 7,
    266–267

Gable, Clark, 191–192
Gailbraith, John Kenneth, 263
Gannett Corporation, 79, 80
General Accounting Office study of
    privatization costs, 229–230, 234
General Electric, 5, 143, 144
Gerbner, George, 74–75, 83, 108
Gilligan, James, 46
Gingrich, Newt, 122, 130

Gitlin, Todd, 76, 80, 109
Giuliani, Rudolph, 189
Glasser, Ira, 184
Golden, Joe Bob, 47
Goldfarb, R.L., 63
Golub, Andrew, 42–43
Good Murders and Bad Murders, 64
Gordon, Bruce, 75–76
Gramm, Phil, 147
Gross, Larry, 108
Grossman, Lawrence, 60, 113, 144
Groundhog Day, 138
Guggenheim, Charles, 124

Habeus corpus, 173
"Hard-on-crime" position, 4
    bipartisan support for, 135, 136
    and consequences of challenging,
        134–135
    and lobbyists, 144–145
    political use of, 5, 97, 115–151, 169
    and sentencing laws, 102
Hatch, Orrin, 153, 155
Hawkins, Gordon, 177
Health care, 14–15
Helplessness, learned, 110–111
Higgins, M. Wayne, 230
High Plains Juvenile Facility, 212–215,
    219, 226–227, 245
Hinds, Michael de Courcy, 128–129
Hinton, Sue, 260
Hispanics
    disproportionate population in prisons,
        6
    and racial profiling, 189
    and sentencing, 186
    See also Race
Historical view of
    crime and prisons, 239–242
    rehabilitation, 195–198, 241
Hitchens, Christopher, 172
Hoelter, Herb, 38
Horton, Willie, ads regarding, 6, 96, 136,
    154, 156, 280

Hromas, Scott, 40
Human Rights Watch, 46

Imse, Ann, 212, 213, 227
Incentives, 96–97
Incumbency, 133–134, 138
Independence Institute, 154
International opinion of U.S. Justice
    system, 6
Interstate movement of prisoners,
    208–210, 215
Investor class, benefiting from prisons,
    22–26, 253–255

Jacobson, Michael F., 68, 80
James, Samuel, 197
Johanns, Mike, 173–174
Johnson, Bruce, 42–43
Johnson, Lyndon B., 108
Johnson, Richard, 205–206
Jones, Ron, 259
Jordan, Ron, 235
Journalists and compliance with media
    profiteering, 77–81
Joyce Foundation, 132
Judicial system and mandatory
    sentencing, 164–166

Kaniss, Phyllis, 63
Kaplan, Sheila, 68
Keating, Frank, 148
Keenan, Patrick, 172
Keeper's Voice, 119
Keillor, Garrison, 62–63, 65
Kennedy, Anthony, 153
Kennedy, Ted, 135
Kerlikowske, Gil, 34
Kerr, Steven, 269, 273
King, Ronald, 48
King, Tom Will (Bill), 47–48, 49
Klaas, Polly, 157–158, 280–282
Kopel, David, 154, 155, 177,
    178
Krisberg, Barry, 39

Labor, prisoners as, 18–19, 196–198, 232–233
  and out of state prisoners loophole, 232–233
Lake, Celinda, 106
Lamb, David, 16
Lecter, Hannibal, 101
Letts, Spencer, 165–166
Levin, Barry, 48
Levine, Grace Ferrari, 110–111
Lewinsky, Monica, 126
Limbaugh, Rush, 80
Lobby, prisoner, 142–151
Logan, Charles H., 262

MacNeil, Robert, 55, 277
Mademoiselle, 68
Maher, Bill, 118
Making Local News, 63
Maloney, Matt, 212
Mandatory sentencing, 4, 154–155, 156, 163–167, 249
  See also Sentencing
Mander, Jerry, 83, 85, 86
Mannix, Kevin, 19
Marijuana offenses, 193
Marketing Madness, 68
Marler, Betty, 213
Marquette University, 68
Mathiesen, Thomas, 49
Mauer, Marc, 50
Mazur, Laurie Ann, 68, 80
McBride, Joseph, 68
McCaffrey, Barry, 144, 192
McCarthy, Joseph, 123
McCarthy, Patrick, 251
McChesney, Robert, 72, 73–74
McKelvy, George, 210–211
McWherter, Ned, 147
"Mean world syndrome," 107–113
Media industry
  and advertiser control of content, 67–70
  and change to profit driven nature, 54, 57–63, 73

  choosing the message of, 63–70
  and corporate mergers, 3, 70–72, 278
  and crime profiteering, 20
  and deception regarding crime rate, 181
  increased use of crime-oriented content, 3, 55–57, 73
  international nature of, 73–77
  and journalists acceptance of news profiteering, 77–81
  lobbying efforts of, 60, 143–144
  and public's worldview, 54, 106–107
  and reward system for violence, 269–272
  uniformity of content of programming of, 70–77
  See also Television
Media Monopoly, The, 71
Mercedes-Benz, 68
"Mere thought," 98
Merrill Lynch, 5, 246
Metz, Craig, 140
Miller, Jerome, 186
Miller, Mark Crispin, 61–62, 69
Minorities. *See* Blacks; Hispanics; Race
Missle-gap, 30
Mistreatment of prisoners, 45–49, 202–217
  in Texarkana, 199–201, 211, 218, 221
Mitchell, George, 139
Moore, Adrian, 245
Moore, Margaret, 205
Moore, Michael, 19
Moran, James, 231
Morgan, Michael, 108
Morris, Dick, 122–123, 131
Morrison, Edward, 159
Moyers, Bill, 142
Murder and the media, 65–66
Murdoch, Rupert, 80
Murray, Bill, 138
Murrow, Edward R., 80

National Association of Criminal Defense Lawyers (NACDL), 162, 166

National Commission on the Causes and Prevention of Violence, 108
National Council on Crime and Delinquency, 39–40
National Crime Victimization Survey (NCVS), 27, 35, 43
National Criminal Justice Commission (NCJC), 31, 91, 136, 170, 179–180, 255
National Development and Research Institute, 42–43
National Institute of Justice (NIJ), 36–38
National Rifle Association (NRA), 144–145
  and three strikes laws, 160, 163
National Television Violence Profile, 95–96, 103, 108–109
Naureckas, Jim, 61, 77
New Prince, The, 123
News Corporation, 80, 143
New York and lease-bonds, 249–251, 253–254
Nichol, Gene, 173
Nichols, John, 128, 129
Niebuhr, Reinhold, 239
No Equal Justice: Race and Class in the American Criminal Justice System, 188–189
Nonviolent criminals, 155, 167, 194
  and sentencing laws, 178
  and three-strike laws, 160
  and truth in sentencing laws, 169
Northeast Ohio Correctional Center, 10
Northfield Dam, 265–266
Numbers incarcerated. *See* Population

Ogletree, Charles, 189
One-sided messages, 101–102
Operation Rescue, 127
Oxford History of the Prison, The, 240

Paramount Pictures, 68
Parole, abolishment of in federal system, 154

Pataki, George, 250–251
Patriot Games, 68
Penal systems, international, 1–2
Perpetual nature of prisoner machine, 3, 6
Persuasion, 90–91
  methods of, 94–113
  three-pronged process of, 96, 116–117
Petty, Richard E., 95, 96, 97, 98, 117
Philadelphia, crime reporting in, 34
Philip Morris Company, 68, 69
Plato, 90
Poitier, Sidney, 191
Policy changes to end perpetual prisoner machine, 268
Political action committees, 124, 133, 134
Political consultants, 3, 117, 119–126, 127
Politicians
  and reward system, 273–274
  and use of issue of crime, 5, 97, 115–151, 169
Polls, public opinion, 3, 4, 127, 130, 280–282
  and crime, 28, 270
  five tools of, 124–126
  increasing importance of, 4, 117, 131
Population, prison, 1, 4, 5, 7, 12, 17, 27
  and classification of inmates, 204–206
  composition of, 181–192
  and the crime rate, 27–52
  future predictions of, 7, 266–267
  replacing of violent with non-violent, 178–179
  and size of prison system, 251–252
Poverty, 102
  as principal factor in imprisonment, 6, 182
  and sentencing, 178, 184, 185, 188
Prison Blues, 178
Prison construction, 4–5, 13, 219, 251–252
  in California, 158–159
  and 1994 crime bill, 171
Prisoner classification, 204–206

"Prisoner code," 44
"Prisoner machine," 2–3, 7
Prison-industrial complex, emergence of, 3
"Prisonization," 44–49, 102, 168
Privacy, right to, 111–112
Private-prison corporations, 5, 17, 21
    care of prisoners in versus shareholder profits, 201–217
    and cost to public sector to oversee, 230–231
    and efficiency versus bureaucracy, 224–226
    federal government plan relative to, 236
    and financing with lease-payment bonds, 242–252
    historical view of, 196–198
    and housing of out-of-state prisoners, 215–217
    and lease-bonds, 244–252
    and lobbying, 146–150
    and non-disclosure of prisoner status, 204–208
    and non-reporting of problems, 203, 204, 207, 208, 210–211, 214, 216–217, 218, 221
    physical conditions of, 201–202
    and prisons of compared to public prisons, 218–219
    and the reward system, 274–275
    and saving of money, 5, 223–237
    and violence, escapes, and riots, 207–208
    See also Corrections Corporation of America; Wackenhut
Private Prisons: Cons and Pros, 262
Profit as motive behind increase in prison population, 2, 10–11
Prosecutors and political advantage, 166–167
Public awareness, of violence emphasis in media, 276

Public opinion, 3, 4, 117, 118–119, 165
Public Perspective, 56
Pung, Oroville, 259

Race, 6–7
    and the death penalty, 172
    and future prison population, 266–267
    and sentencing, 182–192
    and television depiction of crime, 93–94
Racial profiling, 189–190
Ramsey, JonBenet, 60, 66, 70, 78–79, 271
Rapes, 16, 46
Reagan, Ronald, 28, 70, 120–121, 164
Real-estate investment funds (REITs), 13, 232
Real War on Crime, The, 170, 180
Rebound, Inc., 212, 214, 219, 221, 227
Recidivism, 37–38, 102, 169–170
Rector, Ricky Ray, 172
Rehabilitation, 43–49
    and family structure, 208–210
    historical view of, 195–198
    and politicians, 102–103
    and the reward system, 274–275
Rehnquist, Justice, 112, 161–162, 163
Reno, Janet, 166
Reporting of crime, 31–36
Report of the National Criminal Justice Commission, 97
Report on the Prisons and Reformatories of the United States and Canada, 198
Republican Party, 129, 130, 135–136
Reward system, 268–279
    and the media, 269–272
    and politicians, 273–274
Reynolds, Mike, 157
Richardson, Edmund, 197
Riggs, Michael, 156–157
Rise of the Political Consultant, The, 120, 121
Robertson, Pat, 80

Rochelle, Robert, 147–148
Rockefeller drug laws, 249
Rocky Mountain Boys Ranch, 217
Rocky Mountain Media Watch 1997
    study, 109
Rollo Code of Morals, The, 240
Romer, Roy, 257
Rothman, David J., 240
Rupert, Dorothy, 251–252
Rural communities, 16–17
Russia, numbers of prisoners, 1

Sabato, Larry, 120–124, 134
San Quentin State Prison, 5, 19
Sauter, Van Gordon, 112
Schiller, Herbert I., 261
Schiraldi, Vincent, 256
Schwarz, John, 257
Seagram and Sons, 143
Seldes, George, 57–58, 77
Seligman, Martin, 111
Sentencing, 102, 153–175
    as reason for increased prison
        population, 50
    and "truth in sentencing," 167–171
    See also Death penalty; Mandatory
        sentencing
Sentencing Project, 182–183
Sentencing Reform Act, 154–156, 182
Serling, Rod, 80
Sessions, William, 149
Sex and the media, 74
Sexual assaults, 45–46
Signorielli, Nancy, 108
Silence of the Lambs, The, 101
Silva, Duane, 159–160
Simpson, Nicole, 104–105
Simpson, O.J., 104, 271
Slavery, 186–187, 191–192
Social programs
    decrease of as factor in increase of
        prisoners, 6

diversion of funds from, 5–6, 246,
    252–261
Source of a message, as persuader,
    97–98
Spence, Floyd, 140
Spencer, Stuart, 122
Springfield, Oregon school shooting, 105
Staebler, Neil, 120
Staffing, inadequate, 211–213
Stone, Christopher, 47
Stone, John, 258
Stone, Oliver, 73
Storytelling, 83–85
Stossel, Scott, 62, 74, 76
Street crime, 54, 106–107
Sullivan, Michael, 215
Sundlun, Bruce, 156
Suren, Bob, 63

Taft study of private prisons, 236–237
Teeter, Robert, 128
Telephone companies, 14
Television
    and creation of alternative
        programming, 277–278
    and crime coverage formula, 91–94,
        293(n13)
    and manufacturing of worldview,
        83–113
    and persuasion, 90–91
    and persuasion factors and crime,
        94–113
    violence on and aggressive behavior,
        88–89
    See also Cable television; Media
        industry
Tennessee and private prisons, 147–148,
    235, 236
Terkel, Studs, 199
Terry, Randall, 127–128
Texas Sunset Advisory Commission study
    of prison costs, 228, 234

Thompson, Tommy, 215
"Three-strikes" laws, 4, 24, 102, 157,
    161–163
  and California, 145–146, 156–163, 220,
    256, 281–282
Time Warner, 143, 278
Tonry, Michael, 167
Trade shows, 11–12, 14
Transportation of prisoners, 15–16
Truman, Harry, 201
"Truth in sentencing," 4, 167–171
"Twenty-First Century Law Enforcement
    and Public Safety Act," 117

Unicorp, 18
Uniform Crime Report (UCR), 31–32, 33
  and falling crime rates, 38–39
Urban Development Corporation,
    249–250
USA Today, 79

Vera Institute of Justice, 47
Victims in the News: Crime and the
    American News Media, 67
Violence, 46
Violence
  and the media, 56–57, 63–67, 73, 76
  public's rewarding of in media,
    270–271
  use of by media creates distortion, 87
Violent offenders
  and alcohol, 193–194
  early release of, 167, 179
  focus on of war on crime policies,
    179–181, 194
  sentencing of, 178
Virginia
  and private prisons, 235
  and truth in sentencing, 170
VitaPro Foods, 14, 150–151
Voltaire, 252

Voter turnout, 127–129, 130–131
Voting rights, 267

Wackenhut Corrections Corporation, 5,
    18, 148
  and control of prison industry market,
    218
  and real-estate investment trusts, 13,
    232
  and Taft prison facility study, 236
Wag the Dog, 194
Walters, Barbara, 64
"War on Crime," 28, 36, 50, 117, 256
  attempts to prove its effectiveness,
    33–34
  and efforts to prove it targets violent
    crime, 179–181, 194
War on Drugs, 189
Weber, Vin, 139
Welch, Jack, 113
Western Missouri Correctional Center, 16
Westinghouse and lobbying expenditures,
    143, 144
Whitacker, Clem, 120
White, Alphonso, 206
Wigand, Jeffrey, 69
Williams, Hayes, 173
Wilson, James, 40
Wilson, Pete, 145, 157–158
Wilson, W., 64
Wines, Enoch, 198
Wines and Dwight Report, 198

Xena: Warrior Princess, 75

Youth Education, 214

Zavaras, Ari, 257
Zimring, Franklin, 36, 37, 177
Zinn, Howard, 128
Zogby, John, 279–280